Overcoming Toxic Emotions

Overcoming Toxic Emotions
A Christian Ethical Framework for Restorative Peacebuilding

Raymond Olúsẹ̀san Àìná

FOREWORD BY Johan Verstraeten

WIPF & STOCK · Eugene, Oregon

OVERCOMING TOXIC EMOTIONS
A Christian Ethical Framework for Restorative Peacebuilding

Copyright © 2022 Raymond Olúsẹ̀san Àìná. All rights reserved. Except for brief quotations in critical publications or reviews, no part of this book may be reproduced in any manner without prior written permission from the publisher. Write: Permissions, Wipf and Stock Publishers, 199 W. 8th Ave., Suite 3, Eugene, OR 97401.

Wipf & Stock
An Imprint of Wipf and Stock Publishers
199 W. 8th Ave., Suite 3
Eugene, OR 97401

www.wipfandstock.com

PAPERBACK ISBN: 978-1-6667-3301-3
HARDCOVER ISBN: 978-1-6667-2724-1
EBOOK ISBN: 978-1-6667-2725-8

05/27/22

In memory of

My parents, Veronica Olajumoke Aina
and Raphael Omotosho Aina

My brothers, Fr. Cosmas Olufemi Aina
and Richard Abiodun Aina

And

in thanksgiving to God,
for my 50th birthday

Contents

Foreword by Johan Verstraeten | ix
Acknowledgements | xi
Abbreviations and Acronyms | xiv
Prologue | xvii

General Introduction | 1

1 Nigeria's Dance of Death: Responses to Its Unjust and Violent Past | 12
2 Restorative Peacebuilding in Nigeria: The Best Road Not Taken? | 38
3 A Christian Ethical Appreciation of Archbishop Desmond Tutu's Theology of Restorative Justice | 59
4 A Theological Ethics of Restorative Justice in Peacebuilding | 105
5 A Christian Ethical Exposition on the Three Pillars of Restorative Justice | 124
6 A Theology of Reconciliation for My Neighbor-Turned-Enemy | 139
7 Nigeria and Beyond: An Agenda for Christian Ethics in Restorative Peacebuilding | 167

General Conclusion | 203

Appendix 1: Restorative Justice's Hope & Promises | 231
Appendix 2: A Theological Ethical Proposition for Reconciliation | 233
Bibliography | 235
Index | 253

Foreword

THIS OUTSTANDING BOOK IS an original and outstanding contribution to the discussion about restorative justice as a crucial component of peacebuilding and conflict transformation. It is written by Rev. Dr Raymond Aina, whom I have known in Leuven as a most intelligent doctoral student.

Aina focuses on *toxic emotions*, a rather new topic in peace research. His approach is transdisciplinary. He combines theological insights with historical, juridical and ethical reflection. He carefully analyzes facts, ideas, and texts. On the one hand, he is very precise. On the other hand, he never loses his way in details and he keeps the red thread of his argument continuously in mind.

With a critical gaze, Aina scrutinizes uncritical assumptions, for example about the political use of a forgiveness discourse, and when necessary, he does not hesitate to challenge authorities like Desmond Tutu. But his criticism is never without due respect to the nuances of a rejected or criticized argument.

Aina's book provides an excellent theoretical clarification of the victim-oriented concept of restorative justice, and it opens a broader hermeneutic horizon via a profound Trinitarian theology. Notwithstanding its theoretical excellence, Aina's book is a work with practical implications. It emerges from a real concern for the future of Nigeria. As such, it is also an excellent example of contextual thinking.

In short, this thought-provoking book is a "must" for everyone interested in peace research, restorative justice, and the role of toxic emotions, and particularly for everyone who cares about peace in Nigeria.

Johan Verstraeten
Katholieke Universiteit
Leuven

Acknowledgements

IF ANYONE HAD TOLD me this time last year that I would be writing these words by this time, while still holed up here in the seminary, I would have done the same thing I had done for close to a decade—*laugh out loud, laugh it off!* Then, two beloved colleagues and confreres, Efeturi Ojakaminor, OMV, and Idara Otu, MSP, came along like stubborn guardian angels, insisting I would do it. I remember that morning on October 22, 2019, that Ojakaminor drove from Suleja to Gwagwalada. He solemnly handed me a typed letter from him with a renewed request: "Please, begin the project of writing a book on Moral Theology." This touched me, but then I still dithered. I was looking forward to a well-deserved sabbatical leave to do it. When it was clear in February 2021 that I wouldn't have that sabbatical, Otu drew that commitment from me to do this—with or without the sabbatical. He walked me through the initial writing of the book project to Wipf and Stock. Their persistence, like the widow in the Gospel of Luke (18:1–8), forced me to do something. Now I deliver the fruit of their persistence—*With a grateful heart for helping me break my self-imposed jinx!*

This book is a development of my doctoral dissertation over a decade ago, under the tutelage of a remarkable *magister*, em. Prof. Johan Verstraeten at the Katholieke Universiteit Leuven, and a decade of post-doctoral research and teaching in Nigeria. Prof. Verstraeten birthed my area of specialization and research focus. I am thankful for his diligent, patient, yet uncompromising assistance (on the fundamentals of faith and research) in the course of this project. My Yoruba elders say: "Even if a child has clothes as much as the elder, the child can never have as many rags as the elder." 'Rag' is the metaphor for experiences of life. I have been richly blessed by the 'rags' of Prof. Verstraeten. No one was better suited to pen the foreword to the work. *Bedaankt*, Prof. Verstraeten.

I can't forget to thank the faculty of theology and religious studies of KU Leuven; and my Board of Examiners over a decade ago for our lively conversations that challenged me to tie up some loose ends. It's been worthwhile for me. I am immensely grateful also to the MWI Aachen for its scholarship grant for my doctoral research. Thanks too, for the post-doctoral collaboration—the "Religion and Violence in Africa" project, which the Research Department of MWI Aachen, Germany coordinates, on the intersection of religions and violence in Africa. I am grateful to Bishop Matthew Kukah, who enthusiastically agreed to go through the manuscript and pen some words when required. Bishop Kukah was the Secretary of the Oputa Panel that experimented with restorative justice in peacebuilding when Nigeria returned to civilian rule in 1999.

I salute my former Superiors General, and the current one, Revd Dr Callistus Isara, MSP, and their respective Councils, for the confidence and privilege to study at the KUL, and for the decade-long post-doctoral teaching and research at the National Missionary Seminary of St Paul. I cannot forget my confreres in the South African and Botswana missions who facilitated and took care of my observatory trips to South Africa twice between December 2008 and September 2009. They helped to give this work some contextual feel and insights. My friends in MSP, Peter Oyenugba and Paul Dadson, have been friends indeed for they were there during my needy times to this moment. Without being asked, Paul and Peter, together with my nephew, Babatunde Aina, took care of my financial worries for this book project so that I wouldn't get distracted. *Una doh—I twale for una o.*

I have been blessed with the crop of colleagues and confreres on the faculty and my community here at the National Missionary Seminary of St Paul, Abuja. For their support and push, I say, "Thank you, sisters and brothers"—Josephine Nwaogwugwu, Nneka Uzukwu, Mary Benedict Isara, Eugenia Ejiogu; Augustus Essien, Michael Etokakpan, Brian Okon; Daniel Ihunnia, Emmanuel Mbam, Linus Kpalap; Pius Ekpe, Nduka Uzor, Innocent Odiaka, Cosmas Nwosuh, John Paul Arowosoge, Godwin Akpowho; Benjamin Okon, Clement Kanu, and Joseph Okere. Efeturi and Idara have been amazing in proofreading the recent drafts.

To my siblings—the late 'Biodun, 'Dele, 'Funmi, the late 'Femi, and Akin—and their families: thanks so much for keeping me going, especially during my times of loneliness and heavy heart with our recent bereavement. Without your calls and chats, and, of course, prayers, who knows how things would have turned out? *E se pupo.*

I appreciate the following colleagues and friends whose critical remarks and corrections enriched the original research: Laurent Balog, Ignatius Edet, David Kirchhoffer, as well as the members of the Missio Aachen research group on the "Religion and Violence in Africa" project. Thanks also to some of my friends whose lives and friendships strengthened me in the last few months—Mike (*Jigan*), Kate, Raphael, Ojiaku, Segun and Toyin, Udodirim, Tony and Toyin, and Bibiana. The same goes for my past and present students at the National Missionary Seminary of St Paul, for their outstanding scholarship and passion for a better world. Their scholarship and passion for the missions have been my sources of immense inspiration and encouragement. *I tank una plenti plenti!*

How can I forget the adorable kids of my nieces and nephews? My experiences of them in the last few years have deepened my hope that, as Lagbaja, the Nigerian masked musician, once proclaimed, "*Naija don sweet bifo; Naija go sweet again.*" They represent a new generation that might have "a different spirit" from the previous generations—a generation that may be fully alive, more reconciled, less dogmatically ethnocentric, and more linguistically pluralist. May they and their generation reach the Promised Land of Loving Justice, Peace, and Reconciliation, which the generations of their parents and I still grope and struggle towards.

The Yoruba say, "The biggest masquerade comes out last from the sacred grove." The greatest imaginable thanks go to *Olódùmarè*, the Enabler of all who achieve any worthwhile goal: To him be glory and praise forever. May his justice and peace reign in our hearts and our land.

Raymond Olúsẹ̀san Àìná, MSP

Abbreviations and Acronyms

AG	Action Group—a defunct Nigerian Political Party
ANC	African National Congress—the ruling party in South Africa
Baruti	A Sesotho/Setswana word popularly used to designate pastors; religious figures (singular: *Moruti*)
Boko Haram	Literally, means "book is sinful." It's the popular name for a Nigerian Islamic terrorist group, whose official name is *Jama'atu Ahlis Sunna Lidda'awatiwal-Jihad*—"People Committed to the Propagation of the Prophet's Teachings and Jihad"
CAN	Christian Association of Nigeria—umbrella ecumenical body for Nigerian Christians
CATHAN	Catholic Theological Association of Nigeria
CDD	Center for Democracy and Development—a Nigerian civil rights campaign group
COR	Cross River-Ogoja-Rivers—a socio-political group of ethnic minorities South-South of the Niger; agitating for autonomy from the Igbo before and during the First Republic
CSN	Catholic Secretariat of Nigeria
CST	Catholic Social Teaching/Thought
DP	Democratic Party—a South African political party, now known as Democratic Alliance (DA)

Eiye Kinkin	A Yoruba expression for any tiny bird—a euphemism for marginalized persons/peoples
Gacaca	Post-genocide Rwandan adapted restorative justice and traditional conflict resolution mechanism
HRVIC (aka Oputa Panel)	Human Rights Violation Investigation Commission (Nigeria's TruthCommission)
ICR	Interactive Conflict Resolution
IFP	Inkatha Freedom Party—a South African political party
IGAD	The Intergovernmental Authority on Development—in Eastern Africa
JDPC	Justice, Development and Peace Commission
JPR	Justice, Peace and Reconciliation project
Kill & Go	A derogatory term for members of the Nigerian Military Police
MSP	Missionaries of St. Paul of Nigeria
NCNC	National Council of Nigeria and the Cameroons later renamed National Council of Nigerian Citizens—a defunct Nigerian Political Party
(N)RSV	(New) Revised Standard Version of the Bible
NPC	Northern Peoples Congress—a defunct Nigerian Political Party
RCC	Roman Catholic Church
RJ/CJ	Restorative Justice/Criminal Justice
Rainbow Nation	A popular nickname for post-Apartheid South Africa
PTSD	Post-Traumatic Stress Disorder
SACC	South African Council of Churches
SECAM	Symposium of Episcopal Conferences of Africa and Madagascar
TC/TRC	Truth Commission/Truth and Reconciliation Commission

The Report	The eight-volume report of Nigeria's Human Rights Violation Investigation Commission
WCC	World Council of Churches
WWI	World War I
WWII	World War II

Prologue

THE PERPETRATOR said, "You talk of justice and reconciliation. Where is the boundary? How can you want to punish me, yet still talk of forgiving me? What is the point of Reconciliation when I am going to pay and am already paying for my offences? Reconciliation—does it matter to us?"

The Victim mused, "What can the offender do to bring back what is gone? I will be betraying the emotions of my departed relatives who died because of him if I forgive him. That betrayal, for me, is a higher injustice because it will be sharing in the guilt and injustice of the offender. No, I cannot dare; I cannot betray my loved one or soil her memory by some forgiveness. My Vengeance is basically in refusing to forgive, even if I will accept not to revenge. I do not need to forgive him; he does not need forgiveness. I choose not to forgive him. What does that take away from society? After all, I am not planning to avenge."

At this point, *the Perpetrator* retorted, "To claim to forgive me while I am undergoing punishment is meaningless and an insult to me—because that is taking me as a fool. Maybe after completing the punishment and I am disposed (and not just me but my family and constituency) . . . maybe then I may think about that. After accepting I did wrong and I am still paying for it, forgiveness and reconciliation are now proposed. There is a disruption of rhythm here. Acceptance of culpability leads to Reconciliation. But the language of 'paying for it' is a *non sequitur*. My final word here is: Let me be; let her be; let us be. Let the society be."

The Elder explained, "The so-called 'paying for it' you are referring to is not penal as I think you may perceive it. We believe in the milk of humanity flowing in you—and it is an accident in history that this milk of humanity got tainted. You have shown now clearly that human blood runs through your veins."

"Are you trying to patronize me?" interjected *the Perpetrator*. "Are you patronizing me with this milk and blood stuff because I do not fall for such cheap blackmail?"

The Elder replied, "I am saluting your courage—not patronizing you. That would be insulting you. As I was pointing out, we believe that you can look through the eye of your sister's sufferings and pains and then we leave it to you and her to explore the best way these sufferings can be healed. This is what we mean by restorative justice. We believe this is what can put an end to or at least truncate the spiral of violence in our community. Rings of violence are not the best heritage for our children. We had that heritage—are we better off?"

The Victim protested, "Oh ho! The whole point is not about me, about my people but for the whole society. Suppose our pains and anger are not threatening society, we will be sulking alone. What a selfish and ungodly proposal."

"On the contrary," replied *the Elder*, "we are concerned about you but we are looking at it from another angle. You are very integral to our society. We are aware that you are nursing both physical and emotional wounds. There are few chances of your reaching the peak of your human potentialities in all aspects. It will be selfish and ungodly for the rest of us if we looked the other way. Our elders have a saying: 'what affects the eyes affects the nose.' We are one. That oneness in the community is what we are trying to build. If you are in the best of shape, we are also; if any part of the community is not in good shape, all of us are not as well. That is the solidarity of our common humanity. This is the spirituality behind the whole process of restorative justice. This interface is an instance of restorative justice on the way towards reconciliation.

The Victim said, "That sounds brilliant; maybe, we may just go along and see how it turns out."

The Perpetrator shrugged, saying, "I guess I will do the same so long as it is not a carefully concocted plan to bring me to ridicule and public opprobrium."

The Elder smiled for the first time as he said, "Thank You both. That means I can give an outline of the 'rules of engagement'; what this process is not; what it is; and the substructure upon which we are attempting to build a new and positively alternative way of life for durable and sustainable peace in our community."

General Introduction

> We're trying something different, and it really seems to work. We are getting the victims and offenders to sit down with each other, and the offender is being held directly accountable to the victim. . . . For the first time, I feel I can live out my Christian faith in my work. —A Probation Officer.[1]

WHEN NIGERIA RETURNED TO democratic rule in May 1999, one of the first executive decisions of the new government was to set up the Human Rights Violations Investigation Commission. The brief of the Commission was to kickstart a process of national reconciliation by promoting truth-telling as integral to justice for victims of human rights abuses. The Commission raised more questions than answers, especially on the tensions between, on the one hand, the diabolicization of some perpetrators, and, on the other hand, banalization (with expressions of apologies and forgiveness). Hence, the HRVIC and its language of national catharsis raised for me personal ambivalence regarding justice, reconciliation, and forgiveness long before its *Report* became public, and before I heard of restorative justice.

Restorative justice brings together the various parties in a conflict to the extent that it enables parties to create harmony even in the face of possible chaos by paying attention to the human person adequately considered. The restorative justice approach is a relatively new one that found its way into legal terminology in the last twenty years of the last century. One of the reasons for its emergence was the contention that the prevalent judicial processes "steal conflicts"[2] from the primary stakeholders (i.e., victims) who are turned to state witnesses. The aim as such was to rediscover the personal dimension of conflicts and crimes by seeing these more

---

1. See Schweigert, "Undoing Violence," 207–8.

2. Nils Christie first used the phrase to mean judicial processes do not take sufficiently into account the position of the victims, particularly their multifarious wants. This leaves the victims unsatisfied. Cf. Christie, "Conflicts as Property," 1–15.

as hurts that needed to be healed. This aim of restorative justice is one of the reasons why the probation officer, quoted above, is more at home with her Christian faith, such that she does not have to live a schizophrenic life—living by some kind of restorative justice in her private life, but enforcing a retributive justice in her legal duties.

Restorative justice is a new way of looking at criminal justice. It is a valued-based approach to responding to wrongdoing and conflict, with a balanced focus on the offender, victim, and community. Restorative justice focuses on transforming wrongdoing by healing the harm, particularly to relationships, that is created by harmful behavior. The primary stakeholders in restorative justice processes are the person(s) who caused the harm (offender), the person(s) harmed (victim), and the affected community. It provides an opportunity for victims, offenders and sometimes representatives of the community to communicate about an offence and how to repair the harm caused. This can lead to the offender making reparation—either to the victim, if the victims wish, or the wider community through community service. By collectively identifying and addressing harms, needs, and obligations resulting from wrongdoing, we can create healing and put things right again.

Beyond its original context (penal; criminology), restorative justice has entered the peacebuilding fray as a corrective to a deficiency in dominant peacebuilding approaches. Loads of strategic peacebuilding and transitional justice methods spend energies and resources to put the world back into working order without adequately getting the person into shape. Restorative justice, as a metaxological approach with a relational character, operates with the recognition that if one puts the person right, one is indeed repairing the world. Its most telling contribution is the South African Truth and Reconciliation Commission (TRC). A less known but equally decisive contribution is the Nigerian Human Rights Violations Investigation Commission (HRVIC). Restorative justice can be involved in peacebuilding projects today because it resonates with some developments in contemporary conflict resolutions theses.

First, contemporary conflicts are asymmetrical and mostly intrastate; escalating within states where people have been long exposed to power imbalance exemplified in socio-economic deprivation, socio-cultural marginalization, and increased loss of control over revenue derivation that can guarantee a good and secure life. Second, these conflicts, especially when they turn violent, highlight their complexities and irresolvable natures due to a mixture of objective interests and subjective factors. Subjective factors are to a great extent identified by clashes of toxic emotions. Hence, if these conflicts and clashes of emotions will be resolved, there must be a conflict resolution method that gives a strategic place to the subjective factors. This has led to the development of "interactive conflict resolution" processes.[3]

Restorative justice, due to its strategic relationality, holds a lot of promises in helping the case of interactive conflict resolution. It is within this context that one can understand why transitional societies like Nigeria and South Africa opted for restorative justice as a peacebuilding project. Indeed, the HRVIC option motivated this book's thesis because it helped to highlight the effects of subjective factors in Nigeria's asymmetric violent conflicts for over five decades; the futility of glossing over these; and the challenge posed to religions, especially Christianity and its theology if they will be relevant in contexts like Nigeria.

Motivations

When in 2004 I arrived at the Katholieke Universiteit Leuven to begin my Licentiate studies in moral theology, I finally chose as my research project the relationships between justice, peace, forgiveness, and reconciliation in a way that eschews the binary opposition of either diabolicization or banalization. As one belonging to the post-Civil War generation, restorative justice, its strategic relationality and emphasis on concrete persons and their interests and needs (both objective and subjective), held a huge attraction for me for the sake of a generation *burdened with memory* but not yet comforted with the *muse of forgiveness*.[4] At the end of my licentiate studies and its thesis, there were outstanding issues.

First, I realized there is the paucity of systematic and thoroughgoing Christian ethical response to data thrown up by victimology and traumatology—two disciplines crucial to restorative justice discourse. Today, the discussion on restorative justice, regarding justice, is a matter for social scientists and legal practitioners. Perhaps, this paucity contributes to the nonvalorization of (Christian) religion in restorative justice discourse among serious-minded criminologists and political realists. Second, as a Nigerian, burdened with its past, I am desirous for it to reach nationhood and not just remain a mere geographical expression.[5] Nigeria has a nation space but not

---

3. Fisher, "Interactive Conflict Resolution," esp. 230–64.

4. This plays on the title of Wole Soyinka's monograph on the tensions noticed with South Africa's TRC and the implication for wider campaigns for reparation in postcolonial African nations. See Soyinka, *Burden of Memory*.

5. Chief Obafemi Awolowo is one of the founding fathers of modern Nigeria. One of his mostly quoted statements is that Nigeria is not a nation, with its people having a national identity, like the English, Germans, Welsh, and Irish. Rather, Nigeria is "a mere geographical expression" and "an appellation" used to describe peoples amalgamated

nationhood because of residual issues of the past. What then can Christian ethics in contexts like Nigeria say to a pointed question of restorative justice: what is the role of criminal justice ethics and system in peacebuilding—is it merely processing for penalty and punitiveness (retributive justice)?

Third, Nigeria is trapped now in the most virulent religion-inspired violence in decades.[6] Islam has been most implicated in the connections between religion and violence in post-colonial Africa. Some violent intra-national conflicts do not have intrinsic connections between religion and violence. However, violence implicates religion via manipulation of religious identity. Islam is easy to manipulate because of its lack of centralized organization. Christians are mostly victims of religious violence in contemporary Africa. Notwithstanding, Christians are at the forefront of advocating for and investing in conflict resolution. What kind of ethics of peace or theology of reconciliation should one expect from the religion of victims of religious violence? How can the religion of victims of interreligious violence propose an ethics of peace and conflict resolution without capitulating to the aggressor? Why should Christianity in post-colonial Africa not resort to the biblical morality of *lex talionis*? How should the Christian Tradition relate with a religious foe that remains unrepentant of its imposed shame and debilitating worthlessness on Christian victims? How can Africans move beyond or contain the destructive power of religion in their midst?[7] How do we resolve the tensions in Christian theology of reconciliation and ethical realism regarding non-retaliation and just war thinking? How can Christians, as mostly the victims, have a shared identity with their perpetrators who are not apologetic for their actions? Of course, Nigeria's dance of death since the 1960s, especially between 2009 and 2021, provoked these questions. They are not peculiar to Nigeria, and Nigerian Christians.

Given these three issues, there is the need for a theological-ethical framework for restorative justice that will serve as a kind of parameter where fundamental theological and ethical issues are addressed. This is now necessary because most of the extant researches today on justice and peace focus on reconciliation, forgiveness, and democratic governance, not the kind of justice per se that is needed. This book, therefore, is a crucial contribution towards a theological-ethical framework that specifically

---

to form an entity, simply to distinguish them from those outside those amalgamated boundaries. Hence, the political setup most suited for this entity is federation like Switzerland. Awolowo, *Path to Nigerian Freedom*, 47–48, 50, quotation on 47, 48.

6. I have explored some of these conflicts in my previous works. See Aina, "Religion, Politics and the Angst"; Aina, "Good Governance"; Aina, "Killing for God".

7. This echoes the three-volume work on the relationship between violence and religion. See Ellens, *The Destructive Power of Religion*.

addresses the role and ambiguities of restorative justice, especially in transitional societies like Nigeria. For instance, there is the tension between procedural fairness in the justice process and restorativeness among parties involved, as well as the ambiguity of the place (or the incongruity) of punishment in restorative justice.

On Overcoming Toxic Emotions

The motivation for this book's main title comes from an unusual source. Originally the title did not contain "overcoming toxic emotions." However, a chanced reading of a book by a late relational psychoanalyst, Stephen Mitchell, changed that.[8] In this book, Mitchell tries to understand how an intensely positive phenomenon, falling in love, can end up in bitter aggression and deep-seated hatred, bordering self-destruction. He explores the theories of "hawks" (human beings are naturally wolfish) and "doves" (humans are naturally pacific; violence is an external contagion).[9] Rather than being exclusive of each other, human beings oscillate between the hawkish position (aggression for the sake of power and dominance, as in law and order) and the dovish position (aggression as a response to the sense of "frustration and deprivation").[10] These positions alone do not tell the whole story.

From his experience as a relational psychoanalyst and marriage counselor, and studies in political violence, Mitchell concludes: "The worst aggression does not just erupt, now here, now there, in a random fashion; it is part of a cyclical pattern of trauma, endangerment, and revenge, leading to more trauma, endangerment, and revenge."[11] Murderous rage usually erupts not as a result of a threat to bodily existence, but due to "perceived lack of respect . . . the threat is not to survival but to dignity and self-respect."[12] Hence, the relentless push for revenge among human beings can be located in the commitment towards redressing past humiliation, even to the point of endangering those taking the revenge.[13] The experiences of endangerment (a sense of self-respect and dignity is under threat) provoke anger and a plethora of responses.[14] Ultimately, intense hatred is rooted in "humiliation

---

8. Mitchell, *Can Love Last?*
9. Mitchell, *Can Love Last?*, 123–25.
10. Mitchell, *Can Love Last?*, 126.
11. Mitchell, *Can Love Last?*, 128.
12. Mitchell, *Can Love Last?*, 129.
13. Mitchell, *Can Love Last?*, 129.
14. Mitchell, *Can Love Last?*, 130.

and endangerment to the self."[15] Hence, to make one's responses and counter-responses reasonable, we organize the past experiences into narratives around the axes of self-pity or guilt. To understand the narratives of the past, one must pay attention to the centrality of these axes.[16]

Reflecting on Mitchell's positions, I realized a significant aspect of violent conflicts that had been neglected, more so in Christian ethics: the role of emotions, especially toxic ones. They are a reasonable measure of human value, and without unearthing these emotions to make sense of them, violent conflicts persist and there is no sustainable peace. Hence, this book's title reflects this insight as part of its critical contribution to the Christian ethical framework on restorative justice and its relevance in Nigeria.

Theological Approach, Method and Presuppositions

We need to be "catholic in our method"[17] to understand how people, in specific contexts, interact and experience their political fissures and the *afterwords*. As a book on Christian ethics, its overarching approach is one of the historical Consciousness. This approach is multidimensional, rather than being one-dimensional. A one-dimensional approach, especially involving an inquiry on social phenomena, leads to a generalization that glosses over the complexity of issues. Accordingly, to understand what is going on, a multidimensional approach enables the inquirer(s) to "elucidate what is difficult to comprehend" and analytically organize what appears haphazard. It is only after this understanding (the descriptive) that discussion on the ought (the normative) should realistically begin.

The multidimensional historical consciousness approach, popularized in the fifties and sixties by theologians like Bernard Lonergan,[18] and Personalist moral theologians,[19] recognized some theses. These are:

i. The Christian religion is in a changed world. Hence, there is the need for genuine moral theology in this changed world;

ii. The accentuated awareness of historicity called for new theological anthropology for Christian ethics, which must incorporate findings

---

15. Mitchell, *Can Love Last?*, 143.
16. Mitchell, *Can Love Last?*, 145–48.
17. Chabal and Daloz, *Africa Works*, xvii.
18. See especially Lonergan, "Transition," 1–9.
19. See for instance Böckle and van Ouwerkerk, *Moral Problems*.

from "positive sciences, such as sociology, biology, psychology and medicine"[20] and

iii. Christian ethics must be open to an interdisciplinary conception of the multidimensional human person, her/his needs and desires. According to Lonergan, the Christian ethicist must work in collaboration with other scientists. For instance, the ethicist should offer her/his ethical judgment after, not before, considering available data from the scientists on practices, presuppositions, and consequences of the phenomenon under study.[21] This signals the transition from naïve realism to "critical realism, a realism that knows the real because it knows what is true."[22]

As such, our preferred theological approach especially in Christian ethics is willing to propose an ethics of the meaningful that is intelligible and credible, even beyond the immediate tradition. If one recalls Lonergan's admonition offered above to the Christian ethicist on how to proceed before ethical judgment, the reader will recognize that this book gathers the data and analyzes the data (chapter 1). Yet, it must not be lost on the trans-disciplinary Christian ethicist that this task remains a theological one. Hence, it must interpret and offer positions or counter positions based on multiple theological and ethical principles. Accordingly, this book is hermeneutical. It interprets the data on the genealogy of Nigeria's violence, and Archbishop Desmond Tutu's praxis of restorative justice, for instance, through the prism of the Christian history of salvation, received as an African (Yorùbá) Christian.

From the foregoing, this book argues that restorative justice's principal inspiration is the challenge it poses to theology, especially Christian ethics. Framed as a question, it asks: what does theology say or what has theology got to contribute to the discussions and issues raised about mass violence and the imperative of justice? Restorative justice inspires Christian theology (especially ethics) in three ways.

The first inspiration is the push to a systematic engagement with Archbishop Tutu's imagination of restorative justice in peacebuilding since his positions have inadvertently become paradigmatic Christian theological ethical contributions. It is high time Archbishop Tutu's imagination and contributions were theologically held up to scrutiny.

---

20. Böckle and van Ouwerkerk, "Preface," 2.
21. Lonergan, "Moral Theology," 307.
22. Lonergan, "Moral Theology," 309.

The second inspiration from restorative justice is the push again to take another long and hard look, this time into the Christian tradition, and see a classic or root metaphor that might be viable in public for Christian ethics concerning restorative justice. This inspiration is a contribution of systematic theology to the discussion on the religious standpoint and arguments for or against restorative justice. The input is from the perspective of the Christological tract referred to as the hypostatic union. The hypostatic union can serve as a sufficient theological frame for restorative justice given that Christ brought reconciliation between the estranged parties (God and humanity) because the two natures, i.e., two distinct spheres of reality—divine and human—were united in the person of Christ.

The third inspiration consists of fundamental theological rethinking of some inherited notions, to the point of making distinctions between some of them, although they are usually coupled together, e.g., reconciliation and forgiveness; justice and peace; truth and justice. However, the book argues that making a distinction between these does not necessarily mean separating them. Making distinction shows the correlation and interrelationships between these concepts invoked about reconciliation. The third inspiration eventually leads to some concrete proposals for religious actors (especially the church) in Nigeria towards overcoming toxic emotions and exorcising the spirit of impunity.

Proposed Reading Lens

Given that

> *Neighbors-turned-Enemies view themselves via "Victim-Perpetrator" lens, thus living in a toxic relational environment,*

How do we evaluate the transformation of poisoned relationships and toxic environments?

This book proposes

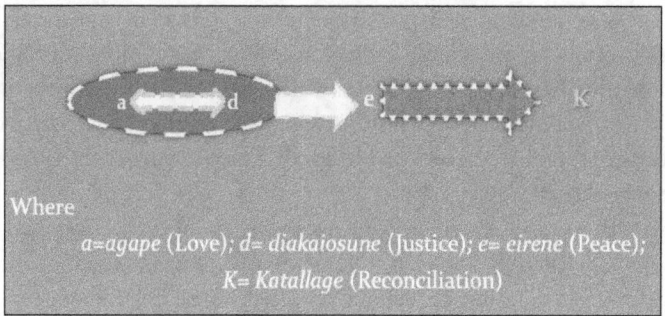

Courtesy of the Author

A Thesis

Love (*a*) and Justice (*d*) mutually reinforce each other. The mutual reinforcement between the two makes Peace likely. An environment of Love and Justice experiencing Peace has a *higher likelihood* of moving towards Reconciliation (*K*). To argue its thesis, this book as part of the inspirations and challenges of restorative justice reflects on how Christian theological ethics can realistically respond to the issues of Go(o)d, evil, victimization and justice based on the criminological imagination and practices of the restorative justice movement. This is to suggest how (Christian) theological ethics can approach issues critical criminologists are bringing forth today based on their work with victims of conflicts and various violations.[23] When theological ethicists bring their imagination in contact with criminological and victimological imaginations and trends, then they (theological ethicists) can be seen as serious dialog and justice project partners for collective victims/survivors.

The first chapter offers Nigeria's history of violence, and how the country has been dealing with this history. The chapter offers an ethical perspective on the various ways of confronting the reality of violence in Nigeria, a preeminent cleft country characterized by civilizational faultlines and prebendal politics. When Nigeria experimented with the restorative justice movement and inspirations between 1999 and 2002, the country had this history of fratricide in view.

---

23. Elsewhere I have engaged with the promises, ambiguities, and inspirations of the restorative justice movement, especially in peacebuilding. See Aina, "Nigeria's HR-VIC;" Aina, "Overcoming 'Toxic' Emotions."

The second chapter demonstrates how a particular transitional society—Nigeria—domesticated insights in contemporary critical criminology on unearthing the roots of manifest social harm. The chapter conceptualizes the kind of healing justice that transitional societies like Nigeria need, or how to conceptualize those who are entitled to it, or to whom is owed the ethical obligation of reparation.

The third chapter critically engages with Archbishop Desmond Tutu, since his Christian ethical contributions have become paradigmatic of a Christian understanding of restorative justice in peacebuilding, especially in Sub-Saharan Africa. This chapter confronts those who subscribe to Tutu's paradigmatic approach with the conceptual haziness inbuilt in it. Yet, it is insufficiently scholarly and irresponsible to deconstruct Tutu's magisterial paradigmatic approach without a clear proposal for Christian theological ethical imagination and framework that might hold more promise for the sake of being realistic and attentive to grey areas criminologists wrestle with.

Chapter 4 argues that, with the help of a central Christian doctrine, we can move beyond Tutu's conceptual haziness towards justice that heals in dialog beyond the frozenness of death. The chapter articulates a Christian theology of restorative justice inspired by the hypostatic union. This is premised on what can be seen as authentic and realistic theological ethics in transitional societies.

Chapter 5 provides a conceptual framework that should guide actions inspired by restorative justice. Each component of the proposed framework is followed by a Christian ethical reflection on the meaning and plausibility of "justice that heals," "justice and dialog," and "justice beyond frozenness of death." Chapter 6 focuses on the Christian theology of restorative justice, anchored on a theology of reconciliation for enemies who will remain neighbors. In particular, the chapter revisits Aquinas's discourse on the normativity of vengeance (*vindicatio*). I place this discourse alongside Emmanuel Levinas's excessive responsibility to violations. The chapter argues that Aquinas and Levinas are capable of reinforcing each other in the Christian theological ethics of reconciliation.

Chapter 7 outlines the role and responsibilities of the church in overcoming toxic emotions in contexts like Nigeria. The church in transitional societies must find bold and creative ways to institutionally embody the compassion it so much preaches and writes about. The chapter revisits the debate about the place of justice in the ecclesial mission of evangelization. It argues that an equilibrated Christian identity demands us to move beyond the notable disproportionality between justice and charity. The chapter addresses current debates about just war thinking in Catholic Social Tradition.

The book ends by presenting some of its fundamental findings while offering some reflections on the relationship between Christian reconciliation and the conditions for post-conflict justice on the way to reconciliation. The general conclusion presents visions and hopes for a reconciled world, where people move beyond being satisfied with the common ground to moving to the higher ground; from conciliation and cessation of overt hostilities to positive justice and reconciliation. It restates the centripetal and transformative role of religion in transitional societies. I end with a position on the current debate on the relationship between forgiveness, justice, and reconciliation. My wager anchors on the lessons we can learn from the restorative justice movement, the hypostatic union, and Pope Francis's *Fratelli Tutti* for ecclesial mission and Afro-Christian ethics of reconciliation in Nigeria and beyond. This should be viewed as a creative and proactive response to recommendations for programmatic action for transitional societies so that their diversity and unity may no longer be undermined.

1

Nigeria's Dance of Death

Responses to Its Unjust and Violent Past

"To keep Nigeria one / Justice must be done."[1]

But in Its absence . . .

"The old is dying and the new cannot be born; in this interregnum, there arises a great diversity of morbid symptoms."[2]

IN 2014, THE NOW-DEFUNCT TonyBlairFoundation.org published ten must-reads on religious conflicts in Nigeria. The books are interdisciplinary in scope.[3] These books offer both insider and outsider perspectives on Nigeria's history of violence, and how the country has been dealing with this history. This reading list was not intended to be exhaustive, because it was not. On the contrary, it significantly illustrated trends in scholarship regarding dimensions of narratives of violence in a cleft country. This foundational chapter offers an ethical perspective on the various ways of confronting the reality of violence in Nigeria, a preeminent cleft country characterized by civilizational faultlines and prebendal politics.

Why do we revisit our history of violence? It is a necessary step towards reconciliation of ruptured relationships and a breaking of the cycle of

---

1. Wole Soyinka made this statement in 1969, upon his release from over two years of solitary confinement due to his protest against the Civil War. Soyinka's assertion above was his "antidote" to a national jingle during the war: "To keep Nigeria one / Is a task that must be done." Soyinka, *You Must Set Forth*, 142. The "antidote" is premised upon his conviction during his prison days that there must be determination to eradicate "fundamental inequities which gave rise to the initial conflicts." Soyinka, *Man Died*, 181.

2. Achebe, *Home and Exile*, 80.

3. See Campbell, "Ten Books".

vengeance. A Nigerian musician, Lagbaja, aptly expresses this necessity in his track, "Me and You No Be Enemy (We Be Family)."[4]

This chapter on Nigerians' heritage of violence reminds us of the complexities of violence and peace in a significantly Christian yet bleeding continent. Nevertheless, since this is a book in Christian ethics vis-à-vis transitional justice, we should provide from the outset a Christian ethical understanding that informs the claim and thrust of this chapter. This is necessary to delimit the scope of the historical data about Nigeria's past.

An Ethical Framework for Peaceful Relationships

The past is not past because people are caught in the dilemma of holding to and fighting for their version of truth and justice—as a way of coping with a traumatic past. So, the past is not allowed to pass because it has become a way of honoring the memory of victims of the past. In the process, we find the dynamics of collective memory, which often take an untoward aggressive turn. Individual remembrances that become normative over time inspire this collective memory. This is called a stipulation. Stipulation states that a remnant of history is "important, and this is the story about how it happened, with the pictures that lock the story in our minds."[5] This collective memory is inherited long before we become aware of the significance of the story we are told or the repercussion of the version of the story related to us. A typical example is our birth. We do not recollect how we were born, but we are told of it so often that we know it well and become passionate about it when we subsequently narrate it later in life as if we witnessed it.[6]

There is a flipside to stipulation. A disproportionate concern with this kind of version of the past can lead to excessive memory. Hence, old conflicts never die; and the wounds never heal. Paul Ricœur warns us against this kind of excessive memory due to the nature of truth. According to

---

4. See Labaja, "We–Lágbájá," https://www.lagbaja.com/media/lyrics-we.php. The track is a combination of the Yorùbá language and Pidgin English (an indigenous contraption of the English language). The translation runs thus: "If you kill me, they [my people] will kill you. Then your people will revenge, and then my people will avenge. Then your people will retaliate. Revenge, avenge, revenge, retaliate—that is how the madness will continue. Why do brothers kill themselves? We are one family. Regardless of where you come from, regardless of your nationality, all of us are the same." Lagbaja, the musician, rendered the song in commemoration of the spate of ethno-religious violence and reprisal attacks that rocked Nigeria between 1999 and 2001.

5. Sontag, *Regarding the Pain*, 86.

6. Suleiman, *Crises of Memory*, 4.

Ricœur, "truth" is the "fragile constitution of historical knowledge."[7] Excessive memory tampers with truth's fragility. This happens, from the perspective of Ricœur, when there is disproportionate attention to the "depth of fault" without the corresponding "depth of forgiveness" characterized by consideration towards the guilty.[8] This disproportionate attention, which results in excessive memory, is caused by what Ricœur elsewhere refers to as hurting remembrances and unlabored "work of memory and work of mourning."[9] This obsessive memory, agreeing with Suleiman, is a sign of "'a retreat from transformative politics.'"[10] This usually exhibits itself in the "form of group memories vying with one another for recognition of the groups' suffering, 'reflects a new focus on narrow ethnicity' and acts as an obstacle to democracy."[11] Addiction to memory, with its tempting emotion of melancholy, arises as a result of sacralization of memory and the duty to remember. These do swiftly and unwittingly degenerate into "kitsch, the very purpose of critical self-reflection."[12] This kitsch fearfully leads to political instrumentalization. Suleiman's assertion is apt as we examine Nigeria's past and current state: "collective memory of ethnic humiliation or of religious conflict can be put to cynical political uses."[13] The past holds the present captive and even determines how the future plays out. The years 1966/1970[14] are gone. We are in the second decade of the twenty-first century. Have Nigerians not moved ahead? Some honest skeptics can ask—questioning the claim that the past is not past but ever-mutating in Nigeria.

Even if chronological time (e.g., 1966, or 1970) passes, existential time can remain frozen. Existential time can be defined as *a significant*

---

7. Ricœur, *Memory, History, Forgetting*, 498.

8. Ricœur, *Memory, History, Forgetting*, 468, 473. This consideration within justice is an instance of forgiveness *in cognito*. On this and other traces of forgiveness, see Ricœur, "Difficulty to Forgive," 10–15.

9. Ricœur, "Memory and Forgetting," 6–7.

10. Suleiman, *Crises of Memory*, 5.

11. Suleiman, *Crises of Memory*, 5.

12. Suleiman, *Crises of Memory*, 5.

13. Suleiman, *Crises of Memory*, 7.

14. As will become clearer in this chapter, 1966 and 1970 are significant for post-independent Nigeria. In 1966, Nigeria witnessed unprecedented murderous political crises, which drove Nigeria to the brink of disintegration with the internecine war of 1000 days (the Civil War) between 1967 and 1970. The war ended in January 1970. The factors for the crises, the effects of the crises, the post-*bellum* situations, and the responses principally inform this chapter. Hence, we shall refer often to 1966 and 1970. For a historically thorough account of the events between 1966 and 1970, see the magisterial two-volume work of Kirk-Greene, published within months of the end of the civil war. Kirk-Greene, *Crisis and Conflict*.

moment that shapes, sustains, and protects a particular notion of individual or collective selfhood (i.e., identity) to the extent that other events, moments, and histories are judged by such crucial moments. Hence, such existential time resists a positive metamorphosis due to a perversion of memory that is a result of twisted values. Existential time and its perverted memory create the endless violence of identity—either religious, communal, ethnic, or class in places with a multicultural and multi-religious context like Nigeria. Indeed, the violence of identity, based on a perversion of collective memory, can be very difficult to overcome in places like Nigeria, especially "if one group competes with another."[15] This competition breeds crises of legitimacy for constituted authorities among the peoples who reject them as improper to rule or as not ruling properly. In this way, the spiral of instability and violence is assured.

To test the claim as enunciated above, I shall present the approaches Nigeria (particularly the successive governments of the Republic) has taken to deal with violence, conflicts, and atrocities perpetrated, the justice that victim-survivors experienced, and the symbolic actions accorded the absolute victims (the dead). Whatever this excursus shall yield will inform the kind of role restorative justice has played and can further play in Nigeria. It will equally lead the reader to question if Christian ethics of reconciliation in the context of some post-conflict climes today can realistically tackle the issues we raised in the general introduction about Nigeria.

There is a caveat expectedly. I am an Afro-Christian ethicist. Hence, my interpretive framework shall be informed by my Christian tradition as much as by my Nigerian (Yorùbá) root. For instance, my view of violence is close to that offered by the *Theological Dictionary of the Old Testament*. The *Dictionary* defines violence as "the cold-blooded and unscrupulous infringement of the personal rights of others, motivated by greed and hate and often making use of physical violence and brutality."[16] Even if this definition is limited,[17] the definition offers a clue into what can be regarded as crucial indices of violence and violations in Nigeria. These indices are:

a. "cold-blooded": this suggests that agents of violence are blind to the bleeding and weeping face of the "other," i.e., the victims;

---

15. Falola, *Nationalism and African Intellectuals*, 169.

16. Haag, "Chāmās," 482.

17. It is micro-focused. It does not include a violation of a corporate entity, e.g., ethnic groups, religious groups, or communities that suffered "collective punishment" for the crimes of individuals. These distinctions are critical in the context of Nigeria, as will become clearer in this book.

b. "unscrupulous": Violence presupposes an absence of virtues that make human flourishing possible;

c. "motivated": Violations are not rash; they are rationally based on an internal movement of perpetrators—though due to a perversion of values—thus perpetrators bear some degree of responsibility;

d. "greed and hate": These two human passions are pivotal to understand the basis and depth of violations and injustice meted out to fellow human persons;[18]

e. "unscrupulous infringement of . . . personal rights": Any human act that unjustifiably invades a person or persons' legitimate existential and physical space is an act of violence, and a violation of the victim(s)' dignity;

f. "often making use of physical violence and brutality": This index shows that violence does not necessarily begin with physical actions. There are non-physical ways of violating people. Physical actions are habituated instrumental activities to bring about the desired consequence.

The last point above is interesting because it reiterates what many unsung victims know from their experiences. There are instances of unspeakable horrors, an invasion of one's existential and political spaces, without experiencing a single gunshot or physical torture. It is an insight that Adam Curle mentions in an article he contributed in *The Year Book of World Affairs* (1976) where he discussed the scope and purpose of "Peace Studies" as distinct from "International Relations," "War Studies," and "Strategic Studies." The kind of violence that "Peace Studies" should attend to includes starvation and malnourishment arising from deliberate government neglect, humiliation, and distortion of people's perception of reality due to propaganda. Indeed, Curle remarks, many "die because of these conditions. Circumstances such as these inflict such damage on human life, health, capacity for creative and happy existence and work, and for the development of potential, that I find it impossible to refer to them as peaceful."[19] Today, there are increasing sensitivities close to Curle's, like those from restorative justice advocates, and theorists of interactive conflict resolution. In the same vein, this chapter, indeed this book, as a whole, shares this sensitivity.

---

18. According to the Oputa Panel Report, volume three, titled "Research Reports," the Igbo of Nigeria believe that "deep-seated hatred" is the prime motivational factor for the murderous hostility they have experienced from other ethnic groups, especially in Northern Nigeria since 1945. See HRVIC, *HRVIC Report: Volume Three*, ch. 6, nos. 6.16–21.

19. Curle, "Peace Studies," 10.

To pursue an ethical framework, which will unearth peaceful and unpeaceful relationships, and to create peaceful relationships that should contribute to a change in the balance of power,[20] we must understand human psychology that makes unpeaceful relationships and violations happen in the first place. Jonathan Glover, in his *Humanity*, acknowledges that if we want to understand and respond adequately to violations and brutality in their myriad forms, we need to understand human psychology and factors that make cruelty possible in human beings. These factors are: "love of cruelty" (hatred—"Deep in human psychology, there are urges to humiliate, torment, wound and kill people"); a sense of self-inadequacy that asserts itself through "domination and cruelty;" and the gradual erosion of previously clear "moral identity."[21] These factors give an inkling into why physical acts of cruelty may be occasional, or why they are the last in a series of violent behaviors towards victims. Furthermore, these factors play out by stripping victims or the target groups of their "protective dignity," sometimes through emotional assaults, and later physical acts. However, violators can resist that part of their human psychology "that makes atrocities possible."[22] Hence, no human person, no matter how depraved, is beyond conversion, redemption, and renewal.

Even if Glover's thesis seems disturbingly pessimistic of the human person, his last point acknowledges that the human person does not become completely consumed by or subsumed in her/his evil acts to the point that s/he cannot disconnect from them. Furthermore, human beings, as ongoing existential projects, remain ever-open to the unexpected interruption of the other than the self. The other's unexpected interruption, at times, can be redemptive. The inadvertent bloodied or weeping interruption of the other can rescue the perpetrator(s) from self-destruction. Glover gives an anecdote to substantiate his claim. During the twilight days of the Apartheid regime in South Africa, the police were attacking "with customary violence" some persons holding a public protest. In the ensuing melee, a policeman (a White) was pursuing a woman (a Black) with his club. As the lady ran, one of her shoes fell off. That unexpected incident proved to be a turning point, beyond the wildest dream of the pursued woman: "The brutal policeman was also a well-brought-up young Afrikaner, who knew that when a woman loses her

---

20. These are part of what Curle considers as the "core and principles of peace studies." Cf. Curle, "Peace Studies," 10–13.
21. Glover, *Humanity*, 33, 35.
22. Glover, *Humanity*, 36, 38.

shoe you pick it up for her. Their eyes met as he handed her the shoe. He then left her, since clubbing her was no longer an option."²³

At this point, the reader can quickly get a glimpse of the thesis of this book: *relationality is crucial for the recognition of the dignity of victims, and the renewal of the humanity of perpetrators, who choose to become responsible*. Responsibility comes from two English words—response (action) and ability (faculty). Hence, responsibility is *the capability to act in reply to the suffering of the other*; and this *response-ability* is deeply anthropological, and not merely supererogatory.²⁴ To be human is to have the ability to respond to the blinding tears of the other. This Other than the self, in the Levinasian sense, reveals itself as a command before thought. The command before the thought is grounded in the pre-originality of Other, implying that the Other's call to responsibility does not issue from my intentionality: "in the 'pre-history' of the ego posited for itself speaks a responsibility, the self is through and through a hostage, older than the ego, prior to principles."²⁵ Hence, the call of responsibility from heteronomy is beyond one's plan. Rather, it is a "pre-reflective summoning of moral conscience" that is an expression of devotion to God since responsibility calls us to be devoted to the Other-as-Neighbor.²⁶

To lose the ability to respond to the tearful faces of the Other is to become less than human created in the image and likeness of God. So, the kind of interruption of the Black woman in the story related above becomes a graced moment for the brutal policeman to renew his humanity i.e. "response-ability" to the piercing gaze of the one whose shoe fell off. Accordingly, *a just process of conflict resolution that can bring sustainable peace and reconciliation should have an in-built strategic relationality between stakeholders.*

Furthermore, no matter our moral indignation about the wicked and atrocious activities of perpetrators, we may not pronounce a final word on them. This echoes Ricœur's words about consideration and his depth of forgiveness referred to earlier. If we acknowledge the possibility of humans, no matter how low they have sunk in their depravity, to be *response-able* again, then we can no longer allow ourselves to operate an ethical and judicial system of diabolicization if we want to build a just and human society in perennially at war places like Nigeria. Thus far, I have highlighted the

---

23. Glover, *Humanity*, 37–38, quotation on 38.

24. Viktor Frankl, a Jew, and Holocaust survivor, penned these words: "Being human means being conscious and being responsible." Sacks, *To Heal*, 3.

25. Levinas, *Otherwise than Being*, 117.

26. Vogel, "Jewish Philosophies After Heidegger," 131.

Judaeo-Christian inspiration for the claims and hermeneutics of this chapter, and consequently of this book.

At this point, I wish to share an African inspiration for the theological-ethical position in this chapter as well. It is a mythopoetic rendition from Yorùbá oral tradition. This rendition is referred to as "*Ìtàn Ọba Aláràn-án àti Ẹiyẹ Kíńkíń*"—"The Story of King *Aláràn-án* and the Tiny Bird."[27] This story is used in Yorùbá traditional conflict resolution to upbraid those who ignore the insignificant in the search for peace and stability. The story offers insight into some statements that shall be made later in this chapter on the persistence of violence and mass atrocities in Nigeria. *Ọba Aláràn-án* had a community project. He wanted a portion of the village's forest to be cleared and prepared for the village's market. He summoned all in the village, except *Ẹiyẹ Kíńkíń*, to participate in this community project. *Ẹiyẹ Kíńkíń* was angry and felt insulted by this exclusion. Hence, it devised a means to sabotage the community project as a protest. Consequently, at the end of every day's work by the villagers, *Ẹiyẹ Kíńkíń* would appear from hiding and sing to the grass:[28]

Lead: *Ọba Aláràn-án bewe* (King *Aláràn-án* commissioned a task)

Refrain: *Kíńkíń* (*Kíńkíń*)

Lead: *Ó bẹ̄ kèrè ẹiye* (He commissioned all birds)

Refrain: *Kíńkíń* (*Kíńkíń*)

Lead: *Ó bẹ̄ kèrè ẹiye* (He commissioned all birds)

Refrain: *Kíńkíń* (*Kíńkíń*)

Lead: *Ó dèmi Kíńkíń si* (He left me *Kíńkíń* out)

Refrain: *Kíńkíń* (*Kíńkíń*)

Lead: *Koríko dìde* (Grass, sprout)

Refrain: *Kíńkíń* (*Kíńkíń*)

Lead: *Èrúwa dìde* (Savannah grass sprout)

Refrain: *Kíńkíń* (*Kíńkíń*)

After singing, the grass would sprout. This went on for a long time that *Ọba Aláràn-án* got worried. So, he decided to enquire from the *Babaláwo*.[29]

27. I shall use the version in Adeleke, "Lessons," 183–84.

28. See Adeleke, "Lessons," 184.

29. *Babaláwo* means literally "father of mystery" of the *Ifá* Literary Corpus. This literary corpus is a divination system. Apart from this, it is also a traditional Yorùbá philosophy and thought system that "represents the traditional worldview.... Even

After divination, the *Babaláwo* revealed to King *Aláràn-án* that it was the handiwork of *Ẹiyẹ Kínkín*, to punish the king for the non-recognition of *Ẹiyẹ Kínkín*. Recognition must not just be proclaimed or nodded at. It must be profoundly rooted in the corporeal. Hence, to stem the disaster of reversal on their community's project, *Ọba Aláràn-án* must apologize to *Ẹiyẹ Kínkín* and be made to feel belonged by including it in the community project. The king did this. The community experienced peace and progress. The community accomplished its project.

We glean a significant lesson from this story. It is very dangerous to practice selective marginalization of individuals/groups because they are not considered to be important in the calculus of common projects. Insensitivity to insignificant people drives such people towards extremism.[30] This lack of recognition must be repaired both corporeally and symbolically as *Ọba Aláràn-án* was enjoined to do, which he did. This story reinforces another Yorùbá proverb usually invoked during conflict resolution: "*A-jẹ̀bi má mò ní kó ogun ja ìlú*"—"one who is guilty and does not know and does not care brings war upon the town."[31] Accordingly, there is the assurance of stability and relief for the whole community once the offending party/parties recognize(s) its/their guilt and decide(s) to participate in redressing the residual effects: "As demonstrated in the myth about *Kínkín* . . . the recognition of all individuals/groups in a given society is crucial to development and coexistence. This is especially relevant to identity-based conflicts that can be local, national, or regional in scope."[32]

---

today Ifa is recognized by the Yoruba as a repository of Yoruba traditional body of knowledge embracing history, philosophy, medicine, and folklore." So, the *Babaláwo* is one versed in the *Ifá* corpus to the extent he has reached the level where he can discern what *Ọrúnmìlà*—the God of Wisdom, and the owner of *Ifá*—reveals for those gifted with discernment. Abimbola, *Sixteen Great Poems*, 32.

30. This is one lesson that can also be learnt from a proverb invoked at the end of a story involving a husband who was insensitive to the emotions of his wife. The proverb goes thus: "*Mọ ìwà fún oníwà ni ọ̀rẹ́ fíí pẹ́*"—"The understanding and tolerance of a friend makes friendship last long." In this story, the husband's rooster was messing the couple's home and the woman was forced to be cleaning it all the time. She complained but the husband didn't care. The woman was driven into action. She decided to buy a goat and put it in their room. However, the husband could not take it, and the wife emphatically told the husband to bear the effect of her goat's droppings since she had been bearing the effects of his own insensitivity. Hence, if there would be peace and relief in the family home, both parties had to pay attention to each other's emotions and the effects of their pets' actions. They must take concrete actions to remove the effects without necessarily endangering the pets. On this story, see Agbaje, "Proverbs," 242.

31. Adeleke, "Lessons," 187.

32. Adeleke, "Lessons," 189.

The rest of this chapter shall examine some of the responses in Nigeria to violence and institutional acts of degradation to see if these responses paid attention to the ethical perspective above on the human person and the human community. Since Nigeria's violent past is huge, the chapter will necessarily make a selective examination of post-Civil War response (1970) as its principal focus, while relating this to responses to later violence like inter-ethnic conflicts, acts of violence arising from militant self-determination of some groups, and the locust years of the military regime, especially the Babangida and Abacha years (i.e., 1985–98).

My proposal is *individual, collective, and/or institutional responses to a violent past, which do not have at their core the human psychology of doers of evil and the communities that formed that psychology, will not succeed in creating an environment of a sustainable just peace.* Various Nigeria's responses to violence and mass traumas have been more on the instrumental level, thus ineffectual, sporadic, psychologically hollow, and ethically unsatisfying. To that extent, various forms of violence have been recurring decimals in Nigeria. Perhaps, Nigeria is not fated to doom and implosion. Yet, institutional responses to violence and discontents have not shown courage and creativity in unearthing the various psychologies motivating violence and social irruptions, nor has the country created a justice process and system that is sensitive and adequate to deal with issues relating to violence and discontent, especially reparation and dispossession. For instance, restitution, e.g., of land/property as part of the sacrosanct restorative justice is very justified. Nonetheless, it can be argued that restitution at whatever cost can jeopardize foreseeable peace, especially if the violator (or the second or third party) holds military and socioeconomic ace. In that sense, why not let go of justice (restitution) for the sake of peace? Or why do people not just keep quiet about restitution for the sake of "national reconciliation" as was the case in Nigeria after the end of its Civil War in 1970 and subsequent inter-ethnic and inter-religious conflagrations?

These are parts of the issues at stake that demand creative options. Although I stated elsewhere that Nigeria might not be fated to doom, it is perennially pressing the button of self-destruction. This is one of the numerous paradoxes that characterize Nigeria. Though Nigeria has a semblance of stability because there are multiparty elections, it abysmally ranks low in democratic culture.[33] James O'Connell, in his pre-Civil War article on Nigeria, regards the following three factors as responsible for the fragile stability of Nigeria in the sixties: "constitutional imbalance and the decay of constitutionalism; the frustrations of insecure or disappointed

---

33. Aina, "Nigeria's Post-Amalgamation," 14–31.

economic expectations, and the poor caliber of political leadership."[34] It is striking that these factors more than six decades ago are still relevant today. Accordingly, there is the need for creative imagination to deal with prolonged human rights violations and a culture of impunity. However, before we create the imagination for proactive initiative for Nigeria's intractable past, we should know where the past is coming from and what made the past's conflagrations possible in the first place.

Mass Violence and the Role of Emotions in Nigeria

Many commentators rightly observe that manipulation of primordial ties (e.g., ethnicity and religion) and the existence of poverty are responsible for Nigeria's intractable conflicts and mass atrocities.[35] Since the principal focus of this chapter concerns *postbellum* Nigeria (1970 and following), I shall briefly present two interlocutors to buttress this point. The late Nigerian Playwright, Ola Rotimi, presented a provocative play after the Civil War, titled *The Gods Are Not to Blame*—an adaptation of the Greek myth *Oedipus Rex*.[36] In the play, Rotimi conveyed the message that the destiny fashioned for the land by the "Gods" (i.e., "British colonialists") was not to be blamed for the calamity that befell the land. Rather, it was the arrogance, disrespect, hot-temper, and unquestioned acquiescence to the cultural ethos of the major protagonists that caused the calamity. Rotimi's colleague, Soyinka, disputes this position. Soyinka puts the blame squarely on the shoulders of "the Gods," who taught Nigerians the art of election rigging (with the 1959 elections),[37] and on one

---

34. O'Connell, "Fragility of Stability," 1033. On poor caliber of leadership afflicting Nigeria, compare Oputa Panel *Report* about the frustrations of the younger generation short-changed by the older political class—and these frustrations make it easy for them to be manipulated to create chaos. See HRVIC, *HRVIC Report: Volume Seven*, ch. 1, nos. 8–10.

35. See for instance Korieh and Nwokeji, *Religion, History, and Politics*; Uwazie et al., *Inter-Ethnic and Religious Conflict*; Smith, *Culture of Corruption*; Suberu, *Federalism and Ethnic Conflict*.

36. Rotimi, *Gods Are Not to Blame*.

37. Soyinka shares a revelation that simply confirms what many Nigerian historians and first-generation politicians had long suspected. "The elections [in 1959] that placed a government in power at the centre were rigged" because "John Bull was not about to leave an independent Nigeria under the control of any uppity radicals, as the southern nationalists—the East and the West—were perceived." Harold Smith, a former colonial officer, went as far as asserting: "It was the British who taught Nigerians the art of rigging." Smith, a former colonial officer, revealed this in his 1992 memoir. The British government suppressed this memoir before its publication. Soyinka knew about this because Smith sent him the manuscript. Soyinka, *You Must Set Forth*, 54.

of the Nigerian protagonists: those that claimed they were "born to rule" in Nigeria, i.e., the purported "Kaduna-Mafia."[38]

Nevertheless, it is not enough to prove the link between manipulation of ethnicity/religion, or poverty, and mass atrocity. Others in similar situations like Nigeria do not implode like Nigeria (e.g., pluralist countries in Europe, or poverty-stricken places like India). Hence, facts alone (e.g., manipulation of people) do not always lead to a definitive conclusion. I suggest that the task of social commentators or political analysts should be complemented by that of social ethicists who should seek to excavate these ties and the economic conditions to discover the underlying social and human psychologies that make people so susceptible to manipulation of their primordial ties or their economic conditions. Furthermore, unearthing human psychologies should probably unravel why people persist to give in to manipulations when it has even been exposed that those opportunists are simply manipulating them. Ethicists, unlike social scientists and public commentators, have the task of unraveling and giving an articulated ethical reflection on the myths and values informing public practice and ethos affecting their respective contexts for good or for ill. Understanding the values and rationality behind atrocious acts of otherwise normal people is part of ethical resistance to such acts. John Bowker suggests three fundamental questions that can help in unraveling the values, causes, and constraints that lead to conflicts: "To what do people with competing ideas appeal to support or justify what they are saying? What warrants do they offer for their assertions? Are those warrants sufficient or adequate for the task?"[39] A sure place to begin is the prevailing psychology of stakeholders, because "reason is not sufficient to deliver us from evil."[40] Redemption from evil needs both the cognitive and emotive faculties of persons and not just the cognitive faculty alone.

This claim is inspired by an ethical insight about the moral perception of the human person that points out how "a situation affects the weal and woe of the human beings involved in it."[41] Moral perception is rooted in the dynamically receptive capacity of the human person. Accordingly, in confronting the past, we must pay attention to the role of emotions. Whether real or imagined they serve crucial functions.[42] They serve as a rational measurement of value, not just individually but also relationally

38. See for instance, Soyinka, *You Must Set Forth*, 54; Soyinka, *Man Died*, 177.
39. See Bowker, *Sacred Neuron*, 7.
40. Bowker, *Sacred Neuron*, 11.
41. Vetlesen, *Perception*, 162.
42. In the Nigerian context, see Kirk-Greene, *Genesis*.

and socially. Every human person and group has the capacities and dispositions to experience and act on any human emotion. No one has immunity from emotions, and actions that flow from these, because emotions "are indispensable apprehensions of moral reality."[43] Hence, since "emotional cognition" is a human attribute,[44] differences come only when it comes to the kind of acceptable actions that emotions inspire. Those who do not pay attention to generated, but especially latent, emotions cannot properly understand the past they want to overcome or create a durable justice system that would take care of that thorny past.

One might be struck by the forthrightness of some remarks by the Northern delegation to the inconclusive constitutional conference of September 1966:

> We all have our fears of one another. Some fear that opportunities in their own areas are limited and they would therefore wish to expand and venture unhampered in other parts. Some fear the sheer weight of numbers of other parts. . . . Some fear the sheer weight of skills and aggressive drive of other groups. . . . These fears may be real or imagined; they may be reasonable or petty. Whether they are genuine or not, they have to be taken account of [sic] because they influence to a considerable degree the actions of the groups towards one another and, more important perhaps, the daily actions of the individual in each group towards individuals from other groups.[45]

This was a clear articulation that sought to explore the role of emotion (in this case fear, or *angst*) in the political debacle of 1966. This insight is compelling in understanding Nigeria's troublesome past, up till the end of the Civil War in January 1970, and till 2022.[46]

Human psychology possibly helps the manipulation of ethnicity and religion, which inspire mass violence and atrocities. One can articulate this thus: *the toxicness of humiliation, shame, and worthlessness has a corresponding strong desire for extrication or at least deployment somewhere*. Even if there are no institutional spaces for removal or displacement, this toxic

---

43. Vacek, "Passions," 68.

44. Vacek, "Passions," 72.

45. "Memorandum submitted by the Northern Region" cited in Kirk-Greene, *Crisis and Conflict*, 1:14–15.

Kirk-Greene repeats this statement in his research report on the connection between Nigerian Civil War and the role of emotion (especially fear). See Kirk-Greene, *Genesis*, 20. James Wunsch mentions this fear and politics of paranoia as contributory factors to ethnic conflicts in Nigeria. Cf. Kirk-Greene, *Genesis*, 21; Wunsch, "Nigeria," 172.

46. I have explored this elsewhere. Aina, "Religion," 333–49.

material will be deployed all the same through other means. Therefore, no matter how strong punitively institutions or legislations are if these institutions do not create spaces for the displacement of toxicity, nothing can deter those determined to displace the imposed toxic emotions. It is a healthy and justifiable desire to displace the imposed toxic emotions. When the displacement goes awry it is because the state and its institutions failed to acknowledge this desire and respond adequately.

One can glean from the above assertion that the toxicity of humiliation and the desire for its removal or displacement are major contributors to the hatred chain. The more persons or peoples feel toxic and worthless, the more they are prone to violently displacing their toxic state and worthlessness. They are less interested in the inclusionary transformation of their emotions. The higher the level of trauma, the lower the openness to peace-building and reconciliation among divided parties. Consequently, there is an implied ethical imperative derived from the observation above. However, the imperative appears quite problematic. Hence, I shall present later a more preferred imperative in dealing with toxic emotions.

Toxic Emotions and an Ethical Imperative

Actions inspired by toxic emotions reveal an ethical imperative, which can be formulated thus: *Act in such a way to eliminate emotive toxicness or at least reduce the toxic level.* This ethical imperative reveals an ethical responsibility that is primarily directed to those with toxic emotions. It does not address the universality of this ethical imperative. Left at this level, this ethical imperative becomes a ground for a rewriting of ethics as that of relativism. Actors do not have any room for shared ethics of the human family (an example will be the "might is right" ethical logic). Hence, the primary responsibility is to sufferers of toxic emotions. The means for displacing or reducing this toxic level is inconsequential. The question rarely arises collectively within the group about the ethics of things in service of the end. Dissenters, who insist on discussing the ethics of means, are hardly tolerated. Consequently, people are fed on a staple diet of the formulated imperative above.

This is possibly why normal people do abnormal things to neighbors who belong to rival traditions that had caused their toxic emotions. Normal people with toxic emotions imbibe the proposed ethical imperative to remove this toxic condition from their group—by displacing it on others that caused their condition in the first place. They do not remember that they had been neighbors for decades or generations. They accept this ethical imperative because they belong to rival traditions (cultural, ethnic or religious).They cannot forget that. The ethical imperative becomes powerfully evocative when those constructing this new ethics invoke any proverb similar to that of the Yorùbá: "*Odò tí ó bá gbàgbé orísun rẹ̀ á gbẹ*"—"A river that forgets its source will dry up." So, neighbors must not forget their respective sources. When this source is polluted, people belonging to this polluted source are obliged to do something about this pollution. It can mean transferring the pollution to their neighbors' source. Unfortunately, their neighbors suffer gravely in their hands. This is about memory, honor, and shame. This ethical reasoning becomes so powerful with time when respectful voices within the suffering group articulate and campaign for this through the triumvirate of politicians, intelligentsia, and the media.

This was the dynamics in post-WWI Germany. Germans collectively experienced the toxic emotions of humiliation and shame coming from the retributive justice of the Versailles Treaty. Hence, Germans responded to the call to reject and displace these toxic emotions. This was one of the reasons for the popularity of the Nazi program among ordinary Germans such that they collaborated actively in the Nazi actions that eventually became the Holocaust and crimes against humanity.[47] A similar dynamic was also at work in the period leading to the Rwandan genocide. Through the Hutu Hate radio, the triumvirate mentioned above played on the fears of the Hutu people by emphasizing the threat of the pollution of Tutsi "cockroaches." These fears were played up and the source was projected on the Tutsi. Hence, Hutu could end up massively participating in a unique genocide. Close, intimate, and cruel killings are done largely by using machetes to hack down neighbors while looking them in the eye. Events in Nigeria between January 1966 and January 1970 followed the dynamics above because most of the killings of Northerners and Southerners were done with machetes, at close quarters and with mindless cruelty.

Given the instances narrated above, Soyinka confronts us with the morbidity of death encapsulated in the "I'm Right; You're Dead" rhetoric fueling both terrorist attacks and the counter-terrorism of the Empire.[48] What this ethos fails to realize is that victimized people can be forced to opt for a somber ethical logic expressed in this Yorùbá dictum, "*Ikú yá ju ẹ̀sín*"— "Better dead than public humiliation." This is what makes sustainable peace so difficult to come by. There is no hope for peace as long as public humiliation continues and no justice that wipes away this public humiliation of those experiencing the toxic emotions. Such is the power of toxic emotions.

---

47. See Pollefeyt, "Forgiveness," 136–40.
48. Soyinka, "Climate of Fear."

This, unfortunately, is the case when people are trapped in the ethical imperative formulated earlier. If people burdened with toxic emotions are left with no alternative to the ethical imperative formulated above, there is little chance of just peace and reconciliation. Consequently, we need to explore the possibility of an alternative ethical imperative, inspired by the Christian tradition of divine-human reconciliation. Hopefully, this ethical alternative might be liberating and transformative for such people as Nigerians, as we attempt in the subsequent chapters of this book.

Toxic Emotions and a Preferred Ethical Imperative

The ethical imperative in the preceding subsection acknowledges the undesirability of toxic emotions for human wellbeing. Hence, there is the ethical responsibility to clean up the toxic material. This is against the backdrop that toxic emotions are obnoxious habits that had been cultivated in persons. If not overcome, these toxic emotions can prove very fatal. This makes sense from the genius of the scapegoat ritual in the book of Leviticus (6:1–10). Confronted with the danger of a people going through life burdened with potentially destructive emotions coming from human actions, Israelites were commanded to symbolically transfer these toxic emotions on a goat. They then drive it into the wilderness. This enabled the people to feel fresh and start afresh every year. Unfortunately, with time, this scapegoat mechanism took a sinister turn. Human person(s) replaced the goat, yet with the same logic: it was better for one creature to die than for the whole community to perish due to toxic emotions and their effects. The turn in self-preservation and obligation to reject worthlessness became sinister precisely because it failed to recognize an equally pertinent ethical responsibility: *to ensure that what one protests against and rejects is not made to be experienced by one's neighbors (either as individuals or as groups).* This ethically informed caveat should be understood against the backdrop of the Christian tradition on divine-human reconciliation.

Through his ministry and actions, Jesus evoked some toxic emotions among a host of people.[49] To deal with these emotions, they sought to eliminate them by transferring them to Jesus. On the cross, Jesus publicly acknowledged his own toxic emotions—of humiliation, suffering, and abandonment: "My God, my God, why hast thou forsaken me?" (Mark 15:35). However, God remained silent, non-interfering in the face of the public

---

49. I ask the reader to recall, for instance, the kind of sentiments expressed during the fourth week of Lent that sets the tone for what was to come to Jesus. See especially the first reading (Wis 2:11–22) for Friday of the fourth week.

humiliation and shame of his only Son. Yet, God was not passive. There was a divine protest against the toxic emotion his Son was made to experience. The resurrection was the ultimate protest against and a rejection of the toxicity. By raising Jesus from the dead, and with a glorified body, God acted to eliminate the toxic emotions of the Son, but without generating or transferring such toxicity to his neighbor—humans.

The resurrection was the moment of redemption for humanity, which gave the possibility for reconciliation between God and humans. I will develop this point in chapter 4 when I turn to the place of the Christological doctrine of the hypostatic union in restorative peacebuilding. In the meantime, this divine-human reconciliation should be understood against the backdrop of an ethical paradigm (diabolicization) that demonizes persons. This paradigm operates an ethical dualism that follows the logic of retaliation and reprisal, with no room for rebuilding trust (reconciliation), and possibly forgiveness. Hence, redemption for the human race from the vicious cycle of toxic emotions lies in de-diabolicization. According to Didier Pollefeyt, this is the first step towards "the recognition of the desire for the good in the other (and not only the evil)."[50] This, continues Pollefeyt, is "the *conditio sine qua non* [for] real peace and forgiveness."[51] Although Pollefeyt writes on how to make this happen between human persons after a violent past like the Holocaust, his words are apt for the relationship between God and humans after the death of Jesus, for two reasons. First, God, as revealed in the Scriptures, is ethically qualified. So, God's response to the suffering and death of his only Son has to be viewed ethically. Second, if one accepts the claim above, then one can recognize that what Pollefeyt articulates has been practiced before the post-Holocaust period. Hence, God's ethical response in the suffering, death, and resurrection of Jesus is the lesson God has left humans. This claim emphasizes that emotions, and actions arising from them, are closely linked to an ethic of vice or virtue. Responses to toxic emotions, either through an ethical paradigm of rationalization (relativism) or diabolicization (objectivism), flourish through the cultivation of an ethic of vice.[52]

Accordingly, we articulate a preferred ethical imperative in dealing with "toxic emotion." This preferred ethical imperative is sensitive to the

---

50. Pollefeyt, "Forgiveness," 131.

51. Pollefeyt, "Forgiveness," 131 (emphasis original).

52. Paradoxically, the creators of such ethic present it to the people as an ethic of virtue. For instance, Pollefeyt notes in his critique of Peter Haas's ethical interpretation of the Nazi ethic that "Nazi propaganda portrayed the extermination of the Jews as a good by connecting it to the ethical principle of the right to self-defense." Pollefeyt, "Morality," 121.

ethical responsibility demanded by imposed toxic emotions. On the one hand, it cautions against a sinister turn implied in the ethical imperative formulated earlier. On the other hand, as a responsible ethic of virtue, the preferred ethical imperative is an inspiration from God's ethical response to the toxic emotions imposed on his only Son. The preferred ethical imperative can read thus: "*Act [in such a way] to eliminate emotive toxicity or reduce the toxic level such that your action does not generate or transfer such toxicity to your neighbor.*" This echoes the universal Golden Rule: "Do to others as you would want to be done to you"—or according to the Yorùbá: "*Oun tí a ò gbọ́dọ̀ jẹ, a ò gbọ́dọ̀ fi lọ́ ẹlòmíràn*"—"What we are forbidden to eat must not be suggested to others."

One can recognize that this ethical prescription echoes Kant's categorical imperative: "Act only according to that maxim whereby you can at the same time will that it should become a universal law."[53] However, it goes beyond the Kantian imperative, which accords priority in ethics to respect for others. Kantian ethics does not have space for "emotion" in ethics. So, it is counter-intuitive to affirm respect for others without showing concern for the blinding tears and woes of others. Hence, the ethical imperative formulated above acknowledges that beyond respect for others, one must have concern for them. This ethical preference reveals the interplay between "the faculties of reason and emotion in moral performance."[54] Accordingly, emotions are ineluctably central to the founding of ethics and ethical decision-making.[55] Consequently, the ethical preference as formulated above provides a possibility for an objective morality that finds its commonality in the shared human experience of suffering, which counteracts the internally destructive ethical relativism revealed in the actions of ethnic and religious irredentists.

The objective morality suggested in the ethical imperative above does not imply passivity merely for the reason that it rejects transferring toxicity to others. It demands action. However, it is a responsible action that has eyes also on the vulnerability of others. This "ethical movedness," especially towards one's neighbors who belong to rival traditions, is a great blessing.[56] It provides

---

53. Cited in Cottingham, *Western Philosophy*, 512.

54. Vetlesen, *Perception, Empathy, and Judgment*, 3. I agree hence with Ricœur's critique of Kant's Categorical Imperative as offered in Maureen Junker-Kenny's reflection in *Memory, Narrativity, Self*. The Categorical Imperative, though a "highest principle of action," fails to recognize the otherness of persons and the need for context-dependent decisions beyond context-independent norms. See Junker-Kenny, "Capabilities," 174–76, quotation on 174.

55. Cf. Vacek, "Passions," 72.

56. Burggraeve, "Conversational God," 352, 353.

a possibility for conflict transformation, and a post-conflict justice with a win-win outcome. This takes inspiration from Ricœur's position referred to earlier with regards to maintaining a delicate balance between the "depth of fault" and the "depth of forgiveness." Consequently, one can recognize that what Nigerians need are prophetic witnesses, both as persons and as institutions when dealing with the effects of emotions in their society. These prophetic witnesses are devoted to the creation of an ethic of virtue, inspired by the preferred ethical imperative above. Yet, these witnesses are at the forefront of promoting loving justice for persons and peoples torn apart due to transgressions against the right demands of relationships. I elaborate in chapter 7, which proposes a credible ecclesial mission in Nigeria today. In the meantime, this kind of response to the power and role of toxic emotions in Nigeria's violent past and the difficulty in pursuing justice demands that these emotions must be named. Darkness is powerful as long as it is not held up before the light. Since analyses of the Nigerian situation have focused so much on numerous conspiracy/manipulation theories, the toxic emotions mutate and crisscross diverse groups in Nigeria undetected. This is why they are so destructive, and violence is never far from the surface.

We can begin by asking some questions: "What do we make of these toxic emotions among Nigerians?" "What should be done with them?" "How can Nigerian peoples overcome these emotions without necessarily transferring them to others?" "What kind of justice system is at work in Nigeria but has been unable to give proactive and sustainable answers to the questions driving this book as a whole?"

Ethnic Violence and the Problem of Justice: Some Historical Statements

Ethnic divisions are deep and easily exploited by today's educated political elite who see in ethnic consciousness a potential tool for mass support in politics.[57] With such instrumentalization of ethnic consciousness, actors will generally gloss over atrocities because of an underlying ideology and strategy motivating those atrocities as highlighted below.

1. If perpetrators of atrocities or mass violence are from the domineering ethnic group, then they will be seen as heroes who are advancing the cause of the group. Hence, attempts to bring them to justice will be scuttled.[58] This leaves the victims from the other ethnic groups seeth-

---

57. Aina, "Religion," 336–42.
58. "Interview with Major Nzeogwu," in Kirk-Greene, *Crisis and Conflict*, vol. 1,

ing in anger and frustration that they could not receive justice because they do not control the levers of political power, or the institutions for redress are not controlled by them. Nevertheless, they take exception to the impunity forced on them. Resistance to the impunity of the domineering group will be conveyed through:

   a. sporadic attacks on the vulnerable members of the domineering group, while in the meantime
   b. they plan to compromise, jeopardize, decimate, and wrest power from that "humiliating" group.[59]

The aim is to sever the arrowheads of the group—political leaders, bureaucrats, and senior military officers. This creates a power vacuum and the "humiliating" group is left in confusion.

2. During the interregnum, the previously humiliated group takes control of the reins of power. It sets out immediately, either brazenly or tacitly, to settle old scores. Consequently, other sets of victims are created, who in turn demand justice. Unfortunately, they will not get it as long as their groups remain in a humiliating position. The 1962/63 crisis in the Western region is an example from Nigeria's First Republic. The federal NPC-NCNC coalition's intervention in a regional affair of AG-controlled enclave broke an unwritten rule: non-encroachment by one party into the political base of another ethnic-dominated party.[60] However, breaking this unwritten rule has been seen as retribution for the sustained and troublesome opposition of AG at the center, and for consolidating its hold on western Nigeria. Yet, it was making inroads in other regions by preying on the intra-regional inter-ethnic conflicts, e.g., in the north (Hausa/Fulani vs. Middle Belt peoples) and in the east (Igbo vs. COR group).[61]

3. It is on record that after the January 1966 coup, many southerners taunted their northern neighbors over the death of the prime minister,

---

139; Soyinka, *You Must Set Forth*, 99–100.

59. For instance, Kirk-Greene writes in the aftermath of January '66 failed coup and subsequent Military government of Aguiyi-Ironsi: ". . . the North knew how—and was already beginning in its leadership circles—to apply the break to Southern acceleration." This came on the heels of the Northern advice, expressed in the Editorial of the North-based *New Nigerian* daily on March 1, 1966 to Aguiyi-Ironsi: "hasten slowly." See Kirk-Greene, *Crisis and Conflict*, vol. 1, 45.

60. Okpu, *Ethnic Minority Problems*, 163.

61. See Okpu, *Ethnic Minority Problems*, ch. 3; Suberu, *Federalism and Ethnic Conflict*, 28.

Tafawa Balewa, and the premier of the Northern Region and the late Sardauna of Sokoto, Ahmadu Bello. The *New Nigerian* newspaper recorded this.[62] That humiliating act towards these victims, who had close to iconic statuses among the Hausa/Fulani people, was not met with judicial action. That would not be forgotten; just as northern people would be reminded that this was a repeat of a similar public humiliation of northern political leaders during the 1954 constitutional assembly in Lagos. The northern delegates had come with a proposal for a confederal, even secessionist, clause. The proposal was roundly rejected. As the northern delegates left the hall, southerners outside threw stones at them as well as uttering humiliating words. This act was remembered by the Hausa/Fulani people for years to come.

4. To make matter worse, Aguiyi-Ironsi with the famous Decree 34 of 1966 turned Nigeria from a federal state, though a faltering one, to a unitary state with one central command after the military tradition. The consequence was the unification of all national services, especially the civil service and Nigerian police.[63] This move came to be read as another revenge act against the domineering northern region which had used its disproportionate size to control almost every aspect of the nation. With the unification act, the north suddenly found itself marginalized because of the south's head start in the modernizing/modern institutions introduced by the British during the colonial era, especially education.[64] So, the north, no longer insulated from the competitive and ambitious south, found its public service was taken over by southerners who flooded the region. This generated further humiliation for the north and signaled that the south was profiting increasingly from the south-perpetrated victimization of the north. Instead of actions of justice for what the north experienced on January 15, 1966, the regions of the perpetrators got more rewards.

5. With no decisive action taken, no. 1 above becomes sensible. An interpretation given after the failed January 1966 coup and subsequent actions ran along the following lines. The actions were meant to pass

---

62. See Kirk-Greene, *Crisis and Conflict*, 1:138–39. The flamboyant demeanor of Kaduna Nzeogwu during a BBC interview on January 22, 1966 (just a week after the failed coup) as he recalled his execution of the coup in Kaduna, especially the portrayal of the late Sardauna of Sokoto, the revered Ahmadu Bello, as crouching "among the women (of his harem) and children hiding himself" was incensing—at least to the northerners. On the text of the interview, see Kirk-Greene, *Crisis and Conflict*, 1:138–39, quotation on 138.

63. For the full text of this decree, see Kirk-Greene, *Crisis and Conflict*, 1:169–73.

64. See Suberu, *Federalism and Ethnic Conflict*, 31.

as retribution from the south, especially the Igbo, for the political humiliation suffered in the hand of the north-dominated federal government. Hence, the victims of that coup could not realistically hope for legal, not to talk of substantive, justice. The perpetrators were not treated as they should have been by the law. The consequence was that the victims' group would respond with time. That happened on July 31, 1966, when another coup, led by northern junior military officers, decided to wipe the tears of humiliation and shame of the region by revenge. They killed the military head of state, Aguiyi-Ironsi, and the military governor of the western region. With the success of the coup, the dam of hatred that had built up in the north broke. Hausa/Fulani people went on a rampage, killing en masse many southerners, especially those of the Igbo extraction.

6. Yesterday's victims denied justice, and subjected to a series of humiliation (either by omission or commission), became today's monstrous perpetrators.[65] Even if in no way whatsoever justified, one should understand why the military governor and other authorities in the north did little immediately after the mass atrocities against southerners, mostly Igbo, began. They were simply following the logic in nos. 1 and 2 above. If the ritual of justice had been performed after the January 1966 coup, the magnitude of hatred, reprisals, and mass atrocities would probably have lessened. The accusation of genocide (by the Igbo against the Hausa/Fulani) would probably not have arisen because hatred was not directed at the southerners, especially the Igbo, per se. The mass atrocity was an unjustifiable and monstrous response to an unmitigated sense of humiliation and lack of experience of justice. Without reparative justice, after northern leaders were killed, the people of northern Nigeria felt being in states of unimaginable shame and humiliation. This is why one should take exception to the partial reading and interpretation of events between January 1966 and January 1970. Wole Soyinka, for instance, publicly and understandably agreed with the Igbo's decision to secede from Nigeria. "When a people have been subjected to a degree of inhuman violation for which there is no other word but genocide, they have the right to seek an identity apart from their aggressors."[66] This is

---

65. Adiele Afigbo avers that uprising and mass actions, even violent ones, are statements about the failure of legal justice: "The fact of the matter is that uprisings, rebellions and revolutions, whether popular or unpopular, are an attempt to dramatize in blood and broken bones the shortcomings or failings of a particular political order and if possible to abolish such shortcomings." Afigbo, "Popular Uprising," 572.

66. Soyinka, *You Must Set Forth*, 101.

troubling. It seems that for Soyinka and popular hagiography (passing as historiography), only one side has gripping stories of humiliation and collective shame to tell. Scholars who research Nigeria's past to find a way forward pay little or less attention to the anguish and "a degree of inhuman violation" of the north. It is as if the north, by the fact of the projection of its regional dominance onto the national stage, can only be seen as what I may call the primordial perpetrator. So whatever it suffers, though unfortunate, is nothing compared to what it had done to other parts of the nation. This one-factor thesis and justified response is nothing but ignorance of "political historiography" and an instrumentalization of memory.[67]

7. If post-conflict actions taken by either the victors or the vanquished will carry some legitimacy or draw some sympathy, then the actors' vision of "peace" and "justice" will have to be sold to the people. Thus, we glimpse the commodification and instrumentalization of memory by the triumvirate: political leaders, the intelligentsia, and the media.[68] Indeed, "the real can be mythologized just as the myth can engender strong reality effects"[69] depending on the approaches adopted between the revolutionary, the counter-revolutionary, and the revisionist. This is where one finds some ideological trend noticeable today, especially in Africa: Post-conflict memoirs (or narratives) of certain parties in conflicts are published, or are marketable.

Nigeria's Crises of Memory and Poor History of Transformative Conflict Resolution

Post-independence Nigeria has a poor record of conflict resolution to unburden a traumatic past for victim-survivors or secondary victims. Daily, the poor record keeps alive the memory of victims who met violent death but were not accorded respect and recognition even in death through a vindicating justice process. As argued in the preceding section, Nigeria's history is littered with the corpses and memories of victims of a violent past deprived of justice. Hence, Nigeria is suffering from various crises of memories. A crisis of memory is "a moment of choice, and some times of predicament or conflicts, about remembrance of the past, whether by individuals or by groups"[70]

---

67. Amoda, "Relationship," 155.
68. Dinerman, *Revolution*, 232–33.
69. Cited in Dinerman, *Revolution*, 27.
70. Suleiman, *Crises of Memory*, 1. The crises of memory arise when parties find

rooted in the "interpretation and public understanding of an event firmly situated in the past, but whose aftereffects are still deeply felt."[71]

Memory then is interconnected with trauma, testimony, amnesia, and the (im)possibility of forgiveness. When these intersect but are handled poorly, violence is certain to erupt due to the conflicting recollection and interpretation of a problematic history. Conclusively, the tendency to distort communication in post-conflict settings seems to leave a message that some post-Civil War Nigerians find ethically troubling. It is not just bad politics and grave impediments to historical understanding. It suggests that whatever one does in liberating one's group from real or felt threat is permissible, even unquestionable. Additionally, just one side has gripping stories to tell. Narratives in whatever form presuppose the awareness of emotions' role in dealing with the past and in keeping memories alive. We love to tell stories but hardly do we pay attention to what the emotions conveyed in the stories do to us and our future. This blind spot exists because some of these stories are mythical, not real. We try to make sense of our lives long after some decisive events had happened. When we narrate these stories, we are simply engaging in mythical storytelling—not necessarily the real story. Mythical stories are not necessarily lies or fabrications. They are some idealistic presentation of facts to bolster an argumentation, or a project, or a way of life. Kathleen Daly refers to them as stories of origins.[72] These must be balanced with real stories. These are independent stories that validate or contest mythical claims. This comes with a risk: the project of mythical stories may "die" prematurely. But the risk is worth taking. If we do not pay special attention to the dynamics of "mythical" stories, emotions embedded in these stories will continue to escalate the centrifugal pull in the polity.[73] The next subsection explores how emotions embedded in Nigerians' mythical stories have impacted *postbellum* justice in Nigeria.

---

themselves locked in two extreme ways of dealing with memory. One extreme is "presentism" that claims that the past is present and modified to serve the interest of the present. The other extreme is "taxidermism" that claims that the past is refractory. Hence, it resists undue manipulation. See Dinerman, *Revolution*, 27.

71. Suleiman, *Crises of Memory*, 1.
72. Daly, "Restorative Justice," 55–79.
73. Daly, "Restorative Justice," 56–57.

Dealing with a Cause, Not a Case: Deficiency of Ethical Imagination

As used here, case is "a problem-event that has animated some kind of judgment."[74] A case implies an issue to be solved; while a cause implies an ideological position to be pursued and supported. For instance, if mass violence was a cause, the government would suppress it, even ruthlessly (e.g., the Civil War, *Maitatsine* riots, ethno-religious violence, Niger Delta militancy, *Boko Haram*, IPOB and other secessionist groups). If successfully done, it is business as usual, at least from the government's perspective. Further actions, like reconciliation, understood a rebuilding of trust—between the Nigerian State and its citizens; between the Nigerian State and ethnic groups; among ethnic/religious groups—would be regarded as value-added. If, on the other hand, mass atrocity and what led to it was a case, the parties would come back to the issue.[75]

As demonstrated above, Nigeria's official response to the mass violence of self-determination has been that of a cause: the cause of self-determination (Biafra, Niger Delta, *Boko Haram*, IPOB) vs. the cause of national unity. Hence, once the cause of the national unity is achieved over that of sectional agitators, usually through the use of military force, there is a movement towards consolidation of "national unity" via structural capacity building. Nigerians have been inundated with the news from the Buhari government that *Boko Haram* had been technically defeated by the end of December 2015 because the terrorists no longer held on to territories due to the aggressive military campaigns. Nigerians were expected to assume all had returned to normal. Nigerians were expected to be popping champagne for the government. Things got worse due to Buhari administration's sham braggadocio and its "cause" approach.

Since the seventies till 2022, there has been an absence of case imagination. This meant the loss of the courage to pursue *sanatio in radice*. By now, one can grasp a fact. Impunity and cause go together. The *de facto* cause approach to mass violence and gross violations of human rights in Nigeria from 1966, reaching its zenith in *postbellum* 1970, has inspired subsequent governments in Nigeria to date. Despite largely unilateral (almost always emanating from the state) laudable pronouncements, Nigeria lacked the strategically relational and structured interactive processes for overcoming toxic emotions that have trapped many Nigerians. They see their ethno-religious conflicts and gross violations of rights as cause, not case.

---

74. Berlant, "On the Case," 663.
75. On this see, Kirk-Greene, *Crisis and Conflict*, 2:467–68.

Consequently, from the 1980s, religion became strongly co-opted to realize a cause or to repel perceived unjust cause.[76] Furthermore, despite policy statements and social re-engineering, Nigeria remains a study in paradox. Nigeria is a continental power in human resources, economy, and defense. Yet, it ranks low on the Global Peace Index (GPI) and Human Development Index (HDI). The GDP may increase and political institutions even get stronger. Without decisively attending, in interactive and respectful manners, to subjective interests that fuel unrest, like access to the public goods of the state and an increased stake in the common good of the state, intractable conflicts will not be solved. This expresses the futility of investing in structures and infrastructural reconstruction without investing in the persons who would control those structures in future. Without the institutional provision of a dialogical interface, collective memories of trauma persisted and the clash of narratives continues to fuel conflicts of traumatized and unhealed persons and peoples. This has come to characterize the fast, interventionist and palliative responses of successive governments in Nigeria, particularly during the military dispensation. The nature of military rule made it difficult for military governments to get their priorities right. No military junta anywhere has set up a democratic-like *postbellum* multilateral initiative to respond to individual and collective atrocities.

Conclusion

This background chapter has pursued a line of argumentation that the problem with Nigeria as it experiences periodic mass violence and victimization lies in its past. Expansive justice is very knotty, in places like Nigeria, with its long history of mass atrocities and impunity across its various ethno-religious divide. It is equally challenging on how to define the kind of healing justice countries like Nigeria needs, or how to conceptualize those who are entitled to it, or to whom is owed the ethical obligation of reparation. The next chapter explores the conceptualization of restorative justice, especially as it became associated with peacebuilding. Restorative justice is the fruit of a critical criminological imagination, which aims at evolving structures within the human community that seek the pursuit of post-violence peace and reconciliation. Therefore, the next chapter is on the criminological imagination aimed at developing sustainable peacebuilding practices in the throes of a violent past. This criminological imagination, represented by restorative justice in contexts of mass violence, dares to extend the net of victim focus beyond the privatized victim perspective, which evolved in the sixties and seventies.

---

76. I have explored this elsewhere: Aina, "Killing for God," 95–103.

2

Restorative Peacebuilding in Nigeria

The Best Road Not Taken?

THIS CHAPTER ARTICULATES THE kind of justice that cares for victims' needs, such that it can develop a new understanding of the future by reframing the past and preparing hearts for compassion instead of hate. The first subsection conceptualizes restorative justice at the service of conflict transformation. The second subsection focuses on how a transitional society (Nigeria) drew inspiration from the conceptual description of the justice victims need. Nigeria's inspiration attempted to apply it at the dawn of a new democratic era in 1999. As used here, restorative peacebuilding refers to a process-oriented approach to contentious problem-event, on the way towards reconciliation, i.e., renewal of trust among neighbors turned enemies. Restorative peacebuilding is crucial for estranged parties that are embedded and interconnected within various levels of systems and sub-cultures. Significantly, this process is inspired by restorative justice's four principles: harm-focused; relational; participatory; and democratic.[1] These have the possibility of engendering sustainable peace. How did the country fare with its experiment of restorative peacebuilding?

Justice That Serves Victims and Restorative Justice Imagination

Given the nature of contemporary violent conflicts (intrastate, asymmetric, state crimes), justice that serves victims must factor the state as a (possible) perpetrator/victim into its concept of crime and resolution. The international community with its normative international law, especially on human rights violations and reparations, has considered this. It includes the state in the

---

1. UNODC, *Handbook on Restorative Justice*, 4.

calculus of assigning responsibility as part of satisfaction for a crime.[2] Similarly, the United Nations has adopted some principles on remedying human rights violations by state and corporate bodies, with attention on those with "command responsibility" in an intra/inter-state crime.[3] The UN "Basic Principles of Justice for Victims and Abuse of Power" conceive remedying harm along four axes: a) access to justice (legal process); b) reparation; c) access to information; and d) non-discrimination among victims.[4]

We can infer the notion of justice that serves victims from the above. It boils down to a question. *In the face of intractable generation-old conflicts, what must be done to avoid an immanent apocalyptic scenario of an inevitable all-annihilating war as the only way to end these conflicts?* Some like the UN opt for a structural/institutional (so-called hardware) approach towards viewing justice that serves victims. For instance, William Schabas in his assessment of the UN special tribunals for Yugoslavia, Rwanda, and Sierra Leone opines that the aim of international criminal law and its organs is basically to bring those who have committed war crimes/crimes against humanity to justice and to deter future occurrence.[5] To "bring to justice" is about punitive sanction that is tough to the extent of instilling fear or discouraging those who may be tempted in future that such crimes do not pay, i.e., the costs will always, in the long run, outweigh what gain they are after. This view of justice as retribution and deterrence is utilitarian, premised on a programmatic and minimalist view of the rule of law.[6] The assumption is that (international) justice is about ending impunity, maintaining order, and restoring peace, which is defined in the negative sense, i.e., absence of war or cessation of overt hostilities. In the hardware approach, actors conceive reconciliation as "the restoration and maintenance of peace," which is *ad rem* with the principles and purposes of the UN as an international body.[7]

In contrast to the hardware approach, some prefer a relational, i.e., subject/person-centered (so-called software) approach.[8] The actors here

---

2. Cunneen, "Exploring the Relationship," 357.

3. See for instance, Schabas, *Genocide in International Law*; UNODC, *Handbook on Justice for Victims*.

4. Cunneen, "Exploring the Relationship," 358.

5. On the contemporary understanding of crimes against humanity that can be committed intrastate and in peacetime, see Werle, *Principles*, 222, 225; Schabas, *U.N. International Criminal*, 23n23.

6. For more on this see Mani, *Beyond Retribution*, chs. 2, 3, and 4.

7. Cited in Schabas, *U.N. International Criminal*, 8.

8. On the "hardware" and "software" approaches, see Lopez, *No Peace*, 22–24 (esp. n42).

conceive reconciliation as rehabilitation (or reintegration).[9] This approach is relationally sensitive. It holds that the reconciliation process must necessarily include the rebuilding of trust and reintegration. One of the reasons that several transitional societies at the end of the last century opted for restorative justice was that they found the primary role of the International Criminal Court as inadequate for their intrastate and asymmetric violent past. According to Yves Beigbeder, given the ICC's primary role, reconciliation, which takes years, can be achieved only by vision and political will. It is not the job or the result of criminal justice and its organs.[10] This means that for Beigbeder, like many others, a minimalist approach to the rule of law is the primary characteristic of justice.[11] Instructively, the Rome Statute (1998) that established the International Criminal Court appeared to show interest beyond mere prosecution, sentencing, and punishment. It framed part of ICC's work in the language of restorative justice, with its adoption of three key restorative justice's terms: "participation, protection, and reparations."[12]

Findlay and Henham's book seems to be the most articulate and daring attempt to bring restorative justice face-to-face with international criminal justice and the presuppositions behind it. Their premise is that there is the need to transcend the "normal" processing for penalty and move towards processing for truth.[13] This proposal makes them present what they call the "comparative contextual analysis" (CCA) methodology. Throughout their book, they used this methodology to suggest the place of restorative justice, assess the dominant international criminal justice, and the possibility and imperative of harmonizing restorative justice aims. They argue that it is possible to blend these with the retributive choices without necessarily subsuming restorative justice into the dominant justice system. They hope by doing this that the trial processes locally, nationally, and internationally can be transformed. Accordingly, it will give international criminal justice in whatever form, especially the ICC, greater and ongoing legitimacy. Hence they offer in their conclusion that "within a paradigm which envisages a constructive and strategic role for trial justice in the healing and rebuilding of broken communities and lives, lies the real route to a credible ideology and practice for the control

---

9. Schabas, *U.N. International Criminal*, 559.

10. Beigbeder, *International Justice*, 234. This opens the room for the accusation of the selectivity of justice and judicial decisions even in the UN and the Security Council. See Schabas, *The U.N. International Criminal*, 71.

11. Beigbeder, *International Justice*, 1. On this view and its pitfalls, see Angermaier, "Book Review," 232–33; Mani, *Beyond Retribution*, 26–27, 29–31.

12. Kiess, "Restorative Justice," 116–42, quotation on 128.

13. Findlay and Henham, *Transforming International*, 313.

and management of war and social conflict."[14] However, the ICC has not lived up to "its restorative potential,"[15] because it has not been thoroughly transformed in the light of restorative justice advocacy.

The bottom line is that criminal justice remains uninterested in reconciliation because it contains a lot of irrational and non-linear factors. As such, victims play "auxiliary roles" in the justice that should ordinarily serve them. However, if judicial institutions are part of the avenues by which love and peace are expressed structurally, judicial institutions cannot cease to embody the political imagination and will for reconciliation. As long as we calculate justice based on the number of successfully prosecuted criminals, we let criminal justice and those who run it off the hook too easily. The fast, interventionist and time-conscious feature of criminal justice depicted by the hardware approach must give way to an expansive one that is interested in the bigger picture. This is not merely a utopian or secondary feature of justice. When justice is non-redemptive, how can it foster sincere acknowledgement and openness to post-conflict embrace?

Human justice without the software approach is useless because redemptive justice is the means to peace, and part of the longer route towards reconciliation. The software component of reconciliation, which consists of many irrational and unpredictable factors, especially contending toxic emotions, may be the hard stuff in the long run. The EU book *Towards Better Peacebuilding Practice* acknowledges this much. The money and structural reforms in post-violence societies come to naught if actors do not attend to the irrational factors that influence or impede peace. This is because the hardware approach and its institutions and structures working for peace do not easily focus on irrational factors for peace or violence.[16] Some of these factors (e.g. getting people to overcome hatred, taking responsibility for an irresponsible past, forgiveness, and fear) are matters of the heart, imagination, and spirituality. If people have not been empowered to transcend their fears and anger, the hatred chain and vicious cycle of toxic emotions remain.[17]

What people caught in the vicious cycle need is justice that includes both the hardware and software approaches. On the one hand, justice

14. Findlay and Henham, *Transforming International*, 356.

15. Kiess, "Restorative Justice," 142.

16. In his comparative study of South Africa's and Nigeria's experiments of restorative justice, Benyera argues that some notable members of the international community that control the international justice systems are more interested in the economics of reconstruction, with their conditionalities for rebuilding. Benyera, "South Africa's Truth," 198–99.

17. See Mathews, "What Lessons," 147–48.

includes the inter-personal interaction and positive structural expression of the interaction. On the other hand, the post-violent structures respond to the desired vision for the future together.[18] This indicates that victims' needs are connected with community building. This communitarian vision, therefore, of justice ensures that the society pays attention to victims' needs (and even perpetrators' needs also, since they too are human persons with worth and needs). When a transitional society does something about these needs through multiple means and agencies, it is contributing to a collective building up of a peaceful post-conflict community.

This communitarian vision recalls what Charles Villa-Vicencio refers to as "law beyond law."[19] This is a moral norm that transcends mere legal positivism. On the contrary, "law beyond law" motivates us to envision "'the best route to a better future'. . . . Effectively, it concerns 'the people we want to be and the community we want to have.'"[20] This kind of justice, based on understanding, and not vengeance, on reparation and not just retaliation, on *ubuntu* and not victimization,[21] is a justice that desires a possible decent human society.[22] Post-apartheid South Africa towed that part for a better future. Nigeria followed suit at the dawn of a post-military era.

Post-Military Rule Response to the Ghosts of the Past: Nigeria's Human Right Violation Investigation Commission (HRVIC)

Nigeria had been under military rule intermittently between 1966 and 1999. When the country returned to democratic rule in 1999, the country sought to deal with various human rights violations since the military institution took the reins of governance. What were the options available to Nigeria? Should it be simply a choice between retribution and amnesia? The new democratic government of Olusegun Obasanjo opted for a third way. As discussed exhaustively elsewhere, the third way pursued an expansive view of post-conflict justice, under the rubric of responsive law.[23] The views pursued were:

18. Lopez, *No Peace*, 25 (especially diagram titled "Peace-Home Model").
19. Villa-Vicencio, "Transitional Justice," 388.
20. Villa-Vicencio, "Transitional Justice," 388.
21. Cited in Villa-Vicencio, "Transitional Justice," 388.
22. This kind of justice, Villa-Vicencio contends, is octagonal, consisting of: retribution; deterrence; exoneration; compensation; distribution; rehabilitation; affirmation; and restoration. Villa-Vicencio, "Transitional Justice," 387, 389.
23. Aina, "Nigeria's HRVIC," 55–86; Omale, *Restorative Justice and Victimology*,

i. Accountability, i.e., the disclosure and acknowledgement of wrongs and the effects of imposed emotional *toxicness*;

ii. Confronting mythical stories and stereotypes of the over two hundred and fifty ethnic groups in Nigeria—stories that fuel primordial conflicts and violations;

iii. Responding to legitimate (and exaggerated) claims for institutional justice (i.e., punishment, material, and symbolic reparations), for individuals and communities due to the criminality of the Nigerian State and its agents; and

iv. National Reconciliation and the possible development of a national consciousness beyond parochial interests and primordial loyalties.[24]

The Commission submitted its multivolume *Report* to the president, Olusegun Obasanjo in May 2002.

The Report consists of seven volumes. Volume 1 covers the historical context of the Commission's mandate. Volume 2 gives the international context of human rights and violations, which in turn serves as the guideposts and challenge for Nigeria's attempt to respond to its past. Volume 3, titled "Research Reports," condensed the various reports of volunteer and commissioned researchers who attempted to articulate various human rights violations that were not covered or insufficiently covered by the petitions the Commission received. Volume 4, titled "Public Hearings" is a 347-page case-by-case record of the Commission's public hearings in five cities spread across Nigeria. The hearings were held in Abuja, Lagos, Port-Harcourt, Enugu, and Kano to bring the Commission closer to the people and to give voice to the weak. Volume 5 contains the brief of some memos and petitions received, for which the Commission made specific recommendations. Volume 6 covers the philosophical and theoretical problems associated with reparative justice that is central to the aspirations of many petitioners and other stakeholders at the Commission's hearings. Volume 7 is the summary, conclusions and recommendations of the Commission on how to begin the journey towards nation-building and national reconciliation founded on justice, and ethical consideration of those suffering due to the past. The *Executive Summary*, titled "Synoptic Overview of HRVIC Report: Conclusions and Recommendations (including Chairman's Foreword)," preceded these volumes.[25]

70–71.

24. Aina, "Nigeria's HRVIC," 57–58.

25. The full text of *The Report* was initially on the Commission's website, but the website no longer exists. *The Report*, however, is on a website owned and managed by

Nigeria's Post-Colonial Criminal Justice System: A Case for Restorative Justice

The Report strongly avers that the criminal justice process in Nigeria must move beyond the minimalist construal of the rule of law to a maximalist one[26] if the criminal justice system hopes to redeem itself from the negative perception Nigerians have of it. Indeed, the criminal justice system in Nigeria has short-changed Nigerians. Many Nigerians experienced dispossession of their means of livelihood and meaning, especially through degradation of their environment, without consideration and compensation ordered by the justice system.[27] However, *The Report* considers the failure of the criminal justice system as part of the legacy of colonial intervention among Nigerian peoples. So, Nigerians paid for the "colonially-inherited structure and character of post-colonial Nigerian State, and . . . the manner of its continuing incorporation into the world system."[28] For instance, through the system of indirect rule introduced during the colonial period, the criminal justice system, which invested executive powers on certain individuals (e.g., traditional rulers, and warrant chiefs), broke traditions unheard of. It left a "legacy of protests, revolts, and bitterness against the system."[29] In addition, the post-colonial criminal justice system has been predominantly legal and adversarial, disconnecting itself from social justice (responsive law), because it follows the principal trend in the Western criminal justice system. The system is based chiefly on two principles of nonaccountability and professionalism.[30]

Due to its adversarial nature, the criminal justice system expects legal counsels to follow the principle of nonaccountability: "when acting as an advocate for a client . . . a lawyer is neither legally, professionally, nor morally accountable for the means used or the ends achieved."[31] The principle of professionalism equally states: "When acting as an advocate, a lawyer must, within the established constraints upon professional behavior, maximize

---

Bolaji Aluko, a professor of chemical engineering at Howard University, Washington, DC. See "All About the Oputa Panel."

26. HRVIC, *Synoptic Overview*, no. 40. This implies, for the Commission, that one cannot disconnect CJ from issues of Social Justice.

27. See HRVIC, *HRVIC Report: Volume Three*, 7.

28. HRVIC, *Synoptic Overview*, no. 39.

29. HRVIC, *HRVIC Report: Volume One*, ch. 3, no. 3.45.

30. Cf. Schwartz, "Professionalism," 671–74.

31. Schwartz, "Professionalism," 673. David Luban in his monograph *Legal Ethics and Human Dignity* reflects on these two principles. He states outright that these principles underpin lawyers' action in a trial. See Luban, *Legal Ethics*, 20.

the likelihood that the client will prevail."[32] However, the Commission states that the pre-colonial justice system before its dislocation by colonialism was participatory, inclusive, and at a dialogical interface. Before colonial rule, the primary nations that eventually made up Nigeria maintained "a justice system that was primarily based on a tripartite model (i.e. involving the community, victim and offender in the negotiation of justice and its administration). Prisons were non-existent."[33]

From this quotation, one can catch a glimpse of the restorative justice sensitivity and disposition of the Commission. This quotation resonates with one of the theses of restorative justice: the restoration of dislocated justice sphere among non-Western, post-colonial peoples.[34] Restorative justice, some of its advocates claim, is a restoration of the complex relationship between law, religion, and culture, and sensitivity to many post-colonial societies, and racial/ethnic minorities in the Anglo-Saxon world. It comes as no surprise that the restorative justice movement looks attractive for many post-colonial societies because they see in this movement a possibility of restoration of their indigenous penology and jurisprudence which held law, religion and culture together.[35]

Despite this attraction, one should be aware of the dangerous romanticizing of the pre-colonial justice system since it contained many ambiguities and degrading elements and outcomes.[36] This is one caution one finds absent in the Commission's appraisal of and comparison between the pre-colonial justice system and the colonial-inherited one. Nevertheless, having established the historical roots of the inefficiency of the post-colonial criminal justice system, *The Report* takes a sustained critical look at the criminal justice system. One of the principal observations of *The Report* is that justice institutions in most cases deliberately attempted to protect perpetrators because the office of Attorney General and Minister/Commissioner of Justice are fused into one, and the one holding it is always a political appointee, thus compromising the necessity for rule of law.[37] The criminal justice system, therefore, especially under military rule, where

---

32. Schwartz, "Professionalism," 673.

33. HRVIC, *HRVIC Report: Volume 3*, ch. 7, no. 7.4. Chapter 7 of volume 3 presents various atrocious human rights violations in Nigeria's prisons, the historical roots for the prisons, the challenges towards reparation of past injustices, and building a justice-based prison system.

34. Aina, "Nigeria's HRVIC," 65–66.

35. UNODC, *Handbook on Restorative Justice*, 12.

36. Cf. Fadipe, *Sociology of the Yoruba*, 223–37; Allen, "International Criminal Court," 158–59, 161; Juma, "Legitimacy," 183.

37. HRVIC, *Synoptic Overview*, nos. 109, 112.

most mass atrocities happened, was largely ineffectual in seeking redress because the courts became "toothless bulldogs."[38] Consequently, there were many instances of "conspiracy against justice in many parts of the country," which frustrated hapless victims who demanded justice.[39] Justice, therefore, was compromised. The criminal justice system ceased to be the last bastion of hope for the common citizen, especially the victims of the state and powerful non-state actors. Impunity and abuse of power even before the law became key end products.[40] Agents of the state and powerful non-state actors had no fear of punishment or "the applications of sanctions for violating the human rights of other citizens."[41]

Some common examples of impunity documented in *The Report* are:

- "[E]xtra-judicial killings," which contravened the International Covenant on Civil and Political Rights (ICCPR), and that of the African Charter (art. 4). These stipulate "the right to life is non-derogatory and cannot be suspended under any circumstances."[42]

- Disregard due process. Due process implies that legal actions shall be conducted by laid down procedures. The various organs would work within the legal limits.[43] However, when the state is the guiltiest of mass murders and gross derogation from citizens' right to life as articulated in ICCPR, due process is compromised or completely disregarded as was the case in Nigeria. Calls for investigation, and calls for justice

---

38. HRVIC, *Synoptic Overview*, no. 107. This happened because the Military regimes fused legislative functions with executive one ("Legislative supremacy"), and this made the judiciary hamstrung since military decrees had ouster clauses which prevented the judiciary from reviewing some of the legislative actions carried out by the military regimes. This scenario, according to Oputa Panel, was "a fundamental derogation from the *principles of powers and judicial review, which define a federal system of government.*" HRVIC, *HRVIC Report: Volume Two*, ch. 7, nos. 7.4–6, quotation from no. 7.6 (emphasis original).

39. HRVIC, *Synoptic Overview*, ch. 2, nos. 54, 56, 57, quotation from no. 56.

40. HRVIC, *Synoptic Overview*, no. 108.

41. HRVIC, *HRVIC Report: Volume 2*, ch. 7, no. 7.1.

42. HRVIC, *HRVIC Report: Volume 2*, ch. 7, no. 7.33. The ICCPR (1966) on non-derogation from the right to life (arts. 6–7) rejects torture and degrading treatment or punishment. These articles used "cruel," "inhuman," and "degrading treatment" as alternatives of "punishment." According to ICCPR, one can conclude that "punishment" is synonymous with cruelty, inhumanity, and degradation. Therefore, advocates of restorative justice may be right with their claim that they do not do punishment—if one takes punishment to mean those things articulated in article 7. The dominant criminal justice is not free of this. This claim, nevertheless, is not without some sustained objections. On the articles of ICCPR cited here, and for fuller details, see Suy, *Corpus Iuris Gentium*, 430–31.

43. HRVIC, *HRVIC Report: Volume 2*, ch. 7, no. 7.39.

as punishment, reparation, vindication, and truth, were met with "apathy" and anxiety to "cover any abuses and violations of human rights by policemen and policewomen [rather] than to investigate and punish erring" state agents.[44] Consequently, the principles of fairness, equity, and justice were arbitrarily invoked. This led to what one can call the pragmatic ideologization of national interest and sovereignty that sacrifices rule of law in the name of national security.

Impunity became a major obstacle to remedial justice (reparation and restoration).[45] So, citizens lost trust in the government. Citizens found alternative means to exact justice. For instance, citizens turned to their military friends: "Ordinary citizens also fell back on their connections with military personnel to assert their authority and power over fellow citizens."[46] At other instances, people turned to ethnic militias, university campuses' cults, and retributive reprisals attacks along ethnocentric lines. Those who had not gone violent opted for cynicism and apathy encapsulated in the designation "Nigerian character": if you cannot beat them, join them; use what you have to get what you want.[47]

Summarily, the loss of confidence in the government's regard for due process and readiness to combat impunity at all levels, according to *The Report*, led to the "scourge of ethnic chauvinism, political intolerance and economic devastation that detract or diminish from the worth of the person as such."[48] The reactions of citizens to impunity as presented above show that impunity by the state and its functionaries, whom all have "a higher degree of responsibility and public trust,"[49] is a criminal breach of trust. Consequently, in the long run, this kind of impunity weakens "the social fabric," emboldens citizens for disloyalty, and generally makes citizens lose confidence in the state and its legal process. Citizens realize that they cannot own the process. Yet, this is a crucial index in accountability in an ethically responsible justice system, especially with regards to victims and the need for remedial justice.[50] *The Report* succinctly sums

---

44. HRVIC, *HRVIC Report: Volume 2*, ch. 7, no. 7.36; HRVIC, *Synoptic Overview*, ch. 2, nos. 27–29. Quotation from HRVIC, *HRVIC Report: Volume 2*, ch. 7, no. 7.36.

45. HRVIC, *HRVIC Report: Volume 2*, ch. 7, no. 7.24.

46. HRVIC, *Synoptic Overview*, ch. 2, no. 35.

47. Apathy and cynicism are the principal motivators for the preponderance of corruption at almost every level of Nigerian public sector. On this, see Smith, *Culture of Corruption*.

48. HRVIC, *HRVIC Report: Volume 2*, ch. 8, no. 8.4.

49. HRVIC, *HRVIC Report: Volume 2*, ch. 7, no. 7.25.

50. HRVIC, *HRVIC Report: Volume 2*, ch. 7, no. 7.26.

up the collateral cost as "collective amnesia, pent up anger, agony, hatred, resentment, and revenge, all ready to burst and consume the nation in yet more traumatic decimating explosion."[51]

The Report, accordingly, situates its existence and its *raison d'être* within the context of collective impunity (what the Commission calls "the ugly past of collective violence")[52] which characterized Nigeria's life from January 1966 to May 1999. Nigeria's traumatic and ugly past could not be ascribed to just a few actors. That was why the new democratic government in 1999 tinkered with an innovation—at least to Nigerians. It wanted to move beyond widespread impunity without endangering the "Nigeria Project" (i.e., nation-building). This is one of the most compelling promises of restorative justice, according to *The Report*.

Restorative Justice at a Public Interface: Beyond the Past of Collective Impunity

The Commission situated itself within the growing attraction for Truth Commissions. To the Commission, these were innovations to move beyond an ugly past of mass atrocities by neighbors sharing the same political space. Thus, in the face of "the ugly past of collective violence," it was necessary to come up with and be engaged in "some form of healing process and reconciliation in countries that had experienced violent conflicts and gross violations of human rights."[53] As stated in chapter 1, the current criminal justice system in Nigeria could not deal with the ugly past of collective violence. Criminal justice as structured even today is uninterested in reconciliation.[54] Unsurprisingly, as of 2001 (when the Commission) rounded up its work, there were about nineteen countries with Truth Commissions—temporary bodies, with official status and at times "quasi-judicial truth-finding functions and powers."[55] These were necessary on the assumption that countries burdened with an ugly past of collective violence need such structures to heal the wounds citizens collectively inflicted on themselves. *Postbellum* healing was "a precondition to moving forward in a spirit of national unity and reconciliation."[56]

51. HRVIC, *HRVIC Report: Volume 2*, ch. 8, no. 8.11.
52. HRVIC, *HRVIC Report: Volume 2*, ch. 8, no. 8.5.
53. HRVIC, *HRVIC Report: Volume 2*, ch. 8, no. 8.5.
54. See Findlay and Henham, *Beyond Punishment*, 2; Werle, *Principles*, 222, 225; Schabas, *U.N. International Criminal*, 23n23.
55. HRVIC, *HRVIC Report: Volume 2*, ch. 8, no. 8.6.
56. HRVIC, *HRVIC Report: Volume 2*, ch. 8, no. 8.7.

The articulation of the rationale for a justice process at a public interface involving numerous stakeholders for the sake of interactive conflict resolution of the ugly past and reconciliation between stakeholders (individuals and corporate) resonate strongly with the vision and praxis of restorative justice. There are other expectations from a public enquiry like the Oputa Panel and Truth Commissions that echo strongly the theses and promises of restorative justice. The principal expectations listed by the Commission, which informed its work and outlook, are:[57]

- Restoring the dignity of victims;
- Creating opportunity for perpetrators to "expiate their guilt";
- Facilitating national catharsis and development of a culture of respect for human rights against the prevailing culture of impunity;
- The naming of perpetrators and disclosure of the truth about their atrocities are punishment. This can reduce the urge for retribution.

These expectations echo restorative justice as a mechanism for responsive law, hence making a strong case for it moving beyond micro issues to restorative peacebuilding. The promises of restorative justice outlined above seem to have been achieved by the Commission if one critically views *The Report*.

With the opportunity and space given to victims of the past's violations to make written petitions to the Commission and even appear in person in the various venues of public hearings, one can say the dignity of victims silenced by the previous culture of impunity was finally recognized.[58] Getting their story out was part of the therapeutic tendency claimed in restorative justice.[59] Disclosure of truth, as tenuous as this is because of subjecting truth in "politically and emotionally charged situations," happened in some cases.[60] This brought some reconciliatory gestures between some victims and some perpetrators.[61]

---

57. See HRVIC, *HRVIC Report: Volume 2*, ch. 8, nos. 8.12–14, quotations from nos. 8.12, 8.14.

58. On what the Commission refers to as the "menace of impunity" involving law enforcement agents of the State, see HRVIC, *HRVIC Report: Volume 2*, ch. 7, nos. 7.24–38.

59. On the therapeutic dimension of victims' disclosure of pain and trauma, see HRVIC, *HRVIC Report: Volume 7*, ch. 3, no. 2. The petitions of victims make up *Brief of Memos*, while the details of the public hearings make up volume 4. See HRVIC, *HRVIC Report: Volume 4*; HRVIC, *HRVIC Report: Brief on Memos*.

60. HRVIC, *HRVIC Report: Volume 2*, ch. 8, no. 8.22.

61. HRVIC, *Synoptic Overview*, nos. 1.31, 32; HRVIC, *HRVIC Report: Volume 7*, ch. 3, nos. 5–6, 82.

Furthermore, the Commission appreciatively attempted to confront, harmonize and evaluate disparate narratives and myths bandied by various socio-ethnic groups in Nigeria. The national narrative crafted in *The Report* in my estimation is a noteworthy exercise towards a national narrative no matter how partial. Getting a more holistic view of violence, and its multiplier effects, from as many implicated stakeholders as possible, is one of the principal theses of restorative justice. One of the restorative peacebuilding's theses is that truth must be reconciled and negotiated along four vectors: inter-subjective; inter-personal; inter-group; and inter-national—to arrive at a near national narrative, just as South Africa's TRC attempted to do. Though a unanimous national narrative may be an illusion in Nigeria, at least for now, the narrative presented by *The Report*[62] is laudable because it can serve as the basis for historical studies on Nigeria. It is a more balanced account that should have served as the basis for civic education and national consciousness, and the bedrock for further political rearrangement in the country without proliferating combustible myths used as part of the instrumentalization of collective memory today.

The Report similarly claims to have achieved some catharsis for the nation, which offered the possibility for purification "at the individual psycho-spiritual level and at the wider community and national levels."[63] For many Nigerians, this catharsis brought about by the open and sometimes sordid disclosure of atrocities by yesterday's powerful men and women and security agencies signaled the beginning of the end of the culture of impunity.[64] Naming and shaming that are part of restorative justice's reintegrative trajectory were equally part of the Commission's practice. However, the problem associated with this restorative justice thesis probably contributed to many alleged perpetrators denying blatantly "the human rights abuses and violations alleged against them by their victims and families."[65] Although the Chairman of the Commission, in his foreword, approvingly cites a remark

---

62. See HRVIC, *HRVIC Report: Volume 2*, ch. 2, nos. 2.6–34; ch. 6, nos. 6.27–48; ch. 7, nos. 7.1–50; HRVIC, *HRVIC Report: Volume 7*, ch. 1, nos. 1–33; ch. 2, nos. 1–84; ch. 3, nos. 53–91; HRVIC, *HRVIC Report: Volume 4*, 268–77; HRVIC, *HRVIC Report: Volume 3*, nos. 1–246; HRVIC, *HRVIC Report: Volume 1*, ch. 2, nos. 2.1–31, ch. 3, nos. 3.1–244.

63. HRVIC, *Synoptic Overview*, no. 1.17.

64. Detailed and sobering evaluation of various security agencies implicated in past impunity can be found in the third and seventh volumes of *The Report*. See HRVIC, *HRVIC Report: Volume 3*, esp. ch. 2; HRVIC, *HRVIC Report: Volume 7*.

65. HRVIC, *Synoptic Overview*, no. 1.18.

of a witness concerning the blatant denial,[66] reasons for the denial are more complex than just lack of courage.

Overall, one may classify Nigeria's Oputa Panel as another instance of restorative justice playing an active and transformative role towards an effective and humane judicial process that "heals the pain that crime causes" during and after an armed conflict.[67] The extent of the Commission's success is another issue entirely because the non-release of *The Report* hinders the various forms of reception (political; academic; ethical; theological) such a monumental document deserves. Accordingly, we may not ascribe too much to Oputa Panel on the active role restorative justice has played or is playing in situations of mass atrocities and intractable conflicts. A recent study goes as far as stating that the HRVIC is a failure since the civil authorities cannot enforce its report. Its work, therefore, is invalid. I do not agree with this stance.[68]

Perhaps the Commission put more faith in the ability of restorative justice playing a crucial role in reviving Nigeria's inept criminal justice system if one judges by the space and researches on restorative justice contained in *The Report*. I shall pay some attention to these, though they are not dealing directly with intractable conflict transformation. Nevertheless, if one recognizes that the rule of law, transparency, and institutional stability that guarantee the sustainability of human life, persons and goods about human flourishing are part of the impact areas in peace-building, then it is not out of place to highlight what *The Report* says about Nigeria's criminal justice system and the role restorative justice can play to ensure the sustainability of these impact areas.

Restorative Justice: An Alternative to an Ineffective Nigeria's Criminal Justice System

If the previous sub-section articulates restorative justice's actual role in responding to Nigeria's violent past, *The Report* similarly notes the role, space, and hope for restorative justice in Nigeria's penal system. *The Report* premised its approval of and recommendation for restorative justice on the institutional problems in Nigeria's criminal justice system: e.g., lack of a central planning body for the criminal justice system; lack of

---

66. "And, as one witness pointed out, it takes more than human courage to admit one's wrong-doing. And so the Commission found out!" HRVIC, *Synoptic Overview*, no. 1.21.

67. Vuylsteke, "Criminologist," 5.

68. See Benyera, "South Africa's Truth," 196.

coordination and cooperation between the Police, the Judiciary, the Director of Public Prosecution and the prison services; the dearth of statistical data, and when available, the inefficient use of such data.[69] These institutional problems consequently contributed to a poor prison system in Nigeria. Overcrowding and a delayed justice process characterized the prison system. Consequently, more than 50 percent of prison inmates were those awaiting trials.[70] Other characteristics *The Report* mentions are inadequate health care, welfare, and rehabilitation packages; overuse of custodial prerogatives by the courts; abuse of power and bail conditions by the police; inadequate access to legal services; and corruption.[71] Furthermore, the juvenile justice system was inadequate. Officials at correctional facilities treated female prisoners poorly. In some cases, these officials sexually harassed female prisoners. The officials lacked gender sensitivity training. Prisoners also lacked vocational/educational skills.[72] Worst of all, the justice institution treated mentally ill prisoners poorly.[73]

Indeed, what Braithwaite says of the criminal justice system in the West applies to Nigeria also: "In an ideal world, the intention should be that the criminal justice system heals the pain that the crime causes, but in reality, the adage is far too often different: because the crime caused pain, we must inflict still more pain on the perpetrator. In this manner we end up in a vicious circle."[74] For the HRVIC, this inhumane judicial system exists in Nigeria because the nation lacks a public awareness regarding how the colonial-inherited criminal justice system is "contra-cultural."[75] Hence, *The Report* expresses the need for "cultural realignment and procedural simplification to enable citizens' understanding and involvement in the formal criminal justice process."[76] To this end, *The Report* recommends alternatives to imprisonment.[77]

The alternatives mentioned are "new models of Justice and community participation," specifically "restorative justice models."[78] According to *The Report*, these alternatives will reflect pre-colonial African jurisprudence and

---

69. Cf. HRVIC, *HRVIC Report: Volume 3*, ch. 7, nos. 7.55–56.
70. HRVIC, *HRVIC Report: Volume 3*, ch. 7, table 4.
71. See HRVIC, *HRVIC Report: Volume 3*, ch. 7, nos. 7.28, 7.34, 7.50.
72. HRVIC, *HRVIC Report: Volume 3*, ch. 7, nos. 7.40–44.
73. HRVIC, *HRVIC Report: Volume 3*, ch. 7, nos. 7.45–47.
74. Vuylsteke, "Criminologist and Honorary Doctor," 5.
75. HRVIC, *HRVIC Report: Volume 3*, ch. 7, no. 7.60.
76. HRVIC, *HRVIC Report: Volume 3*, ch. 7, no. 7.61.
77. HRVIC, *HRVIC Report: Volume 3*, ch. 7, no. 7.69.
78. HRVIC, *HRVIC Report: Volume 3*, ch. 7, no. 7.74.

penology. The new models include victim-offender-community mediation; family group conferencing; community mentoring; and community service. The Commission believes these alternatives "will highlight healing justice and redirect energy from emphasis on revenge."[79]

We need to scrutinize the expectation of healing in the alternatives restorative justice proposed. Restorative justice advocates claim that justice heals. Is healing the job of justice? Austin Onuoha, a Nigerian researcher on restorative justice, observes that "restoration of relationship is not a legislated affair."[80] This restoration demands endeavor and ritual process beyond the speciality of the criminal justice system.[81] If one agrees with Onuoha, and this is contestable, "healing" cannot be a legislated/penal system affair. Perhaps, simply taking on the restorative justice rhetoric, the Commission and its researchers were not aware of unresolved controversies and contentions in the restorative justice movement, especially on the claim on justice as healing. I will return to this debate later in chapter 5, arguing how, from a Christian ethical perspective, it is reasonable and necessary to associate healing with justice.

Beyond the claim of restorative justice to heal victims, *The Report*'s proposal for restorative justice alternatives equally hints at:

1. a community-related restorative justice in Nigeria's judicial system; and

2. a non advocacy of a "Community Justice" that is parallel to the judicial system.

In other words, the proposal implies that the community-related restorative justice initiative will be subsumed in the dominant criminal justice system. This suggestion from *The Report* does not represent an alternative procedure; talk less of advocating for it becoming a standard procedure despite declaiming the current judicial system as contra-cultural. We can judge this endorsement, hence, as naïve because the proposals for restorative justice and how it should function in Nigeria are not situated within the current discussion in criminal justice globally today. For instance, *The*

---

79. HRVIC, *HRVIC Report: Volume 3*, ch. 7, no. 7.74. One can notice a tension here with the Commission's construal of restorative justice's aims. Here, the attention is on healing and redirecting vengeful energy. It does not mention punishment. "Community Service" had replaced punishment. Consequently, *The Report* opts for an ethically reasonable loving justice which, to quote Wilhelm Verwoerd from a similar context, puts "a human face literally and/or figuratively to a horrible deed." Verwoerd, *Equity*, 181.

80. Onuoha, "Dilemma," 84.

81. Onuoha, "Dilemma," 84.

Report does not probe the tension between the adversarial criminal justice system and restorative justice ethos: are they radically incompatible? For example, in principle, the adversarial nature of criminal justice is a form of advocacy, which ensures that no arguments or objections get overlooked. It is part of procedural fairness. Hence, it has its function. Yet, a romanticized construal of restorative justice presents an adversarial criminal justice system as not containing advocacy for victims.

Furthermore, how far can advocates incorporate restorative justice in the adversarial criminal justice system? Should it simply run parallel to the adversarial system? Or to word it differently, *The Report*'s proposal on restorative justice does not display attentiveness to the proper role of restorative justice. John Braithwaite, one of the leading advocates of restorative justice, states: "restorative justice remains an alternative option, not the standard procedure. It is but a creek, and not yet the river."[82] Should restorative justice in Nigeria be "a creek" or should it become "the river"? The issues raised above are pertinent because they bear on how restorative justice will properly function. One can aver that though restorative justice ethos and insights are glimpsed from *The Report*, the Commission discussed these insufficiently.[83]

Nevertheless, it is should be noted that Nigerians are paying keen attention to the kind of proposals contained in *The Report*. For instance, a professor of criminology at the Federal University, Wukari (Nigeria), Don John Omale, is a leading advocate of restorative justice in Nigeria.[84] His doctoral research and post-doctoral interventions have been on how restorative justice can become a viable alternative to penal sentencing in Nigeria. Omale shares the kind of optimism expressed in *The Report* that restorative justice will come to play a larger role in Nigeria's criminal justice system.[85]

If *The Report* appears a bit naïve about the extent of restorative justice in Nigeria's penal system, it is not naïve about the viability of restorative justice-related alternatives. It acknowledges that the viability is not very promising. The Nigerian police is singled out as a crucial obstacle to viability. Principally, the police lack training on the need to move from "reactive policing" to "proactive preventive policing . . . problem-oriented

---

82. Vuylsteke, "Criminologist," 5.

83. The Report claims that restorative justice counters popular criminal justice culture. To what extent is it helpful for a state agency to carry out oversight functions on the restorative justice procedure? We bear in mind that, according to the Commission, the state agencies are the greatest perpetrators of human rights violations and principal source of the menace of impunity.

84. He is one of the contributory experts to the UNODC, *Handbook on Restorative Justice*, iii.

85. Omale, *Restorative Justice and Victimology*, chs. 5, 6, and 7.

policing, which involve police-community partnership."[86] Similarly, the police do not cooperate with informed criminologists, who come up with alternatives: "Worse still, the Nigerian Police are reluctant to collaborate with technically qualified criminologists to design appropriate and reliable criminal and law enforcement information management system."[87] Though this may be changing, it may take some time because problem-oriented policing and police-community partnership may be perceived by the excessively authoritarian and corrupt police as threats to their powers and unquestioned access to extort hapless citizens. This attitude is perceived as "the principal means of obstructing justice."[88]

The Report's advocacy for rule of law, transparency, and institutional stability through the strengthening of Nigeria's criminal justice system is very important against the backdrop of developments globally. In the preface to his *Understanding "Restorative Justice"*, Omale writes that the United Nations' adoption of restorative justice in criminal matters prompted him to attempt to reconceptualize "the entire criminal justice practice in Nigeria where [sic] alternative to penal sentencing and juvenile justice are absent."[89] Indeed, we see clearly what Nigeria/Nigerians are missing by the non-release of *The Report* since the HRVIC received and adopted restorative justice beyond Omale's.

Volume 3 of *The Report* devotes chapters 7 and 8 to analyses that go deeper than Omale's *Understanding "Restorative Justice"*.[90] Despite *The Report*'s extensive analyses on the role of restorative justice as capable of engendering durable alternatives to the penal system in volume 3, HRVIC's recommendations on prison reform did not mention restorative justice and its envisaged role. Similarly, the recommendations on the police did not mention the

---

86. HRVIC, *HRVIC Report: Volume 3*, ch. 8, no. 8.52.7.

87. HRVIC, *HRVIC Report: Volume 3*, ch. 8, no. 8.52.8. Onuoha similarly accused lawyers involved in the Niger Delta-Oil companies' conflict because of pecuniary interests. This is similar to the assertion made by Mark Drumbl on the viability of restorative justice in *postbellum* situation, e.g., post-genocide Rwanda. See Onuoha, "Dilemma," 86; Drumbl, "Restorative Justice," 6–7.

88. HRVIC, *HRVIC Report: Volume 7*, ch. 2, no. 54.

89. Omale, *Understanding "Restorative Justice,"* vii. Omale's ambitious project to reconceptualize "the entire criminal justice practice in Nigeria" was born out of his experience at a "Model United Nations Conference" at New York (April 2003). See Omale, *Understanding "Restorative Justice"*, vii. On the text of UN adoption of restorative justice in criminal matters, see, for instance, UNODC, *Handbook on Restorative Justice*, 113–16.

90. To his credit, however, Omale's later work (*Restorative Justice and Victimology*) is far more nuanced and realistic. Some of his recommendations echo *The Report*, especially *postbellum* victim satisfaction, criminal justice reform, the connection between restorative and social justice, and restorative peacebuilding (reconciliation). Omale, *Restorative Justice and Victimology*, 200–207.

alternatives mentioned in volume 3 (chapters 7 and 8) as part of the nation's urgent needs.[91] Perhaps, *The Report* assumes that "alternatives to penal system" can be presumed in the following recommendation: "We recommend an entire overhaul of the prison system in the country."[92] Despite the hope and breath of fresh air the Oputa panel represented, Nigeria's curse of impunity derailed the promise, and Nigeria is worse for it today.[93]

Restorative Peacebuilding: The Best Road Not Taken

Regrettably, Nigeria's curse of impunity has prevented the official release of the HRVIC *Report* to date. Former military president Ibrahim Babangida fought his way through to the nation's Supreme Court to stop *The Report* from being officially released because of unfavorable evaluations made by the Commission on atrocities committed by state agents during his reign between 1985 and 1993. Thus, Nigeria failed to deal decisively with the ghosts of the past. The country fell back into the pit of amnesia and impunity, experiencing grave insecurity. Insecurity, as experienced in Nigeria, refers to "a condition of dangers that gives rise to lack of confidence, protection and safety. This condition threatens human life, communities, and sometimes even the state through relentless aggression."[94] This is why the country can still be listed as a transitional society despite two decades of democratic rule. Transitional societies are nation-states emerging from the throes of intractable civil or international conflicts, with widespread war crimes or mass atrocities. Additionally, transitional societies can also be states emerging from autocratic regimes to nascent democracies.[95] In this case, Nigeria qualifies as a transitional society, because it is bedeviled with intractable conflicts, with its combustible ethnolinguistic and religious fractionalization. Nigeria remains in transition,[96] due to its indecisive democracy, which is gradually sliding into one of the aberrations of democratic rule.[97]

---

91. HRVIC, *HRVIC Report: Volume 7*, ch. 2, nos. 34–36, 44–46.

92. HRVIC, *HRVIC Report: Volume 7*, ch. 2, no. 44.

93. Despite the obvious promises of restorative justice in peacebuilding demonstrated in Nigeria's experiment, the lack of the political will to go the whole way prevents the international community from listing this experiment as one of the instances of restorative peacebuilding. For instance, the United Nations' *Handbook on Restorative Justice* does not list HRVIC as one of the examples of transitional and post-conflict justice mechanisms. See UNODC, *Handbook on Restorative Justice*, 13.

94. Aina, "Christian Response," 35–36.

95. Cf. Freeman and Djukić, "Jus Post Bellum," 214; Norris, *Driving Democracy*, 50–52.

96. Yusuf, "Country Studies," 333–39.

97. Some of these aberrations are "'semidemocracies,'" "'competitive authoritarianism,'" "'illiberal democracies,'" and "'elected autocracies.'" See Norris, *Driving*

Unsurprisingly, Nigeria has a low culture of positive peace. Positive peace "is the attitudes, institutions & structures that create and sustain peaceful societies."[98] There are eight pillars of or factors for positive peace. These are "Sound Business Environment, Low Levels of Corruption, Acceptance of the Rights of Others, Well Functioning Government, High Levels of Human Capital, Equitable Distribution of Resources, Free Flow of Information, (sic) Good Relations with Neighbours."[99] These eight pillars offer us "a baseline measure of the effectiveness of a country to build and maintain peace."[100] Nigeria lacks this baseline, and the lack of positive peace takes a heavy toll on the country.

In recent years, violence had cost Nigeria billions of naira. For instance, in 2018 violence cost Nigeria 66,602,880,432 naira, representing 7 percent of its GDP.[101] Unfortunately, these economic costs mean that the country has less money to spend on human development. Consequently, Nigeria has become the poverty capital of the world.[102] With many homes struggling to survive decently, we are reminded of the causal link between security and the fate of the *Ẹiyẹ Kínkín* of the world. As argued elsewhere,

> The more people are stuck at the base of the pyramid of wellbeing the more their society is likely to experience recurrence of the five major types of violence mentioned earlier. Hence, there is the likelihood of widespread insecurity when the 'poorest of the poor' increase in number with a diminished possibility of being structurally unshackled.[103]

The poor will always be vulnerable to manipulation by criminal or revolutionary elements. Nigeria is still suffering the result to date because the country keeps searching for how to deal with its history of violence, forgetting that it already has a blueprint.[104]

Democracy, 22.

98. Institute for Economics & Peace, *Global Peace 2018*, 60.
99. Institute for Economics & Peace, *Global Peace 2018*, 60.
100. Institute for Economics & Peace, *Global Peace 2018*, 60.
101. Institute for Economics & Peace, *Global Peace 2019*, 100 (Table D.1).
102. "At the end of May 2018, our trajectories suggest that Nigeria had about 87 million people in extreme poverty, compared with India's 73 million people. What is more, extreme poverty in Nigeria is growing by six people every minute, while poverty in India continues to fall." Cf. Kharas et al., "Start."
103. Aina, "Good Governance," 221.
104. Aina, "Nigeria's HRVIC," 55–86.

Conclusion

Restorative justice, as outlined in this chapter, promised to be more forthcoming with reconciliation after wars and mass violence than the dominant criminal justice system. From the accent on Nigeria's HRVIC, as gleaned from its *Report*, we can plausibly affirm that the HRVIC was faithful to the vision of restorative justice advocates as I offered in the first section of this chapter. Restorative justice is even more promising when one looks at Nigeria at the dawn of the new democratic era in 1999. Nigeria opted for a restorative peacebuilding process based on a non-ideal theory of justice. This theory of justice, which restorative justice demonstrates, acknowledges the plurality of values, which cannot be played against one another. Conversely, it demands "a *reasonable balance* between conflicting fundamental values."[105] It takes "a *purposeful*... approach to rights" as against normative, context-blind justice considerations.[106] Furthermore, this theory holds that "an account of justice must give due consideration to the diverse complexities that arise in the real world. This will better prepare us for taking seriously the distinct demands of social justice."[107] This non-ideal theory of justice is normative, justified, and intelligent. Nigeria's HRVIC equally showed great promise in pursuing this humane, though non-ideal, justice for the sake of overcoming toxic emotions on the way towards reconciliation.

Theologically, therefore, one can appreciate restorative justice's promises because it offers a notion of reconciliation that comes close to a Christian theology of reconciliation. This notion of reconciliation recognizes parties as sisters and brothers, and not strangers. Hence, restorative justice promises and is seen to tackle the dilemma of *patrimonicide* and sibling violence in Nigeria. Still, this chapter showed the challenges regarding the kind of healing justice countries like Nigeria need, or how to conceptualize those who are entitled to it, or to whom we owe reparation as an ethical obligation. Nigeria remains stuck in the absence of structural justice and a lack of positive peace. The following chapters lay out the major themes, contestations, and promises, from the lens of the Christian understanding of healing justice and restorative peacebuilding that should influence transitional societies like Nigeria. We begin with a critical conversation with the recently deceased Archbishop Desmond Tutu on his theology of restorative justice and *postbellum* reconciliation.

---

105. Farrelly, "Justice," 862 (emphasis original).
106. Farrelly, "Justice," 862 (emphasis original).
107. Farrelly, "Justice," 862.

3

A Christian Ethical Appreciation of Archbishop Desmond Tutu's Theology of Restorative Justice

The lion and the boar met themselves at the edge of the path. Almost immediately they began their arguments where they left off the previous time. But this time, they were ready to put an end to it; this time not through words but through a free for all, "winner takes it all" fight. As they were preparing to begin their fight, the lion and the boar saw the eagles and the hawks circling above them urging them on. At that moment they got the message: the eagles and the hawks were urging them on so that they could feast later on any of them that were vanquished. With that insight, both the lion and the boar decided to give up the fight and never to desire fight again. They agreed, "It is better for us to be friends than to become food for vultures and crows."[1]

How could Archbishop Tutu of all people collaborate in an exercise that appeared to turn the grassroots 1955 *Charter of Freedom* into a charter of broken promises? Even if he had no intention of betraying this *Charter*, what kind of theological imagination and discourse did Tutu and other *baruti* had that fitted so well into an agenda of a democracy born in chains? To realize their theological imagination/project, to what extent can theologians and pastors collaborate in a public project especially when it is ethically dubious? Alternatively, what kind of theological discourse can confront transitionologists[2] who subtly "seduce" transitional societies to embrace a justice approach,

---

1. Hettema, *Reading for Good*, 11.

2. These are experts interested in humanitarian interventions that "hop from war-torn country to crisis-racked city, regaling overwhelmed new politicians with the latest best practice from Buenos Aires, the most inspiring success story from Warsaw, the most fearsome roar from the Asian Tigers." Klein, *Shock Doctrine*, 216–17.

like most human rights approach projects, dealing with outward manifestations, and not the root causes of a violent and divisive past?

These are the questions guiding this chapter, as part of this book's critical contribution to Christian ethical reflections on the inspiration of restorative justice beyond its original micro-focused context, despite the telling ambiguities. This is pivotal given the valorization of religion in peacebuilding initiatives today. Religion and theologies will normally play some notable roles in peacebuilding projects in many transitional societies. Archbishop Tutu is a clear case of that kind of pivotal contribution. This chapter is faced with a summary question: *what kind of theology/theological imagination is helpful in the long run in facing the promises and ambiguities of restorative justice?*

Ubuntu and Tutu's Restorative Justice Discourse

One of the striking things about Desmond Tutu's reconciliatory messages was that they were not filled with rage or hatred against a government, policy, and beneficiaries that dispossessed him and his people in the land of their birth. This peaked in his active and influential role during the setting up and actions of the Truth and Reconciliation Commission. This Commission and Tutu have been vilified and praised, depending on the spectrum from which the critics look at both parties. With all his ecclesial and global statuses, Tutu was subjected to land pass laws in his own country. He had to wait for sixty-two years before he could vote for the first time.[3] How could a person vociferously campaign for reconciliation with his oppressors when he and his people had the opportunity to revenge for all the years of degradation and dehumanization? Why did Tutu and his oppressed people agree, like the proverbial lion and boar above, with de Klerk and his oppressive forces and his beneficiary peoples not to engage in a judicial process that would have led to more bloodshed and violence? We can partly locate this in Tutu's African philosophical anthropology of *Ubuntu* infused with a profound Christian theology of personhood and hope.[4] As late as 2018, Tutu's life and thought "oozes *ubuntu*."[5]

---

3. Tutu, *God Has a Dream*, 6.
4. Mojola, "Ubuntu," 33.
5. Mojola, "African Bantu," 60.

Tutu's Theological Contribution: The Trio of Confession, Truth, and Forgiveness

Tutu reveals a Christian notion of reconciliation and restorative justice that emphasizes confession (truth-telling), forgiveness, and communion.[6] It is as if confession and forgiveness predispose stakeholders to the pursuit of justice and not the other way round where justice is an *in-between* word. This interpretation is reasonable because the language of confession and forgiveness predominate in Tutu's theology. During the TRC years, he pursued it insistently. However, the material component of justice had to wait even to make its appearance. It seems this justice is an optional extra, whereas confession and forgiveness are essential. Hence, for Tutu, it appears there is no ethical problem in not tying amnesty to concrete reparations to victims.

This is understandable in Tutu's scheme of reconciliation because this theology follows strictly the dynamic revealed between God-the-victim and humans-the-perpetrator. Confession from humans leads to forgiveness from God, who freely renounces the claim to justice-as-retribution arising from humans' prior transgression. It seems remorse and confessions from humans are enough for God to effect a reconciliation with humans again. This analogically applies to humans, who are all members of God's family. One can locate Tutu's "rainbow nation of God" idiom from this family of God metaphor. Accordingly, Tutu's third-way theology of reconciliation shows a persistent interest in effecting this rainbow nation.[7]

So, Tutu's theology of reconciliation is communion-centric (*ubuntu*). It is strongly in favor of reintegration and embrace, though premised on the conversion of hearts, to create havens for future generations. Within this theology of reconciliation, he emphasizes embrace that implies a sense of responsibility, which goes beyond moral equivalence. Hope is at the core of the sense of responsibility from Tutu's theology of reconciliation. This is because reconciliation (i.e., rainbow nation) as *telos* will come from moral supererogation. Since Tutu's theology of reconciliation placed an accent on hope during the TRC years, he had his eyes on the supererogatory—confession and forgiveness. Hence, it seems that in Tutu's theology of reconciliation, forgiveness, not justice (at least the tangible manifestation), has higher

---

6. Mojola, "African Bantu," 62.

7. The Third Way theology during the apartheid years embraced the larger discourse of practical nation-building. Tutu, like other third-way theologians such as John de Gruchy and Charles Villa-Vincencio, over the years leading up to the TRC years, did not incorporate the left-leaning theologies of reconciliation as in Black liberation theology. See Maluleke, "Reconciliation in South Africa," 111; Maluleke, "South African," 38.

priority.[8] Or to put it in another way, it is as if the spirit is higher than the body. This theology of reconciliation can be illustrated thus:[9]

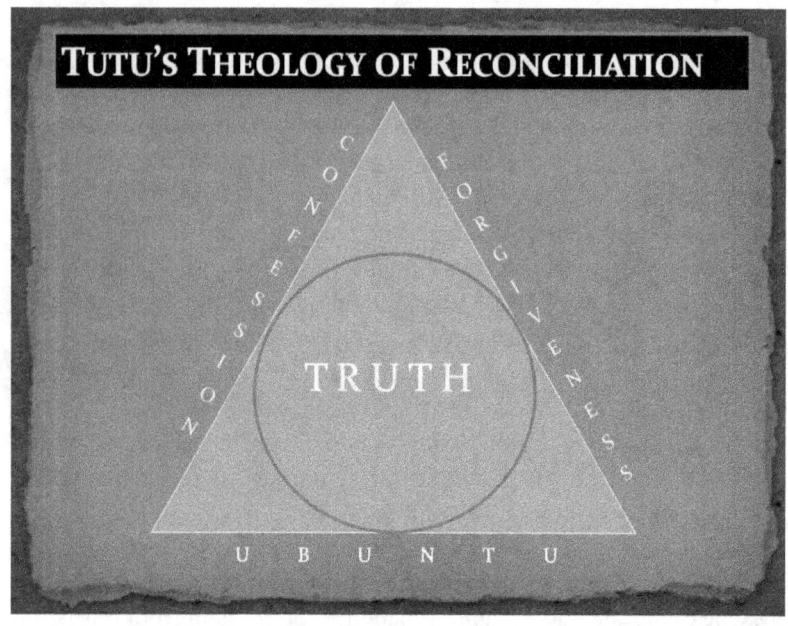

Courtesy of the Author

From the illustration above, the principal features of Tutu's reconciliation, especially in practice, are symbolic, and largely transethical. Reconciliation happens when there is confession (from perpetrators) and forgiveness (from victims), and both stakeholders express the philosophical anthropology of *ubuntu*, in an atmosphere of truth-telling and truth-recognition. We can appreciate his position when we view his postulation from his Christian understanding of sin.

If toxic imperfection is seen as a sin,[10] which is the violation of the law of the covenant, for instance between peoples (connected by *ubuntu*),

---

8. Mojola approvingly notes that Tutu's theological-moral foundation of *Ubuntu* leads to prioritizing forgiveness, reconciliation, restorative justice, and communal cohesion. Hence, there is no reconciliation without forgiveness. Mojola, "African Bantu," 62.

9. This illustration is part of my efforts to understand and interpret Tutu's theology of reconciliation. The reader should not conclude that I agree with this illustration and the explanation that follows.

10. I am following Paul Ricœur's typology of moral evil: defilement, sin, and guilt. See Ricœur, *Symbolism of Evil*, 25–46.

then healing implies repentance and forgiveness. Tutu's religious intuition sees forgiveness as a right to forgo retributive punishment.[11] This gracious forgiveness can bring about repentance, which opens the possibility for reconciliation. From the illustration, truth connects the three angles of reconciliation. Hence, there is no reconciliation without truth. This reminds one of Usman dan Fodio's statements that "conscience is an open wound, only Truth can heal it."[12] Truth disclosed (confession) contributes to the healing of hurts and the cleansing of polluted relationships among South Africa's peoples. When the pollution has been cleansed through full disclosure, forgiveness (as absolution), which lets go of hatred and desire for vengeance for *ubuntu*'s sake, completes reconciliation. Accordingly, with this theology of reconciliation, one regards violations as a defilement of relationship. Hence, the principally symbolic acts of repentance (expressed in remorse), satisfaction (full disclosure of truth) and absolution (expressed in forgiveness) in an atmosphere of renewed *ubuntufication* can effect cleansing of defiled relationships (expressed as reconciliation).

Theologically, we can refer to this as a religious notion of healing. The *TRC Promotion Act* (1995) contains no reference to healing. Yet, the *baruti* on TRC, especially Tutu and Boraine, used the word variously to describe what TRC was doing. However, the religious notion of healing, used at the initial stage of TRC, had a metaphysical sense. One invokes this notion of healing, according to Alfred and Marietjie Allan, to mean enabling the wounds of the past to become less painful for the parties. In this sense, it is the purification of the taboo effects that matter. This is possible by performing the rituals of purification, e.g., satisfying the conditions for amnesty.[13] So, healing implied that the traumas and wounds of sufferers would be overcome for the parties to return to their "pre-trauma functioning level."[14] Although their observation is well-taken, Allan and Allan's definition of healing in the psychological sense is problematic. Anthropologically, and even psychologically, we cannot return to our "pre-trauma functioning level." We cannot return to the level of living as persons before our distended narratives. This is why reconciliation in contexts like South Africa and Nigeria is construed as the rebuilding of trust among persons/peoples. The rebuilding implies a process that may or may not be completed; hence the tensions that arose when the trauma

---

11. Tutu, *No Future*, 272.

12. We culled this from the cover page of a leading Nigerian daily, *The Guardian*. *The Guardian* adopted the words as its motto. The jihadist Fulani, Usman dan Fodio, is the father of modern-day Islam in northern Nigeria.

13. Allan and Allan, "South African Truth," 472.

14. Allan and Allan, "South African Truth," 472.

happened will not go away completely. As long as this is so, we cannot return to that pre-trauma functioning level. Yet, it does not mean we do not experience healing. It depends on what that healing means. I will return to this later when evaluating Tutu's notion of healing.

In the meantime, Tutu's theology of reconciliation recognizes parties to be neighbors (also siblings), and not strangers. The crucial question and dilemma are: What kind of justice system and arrangement can adequately take care of this paradox of My Enemy–My Neighbor?[15] According to Tutu, restorative justice with its strategic relationality and dialogical nature is a welcome help towards incarnating his theology of reconciliation. First, restorative justice promises a forward-looking approach that is suitable for the dilemma of My Enemy–My Neighbor. Second, restorative justice's strategic openness to a dialogical interface can help in dealing effectively with the past such that the triangle of reconciliation as illustrated above can happen. Third, restorative justice, as the midway between "Nuremberg" and "Argentina," is capable of restoring equilibrium among neighbors-turned-enemies. Consequently, Tutu and some with similar theological outlooks recognize the Christian theological tasks of restorative justice-like TRC. We can summarize them thus:

i. Truth must be revealed for reconciliation to happen;
ii. Public repentance is needed;
iii. Genuine remorse and personal repentance are crucial;
iv. Penitents must have a firm resolve to change their ways;
v. Penitent perpetrators must undo their wrongs;
vi. The TRC, by giving penance, plants new seeds "so that all that is left tomorrow is only memories."[16]

---

15. This phrase is not original to me. See Stover and Weinstein, *My Neighbour, My Enemy*.

16. These are the essentials of authentic reconciliation and sustainable nation building from a Christian theological perspective. Senator Moosa, then South Africa's MP and Chair of Select Committee on Justice, outlined this during a conference ("Reconciliation and Healing: TRC and the Church") in 1996, cited in "TRC and the Church," 7. Moosa readily points out that these features must go hand in hand with social justice, due to the reality on the ground—severe poverty, high rate of unemployment, inadequate housing, and the injustice of landlessness. Hence, revealed truth at the TRC is "meaningless" without empowerment that the traumatized majority experience. Accordingly, the TRC was just "one facet of an overall need for reconstruction and development, transformation and nation building." "TRC and the Church," 8.

This Christian theological task, which Tutu ardently spearheaded, combined two, out of the five, typologies of reconciliation critics noticed during the TRC hearing.[17]

On the one hand, there is the non-racial typology characterized by the dissolution of racial identity. The TRC, argues Tutu, was to promote the rainbow society. The perpetrators (especially Whites) who acknowledged their offences would be reintegrated. Communal cohesion is the goal of this kind of typology.[18] On the other hand, we have the religious-redemptive typology. This placed a strong emphasis on forgiveness and honesty, and the rediscovery of individual and social conscience (virtues). This moral awakening, by understanding the import of *ubuntu*, remorse, confession, will come principally from reflection. The TRC, Tutu argues equally, is about confronting people with the past's evil, challenging people to repent, and having a firm resolution not to violate people again. This typology has the risk of equating the incidence of forgiveness with reconciliation.[19]

The two typologies that featured prominently in Tutu's advocacy for restorative justice in post-apartheid South Africa revolved around a single notion of evil. It is a defilement of relationships. Hence, one indicates reconciliation as cleansing, through symbolic acts of healing. The flip side is that Tutu's larger-than-life impact on the TRC and its proceedings meant the domination of the two typologies of reconciliation most appealing to Tutu. Farid Essack, a foremost South African Islamic scholar and political activist, pointed this out during the public hearing of communities of faith during the TRC: "the powerful presence of Archbishop Tutu . . . also meant that the understanding of reconciliation with which the hearings worked was coloured by his own personality."[20]

Although Tutu theologically expressed the need to overcome polluted relationships in post-apartheid South Africa via TRC's task, his concern was not simply religious. This was why Tutu and other *baruti* could partner with those not moved primarily by religion, e.g., the ANC-led government that supported the first typology (non-racial identity). To reiterate, some South African scholars argue that Tutu was not solely driven by religiosity and African inclination. They argue that his focus was more fundamental and anthropological. That was the reason non-Christians and even nonreligious stakeholders could partner with Tutu. Human

---

17. See Hamber and van der Merwe, "Rainbow of Reconciliation," 19–22.

18. Hamber and van der Merwe, "Rainbow of Reconciliation," 19.

19. Hamber and van der Merwe, "Rainbow of Reconciliation," 20.

20. Research Institute on Christianity in Africa, "Faith Communities and Apartheid," 67.

beings, irrespective of the traumatic divide, ought to confront themselves with "the often-neglected connections between *equity, mercy, forgiveness* and amnesty within the TRC process."[21]

Humans are value-creating, meaning-fashioning beings. The values attached to after-word issues or the meanings given to events (before, during, and after a violent past) have to be considered in justice, peace, and reconciliation processes. So, the TRC process was about unearthing the deeper nuances of the moral meaning of a particular response to the issues of the past that eminently resonates with Nigerians' experience: "to resist an overemphasis on retributive individual justice in response to politically motivated violence/violations; the vital importance of restorative justice; the need to give breathing space to mercy and forgiveness."[22] Consequently, Verwoerd emphasizes this point in the face of relentless criticisms against the amnesty process within South Africa's TRC. Between idealism and romanticism, the nation chose the path of realism—even if fraught with lots of unresolved ambiguities. Consequently, Verwoerd offers in his conclusion, "few of us terrestrial beings can afford the luxury of having second thoughts about the need for equity, mercy and forgiveness, and the moral remembrance that underlies these responses to wrongdoing."[23] Yet, Verwoerd reiterates that offenders have to be punished. The issue is about the kind of punishment laden with the moral meaning of equity, mercy, and forgiveness, anchored on *ubuntu*.[24]

Even if TRC's option was not principally about religiosity, Christian theologians and *baruti* like Tutu recognized that the theological virtues of faith, hope, and love are indispensable for reconciliation to happen as envisioned thus far, especially in the illustration above. The theological substructure of Tutu's theology of restorative justice hinges upon the three virtues. Accordingly, Tutu's theology of reconciliation in the context of My Neighbor–My Enemy appeals very strongly to virtue ethics. Without emphasizing virtuous disposition, we continue to witness the dissonance between the ethics of being of persons and the normalized spirit in their institutions. When there is harmony, we can recognize that peacebuilding is about a new beginning characterized by liberation from the burden of the past. When the post-violence justice processes lift the past's burden,

---

21. Verwoerd, *Equity*, xi (emphasis original).
22. Verwoerd, *Equity*, xii.
23. Verwoerd, *Equity*, esp. ch. 1, and conclusion, quotation on 202.
24. See Verwoerd, *Equity*, 129–34. The acknowledgement of punishment notably differentiates Verwoerd from Tutu. While Tutu insists on beyond retribution and no punishment in restorative justice, Verwoerd does not reject punishment, although he adds no degrading punishment as a caveat.

survivors of the burdensome past will grow in their trustworthiness towards one another.

An Evaluation of Tutu's Contribution to Restorative Justice Discourse

> Let us be careful not to mistake hope for achievement.
> —Kofi Annan (2002)[25]

The late Kofi Annan, former UN Secretary-General, uttered the statement above against the backdrop of an excessive sense of exuberance some heads of state displayed after Thabo Mbeki's assertion that Africa had hope. For these heads of state, particularly the late Muammar Gaddafi, the end of White rule in South Africa signaled the triumph of post-colonial hope. Annan was aware of numerous challenges and anomalies all over Africa. Hence, he cautioned against equating hope's widespread applause for evidence of achievement in improving Africans' standard of living. In the context of this chapter, Annan's statement reminds us of the eternal tension between hope and achievements. Hope, in this context, can be defined as an unfounded belief for future good, while expectations and achievements signal the concrete evidence of collective wellbeing for the expectant. It seems Tutu's theology is high on hope as opposed to expectations. How fair is this of Tutu?

Evaluating Tutu's Theology of Restorative Justice

To appreciate the value of Tutu's contribution, we need to revisit the importance of the revalorization of religion in a secularized world.[26] Revalorization of religion is an instance of the deprivatization of religion. Deprivatization, according to José Casanova, is "the process whereby religion abandons its assigned place in the private sphere and enters the undifferentiated public sphere of civil society to take part in the ongoing process of contestation, discursive legitimation, and redrawing of boundaries."[27] Deprivatization is deducible from at least three historical events.

---

25. Meredith, *State of Africa*, 681.

26. Revalorization of religion refers to "the thesis that religion has regained its energy and life after a period of deprivation of life and relevance in public space. The deprivation coincided with the Enlightenment period and its enforced privatization of religion." Aina, "Catholic Identity," 461.

27. Casanova, *Public Religions*, 65–66.

First, the church was active in the movement towards democratic rule "in Spain, Poland, and Brazil."[28] With wit to add, the European Union project was "a Christian Democratic project, sanctioned by the Vatican, at a time of a general religious revival in post-World War Two Europe, in the geopolitical context of the Cold War when 'the free world' and 'Christian civilization' had become synonymous."[29] The church's active involvement was not to guarantee only its rights. It was equally to protect the rights of all aspects of the democratic society. So, in the construction of a liberal democratic society, rather than being private, the church decisively participated and facilitated.[30]

Second, deprivatization occurred when religion (e.g., the church) entered the public sphere to contest and question the state's arrogation of powers regarding weapons of mass destruction and unbridled market fundamentalism, and the adverse effects on the citizens of the world.[31] Third, deprivatization equally occurred to protect fundamental spheres of life the state was encroaching.[32] So, the second and third occurrences of deprivatization were meant to check the liberal state when it was overreaching itself.[33]

Tutu provides an example of how Christian theology can respond when the state misbehaves to the extent of endangering the various levels of relationships existing within the state. Similar to the first example of Casanova's deprivatization, religions in transitional societies will have to contribute towards a humane polity.[34] Nevertheless, it is problematic to embrace Tutu's inspirational example in peacebuilding without a caveat. It is even more problematic to build transitional projects on inspirational religious figures that are not adept at conceptually clarifying issues and concepts invoked in strategic planning and execution of public projects. According to Heribert Adam, in a publication examining how memories of past evils are tackled, the moral stature of some influential religious

---

28. Casanova, *Public Religions*, 57.

29. Casanova, "Religion," 66.

30. Casanova, *Public Religions*, 57.

31. Casanova, *Public Religions*, 58. See Verstraeten, "Fundamental Changes," 176–80.

32. The drafters of the Universal Declaration of Human Rights formulated the document to protect persons and peoples from the kind of violations that preceded or occurred during the tragic WWII. This Declaration, though formulated as a non-religious document, is greatly indebted to religious contributors, like Jacques Maritain and René Cassin, and their religious metaphors. Cf. Verstraeten, "Fundamental Changes," 180–81.

33. Casanova, *Public Religions*, 58.

34. See Aina, "Catholic Identity," 462–71.

figures, like Tutu, has so much enthralled us that we have taken their magisterial religious intuitions as empirical evidence.[35] Some recent publications on Tutu still demonstrate this enthralled perception. Osotsi Mojola, in his evaluation of Tutu's theology and praxis at the service of global justice and human rights culture, holds up Tutu as an unapologetic apostle of *ubuntu* and restorative justice. These promote hope and healing.[36] Tutu is so consistent in his advocacy that he earned himself a popular sobriquet, "a rabble-rouser for peace and justice and freedom."[37] In the same volume, Mofihli Teleki and Serges Kamga effusively praised the *ubuntufication* of the TRC and post-apartheid South Africa. Tutu's inspiration on this is so successful that they can state that *ubuntu* was "a stimulus in South Africa's public service policies through which its values were referenced in order to improve public services to ordinary citizens."[38]

The world needs the inspiration, moral integrity and internationally acclaimed stature of Archbishop Tutu. However, this appeal might be waning. People are beginning to raise critical questions about the imagination and praxis of religious actors like Tutu,[39] who exemplifies Scott Appleby's model of "The Interventionist," i.e., the "Mediator and Magister," in peacebuilding.[40] The questions center on the hopes that appear unsupported by theological finesse that can respond reasonably to the numerous grey areas in transitional societies. So, a key argument in the following pages is that Christian ethicists, who are adept at making distinctions and schematization of the various competing demands for transitional societies, need to be more visible in religious contributions in public. While not necessarily rejecting the interventionist and magisterial role of inspirational religious leaders like Archbishop Tutu, they need to be complemented at least by religious ethicists who, like Paul Ricœur, are mediators "between the poles of the secular and the sacred."[41] Those mediators follow Ricœur's exhortation that

35. "Due to the international stature of the TRC's chair, Desmond Tutu, his hopes and predictions have entered academic literature as empirical facts." Adam, "Divided Memories," 93.

36. Mojola, "Ubuntu," 33.

37. Mojola, "Ubuntu," 34.

38. Teleki and Kamga, "Recognizing the Value," 324.

39. For instance, Cody Corliss avers that the restorative justice Tutu promoted during the TRC and thereafter "is easier in theory than in life, where the scars and pain are not abstract." Furthermore, the restorative justice that advocates tout today anchors on "a romantic version of pre-colonial past, a vision Desmond Tutu echoed when he claimed that Africa just was more concerned with resorting balance than punishing." Corliss, "Truth Commissions," 298–99.

40. Appleby, *Ambivalence of the Sacred*, 239–43.

41. Duffy, *Paul Ricoeur's*, 108.

the hermeneutics at work in the public maintain congruence between truth and method,[42] unlike Tutu's translation method, which as shall be shown below is not strong on clear theological method and sound social-scientific (and even biblical) analyses. My theological evaluation, therefore, inclines towards a theological construal that shall insist on a religious discourse that accepts and develops the penultimate status of justice (even restorative justice). In other words, a nuanced theology of restorative justice, unlike the religious discourse in restorative peacebuilding so far, will accept that even within a theology of reconciliation, the status of justice after mass violence must not presuppose a necessary coupling of forgiveness and reconciliation as Tutu was fond of doing. At this point, let me offer the definitions of justice, reconciliation, and forgiveness that underpin the following critical remarks on Tutu's theology of restorative justice and reconciliation.

On Justice, Reconciliation and Forgiveness

JUSTICE

We can define justice theologically as the commitment in practices and procedures to rebuild/renew relationships that had been unduly damaged by acts of human omission or commission.[43] This theological understanding resonates with the traditional Yorùbá construal of justice. As a noun, it means a state of right atmosphere between persons/peoples that promotes the well-being of humans adequately considered. As a verb, it means recreating the atmosphere for the possibility of living out the demands of right relationships. "Justice" (òdodo in Yorùbá) as a noun evokes fairness, equity, and balance.[44] It is not essentially a decision taken at the end of a trial, i.e., sentence. Yorùbá render sentencing as "ìdájọ́" (judgment).[45] According to Fadipe in his pioneer work, *The Sociology of the Yoruba*,[46] the people refer to justice as òdodo—"peace-making justice."[47] This goes beyond judgment (apportioning blame and praise). It seeks to "conciliate according to the prejudices and customs current in Yoruba Society."[48] Hence, justice emphasizes both the noun (òdodo) and the verb ("ìdájọ́) dimensions of justice

---

42. Duffy, *Paul Ricoeur's*, 108.
43. Cf. Kubicki, "Sacramental Symbols," 177.
44. Cf. *Dictionary of the Yoruba*, s.v. Ododo.
45. *Dictionary of Yoruba*, s.v. Idajo.
46. Fadipe, *Sociology*.
47. Fadipe, *Sociology*, 223.
48. Fadipe, *Sociology*, 223.

for the sake of ethical balancing involved in this aspect of the post-conflict transitional process. This is how justice contributes to peace, and ultimately reconciliation. Multi-dimensional justice is crucial because it is the promise that the past will not repeat itself.[49] Given the exposure anxiety due to prior victimization, justice is the process that, through acts of "mourning" (both individual and collective symbolic acts of commemoration), seeks the recovery of "discretion, dignity, and pride" to the persons and peoples that have been traumatized.[50] Charles Villa-Vicencio, a South African contributor to the *Handbook of Restorative Justice*, might reckon that what Kaufman affirms is part of his octagonal justice, particularly the exonerative, rehabilitative, affirmative, and restorative sides of justice. These sides of justice will lead to the restoration of justice that creates sustainable peace, instead of the perpetual trading of blame.[51] This vision of justice is more pivotal for the peacebuilding process than pure retribution.

Peacebuilding

This is a process-oriented approach to a contentious problem event ordered towards reconciliation, i.e., renewal of multidimensional relationships of neighbors-turned-enemies embedded and interconnected with various levels of systems and subcultures. Accordingly, as against peacemaking, ordered to quell a particularly violent incident, peacebuilding looks beyond the particular problem event and its immediate causes. Instead, it looks at the problem event as cases, which offer opportunities to see the bigger pictures of systems, perspectives, and worldviews fuelling those conflicts. These are usually connected with issues of social justice and the politics of victimization. Hence, peacebuilding is decisively contextual because its processes pay attention to concrete consideration of the situations. Peacebuilding helps to reach the point of "just peace and a peaceful co-existence" by intentional intelligibility.[52] The bottom line, then, is that the peacebuilding approach seeks reconciliation with the least of violence and bloodshed. This peacebuilding concept recognizes the importance of time perspectives. Hence, it spreads its processes and projects along variegated yet interconnected timelines—usually covering between six months and twenty-five years.[53]

49. Arendt, *Human Condition*, 242–43.
50. Kaufman, "Restoration," 229.
51. Villa-Vicencio, "Transitional Justice," 389.
52. De Tavernier, "Love for Enemy," 166.
53. I have been inspired, on the one hand by the distinction between peacemaking

Reconciliation

As peacebuilding's *telos*, reconciliation is the rebuilding of bridging and bonding trust, a part of the social capital, which violent conflicts destroy. The loss of one's assumptive world,[54] with threefold crises (of meaning, life, and death) is one of the effects of trauma. So, trust, despite the past, is indicative of detoxification (*overcoming toxic emotions*). Reconciliation implies previously traumatized people live in an environment of *at-one-ment* with one another. However, this trust is not just a matter of wishful thinking. Some things need to happen for this trust to build up again. Justice, love-as-mercy, and peace are all needed in a delicate but creative balance.[55]

Forgiveness

Forgiveness is an intensely personal action. It is not absolution, nor is it another form of amnesia. Hence, contrary to Yorùbá word for "forgiveness," "*ìforíjì*," being translated as "blotting out,"[56] it is indeed a "crossing out" (*X*), whose variant is pardon (*fijì*). Paul Ricœur, in "Difficulty to Forgive," refers to this variant as "forgiveness *in cognito*; one of the 'traces of forgiveness.'"[57] So, forgiveness, as a gift that crosses out, is a choice. It is an expression of love-as-mercy that lets go (*fijì*) of toxic emotions towards one who had unjustly caused the collapse of one's assumptive world. Forgiveness is

---

and peacebuilding in Aertsen et al., *Restoring Justice*, and the conceptual framework for peacebuilding in Lederach's *Building Peace* (1998). See Rohner et al., "Challenging Restorative Justice," 17–19; Lederach, *Building Peace*, 24, ch. 4, esp. figs 2–3; ch. 6, figs 6–7.

54. According to Jeffrey Kaufman, an "assumptive world" is a "belief construct" that regards reality as valuable, trustworthy and true to give cohesion and constancy to one's identity: "The assumptive world is the ordering principle for the psychological and psychosocial construction of oneself and the human world." Kaufman, "Restoration," 222–23.

55. Acts of *Love-as-mercy* are human expressions that stem the hands of retaliation, thus offering the possibility for justice, which is not just about retribution, although it does not exclude it. On the other hand, *peace* is the cessation of hostilities within a climate of relative calm, with growing recognition and respect of previous neighbors-turned-enemies, who are largely confident in the promise that the past will not repeat itself.

56. Oduyoye, *Vocabulary of Yoruba*, 42.

57. In this sense, agreeing with Ricœur, we forgive and remember, because crossing out (*X*) acknowledges the odious past, and its irreversibility. Yet, it reduces the burden of indebtedness. Forgiveness as crossing out implies a gratuitous offering of a second chance to someone who does not deserve it. Nevertheless, this forgiveness does not preclude various demands of merciful justice, even punishment. Cf. Ricœur, *Memory, History, Forgetting*. For helpful synopsis of this work, in relation to the observation above, see Ricœur, "Difficulty to Forgive," 6–16.

a choice because it is one of the relationship processes one follows after transgressions against relationships. However, it is not everyone who wants or is obliged to go through this specific process of relational repair.[58] So, if one says, without nuance, that "forgiveness is a choice" (cf. Enright), one betrays a liberal bias that "you can be whom you want to be; your happiness or sadness is your own making," irrespective of one's social condition/location. I opt for the more realistic approach of Everett Worthington on forgiveness. This approach explores the limits of agency, especially regarding unforgiveness (refusal/inability) to forgive. "Unilateral forgiveness" does not depend on or necessarily expect a positive response from the one/those forgiven, although one hopes for it. This form of response places the onus of action on the victims. Yet, in my estimation, the unilaterality of forgiveness places a moral burden on those forgiven. Forgiveness places the demands of social justice's ethical demand on the recipient(s) and witnesses. This is the precise moral burden of forgiveness. The forgiving victim symbolically promises to let go of one's toxic emotions and pleads for the recipient to do the needful of social justice's demand. Unforgiveness is a stress reaction. The level of stress increases as the injustice gap increases, while it reduces due to the process of detoxification—i.e., the cooperative process of "removing relational poison,"[59] beginning with justice.

The Problem in "No Future without Forgiveness"

From the expositions on restorative justice in post-conflict settings, with a particular focus on Tutu, we can notice some practical and theological problems. First, reconciliation and forgiveness are almost always coupled together. Tutu's absolute pacifism from the apartheid days to his death is a key reason for this contentious position. As a pacifist, he favors a theology that illogically couples forgiveness and reconciliation as two sides of a coin. Consequently, for Tutu, violence has no space whatsoever. Søren Dosenrode argues that we cannot judge Christians like Tutu who adopt this pacifist position: "It is not for us to judge whether they did the right or wrong thing, whether they did what God wanted them to do or not."[60] Despite Dosenrode's claim, I think part of responsible ethics is to critically appraise Tutu's religious imagination and his ortho-practical interventions.

---

58. Cf. Dindia and Emmers-Sommer, "What Partners Do," 312–13, 319; Fitness, "Emotion and Cognition," 298.

59. Worthington, *Forgiveness and Reconciliation*, 49, 197, 212–17, quotation on 216.

60. Dosenrode, "Instead of a Conclusion," 281.

The controversies about punishment bring out Tutu's absolute pacifist position in his public interventions. He consistently denies punishment a place in restorative justice-like practices (e.g., TRC). This claim is attractive given that it accentuates the connection between reconciliation and forgiveness. It emphasizes the impossibility of reconciliation without forgiveness. However, if one follows the analogy of the sides of the coin to its logical conclusion, the relationship between forgiveness (per se) and reconciliation is not akin to the relationship between a coin and its two sides. Two sides with different "faces" and inscriptions are melted together to form a new entity called "coin." If so, one needs to ask for the name of the entity that has forgiveness and reconciliation as its two sides. This simply questions the easy assumption that forgiveness and reconciliation are two sides of a coin. This is part of the conceptual befuddling dating back to TRC years, with Tutu's invocation of forgiveness and reconciliation. It is as if, like Siamese twins, these are inseparable. Is the Christian theology that couples these always the only valid one? Indeed, is there no future without forgiveness? Contrary to Tutu's "no future without forgiveness," I argue in the following paragraphs: *there can be a future without forgiveness*. Let's recall this book's central thesis: Love (*a*) and Justice (*d*) mutually reinforce each other. The mutual reinforcement between the two makes Peace (*e*) likely. An environment of Love and Justice experiencing Peace has a *higher likelihood* of moving towards Reconciliation (*K*).[61] One missing element in love cannot hold the future to ransom.[62]

With Tutu's theological bias, there is no real awareness of the space between conciliation (*cessation of overt hostilities*) and reconciliation (*resumption of prior [warm and] trustful relations*). This space concedes two things. First, stakeholders have the right to remain strangers. Second, justice (even restorative justice) must not make them friends. Restorative justice is about creating a crime-safe environment, eliciting respect, and reparation from the perpetrator(s). It is about protecting human rights and dignity. Put differently, justice does not make us friends. What we owe one another is justice, not friendship. That is why forgiveness and remorse are not part of restorative justice's core values. Restorative justice, for all its values, falls within the logic of equivalence, while remorse and forgiveness, as peculiar expressions of love-as-mercy, fall within the logic of superabundance.

I premise this theological rebuttal on Nigeria's state as a cleft country. A cleft country is divided along civilizational lines. It is evenly divided

---

61. Where *a-agape* (Love); *d-diakaiosune* (Justice); *e-eirene* (Peace); and *K-Katallage* (Reconciliation)

62. See further Appendix 2 for the breakdown of the various elements of love, justice, peace, and reconciliation I am pointing to here.

between two or more competing cultural and religious value systems.[63] Hence, primordial ties like ethnicity, religion, and even linguistic dialectal differences, are still strong in Nigeria. Also, the country has several centers of power, and the most powerful of these are non-state centers like traditional and religious leaders,[64] who drive bonding trust more than bridging trust. So, what Nigerians most need is justice (as redress, reparation, acknowledgment, respect). Without justice, in this multidimensional sense, forgiveness will even find it difficult to make an epiphany. So, there is a future even without forgiveness in the interim, Hannah Arendt suggests, provided there is respect. Respect is more required in the "larger domain of human affairs."[65] Respect, to Arendt, is friendship minus intimacy and closeness, but what is friendship without intimacy and closeness? Respect implies that in the public domain stakeholders consider the other with whom one has neither intimacy nor closeness, irrespective of the other's "qualities which we may admire or of achievements which we may highly esteem."[66] In today's lingo, this will mean proactive recognition of the other's human dignity irrespective of the state of affairs among stakeholders. This recognition is not a matter of mercy; it is a matter of justice. In the absence of forgiveness, there is still a future; provided justice is present. The recognition of dignity, concretely and symbolically, politically and economically, especially of those who do not count (the *Ẹiyẹ Kínkín*) might in future even lead to an increased manifestation of "love-as-mercy" among survivors of a horrific past.

Perchance, concerning ethno-religious mass violence, the value of plurality can show a way in the quest for a respectful sense of citizenship in Nigeria. This citizenship needs to emerge from decades of confinement and shackles of "class . . . social stratification and exploitation."[67] Yet, this project does not mean Nigerians, or the groups making up the nation, *must* become friends for this to happen. Nigerians, in a constitutionally secular country, can consciously and deliberately develop a culture of "communicative mastery"[68] of their numerous conflicts. Nonetheless, they can retain a paradoxical "solidarity among strangers,"[69] i.e., "strangers who renounce violence and, in the cooperative regulation of their common life, also concede

---

63. Aina, "Religion," 336.
64. Benyera, "South Africa's Truth," 197.
65. Arendt, *Human Condition*, 243.
66. Arendt, *Human Condition*, 243.
67. Habermas, *Between Facts and Norms*, 308.
68. Habermas, *Between Facts and Norms*, 308.
69. Habermas, *Between Facts and Norms*, 308.

one another the right to *remain* strangers."[70] We can say this is the dedication to *national reconstruction in respectful coexistence* as the space between *conciliation* and *reconciliation*, which may blossom hopefully in Nigeria.

If one follows the logic above, then it is not self-evident, as Tutu presupposes, that there is no future without forgiveness. We see one of the dangers from Tutu's contribution. Excessive inspiration from the religious narratives of the *baruti* during the TRC has turned restorative justice into a practice that frames its mandate in binary opposition: either reconciliation built on forgiveness or no future for stakeholders. This binary construal does not have space for *in-between* in restorative justice in peacebuilding. Due to restorative justice's *in-betweenness*, it makes sense to situate it within *diakaiosune* (justice) whereas forgiveness falls under *agape* (love). Love and justice are crucial for *eirene* (peace) on the way to *katallage* (reconciliation). Again this presupposes that theologically there must be a conceptual uncoupling of forgiveness and reconciliation. For practical purposes, as in peacebuilding after a protracted past, reconciliation cannot and must not necessarily be built on forgiveness as if forgiveness can stand on its own and not within other elements classified under *agape*. I offer forthwith the reasons for this claim.

First, reconciliation in transitional societies, as in Tutu's post-apartheid South Africa, is structurally macro-focused with the space for stakeholders to work for the common good—in political and democratic civility. This is crucial for an understanding of peace. Reconciliation as *trustful cooperation* does not presuppose the deep emotions associated with a renewed friendship between individuals after estrangement. This is because deep emotions are properties of individuals, not groups. Or else, one falls into the fallacy of composition.

This fallacy presupposes that interpersonal warmth between persons within a group or groups implies a similar reality within a group or across groups. This position infers those attributes of parts are the same as that of the whole.[71] This is fallacious because "it ignores the difference between parts and whole."[72] The parts (individual persons) are marked by intentionality in addition to other dimensions of human personhood. These dimensions as they inform human persons' choices and actions are mediated by love, which plays out in the relationship between neighbors (understood as members of the human community). On the contrary, the whole (groups) does not have the dimensions of the human person—although human persons make up the

---

70. Habermas, *Between Facts and Norms*, 308 (emphasis original).
71. Govier and Verwoerd, "Trust," 191.
72. Govier and Verwoerd, "Trust," 191.

groups. Accordingly, we cannot, without a caveat or distinction, infer what pertains to the part (human person), e.g., forgiveness, interpersonal warmth, on the whole (groups). This is why one should insist on maintaining the delicate distinction between forgiveness, which happens between persons only, and reconciliation, as the rebuilding of trust after trauma and trial, which can happen between persons, and between groups.[73]

Second, forgiveness is person-centered. It is micro-based, and cannot be structured because of its interruptive character, which makes its epiphany unpredictable. Furthermore, while reconciliation-as-trust can be developed between groups, forgiveness cannot be developed or given between groups. No person can offer forgiveness on behalf of others, except out of emblematic benevolence.[74] For instance, I, as a person with the agency in the present, can forgive others for the effects of past evils that I am still suffering. Nevertheless, I cannot forgive the unforgivable—the evil acts done in the past but whose victims are dead. I cannot forgive on behalf of the dead or those who disappeared.[75] So, the future always carries with it some degree of unforgivable. Nevertheless, this unforgivable will have to be handled skillfully that it does not destroy the future or poison the future generations. Memory purification and transformation should be part of a biblical justice component (i.e., that of humanization). It is possible that as the degree of humanization rises, the level of unforgiveness can reduce to the extent that those in the state of unforgiveness can become ready to offer forgiveness as a gift.

73. Laura Stovel offers similar remarks about this fallacious tendency in the Sierra Leonean TRC report. Stovel is referring to the Sierra Leonean TRC that implored victims to reconcile with perpetrators "for the good of the country." Contesting this fallacy of composition, Stovel offers, "Neither the commissioners nor the report explains how victim-perpetrator reconciliation facilitates national reconciliation. The report only implies that it contributes to individual healing which only indirectly relates to the health of the community and state." Stovel, *Long Road Home*, 214.

74. This qualifies as a trace (shadow) of forgiveness, which is important if group memories will be transformed, according to Ricœur. Yet, this is not forgiveness per se, since forgiveness flowing from the victim deals with personal guilt. See Ricœur, "Difficulty to Forgive," 11.

75. Anthony Bash's theological monograph on how to think of forgiveness in Christian Ethics staunchly defends this kind of position. His work is refreshingly realistic and sensitive to complexities of forgiveness, and unforgiveness, especially insights from clinical psychology, psychotherapy, and social psychology. He dares to state that from a biblical theological point of view, Christians are not obliged to forgive; but exhorted to do so. Obligation and exhortation are not the same. Furthermore, there cannot be corporate forgiveness, on evidence from the New Testament, because groups lack intentionality, capacity to acknowledge responsibility, and cannot repent, as organic moral beings. A group is strictly speaking "a metaphorical entity, and so inanimate." Cf. Bash, *Forgiveness and Christian Ethics*, esp. 93–95, 101–10, 11–40, quotation on 116.

Of course, not every scholar wrestling with forgiveness and reconciliation accepts this position, especially those making case for political forgiveness as part of the reconciliation process. On the one hand, a critical appraisal of these works reveals that the so-called political forgiveness is couched in personal terms—not between groups. It appears some confuse forgiveness between persons from conflicting groups to mean political forgiveness between groups. This, as mentioned earlier about Tutu, is a fallacy of composition. On the other hand, it appears what some refer to as political forgiveness are acts of state pardon (relieving the burden of justified elements of justice, especially personal reparation and retribution) to convicted or indicted perpetrators—for the sake of safety and stability (political expediency).[76] Political forgiveness, for some like Donald Shriver and John de Gruchy, is a political process of transitional justice.[77] With due respect to these opinions, I agree with Bash, that the case they make for political forgiveness as corporate forgiveness "does not stand up to analytical scrutiny."[78]

So, the future is possible, even if there is an inevitable degree of unforgiveness. It does not necessarily follow that the incapacity or improprieties of forgiveness at present blocks the future. It is the lack of loving justice, not simply the absence of forgiveness, which endangers the future. This justice means reparation and recognition for victims and all survivors. It also presupposes due, non-degrading, or symbolic punishment for perpetrators, especially those with command responsibility.[79] The ethical elucidation offered above has a closer relationship with original restorative justice discourse than the *baruti* discourse like Tutu's. Both original restorative justice and this theological ethical elucidation maintain a conceptual distinction and strategic distance about the problematic trio: reconciliation-forgiveness-peace. Yet, for practical and theological reasons, can reconciliation-forgiveness-peace be foreclosed in post-conflict settings? Can restorative justice then offer sufficient assistance to post-conflict areas? These questions can be directed immediately to my position above.

76. Ricœur again refers to this as a trace of forgiveness. According to him, another contentious trace of forgiveness in penal justice and procedure is clemency or "the practice of amnesty in constitutional democracies." This discretionary procedure is a political action as much as a judicial one aimed ultimately at curing "the wounds of the social body." Ricœur, "Difficulty to Forgive," 12.

77. It is impossible to give an exhaustive literature on the subject of political forgiveness. A classic now will be Arendt, *Human Condition*, esp. 236–47.

78. Bash, *Forgiveness and Christian Ethics*, 139.

79. Immaculée Ilibagiza, a survivor of the Rwandan genocide, echoes a similar view when she affirms that pity for murderers, even the circumstantial ones and not the masterminds, does not mean that they cannot or should not be punished for their crimes. Ilibagiza, *Left to Tell*, 196–97.

It may seem that my conceptual taxonomy poses a grave danger for the future of people who will have to live together after a mutually destructive past, like South Africa, Nigeria, and Rwanda.

Of course, restorative justice offers sufficient assistance, though immediately with a caveat: to the extent possible by restorative justice's original focus and the terms of reference of the entity established to process the residual effects of the past. Restorative justice does not offer comprehensive assistance because its focus originally, as stated earlier, does not extend to generational/intergenerational woundedness. Consequently, contrary to Tutu's theology and the uncoupling of reconciliation and forgiveness, invoking restorative justice calls for delicate nuance, especially if stakeholders have to engage in some delicate balancing. Luc Huyse, an authority in transitional justice, counsels that "the crucial challenge is to strike a balance between the demands of justice and political prudence. This is no easy enterprise. It entails a difficult and, on occasion, tortuous cost-benefit analysis. All costs and gains, political and moral, of pardoning and punishing must be balanced against each other."[80] Restorative justice, in its original focus, is not confronted with this kind of balancing.

If there is the exigency to balance the need for justice and political prudence to overcome a suicidal past as in Tutu's post-apartheid South Africa or Nigeria, then a conceptually limited restorative justice in its original context must not be romanticized as Tutu is fond of doing. So, instead of saying forgiveness and reconciliation are two sides of a coin, a more suitable metaphor, at least from a Christian perspective, will be that reconciliation is a three-dimensional gem. This is how we can see the relationship between forgiveness and *katallage* (*K*). Maria Duffy's interpretation of Ricœur's pedagogy of reconciliation in the secular society is instructive. Love is distinct from justice, though interrelated and contributing critically to justice: "Love does not turn into justice, but does appear to be capable of transforming the *sense of justice* that lays at the basis of systems of justice."[81] Love thus educates the principles of justice for the sake of "social reconciliation," which is "the re-construction of the 'moral order.'"[82]

80. Huyse, "Dealing with the Past and Imaging the Future," 322–29, esp. 327–28. See also his evaluation of the TRC, Huyse, "Dealing with the Past in South Africa," 361–64.

81. Duffy, *Paul Ricoeur's Pedagogy*, 115 (emphasis original).

82. Duffy, *Paul Ricoeur's Pedagogy*, 114. This apt interpretation reminds one of Ricœur's concluding remarks on a possible reinterpretation of the Golden Rule from a bilateral logic to that of superabundance. Indeed, unilateral love and bilateral justice will always be in tension. Yet, incorporating "a motive of compassion and generosity in all our codes, penal codes and codes of social justice, constitutes a reasonable task, although difficult and endless." Ricœur, "Golden Rule," 392–97, quotation on 397.

Ricœur already developed this position in *Symbolism of Evil* (1969), in his discussion on the relationship between pardon and punishment, yet with the space for the return of the offender to the community. Pardon is a judicial-ethical response to moral evil. It lessens the weight of guilt, yet it does not exclude punishment. However, it does not foreclose a reception from the far distant land. For this, a pardon is an expression of love-as-mercy. Due to pardon's love-as-mercy feature, return is never far away because pardon offers hope and confidence to re-trace one's steps while accepting in good faith the reparation to be made—the reparation that pardon does not take away.[83] Though Ricœur's contributions referred to here are part of his discussion on how to make sense of evil concerning the human relationship with God, one can appreciate that emphasis in dealing with symbolisms of evil is not on forgiveness categorically. If forgiveness is the letting go of justified emotions of resentment and hatred towards offender(s), then it appears forgiveness does not play a key role in Ricœur's *Symbolism of Evil*. It is pardon-(*even with punishment*)-return that ensures fidelity till the thousandth generation. In other words, it is merciful justice (and all the rituals associated with this) that ensure escape from the captivity of evil to which humans have fallen.

Tutu's Theology of Reconciliation: Symbolism Prioritized Over Materiality?

Tutu's theology of reconciliation accentuates hope, faith and love—in the human person, especially the perpetrators who will confess. However, this hope stresses the confession rather than the reparation aspect. Accordingly, Tutu has been widely criticized for championing a cheap grace through his towering influence at the dawn of a new South Africa and especially through TRC. We can understand the criticisms because of the glaring unjust justice during and after TRC.[84] While perpetrators got their amnesty immediately, victims had to wait till 2004 before receiving material reparation from the South African government. Many still wallow in their poverty. What kind of reconciliation project only glorified handful of victims and a small percentage to offer forgiveness and receive pardon respectively while many who were victims of structural and policy violence remain unfocused, and the majority of beneficiaries (both individuals and corporate) moved on with life as if nothing changed?

---

83. Ricœur, *Symbolism of Evil*, 79.
84. Aina, "Overcoming Toxic Emotions," 210–49.

Tutu's theology of reconciliation has a higher priority for symbolic than tangible justice. Now, I do not favor a binary construal of justice (i.e., the symbolic vs. the material). One of the key promises of restorative justice-like practices (e.g., HRVIC and TRC) is the crucial space for the symbolic component of justice in the transitional process. Nevertheless, from the TRC (and later the HRVIC), it is as if the symbolic is more important than the material. Consequently, it seems a dualistic, or even possibly a Manichean, understanding is inherent in Tutu's theological construal of restorative justice, flowing from this theological notion of reconciliation. It is as if the spirit is higher than the body. If we take another critical look at the illustration above, one will recognize that Tutu's triangle of reconciliation consists of confession, forgiveness, and *ubuntu*. Truth, which ties all the three together, sits within the triangle's space. All the accents on reconciliation in this triangle border on the symbolic—or the spiritual. They are part of the non-material components of justice. This impresses that once truth deals with the spiritual demands of justice, all shall be well. This is not so. One accesses the spirit through the body. Hence, if the Body is not well, it cannot be well with the spirit, even if attention is paid to the spirit's need.

Consequently, reconciliation, as a process, must always demand, at least from a realistic restorative justice theological perspective, that the needs of the body—redressing the state of squalor, rehabilitating and repairing, and holding a society morally responsible and accountable—are as important and non-negotiable as the symbolic needs. When this happens, then restorative justice, beyond Tutu's theology of reconciliation, can accelerate the pace for sustainable peacebuilding and national re-creation. This includes creating a haven of sensitivity and even vulnerability for all the stakeholders where they can voice their experiences of totalizing projects, bereavement, separation, and dispossession, beyond the exclusionary mandates, which Tutu's theology of reconciliation, due to its intersubjective and symbolic priority, had no problems accepting. This theological construal of restorative justice, for instance, will have serious ethical reservations about the way restorative justice has been put to use, and defended even by Christian theologians, in South Africa, Nigeria, and Rwanda. The instrumentalization of restorative justice,[85] even by theologians like Tutu, has severely limited the critical contribution restorative justice is supposed to bring into post-conflict peacebuilding. Since violations are seen through the lens of sin, then healing justice consists of confession-absolution-satisfaction.

---

85. Stovel offers a similar observation. Contrary to claims, she points out that TRC instrumentalized restorative justice, abstracting from it some values, which the TRC then used for its end, which was "to promote national reconciliation and healing." Stovel, *Long Road Home*, 41.

In this scheme, it seems, as noticed in Tutu's theology of reconciliation and defense of TRC's restorative justice, that such religious imagination of post-conflict justice is in a hurry to achieve closure for the larger society. It appears, as suspected in Tutu, that there is discomfort over the lingering fire of resentment and lack of embrace. Hence, there is the quick invocation of forgiveness. It appears grace overshadows the normativity of justice. However, such persons with time get hit with the reality of lack of justice and their hurried stance. The enthusiasm of Tutu at the end of the TRC in 1998 waned, while the material sense of justice became increasingly more pronounced than forgiveness. As early as 2001, Tutu stated that reconciliation must be tangible; those who have been at the receiving end for generations must see a qualitative difference between then (the era of repression) and now (the era of freedom). Reconciliation that comes with freedom, continues Tutu, must translate into clean water, electricity, a decent home, a decent job, affordable education and healthcare. What is political power without the enhanced quality of life?[86] Perhaps, Tutu was acknowledging that the restorative justice intuitions in his contributions did not match the kind of justice and healing needed in post-TRC South Africa. Some years later, Tutu acknowledged that the TRC failed to bring about reciprocity between the racial and ethnic groups in South Africa despite the pragmatic concessions made.[87]

So far, restorative justice, even as theologically presented and practiced, as in Tutu, has been scratching the surface, which is one of the criticisms laid against the TRC. TRC, despite its restorative justice and its *ubuntu*, did not provide full justice for victims. It left victims only with a hope: that through TRC's recommendation as contained in its *Report* the government would ensure social justice for victims, such that social conditions would be something to write home about.[88] Iain Maclean says this justice can only be prefaced with "hopefully."[89] Yet, without justice and expansive reparations that end "the actual injustice and suffering," post-TRC South Africa cannot say to be in a situation of reconciliation.[90] Maclean offers this thesis while commenting on Willa Boesak's ethical reflection facing post-apartheid South Africa and the primary issue of landlessness and forced removals. Boesak argues that the kind of justice that deals with the unresolved issue can be referred to as a nuanced ethic of vengeance. Boesak's argument for

---

86. Amosu, "South Africa."
87. Makofane and Botha, "Christianity," 88–103; Chivers, "Breaking," 20–21.
88. Maclean, "Truth and Reconciliation," 279.
89. Maclean, "Truth and Reconciliation," 279.
90. Maclean, "Truth and Reconciliation," 283.

expansive justice, especially beyond the micro-focused issues that would later bedevil the TRC, sets out to tackle the issue of landlessness, forced removals, and racial stereotypes. He uses a traditional term for justice—vengeance—to articulate his position.[91] However, some like Russel Botman, a Euro-African, mistakenly interprets Boesak's use of the word vengeance to mean retributive justice.[92] What Boesak argues for resonates with Priscilla Hayner's five elements of reconciliation for transitional societies.[93]

Indeed, the symbolic aspects of restorative justice create what in peacebuilding is called a focus and a locus (renewed imagination of the kind of post-conflict society stakeholders ought to build up). Furthermore, without the symbolic aspects, people cannot hope for the creation of shared history and values in a post-conflict community. This kind of community will have a unity based on common and thoroughly all-encompassing humanity and nationhood in which victims and perpetrators can cooperate. These are essential to post-conflict peacebuilding.[94] Nevertheless, achieving intergenerational and group reconciliation in the likeness of the hypostatic union after a conflict is very important if the initial catharsis will be sustained. Thus, restorative justice in the image of biblical reconciliation must take concrete steps towards an equitable and cooperating pluralist community. Sadly, this has been lacking in post-apartheid South Africa. Unintentionally, Tutu's theology, as an example of dominant *baruti* discourse, has contributed to this state or has not mounted sufficient challenge in unmistakable terms.

Tutu's Theology Befuddles Forgiveness, Amnesty and Reconciliation

Tutu's theology of restorative justice defends amnesty theologically that it is an expression of mercy in transitional justice mechanisms. He insists that there could be no hope for reconciliation among divided peoples without political forgiveness. However, Tutu's theology confuses the conceptual difference between forgiveness and pardon (under which amnesty falls). As stated earlier, forgiveness gives up resentment towards a perpetrator, without necessarily giving up the pursuit of punishment, as part of the process of relational repair.[95] Only victim-survivors can offer this. Pardon, on the

91. On Boesak's argument, see Boesak, *God's Wrathful Children*.
92. Botman, "Truth and Reconciliation," 248–49.
93. Hayner, *Unspeakable Truths*, 163–66.
94. Cf. Lederach, *Building Peace*, 33–35.
95. Margaret Walker similarly offers forgiveness as a process of moral restructuring

contrary, is a juridical category that expresses a certain kind of freedom from some demands of justice that a perpetrator receives, based on some normative conditions. These demands include incarceration, lustration, restitution, and compensation. For instance, compensation can be part of a pardon if it is clear that the perpetrator is insolvent. The perpetrator can be pardoned not to make the material reparation but it does not mean that the perpetrator has no culpability nor does it imply that the perpetrator has no responsibility to make things right. It is just that considerations are made for the perpetrator. In international (civil) law, proven insolvency releases the perpetrator from the sacrosanct reparation. Yet, it does not mean that victims lose the right to demand reparation. When such a case arises, the pardoning state has the legal obligation to take over the pecuniary responsibility to those affected by the insolvency-induced waiver. This shows that while consideration might free the perpetrator from restitution, victims cannot be denied their entitlement to reparation.

Victims also can pardon—or precisely, express the desire to pardon. For instance, victims have the freedom to offer the intention to release offenders from some demands of justice for the irresponsible actions of the offenders. Historically, a group of murder survivors ("Murder Victims' Families for Reconciliation") promoted this kind of pardon. Members of this group insist that even if they do not give up the right to have justice meted out, they insist that capital punishment must not be administered. They are convinced of the importance of mercy to reconciliation for the human community. When their passionate plea for this form of mercy went unheeded, they started a public campaign against it. This is one of the earliest groups embodying restorative justice's values. Though survivors can voice *the desire to pardon,* the state is the only competent authority with the prerogative to grant pardon.[96]

Amnesty is an act of love-as-mercy offered by the powerful to the weak. In this case, the state (or victims in some cases) is the powerful, while the perpetrator is the weak. Accordingly, political forgiveness, being a corporate action on behalf of a corporate body, is a misnomer, and even ethically misleading. Due to their lack of conceptual clarity, some *baruti* discourse has confused victims and sometimes created resistance to amnesty. People resist when amnesty is couched in the language of forgiveness and not mercy extended by the state, due to competing demands, based on some

---

after the violent collapse of one's assumptive world. Cf. Walker, *Moral Repair,* 152.

96. Hence, a state cannot forgive. God may forgive for offenses against God's honor. He cannot forgive on behalf of victims. This is part of the *aporia* of forgiveness—that even God may not be free to forgive on behalf of victims in the here and now.

legal conditions.⁹⁷ This assertion is premised on the argument that without space for some principled forms of pardon (e.g., amnesty), a potent tool for reconciliation is vitiated.⁹⁸ However, it seems that some *baruti* discourse on justice and reconciliation after protracted conflict, like Tutu's, uncritically and unrealistically invokes the language of forgiveness, to accentuate the necessity for mercy towards perpetrators. The problem with this discourse is that it seeks to justify its ethically misleading political forgiveness with the concept of Christian forgiveness, i.e., that forgiveness is either freely given or not given at all. It is not premised on conditions.⁹⁹ Hence, amnesty was permissible even without making concrete reparation; and victims were encouraged to forgive even without the remorse of perpetrators so that they (the victims) could be free of resentment; their unconditional forgiveness thus contributes to political reconciliation.¹⁰⁰

97. This is why some critics condemned the Muhammadu Buhari-led government's amnesty program, code-named *Sulhu* for Islamic terrorists in northern Nigeria. The program encouraged jihadists with some level of command responsibility to surrender to the Nigerian Armed forces in exchange for government benefits, including being on government payroll. Most of these "repentant" Islamic terrorists would never be held accountable for atrocities they masterminded or committed. Buhari and his cronies mismanaged the so-called amnesty program. They confused the terrorists' *mea culpa* with the sacrosanctness of justice. They confused standard amnesty provisions for unconditional surrender without accountability. They pursued peace at whatever cost. Paradoxically, we saw the program as a sign of military defeat on the side of the Nigerian Armed Forces. Everyone with command responsibility should not be free of public accountability. The *Sulhu Program* was in violation of international criminal, and humanitarian, laws. On the criticism against the *Sulhu* program, see Anyadike, "Nigeria's Secret Programme."

98. Naqvi, "Amnesty for War," 587.

99. Tutu was pointedly told in Rwanda immediately after the genocide that his "sermon" for forgiveness, irrespective of the past, could not be taken without caveat because there are some atrocities that were unforgivable. Of course, he witnessed resistance probably because of how he framed his sermon: the nation must "move beyond retributive justice to restorative justice . . . move on to forgiveness, because without it there was no future." Tutu, *No Future*, 260. Tutu's mistake, which he made again, in Kenya in 2007 after the post-election violence, was that forgiveness is not the first word after a horrendous past. Rather, it is justice, though eschewing the spirit of retaliation.

100. One of the pointed critiques against this position came particularly from Notrose Konile, victim-survivor (now deceased) during the TRC, who insisted that she could not forgive the officer who participated in the murder of her only son, even if he had asked for forgiveness during a public hearing for his amnesty application. She anchored her objection on the root word for forgiveness in her Xhosa language, *ixolo*. To let go of resentment and to raise up one's hand in surrender both have the same root word, *ixolo*. Hence, she could not fathom TRC asking her to forgive a man who refused *ixolo* to her son when they had the power to do so: "I had a question to the killer that when Zabonke approached, 'Did he not ask for forgiveness?' [*with his hands in the air*]. Here he [*Mbelo*] is asking for forgiveness from me! So my question was, 'Did he not

However, this discourse, as in Tutu's, sidesteps one of the aporias of forgiveness. It is conditional and unconditional, precisely because it is a personal and moral concept, and not juridical or political. As a personal and moral concept, the wounded one has the responsibility to her/himself to offer forgiveness when the one/those threatening the wounded no longer can wound. In other words, forgiveness is possible normally when there is relative respite (the end to overt violence), with relative hope (not necessarily conviction) that the atrocities of the past will not be repeated. Yet, although forgiveness is ethically qualified, it is trans-ethical. That is, the sufferer can equally forgive, with or without the presence of the perpetrator and complicit bystanders, with or without their recognition, remorse, engagement and restitution.

Tutu's theology of reconciliation and restorative justice does not pay adequate attention to this aporia of forgiveness. Yet, a responsible and ethically qualified Christian theology of forgiveness should maintain the aporia of forgiveness. It should not use, as Tutu does, Christ's forgiveness on the Cross as normative. It can even be argued that Jesus appeared forgiving on the Cross because his enemies had done their worst.[101] So, to die in peace, he had the incredible courage to give up resentment towards them. This suggestion is not entirely strange among humans. In the face of mortal, terminal and certain danger and imminent death, something in us—what Christians refer to as the grace of final perseverance—moves the prior resentful person to offer forgiveness and thus die in peace. This is another aporia of forgiveness. Hence, perhaps realistic theological reasoning about forgiveness will highlight the moral of this last aporia: *Baruti*, like Tutu, should encourage people not to wait till imminent death before experiencing a peace that comes from forgiveness; but it should not be couched in a language of normativity. This caveat is added because we can only compassionately exhort for *forgiving-ness*. We may not ethically command or manipulate victims

---

ask forgiveness from you?' . . . But he [*Mbelo*] had no answer. Not even the judge and his attorney—because they had their attorneys." Krog et al., *There Was This Goat*, 200 (emphasis original).

101. Indeed, a skeptic about Jesus's forgiveness can even ask whether Jesus really did forgive. Do we have evidence in the Passion narrative that Jesus really forgave his perpetrators? The oft quoted passage is "Father, forgive them; for they know not what they do" (Luke 23:34). If one takes a critical look again at this passage, what is clear is that Jesus appeals to God on behalf of his perpetrators. He does not utter the words of forgiveness to the perpetrators. However, since Jesus as God-man is one with God the Father, we can argue that the forgiveness shall be bestowed as an action of the Trinity, including the God-man hanging on the cross.

towards forgiveness if the victims do not yet have the assurance of their safety and security, relief and recognition.[102]

Consequently, this is what I find crucially missing in Tutu's theological discourse on forgiveness within the reconciliation project. We should accept that a refusal to forgive due to the absence of forgiveness conditionality mentioned earlier is saddening, but not a moral failure. It is equally not a failure in Christian virtue. On the one hand, it is saddening because second and third parties (perpetrators; the state; or complicit beneficiaries) intentionally delay or neglect the assurance for personal and tangible safety and security, relief and recognition. On the other hand, it is not a moral failure or failure in Christian virtue because the first ethical principle of responsibility is the responsibility to the self. This does not necessarily express selfishness. It does express concern for the self; there is a difference between the two. One who refuses to forgive because of the lack of a favorable environment that gives assurance for safety and relief is practicing an ethically responsible concern for the self.

I offer this critique because of Tutu's grandnarrative of reconciliation that saw the TRC as a miracle. The danger with this is that when a project of justice on the way to reconciliation is cast in the tone of the miraculous, stakeholders find themselves in a fix: who are they to question or criticize grace? It thus silences critical discourse because projects that are considered as miracles are taken out of the orbit of everyday life—since miracles are the temporary suspension of the laws of nature and normalized relationships. Consequently, narrators of miraculous projects expect people to bow down in awe and ask no question about the propriety of the miracle and its components. Cast in this grandnarrative, a lot was open to theological and practical manipulation to realize the miracle. Since God is unfolding a miracle, no one must come in between. Hence, the refusal to own up and the refusal to forgive are seen as delaying the miracle.

---

102. A cross-section of New Testament scholars has a consensus that forgiveness in the synoptic gospels occur within the exhortative discourse on Christian piety and how Christians should behave towards one another, in imitation of God's gratuitousness. Yet, the exhortation, particularly from the moral of the parable of the Unforgiving Servant, insists that forgiveness should not simply be out of obedience to the law (normative command). Rather, it must be based on sincerity (from the heart). This shows the trans-ethical dimension of forgiveness. Christians are expected to go beyond ethical propositions to greater expressions of grace in daily life. Notwithstanding, Christians are not yet in a state of this gracious disposition. They strive daily towards it for the sake of God's kingdom. That is the meaning of Christian piety. Cf. Harrington, *Gospel according to Luke*, 111–13; Keener, *Commentary*, 161, 205, 207, 459; Hendrickx, *Third Gospel*, 316–17, 331–34; Gundry, *Matthew*, 108–9, 374–75; Green, *Matthew*, 77, 81–82.

Accordingly, for Tutu, without critical awareness of the various aporias of forgiveness highlighted above, the refusal to forgive would be a failure in Christian virtue. As a *moruti*, Tutu cannot accept this. Perhaps, again this is because of Tutu's absolute pacifist theology. Forgiveness that brings healing is part of pacifist theology of nonviolent resistance against evil. Healing after violence, according to the pacifist tradition, means experiencing inclusion, thus replacing sentiments associated with exclusion.[103] According to this tradition, then, one needs to forgive to be healed; and if one has not experienced healing, it is because one has not forgiven. Consequently, the individual is at fault for lacking healing.

In my opinion, this position re-traumatizes victims because it imposes guilt on them. However, the religious intuition, like Tutu's, about forgiveness-healing connection has not been empirically demonstrated beyond reasonable doubt. Anecdotes, which Tutu referred to a lot, in *No Future Without Forgiveness*, are not necessarily and scientifically true because various factors bring about positive physiological and psychosocial changes that are normally associated with forgiveness-healing connection.[104] Yet, people have become accustomed to taking Tutu's claim as if they are empirical facts, just as Adam was quoted earlier: "Due to the international stature of the TRC's chair, Desmond Tutu, his hopes and predictions have entered academic literature as empirical facts."[105] Apart from Tutu not showing awareness of scientific explanations to what he normally points to as proof of forgiveness-healing connection, Tutu's theology also misses the point because he paid insufficient attention to another *aporia*—that of healing.

Tutu's Theological Discourse and the Aporia of Healing

Tutu brought concepts like healing in a religious sense from his pastoral background. As a religious concept, healing is a response to a reality of toxic imperfection. Principally, Tutu sees this toxic imperfection as defilement and sin (against *ubuntu*). Since some see the gross violations of the past seen as defilement, then healing implies a purification of the violation of a taboo against codified reciprocal relations in the community. The emphasis is on the fact of violation and not on intentionality. Hence, the one who defiled the community has to be punished. This punishment is part of the rituals of purification for the community to be at peace again, or to appease the justified wrath against defiled interdict. Vengeance, hence,

---

103. Cf. Swartley, *Covenant of Peace*, 59, 89–90.
104. Thoresen et al., "Forgiveness and Health," 255, 257, 258, 273, 275–76.
105. Adam, "Divided Memories," 93.

as expiation removes defilement.[106] However, Tutu does not embrace the symbol of defilement to its logical conclusion probably due to his absolute pacifism, which cannot condone violence inherent in judicial punishment as part of purifying the defilement.[107]

As such, Tutu accentuates the symbol of moral evil as sin—the violation of *ubuntu*, to ameliorate or remove the ethical terror implied in evil as defilement. With toxic imperfection seen as a sin, one also focuses attention on the violation and less on intentionality, due to the symbol of "sin" as an objective reality. This is how we can understand why Tutu firmly insisted during the TRC that the ANC militants were as much sinners as the apartheid government, by the fact of what they did. Intentionality cannot cancel out the fact and consequences of acts. Within this catch-twenty-two situation, his religious intuition offers that for healing to occur for the sinners and those sinned against, there must be repentance and forgiveness. According to Tutu, forgiveness implies the right to forgo punishment,[108] with the possibility of embrace. Here, we get to see what healing means for Tutu. It is restoring the victims, the perpetrators and the ruptured relationships between them to wholeness and health. This happens through the confession-forgiveness trajectory.[109]

We can grasp some tensions already in how Tutu and co deployed healing. On the one hand, the defilement sense, which emphasized rituals, even without attention to intentionality, seemed to invoke justice. In other words, healing comes if the rituals of justice are performed, even if remorse is not present. Now, this position is problematic. It is an insult to think that justice, like restitution and compensation, covers all violations without an acknowledgment of wrong. It was the mistake of the Swiss banks to Jewish Holocaust survivors. By their actions, the Swiss banks reduced life to the "level of commodities" and the human person became "merely a high priced commodity."[110] This misses the sin sense of moral evil. So, with the interpersonal element missing, justice cannot heal and restore. Consequently, reconciliation remains impossible.

On the other hand, the metaphysical (religious) sense of healing points out that justice does not guarantee healing; the supererogatory (forgiveness) is crucial to healing. Perhaps, this is to highlight a provocative position:

---

106. Ricœur, *Symbolism of Evil*, 44.

107. Ricœur refers to this as "ethical terror." Ricœur, *Symbolism of Evil*, 29–33.

108. Tutu, *No Future*, 271.

109. Tutu, *No Future*, 156.

110. See Skotnicki, "How is Justice," 195; Szablowinski, "Apology without Compensation," 345, 348; Danieli, "Essential Elements of Healing," 349.

there can be no peace with justice only.[111] For instance, restitution (e.g., of land/property) is very justified as part of sacrosanct reparation as justice. Yet, restitution at whatever cost can jeopardize foreseeable peace, especially if the violator (or the second or third party) holds military and socioeconomic ace. So, insisting on justice may not repair ruptured relationships. Consequently, people like Tutu (at least during the TRC) assume, therefore, that what heals is not the ethical (justice), but the trans-ethical (forgiveness). For such people, there is no healing without forgiveness. It seems that they passed a message across: if you want to be healed (*and who does not?*), then you must forgive as a matter of imperative to yourself.

This is problematic for three reasons. First, one has a personal responsibility to seek healing; this is an ethical responsibility. However, by correlating healing and forgiveness, Tutu and co raise forgiveness to the level of an ethical imperative, which, as argued earlier, cannot be. Second, this position implies that one is not free to withhold forgiveness. The refusal to forgive further implies that one will be guilty of injustice and lack of charity to oneself. This is unacceptable ethically. Third, the lack of space for the refusal to forgive implies that if someone refuses to forgive, then it is a clear case of an ethical failure and failure in Christian virtue since health and forgiveness go together.

One can understand, though unrelentingly questioning, all the same, Tutu's position on healing that makes forgiveness so central because of its ethical imperative. He cannot accept or understand that forgiveness is a surplus-value. His position might be seen to have some ethical sustainability in the light of Arendt's claim that forgiveness relieves the burden of the irreversibility of human action in history: "The possible redemption from the predicament of irreversibility—of being unable to undo what one has done though one did not, and could not, have known what one was doing—is the faculty of forgiving."[112] A critical look at Arendt's claim shows a consciously nuanced position on forgiveness, which differs significantly from Tutu's, and Tutu might even disagree vehemently with Arendt.[113]

111. Andrew Rigby used to phrase this as a discussion statement for his students during examination: "There can be no peace with justice." Rigby, *Justice and Reconciliation*, 11.

112. Arendt, *Human Condition*, 237.

113. In his *No Future without Forgiveness*, Tutu refers to Arendt's thesis of the banality of evil—to show that those who do obnoxious things are not hydra-headed beings. They are as normal as the next person on the street. Nevertheless, Tutu never refers to Arendt's *Human Condition* where she makes the case for forgiveness in the public realm. One can only wonder why. However, given that he knows about Arendt's works, one might suggest that his theological method does not fit Arendt's position on forgiveness within this method without causing heresy for Tutu. Arendt's position might appear as

First, for Arendt, forgiveness applied to actions with objectively obnoxious consequences, although the actors did not intend these consequences. Forgiveness is for actions with unintended grave consequences arising out of human limitations (e.g., accidents; invincible ignorance; propaganda). Forgiveness here does not mean letting go of moral outrage, resentment and anger. Rather, to use the ethically precise word, this is deculpabilization: excusing the person for the unintended actions that had morally objectionable consequences.

Second, Arendt's notion of forgiveness concerns everyday infractions. It does "not apply to the extremity of crime and willed evil."[114] Arendt arrives at this position upon her reading of the gospel passages that refer to Jesus's teaching on endless forgiveness of trespasses (Luke 17:1–5; Matt 6:14–15). Jesus so taught because "trespassing is an everyday occurrence."[115] However, willful and extreme evil, like the one she had in mind—the Holocaust—is not within the purview of human forgiveness. That will be settled at the last judgment. Strikingly, even from the gospel account, "the Last Judgment is not characterized by forgiveness but by just retribution (*apodounai*)."[116]

Leaving Arendt aside and paying attention to developments in some social science disciplines related to victims' need for proper functioning again, one can further question Tutu's ethical position on forgiveness, especially that it is imperative for victims. Data gathered from traumatology and victimology reveals that forgiveness is not necessarily the component of healing. Justice is. Yet, as I will expatiate in chapter 6, the door is not closed against forgiveness. This brings me back to my earlier appraisal that Tutu's non-appreciation of the *aporia* of forgiveness is related to this position on healing. Tutu does not pay attention to the *aporia* of biblical healing. To understand this claim, we must make some observations on the biblical sense of healing and some Christian theological traditions.

Biblically, healing denotes illness (transgressed evil that defiles personal and human integrity). This is one of the effects of the fall. Millard Erikson, writing from an evangelical background, gives a reasonable construal of healing at least from the perspective of the effects of Christ's incarnation.

---

such to Tutu, especially her stance that even in the Gospel (Luke 17:1–5), Jesus refers to some offenses that are unforgivable in this world. To Tutu, this is unacceptable given his reaction to what the post-genocide Rwandan President told him about unforgivable sins being affirmed in the Scriptures. On Tutu's single reference to Arendt, see Tutu, *No Future*, 144. On Tutu's comments on "unforgivable sins," see Tutu, *No Future*, 260. On Arendt's references to "unforgivable offenses," see Arendt, *Human Condition*, 240n80.

114. Arendt, *Human Condition*, 239.
115. Arendt, *Human Condition*, 240.
116. Arendt, *Human Condition*, 240 (emphasis original).

Healing is part of the atonement package of Christ (others are forgiveness, reconciliation and redemption).[117] Accordingly, healing is part of human entitlement arising from Christ's atonement.[118] Even though Jesus did not directly link healing to individual sin, on many occasions he did "correlate healing with forgiveness of sin."[119] Nevertheless, we can see healing as a conscious action towards alleviating the miseries of life that humans or entities connected with them are enduring.[120]

Similarly, Willard Swartley, a New Testament biblical theologian, writing from his Mennonite tradition, offers that healing is intricately linked with God's gift of peace, which is an expression of the in-breaking of God's kingdom, at least from the perspective of the New Testament.[121] Healing "'includes everything necessary to healthful living: a good health, a sense of well-being, good fortune, the cohesiveness of the community, relationship to relatives and their state of being, and anything else deemed necessary for everything to be in order.'"[122] Summarily, Swartley offers healing as analogous to "the restoration of *shalom*."[123] Violence is the antonym of *shalom*. Hence, healing will be the reversal of the antonym, according to God's will.[124] We can infer some points from this position. Healing affects simultaneously the state of being (individual) and relationships (relational). Healing comprises of the following supererogatory and normative elements: "steadfast love (*chesed*), faithfulness (*emunah*); righteousness (*tsedaqah*), and justice (*mishpat*). These are *sine qua non* for shalom to flourish (Ps 89:14; 97:2b; 85:10)."[125]

We can see a tension here concerning healing. On the one hand, it appears healing is obligatory for anthropological and sociological reasons (Swartley). On the other hand, healing is primarily a gift from God (Erickson). This healing expresses itself concretely out of the human goodwill, due to the virtues associated with the process of healing (Swartley). Since it is God's gift, it cannot be demanded; and it will not always be given, even if one requests it as Saint Paul did (cf. 2 Cor 12:10). This is because some benefits accruing from Christ's incarnation and redemption will not be accessed

---

117. Erickson, *Christian Theology*, 852.
118. Erickson, *Christian Theology*, 853.
119. Erickson, *Christian Theology*, 854–55.
120. Erickson, *Christian Theology*, 857.
121. Swartley, *Covenant of Peace*, 21, 51, 78.
122. Swartley, *Covenant of Peace*, 28.
123. Swartley, *Covenant of Peace*, 28n4.
124. Swartley, *Covenant of Peace*, 29.
125. Swartley, *Covenant of Peace*, 30 (emphasis original).

until the end of time (cf. Rom 8:19–25). Erickson succinctly expresses this crucial *aporia* of biblical healing: "It is not always God's plan to heal. That fact will not trouble us if we but remember that we are not intended to live forever in this earthly body (Heb 9.27)."[126]

Furthermore, since healing is also a human gift, it implies that healing critically depends on human agency, freewill, goodwill and compassion of significant others to those hurting and who should not be neglected. Healing, then, cannot be legislated; no one can mandate it, even if people can demand healing. From a relational and structural point of view, we can only create an atmosphere conducive for humans to bring forth the elements Swartley points out towards those hurting. Consequently, the tentativeness of healing is intricately connected with a double provisionality—of God's grace (Erickson) and human actions (Swartley).

I do not think there are irreconcilable tensions between demand for healing and healing as a gift. Sensitive to the *aporia* of biblical healing and an anthropological fact that not all experience healing even when everything humanly possible has been done, we can appreciate a conceptual difference between justice and healing. Justice is predictable because its normative elements are distinguishable. We are only promised or hope for healing in the justice process. We insist on this conceptual difference because of the danger in making healing, like forgiveness, another ethical obligation exclusively on our part. If (effecting) healing is an ethical obligation on our part, we feel compelled to make it happen in a variety of ways. It may even mean compelling some stakeholders to have those elements for healing noted above, not minding if those being compelled are ready or convinced. For instance, since Tutu and co saw the disclosure of truth as a major component of healing, they laid strong emphasis on disclosure. Even if done without remorse, they reckoned it brought healing to the victims. However, this compulsion and lack of remorse caused more pain.

Similarly, we can notice another danger if healing is obligatory and tied exclusively to justice. It is the danger of the healing process being rushed. Since processing for penalty has a time limit, those who do not see a conceptual and time perspective difference between justice and healing are usually in a hurry to effect healing as fast as possible. For these actors, if the transitional justice process (e.g., a Truth Commission) concludes its work, who will continue the healing? Yet, we must recognize that healing will happen when it will happen, provided there is an encouraging environment for it, whenever it will make its epiphany. It is partly the role of justice to create that favorable atmosphere. Then we understand that though we

---

126. Erickson, *Christian Theology*, 858.

cannot effect healing on ourselves or others via imposition, we have the ethical responsibility to create an encouraging environment, for healing to burst forth, just like the conditionality of forgiveness.

So, Tutu's theological discourse on the forgiveness-healing connection is questionable since healing, at least from a Christian theological perspective, comes ultimately from God. For Tutu, it seems that God's grace will always heal us without exception. Victims just need to forgive. This appears to be a grandnarrative that does not give room for divine freedom, the interruptive feature of grace, and human freedom. Beyond this grandnarrative being theologically problematic as already demonstrated, one has to test it with data from victims who forgave, thus experiencing cathartic healing during the TRC public hearings. Did all of them experience healing as articulated above? How many felt healed in the long term? According to Allan & Allan, as of 2000, no data was available to suggest that "any long-term healing followed for witnesses who experienced catharsis while giving testimony to the TRC."[127] Colvin, writing in 2006, presents the result of his fieldwork among those who appeared before the TRC, told their stories, and were guaranteed to heal. Years after, the momentary catharsis during the TRC had waned. Some witnesses were still searching for healing, because a justice component (i.e., material reparation) was still missing. Victim-survivors demand this justice component from the state and the beneficiaries, for the structural harm they suffered.[128] In a 2006 article, Allan et al. equally point out that healing does not ineluctably connect with forgiveness. After forgiving perpetrators at the TRC, these researchers discovered that the victims were still in search of healing through justice by litigation. This fact led Allan & Allan to assert that "unless victims perceive an apology as authentic it will not facilitate forgiving and the healing victims search for when they embark on litigation."[129]

From these empirical observations, Tutu's grandnarrative on forgiveness-healing connection does not resonate with victims' experiences. Of course, the TRC kickstarted a healing process. However, for such process to be sustained, the transitional society needed "an intensive and sustained therapeutic intervention."[130] However, follow-ups after the exchange of forgiveness and reconciliation were rare. Hence, victim-survivors experienced anger and frustration towards the South African government and apathy

---

127. Allan and Allan, "South African Truth," 473.
128. Colvin, "Shifting Geographies," 166–84.
129. Allan et al., "Exploration of the Association," 96.
130. Allan and Allan, "South African Truth," 473.

towards the "naughty uncle" (Tutu).[131] Victim-survivors concluded that their government (and Tutu) simply used them to achieve democratic stability, with the least possible punitive reactions from the volatile financial market. One sees a paradox about the TRC and Tutu. The international community continues to hold up the TRC as *The Model* and Tutu's moral authority and admiration continue to grow. However, for many South Africans, the TRC is becoming increasingly irrelevant due to great concessions given to beneficiaries of apartheid, who went away with a slap on the wrist. We can understand the increasing irrelevance against the grand promises contained in Tutu's articles of faith; and many bought into this narrative. What this highlights is a problematic ethical reasoning, which even made it plausible in the first place for Tutu to promote the forgiveness-healing connection since his towering presence at the TRC till death.

Tutu's Ethical Reasoning concerning Reconciliation

I tie my interest in Tutu's theological contribution to three of my multiple identities. First, I am a post-War Nigerian *(i.e., born shortly after the end of Nigeria's Civil War)*. With the rest of my generation, we have been fed and are saturated with half-truths and emotion-laden stories of the past, which led to that war, and why inter-ethnic and inter-religious interactions as we grew up to experience them have been that way and could remain that way. Second, I am a pastor *(a Roman Catholic missionary priest)* who was and is persistently confronted with the effects of widespread evils in our midst on individuals and society. Third, I am a scholar and teacher in Christian ethics. Constantly, I struggle on how as a pastor and an ethicist one can make a pastoral and ethical sense of my context, and teach this (either from the pulpit or in the classroom). These multiple identities have some similarities with Archbishop Tutu's.

First, he was born and grew up in a worse hit context of inter-generational and interracial violence. Second, as a pastor, he was constantly confronted with the pains and burdens of his people, which demanded his response. Third, Tutu was a teacher, first as a seminary professor, and later as a bishop and archbishop. This is why I turn to him as a source of inspiration, basically to figure out how to reason ethically about and around the issues raised so far in this chapter and this book on the whole. Nevertheless, one still recognizes a salient point Shirley Du Boulay, Tutu's biographer raised, that he is not a professional theologian in the strict sense: "he is not a black theologian in the technical sense; he has not read

---

131. Maluleke, "Reconciliation in South Africa," 111.

or reflected or wrestled with the issues in sufficient depth.... His thinking is expressed more in sermons, devotional talks and addresses than serious theological writing."[132] So, it is herculean to pinpoint Tutu's ethical reasoning. The best one can hope for is to distil the ethical reasoning at work in his contributions and advocacy.

Earlier, we detected an ethical approach in Tutu's positions on forgiveness and healing. Tutu's predilection for framing *postbellum* afterwords in grandnarrative terms suggests what Christian ethics calls "a moral theology of perfection."[133] Christian ethicists usually use this moral theology to qualify normative/deontological ethics. "Normative" or "obligation" kept surfacing in the discussion on the aporias of forgiveness and healing. According to James Keenan, this kind of ethical reasoning does not pay sufficient attention to "personal historicity" and "human development."[134] Attentiveness to multiple historicity and trajectory of human development are obstacles to any grandnarrative thinking or project. During the TRC and thereafter, some interlocutors pointed out severally to Tutu that the way he framed issues of forgiveness, healing, and reconciliation gave insufficient room for the conceptual difference between these or the necessary nuance concerning forgiveness and healing. He roundly dismissed these critical observations, sticking to his lofty view on reconciliation.

Consequently, one can suggest that Tutu teaches and preaches non-relativized ethics of action, at least when it comes to *postbellum* after-words. Roger Burggraeve, who is the subject of Keenan's article, insists that ethical reasoning related to human persons must pay attention to the "historical dimension of human existence."[135] What Burggraeve argues in his lengthy two-part article is that "'a level of reality'" must be factored into our ethical evaluations when these touch humans, who are situated in time and space; they are changing and developing; and they are affected not only by their "psycho-affective organization."[136] Their social contexts also affect them.[137] However, it seems that for Tutu what Burggraeve calls for is untenable given Tutu's metaphysical sense of forgiveness and healing. Tutu expects everyone who comes forward to tell his or her story to be healed by the cathartic moment and also be able to forgive. He does not pay attention that persons who are affected by their psycho-affective organization and their social contexts

---

132. Du Boulay, *Tutu*, 87.
133. Keenan, "Roger Burggraeve's Ethics," 296.
134. Keenan, "Roger Burggraeve's Ethics," 296.
135. Burggraeve, "Meaningful Living," 8.
136. Burggraeve, "Meaningful Living," 6–7.
137. Burggraeve, "Meaningful Living," 10.

("the collective i.e. meso- and macro-social dimension"[138]) can have various motivations not to forgive and not to experience healing. Tutu's ethical reasoning, then, appears to be more anthropological than sociological. If his theological ethical discourses on forgiveness and healing are open to what Burggraeve refers to as the polysemic dimension of human behavior, Tutu will recognize that holiness and human perfection are not the same.[139]

Hence, he would not have raised forgiveness to the level of Christian normativity, such that one who refuses to forgive (irrespective of the psycho-affective organization and the social contexts) failed to show Christian virtue and African *ubuntu*.[140] Furthermore, he closes off the level of reality that gives space for people to move through their route towards forgiveness, and healing that is humanly possible and meaningful for them. There is a distinction that we can make between what is humanly possible and what is humanly desirable and meaningful in the here and now for concrete persons and groups struggling with the after-word issues of justice, peace, reconciliation (and forgiveness and healing).[141] Yet, traumatized peoples in transitional societies are on the way towards these. So, a theological ethical approach towards them has to be realistic. I take inspiration from Burggraeve:

> Quite a number of people find themselves in the state of a 'confusion of values' because of their psychic-social conditioning; they are hardly capable or even completely incapable of reaching a certain ideal of human quality or 'meaning-fullness.' We should not, therefore, raise the ideal so high and so far away without pointing out the possible intermediate steps, so that people feel that it is unattainable and unreachable in their situation. Whoever counsels people ethically must be close to them where they are 'here and now' and where they are capable of being "tomorrow."[142]

In other words, human growth, especially for those in transition, demands a realistic ethical discourse. This discourse must pay attention to human

---

138. Burggraeve, "Meaningful Living," 13.

139. Cf. Burggraeve, "Meaningful Living," 5, 9.

140. If *ubuntu* is cast so much in the mould of Tutu's religious intuition, and not realism, it can lead to glossing over continuing structural disadvantages, and communitarian tyranny over individual persons in extreme cases. Cf. LenkaBula, "Beyond Anthropocentricity," 381.

141. See Burggraeve, "Meaningful Living," 138.

142. Burggraeve, "Meaningful Living," 152.

growth towards what is humanly possible. Yet, it is via what is humanly meaningful for them here and now.[143]

In the context of this subsection and chapter in general, one can realize that Tutu's grandnarrative approach, which tends to look at things as one indivisible package, could not give space to those who preferred to take the healing route not simply through truth-telling and forgiveness, but through litigation, in the absence of some elements of justice apart from the disclosure of truth. His approach also does not pay attention to those who were (and still are) convinced that it was crucial for their healing here and now to withhold forgiveness, till they experienced stability and relief in the meso- and macro-social dimensions in the long term, even if the offending parties apologized here and now.[144] Tutu's approach is even less equipped to handle the ego-dystonic of the past, who were encouraged to confess to be healed.[145] Yet, the argument for adopting realistic ethics that seeks what is humanly meaningful for these persons and groups partly reveals the provisionality, which comes with historically conscious and realistic ethics of growth. So, the resistance to Tutu's discourse on forgiveness, healing and reconciliation

---

143. See Burggraeve, "Meaningful Living," 155.

144. A woman, whose son was killed (burnt), refused to forgive during the TRC. She chose to take different routes than Tutu (and Mandela) whose lives changed considerably and economically, in stark contrast to hers. She argued: "'it is easy for Mandela and Tutu to forgive . . . they lead vindicated lives. In my life nothing, not a single thing, has changed since my son was burnt by barbarians. . . .Therefore I cannot forgive.'" According to Kay Carmichael, for the woman, the ethical (justice) conditions the supererogatory (forgiveness).Without the change in one's fortune, forgiveness might be difficult under that circumstance: "There was no justice for the woman and she was not in a position to forgive." Surely, Carmichael does not claim that forgiveness has no place after criminal violations. What Carmichael envisions is a model of renewal after violation that holds the spheres of superabundance and equivalence (to use Ricœur's words) in balance. Carmichael, *Sin and Forgiveness*, 131.

145. According to Allan and Allan, the "ego-dystonic" persons are those who committed atrocities in the past. They were convinced they were engaged in a just war to protect their country from rebels—or even criminals. They grew up and worked within a culture and system that proposed to them that White is right, and Black is wrong.

With the sudden turn around, the ego-dystonic during the TRC realized that those criminals were actually heroes, and they, the heroes of the past, became evil men and rotten eggs of the system, according to de Klerk. This was traumatic, and merely confessing their atrocities would not heal them. They suffered a crisis of meaning and selfhood. Suddenly, they witnessed a reversal of the logic. Why should they apologize for actions from that conviction? What then could heal them? Justice (truth-for-amnesty)? Perhaps, what could heal them would be rituals of mourning i.e., establishing justice in the wider sense, in addition to self-forgiveness, and seeing that the masterminds of their ego-dystonism also took responsibility for the crisis. Although justice is part of their healing, what will end it? Perhaps, it is beyond ethics i.e., love-as-mercy. Allan and Allan, "South African Truth," 473–74.

during the TRC and after came down to an ethical discourse that was just unrealistic for many; there was no way Tutu's theological contribution accommodated them without inducing them to guilt.

For instance, Tutu's no future without forgiveness, as discussed above, puts pressure on victims and victimized peoples to forgive because if they persisted in their refusal they are held as endangering the future. This betrays ethics of fear that exaggeratingly focuses on some consequences of human behaviors. It subtly makes people fall in line, by obeying the norm that had been set, in the case involving Tutu, by the Christian tradition and the TRC Promotion Act. This exaggerated emphasis on falling in line contradicts "evangelical message which does not primarily preach a negative ethics of fear but rather a positive ethics of love."[146] The ethical realism that permeates this book challenges Tutu's ethical bent. This ethical realism cautions against adopting an either/or position; it gives no space for growth in an individual's understanding of the challenge of Christ's love. This binary view causes discouragement and alienation in the dominant discourse that emphasizes the either/or approach. Furthermore, ethical realism extends beyond individual considerations to the social system. As long as multidimensional human persons create systems to respond institutionally to complex issues involving human subjects, the evangelical ethics of love must have space too in those systems. If not, there will be a disjunction in ethical responses because, in micro issues, we pay special attention to ethics of love. Yet, in the social system, we see the binary approach inherent in ethics of falling in line.

Instead of binary opposition, a more preferable ethical approach, at least from a Catholic perspective, will be "a both-and attitude towards theory and practice."[147] Ethicists interested in grasping the dynamics of human behavior should spend more time on understanding and clarifying "ordinary, daily behavior and figure out at least some of the reasons why persons make the ethical decisions they do."[148] Nevertheless, this preferable approach in ethical reasoning (i.e., the both-and attitude) is crucial for transition moments or moments of crises and dilemmas. Moments of ethical dilemmas include "conflicts of priorities because of the sheer numbers involved."[149] These moments provoke deeper and structured ethical reflection on what

---

146. Burggraeve, "Meaningful Living," 138.
147. Selling, "Structure," 387.
148. Selling, "Structure," 373.
149. Selling, "Structure," 373.

is going on and things needing to be done or balanced in consideration of competing priorities and long-held principles.¹⁵⁰

Accordingly, people need ethical realism as the appropriate ethical approach at crisis-filled moments like the *postbellum* Truth Commissions and during tensions involving love, justice, peace and reconciliation. This ethical realism acknowledges that we are all naturally flawed.¹⁵¹ Thus, there will not be perfect justice and reconciliation projects. We will make lots of detours, compromises and mistakes on the way to building a delicate but more hopeful, just and peaceful world. Consequently, lots of Tutu's catchphrases were based more on sheer religious intuition and not on thought-out ethical reasoning. I am not suggesting that both are mutually exclusive. Religious intuition can open a fresh perspective for human reason. After all, this is one of the arguments for religious actors to be more active in the public realm dominated by acutely rational *realpolitik*. Nevertheless, one of the arguments of this book is that religious actors like Tutu should take serious Ricœur's admonition: *religious intuition, which might contain some truths, must articulate itself in public with a clear methodical approach if it will stand the test of time and retain its air of respectability*. This is even more pertinent when religious intuition relates to ethics and its systematic approaches to ethical issues.

Accordingly, a more down-to-earth position that would not be perceived as moralizing would realize, as affirmed earlier, that there is a future even without forgiveness, although parties should, like many of us, be helped to "believe in the importance of forgiveness and reconciliation."¹⁵² Some courageous victim-survivors roundly rejected Tutu's claim on forgiveness because it lacked the kind of ethical clarity, analysis and *epikeia*¹⁵³ attentive to the human person adequately considered. However, many who revere Tutu felt alienated by his claim and afraid that they were endangering the future because they were not ready to forgive. In their gut level, some primary conditions necessary for forgiveness were absent and their "naughty uncle" seemed insensitive to the human meaningfulness of their position. Accordingly, Tutu's ethical reasoning was insufficiently meaningful, humanly speaking because it appeared that its theological principles

---

150. This makes sense if the reader recalls the gist of the non-ideal theory of justice mentioned in the conclusion of chapter 2 when summarizing one of the attractions and promises of restorative justice.

151. Selling, "Structure," 386.

152. Selling, "Structure," 386.

153. Keenan refers to this as a virtue of discernment regarding the morally right judgment in a transition moment, as indicative of an ethics of growth. See Keenan, "Roger Burggraeve's Ethics," 303.

(normatively given) did not quite "enter into those areas of life that are beyond the boundaries of Church-taught prescriptive."[154] Considering the current discussion, one can make some conclusions. Fundamentally, Tutu was the "naughty uncle" that carried the emotional baggage of the (Black) community. Yet, he showed a reluctance at crucial moments to "enter into the chaos of another" i.e., being merciful,[155] especially those silenced and condemned to an existence that made the future bleak. Nevertheless, these were expected and cajoled to forgive to be healed, over and above justice, the complex term used for good relations between persons and groups. The justice they demanded (and still demand) "may be applied to an entire spectrum of specific issues in regard to property, time, communication, education, work, mobility, partner choice, family creation, leisure, and so forth."[156] However, many victims of the past realized that these specific issues were excluded from the justice menu, and their "naughty uncle" agreed.

Tutu and "Beyond Retribution" Discourse among Religious Actors

Tutu's religious intuition on transitional justice revolves around the 'beyond retribution' stance. According to him and other absolute pacifists, beyond retribution is the central insight from the New Testament, quite probably.[157] There are a couple of problems with this religious stance. First, the New Testament does not present us with a "beyond retribution" stance. Rather, it is a "not just retribution" stance. Some biblical scholars, in their study of justice/righteousness in the Old and New Testaments, offer that justice has broad meanings and implications. Nevertheless, it is essentially defined by relations and context since it is concerned with preserving, ameliorating, or promoting peace and wholeness of a community of persons bound together by defined relations of trust. In this sense, these biblical terms are not just legal and forensic. They even extend in the same movement towards restructuring of the society and relations if there are inbuilt inequities. Consequently, *justice acknowledges, validates and redresses (victims), repudiates and punishes (offenders), while equally humanizing the society to improve the demands of living together in trust (symbolic) and flourishing (material).* Summarily, the idea of justice/righteousness in the New Testament is not radically different from the Old Testament's: there is still the dialectics of

---

154. Keenan, "Roger Burggraeve's Ethics," 301.
155. Keenan, "Roger Burggraeve's Ethics," 302.
156. Selling, "Structure and Content,"383–84.
157. For a comprehensive articulation, see Marshall, *Beyond Retribution*.

acknowledgement, validation, redress (for victims), repudiation and sanctions (for offenders), and humanization of relationships, systems and culture (macro concerns). So, we are nowhere presented with the unqualified stance of just beyond retribution.[158]

Second, we have already seen the tendency to confuse forgiveness and punishment (i.e., a non-legal phenomenon and a legal concept). We already saw this confusion from Tutu's definition of forgiveness. We see it also in Christopher Marshall's magisterial work, *Beyond Retribution*. Both Tutu and Marshall suggest that forgiveness is an act of release from the victim to the offender, while at the same time surrendering the right to hurt the offender for what the offender did.[159] The problem is that there is little sensitivity to the reality that forgiveness, as an act of love-as-mercy, does not release the offender from punishment, which by definition and reality hurts (or should hurt, without degrading). Tutu's religious intuition is too restrictive (quite abolitionist).[160] It is as if forgiveness and punishment cannot go together. However, from biblical evidence, love-as-mercy and justice go together: *God punishes to the fourth generation but shows mercy to the thousandth generation* (cf. Exod 34:6–7).

Third, the *beyond retribution* metaphor pays insufficient attention to a necessary strategy of bifurcation regarding biblical justice. This strategy has an end with two different means towards realizing it, depending on the subjects. The sincere and remorseful persons shall receive restorative sanctions. These, to Lode Walgrave, a Belgian criminologist, do not necessarily have to include face-to-face encounters. Walgrave premises his position on what he regards as the maximalist position, which recognizes that when voluntariness is absent, restorative justice must not be necessarily weak. It can enforce reparative sanctions ranging from reparative fines and formal restitution to contributing to victims' funds and community service.[161] However, the untrustworthy and insincere persons brought before the justice system will receive retribution. The extent to which the offender

---

158. Cf. Hiers, *Justice and Compassion*; Ziesler, "Righteousness," 655–56; Perkins, "Justice," 475–76; McKnight, "Justice," 411–16, esp. 415; Bennett, "Justice," 476–77; Achtemeir, "Righteousness in the OT," 91–99; Achtemeir, "Righteousness in the NT," 80–85.

159. Marshall, *Beyond Retribution*, 264.

160. Walker aptly observes: "People can and do forgive those who have perpetrated crimes against them, without being inclined to insist on remission of the criminal offender's legally prescribed punishment. Nor should we say that the injured person in forgiving gives up a right to demand any repair from the wrongdoer." Walker, *Moral Repair*, 156.

161. Walgrave, *Restorative Justice*, 23.

responds and is ready to make reparation determines punishment, even in restorative justice, according to this critical realism.[162]

As stated earlier, retribution and restorative justice will always have some relationships. Even Howard Zehr, the grandfather of restorative justice, has acknowledged this fact. In the Afterword to the 2005 edition of his *Changing Lenses*, Zehr takes a more realistic position regarding the relationship between retribution and restorative justice. In the earlier edition, he contended that both were mutually exclusive. However, in the intervening years between the first edition and the revised one, he realized that it is unrealistic to play both against themselves: "Posing them as total opposites also obscures the retributive elements that may be part of a restorative approach."[163] Hence, one sees that the beyond retribution stance of actors like Tutu is not very helpful and efficient.

Fourth, *beyond retribution*, even if practicable, relies excessively on face-to-face encounters, with the hope that there will be acknowledgement. In other words, *beyond retribution* will work with remorseful or at best rational offenders. If these are absent, *beyond retribution* finds itself in a quandary: it does not accept punishment, yet victims want justice. Without space for various levels of distinctions in the justice process, religious metaphors like *beyond retribution* can activate their auto-neutralizing button. Auto-neutralization refers to the phenomenon of a critical concept containing within itself an element that can undermine its critical edge. *Beyond retribution* that has no space for various levels of distinctions of justice (even the merciful one) inadvertently becomes complicit in impunity. Tutu's imagination of "no future without forgiveness" is a case in point. During the TRC, it emphasized exclusively the face-to-face encounter or relational disclosure of truth before mercy (as amnesty) could be offered. It had little to offer, except appeal, regarding those who spurned the process. Or those (either victims or offenders) who were not yet ready for the face-to-face encounter. Yet, concerned stakeholders needed validation/redress, and repudiation/punishment. What about faceless (structural) crimes? This is how one sees that *beyond retribution* has a simplistic approach to complex human expectations of justice on the way to reconciliation.

For religions to flourish in public, particularly with critical criminologists and critical peacebuilding experts, especially in transitional societies, they need to show more adeptness at the complexities of objective factors and subjective interests that must be balanced in the post-conflict justice process. Critical ethical realism is non-negotiable in such public

---

162. Dignan, "Towards a Systemic Model," 153.
163. Zehr, *Changing Lenses*, 272.

religious contributions. Hence, I will suggest later in chapter 7 that religions and the public need more the critical accompaniment of religious ethicists to complement and refine the simple though inspiring contributions of *baruti* like Tutu.

Conclusion

This chapter had two points of departure. First, the world needs the inspiration, moral integrity and internationally acclaimed stature of Archbishop Tutu and other religious actors like him. Second, if we have an inspiration that is not supported by theological finesse, which can respond realistically to the numerous grey areas in transitional societies, that inspiration in due time will be relegated when the world is no longer under the spell of such inspirational figures. Consequently, the positive and proactive potential of religious contributions will be neutralized. The danger then is that dogmatic secularists will point to an instance of this auto-neutralization as another proof that religion is not useful in public projects of the liberal state. Hence, Christian ethicists have grave responsibility so that their religion does not press the button of auto-neutralization. Without necessarily getting panicky about the threat of auto-neutralization, their contributions will add to the quality of arguments for religious contributions in the search for sustainable peace and reconciliation projects in the world today. Such prophetic technical analysts must be sensible by paying attention to the different layers of meaning of key metaphors actors deploy from their sacred texts. They must be attentive also to insights from relevant non-theological disciplines, the everyday discourse of ordinary citizens through various media and literary genres.

This chapter highlighted the various dimensions of the ethical approach in Archbishop Tutu's theological discourse on and advocacy for restorative justice, as well as the after-word issues. The chapter concluded that Tutu's richly inspirational interventions are religious intuitions that needed to be tempered by an ethical realism acutely aware of the human person adequately considered. Deconstruction without reconstruction or credible alternative may sound scientific, but it is moral irresponsibility. Consequently, we must propose a possible alternative theological imagination that can inspire the kind of ethical realism in restorative justice, which this book is pursuing. Thus, in the next chapter, I shall explore an arcane theological analogue, which in my estimation is promising regarding the kind of theological ethical imagination in peacebuilding that might stand the test of time.

4
A Theological Ethics of Restorative Justice in Peacebuilding

THIS CHAPTER OUTLINES A theological vision for restorative justice, which should inspire its theory and praxis. I premise this on what we can see as realistic theological ethics in public. This kind of theology "needs to confront the structures of the public drawing up a theological politics."[1] Nevertheless, we must do this in collaboration with the social sciences to offer an articulate, yet principled, stance on a requisite theological framework in the search for justice and reconciliation, i.e.,

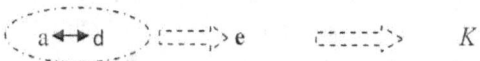

where *a=Love; d=Justice; e=Peace; K=Reconciliation*

Courtesy of the Author

Consequently, Christians' doctrinal affirmations must have bearing on people's concrete contexts. Hence, this chapter digs deep into a particular Christian doctrinal affirmation to offer a reasonable response to historical developments of mass violence and the search for post-conflict justice, peace and reconciliation.

Christians, Violence, and Thirst for Vengeance

Religion, as an ideology, has the proclivity of coloring relationships. First, religion exerts influence on public policies and social ordering. Second,

1. Schwager, "Christology," 356.

religion engineers behavior. It offers identity to adherents such that "it colours human relationships, struggles and competition."[2] Religion, thus, as an identity marker, piths people against one another. Even if there is no direct link between religion and violence, attests Lloyd Steffen, religion supplies some motivations for violent behaviors. Steffen opines, "there is no doubt that religions sponsor viewpoints and attitudes that affect the decisions people make about what to do and how to act, and this is certainly true on the issue of violence."[3] We can safely aver that religion has acted more like a centrifugal force in post-colonial Africa. Instead of preaching and pursuing a united people under God, religion appears intolerant. Consequently, religion's collaborators with the political elite engage in profiling. Profiling is meant to exclude fellow citizens, who happen to practice another religion. Violence has a high probability of breaking out in multi-religious countries like Nigeria when the excluded other resists the profiling and transactional politicking.

With particular reference to post-colonial Africa, Islam is generally implicated and involved in violence in most of the countries caught in religion-implicated mass violence. Victims, in most cases Christians, sometimes respond with retaliatory violence. These Christians' response presents us with the vicious cycle of vengeance and retribution (as self-help) in the absence of formal response to an unjust violation. We are reminded again that impunity is a major cause of and motivation for violence. Aggression against the other, regardless of their religion, is the main issue. Religious conflicts, from various country studies in Africa, on the one hand, and from my experience as a Nigerian, on the other, are about the scramble for scarce resources of the state. Other reasons are the fight for territorial space, an exaggerated sense of entitlement, right, and appeasement. Despite these compelling reasons, the Christian ethic of peace and theology of reconciliation must pay attention to the psychology of religious extremists. Jessica Stern captures it.

> The religious extremists' angst is familiar, as is their fear. What surprised me most was my discovery that the slogans sometimes mask not only fear and humiliation, but also greed—greed for political power, land, or money. Often, the slogans seem to mask wounded masculinity . . . the alienation, the humiliation, and the greed that fuel terrorism.[4]

2. Muhammad, "Religious Conflicts," 21.
3. Steffen, "Religion and Violence," 132.
4. Stern, *Terror in the Name*, xix.

How can Christian theology of reconciliation inspire Christians to protect themselves from the effects of such morbid psychology of religious fundamentalism?

Hypostatic Union Inspiring a Theology of Restorative Justice[5]

The Christian mission of reconciliation is clear in 2 Corinthians 5:18–20, inspired by the divine initiative of reconciliation between the Trinity and humanity.

> All this is from God, who through Christ reconciled us to himself and gave us the ministry of reconciliation; [19] that is, in Christ God was reconciling the world to himself, not counting their trespasses against them, and entrusting to us the message of reconciliation.[20] So we are ambassadors for Christ, God making his appeal through us. We beseech you on behalf of Christ, be reconciled to God.

This passage equally offers us an occasion to reflect on what reconciliation is and how God reconciled estranged humanity with himself (vertical reconciliation). This presents the inspiration for how to pursue reconciliation among human beings (horizontal reconciliation). The Chalcedonian definition of the hypostatic union, which sought to settle the Christological controversies of the patristic period, shall help us appreciate how the divine initiative (vertical reconciliation) in Jesus Christ can open up possibilities for us to pursue horizontal reconciliation, as much as our analogical imagination permits.

Chalcedonian Confession and Its 'Communicatio Idiomatum'

> One and the same Christ, Son, Lord, only-begotten, acknowledged in two natures which undergo no confusion, no change, no division, no separation; at no point was the difference between the natures taken away through the union, but rather the property of both natures is preserved and comes together into a single person and a single subsistent being; he is not parted or

---

5. This builds on earlier researches on the relationship between the doctrine of the hypostatic union and Christian theology of post-conflict restorative justice in transitional societies. Cf. Aina, "Catholic Theology," 81–98; Aina, "Hypostatic Union."

divided into two persons, but is one and the same only-begotten Son, God, Word, Lord Jesus Christ.[6]

The Chalcedonian confession emphasizes the unity of the dual nature of Christ. The church anchors this doctrine on the principle of *communicatio idiomatum*. This term states that the divine and human natures in Christ are distinct. Yet, the divine and human properties can be attributed to each other given their union in the person of Christ. The patristic fathers were not contesting the two natures of Christ. The debate was about "'the mode of union,' i.e. the manner by which separate spheres of realities joined in the person confessed as the Son of God."[7] Consequently, in the drama of divine reconciliation, God "fully recognized and respected" humanity.[8] We can draw a lesson immediately from the *communicatio idiomatum*. God did not sacrifice the distinct properties (divine, human) for reconciliation between God and humans. We must not dissolve differences because of reconciliation. Here, we see the unique paradox of the hypostatic union: at the moment of *kenosis*, something incommunicable, and deeply rooted in the divine sphere of reality, joined with the human sphere of reality and Jesus Christ, the God-man, was the outcome.

If conflict transformation is "a form of 'redemption,' then the hypostatic union, as a new manner of being, challenges stakeholders, especially Christians, to let this manner of being be the pattern of 'redemption' after violence."[9] The hypostatic union did not destroy what already existed. Rather, it renewed "who we are and how we are in relation with our relationships and those we share common actions."[10] Renewal implies how humans live in the world damaged by sin, especially regarding our choices concerning virtue or vice. We can say the hypostatic union revealed the harmony of two extremes "for the sake of reconciliation between God and humanity."[11] The harmony of two extremes in a single *hypostasis* (the Son of God) inspires the Christian conviction that "triumph over estrangement within humanity is always possible regardless of contrary movements in the body-polity."[12] Regardless of the extent of our trauma and our (radical) differences, "'co-existence, co-operation, and co-participation' is possible. This is part of the Christian affirmation of graced *ordo caritatis* that

---

6. Cf. Council of Chalcedon, "Definition of Faith," 86.
7. Aina, "Catholic Theology," 83.
8. Aina, "Catholic Theology," 84.
9. Aina, "Catholic Theology," 84.
10. Aina, "Catholic Theology," 84.
11. Aina, "Catholic Theology," 86.
12. Aina, "Catholic Theology," 87.

is necessary for realizing an ethics of love and responsibility in the world."[13] This is why we can say that the hypostatic union, as "'[t]he most unlikely truth,'"[14] appeals to the human heart and conscience. This unlikely truth is the work of grace, and the human heart perceives that we need grace for human co-belonging. This holistic co-belonging is a pilgrimage; we may never reach it, but it is achievable. The twin belief in divine grace and the fundamental goodness of humanity must be "integral to any theology and praxis of restorative justice from the Christian perspective based on the memory of Christ mediated by apostolic witnessing."[15] For now, this has not happened. The doctrine of the hypostatic union is largely marginalized, for example, in the Catholic theology of justice and reconciliation, and is absent in magisterial teachings on post-violence reconciliation.

I am, therefore, arguing subsequently that the doctrine of the hypostatic union inspires a proposal for a theology of restorative justice. This restorative justice seeks to achieve "just peace."[16] Just peace implies a peace process and a flexible structure that take into consideration the basic principles and desires of the constituting units in a particular conflicting area for the sake of reconciliation, the overall *telos*.[17] Restorative justice should aim at social transformation through the commitment to various spheres of justice to mark a renewal after a violent past. This is a mimesis of the path of the Son of God, which marked the beginning of a new way of countering evil and injustice involving human beings. This mimesis seeks redemption and not annihilation. What follows is a construal of what a theology of restorative justice, inspired by the Christological tract, might look like. This is necessary to address a lacuna, which has partly motivated this book, especially for the sake of a Christological ethical contribution to the growing appeal of restorative justice in peacebuilding.[18] It is even more pressing

13. Aina, "Catholic Theology," 87.
14. Aina, "Catholic Theology," 83.
15. Aina, "Catholic Theology," 87.
16. I use this phrase as John Paul Lederach used and proposed it to mean "an adaptive process-structure of human relationships characterized by high justice and low violence ... a view of systems as responsive to the permanency and interdependence of relationships and change." Lederach, "Challenge," 36.
17. According to Elias Opongo, just peace has some underlying principles, which include "participation, restoration, right relationship, reconciliation and sustainability." Other principles, which appear to betray a Roman Catholic bias, contrary to the original roots, are "the non-violent mechanism founded on [sic] protection of human dignity, promotion of life (both human and ecological) and safeguarding of the common good, all within the prism of the Catholic Social Teaching." Opongo, "Spiritual-Diplomatic," 78.
18. I acknowledge some previous Christological contributions to restorative justice.

to do so when one realizes that the Christian theology of the most popular theologian-advocate of restorative justice, Archbishop Tutu, is fraught with theological ethical problems and dangers.

Deductions from the Classical Hypostatic Union for a Christian Ethics of Reconciliation

Kenosis: Challenge to Victims and Perpetrators

The incarnate Son experienced the brunt of human facticity and brokenness: "tempted in every way, but did not sin" (Heb 4:15) and he was made perfect through his sufferings and temptations. If he did not experience those temptations and tensions that are the lot of human beings, he could not be the "perfect mimetic source of love, trust, and hope."[19] The incarnation, seen from this perspective, shows Christ's life as one that was completely oriented toward giving his life to God and others in faith, hope, love, and self-sharing. Thus, our salvation comes by sharing this life as one like Christ oriented towards God and others in overriding love. Divine compassion is the content of God's movement in the hypostatic union.[20] This compassion is concretely expressed in God's option for (substantial) relationality in the hypostatic union.

This compassion through *kenosis* meant that God accepted limitations that came with a choice. This is a costly relationality for the sake of reconciliation. This confronts those with (racial/ethnic/gender) superiority complexes, especially if they are Christians, about the absurdity of their complexes. For instance, this confronts the mostly Christian churchgoing White South Africans or ethno-religious jingoists in Nigeria that they just don't get it about the consequence of what they proclaim every Sunday or every time they pray the rosary: *the word became flesh*. What they do not get is that in the drama of reconciliation condescension of compassion is very crucial.[21] This *kenosis* consists of letting go, not out of forced humiliation, but for the sake of a new dawn, inspired by compassion, and not patronage. *Kenosis* is essential to dialog and encounters, which are integral to the vision of restorative justice. This form of *kenosis* is hard to come by in human encounters as people attempt to

---

Significantly, the discussions have largely centered around biblical narratives on Jesus's inspirations, and they are micro-focused. Mine is largely doctrinal, and directed to mass violence. See Broughton, *Restorative Christ*; Marshall, *All Things Reconciled*.

19. Collins, "Girard and Atonement," 144.
20. Davis, *Theology of Compassion*, 272.
21. Cf. Schwager, "Christology," 348–62.

come to terms with violence and overcome it. It is not easy to achieve because such an expression of mercy is usually interpreted as a form of weakness. Hence, many feel constrained to opt for face-saving acts like revenge and some other angry ways of displacing toxic emotions. On the contrary, *kenosis* expressed concretely, on the one hand, in love-as-mercy (e.g., empathy; forgiveness; gratuitousness) to the perpetrator, is "the ornament of the brave,"[22] to quote a Sanskrit saying. It expresses love-as-mercy as a self-effacing grace, without drawing attention to itself.

On the other hand, *kenosis* challenges perpetrators (individuals/groups) to go and do likewise. This is an understanding of the Golden Rule. Rather than confining human relations to the logic of equivalence, the Rule transcends it, as a concrete expression of *imitatio Dei*. We can understand this position against the backdrop that humans experience the logic of superabundance (love; gift) before an experience of equivalence (justice; obligation): "The antecedent generosity of the *because* preserves the Golden Rule from the perversion latent in the prospective *in order that*. This salvific motivation constitutes the *reason of the heart* par excellence."[23] It is reasonable to arrive at this understanding since the Rule exhibits the "*paradoxical* structure of the logic of superabundance."[24] Hence, it makes sense, Ricœur continues, that the Golden Rule should motivate "all our codes, penal codes and codes of social justice" even if fraught with difficulties and endless demands. Accordingly, the Rule serves a metaxological role in the tension "between self-interest and self-sacrifice."[25] This implies overcoming some subjective factors that impede justice and reconciliation, due to a pervasive culture of death and its ethical imperative.[26] For instance, some of the subjective factors that played out during the TRC by the leadership of the Dutch Reformed Church included the concern to protect "its own status . . . and concerned about stating its own views and defending its own position"[27] even when this flew in the face of the reality of the leadership's complicity with the Apartheid government. In a later chapter, I shall pose the challenge of *kenosis* for perpetrators and/or complicit bystanders to the church in Nigeria.

---

22. See Henderson, *Forgiveness*, 111.
23. Ricœur, "Golden Rule," 396 (emphasis original).
24. Ricœur, "Golden Rule," 396–97.
25. Ricœur, "Golden Rule," 396–97.
26. For an earlier discussion on this ethical imperative, see chapter 1 of this book, under the header "Mass Violence and the Role of Emotions in Nigeria."
27. Anthonissen, "Critical Analysis," 273.

Radical Otherness and Christian Ethics of Reconciliation

The Chalcedonian definition and other patristic witnesses explored above reckon with a given. In the case of Christ, two complete substances were united, yet there was "no confusion, no change, no division, no separation; at no point was the difference between the natures taken away through the union, but rather the property of both natures is preserved."[28] The unity of the two spheres of realities—divinity and humanity—happened because of an end, i.e., the repair of a ruptured relationship between God and humans, yet without the word ceasing to be what it is. The very personhood of the incarnate word gives enough message: a new creation does not need to dissolve difference. On the contrary, the differences ought to be used creatively to achieve the goal of the new creation. When one looks back at South Africa's or Nigeria's several "nations" in one, it is difficult to attest that these countries have achieved, to the degree possible in human political union, an analogous hypostatic union. We need to pursue this further.

According to the Chalcedonian definition, though the incarnate Son of God did not lose his identity as the second person of the Trinity, the person that existed in time and space was fully human. This intricate union of separate realities (*ousia*) without annihilation and sublimation reveals how God patterns our redemption: no imposition, no violation. From this definition, one realizes that radical otherness came into a reconciled union of qualitative difference. Consequently, if this radicality was possible for God, it is not impossible for humans among themselves. Humans need not limit their horizons insisting on "radical otherness," on the one hand, and projects of totalitarianism and sublimation that seek to annihilate differences, on the other. If the union of timelessness with concreteness was possible in the hypostatic union, then Christians have a responsibility to challenge myths of radical separation (irreconcilable alterities).

One can see that the hypostatic union sharpens how we frame our differences, to substantiate the claim that we are different not by nature but by our relations (mode). When we say our differences, therefore, are strictly modal, it means that on the level of our historical origination we are different. In other words, we come about as human beings in the world through different modes/manners. This does not constitute radical separation or difference, just as we cannot say that children conceived *in utero* and those born *in vitro* possess "different substances or natures."[29] So, our uniqueness concerns human history, i.e., that we come into existence uniquely.

---

28. Cf. Council of Chalcedon, "Definition of Faith," 86.
29. Daley, "Nature," 174.

As such, distinctively Christian ethics must work towards a mode of union among humans that imitates the union of timelessness with concreteness (i.e., hypostatic union). This is authentic human co-belonging. This holistic co-belonging is a pilgrimage—we may never reach it, but it is humanly possible, though negotiated through what is humanly desirable and meaningful. Consequently, what transitional societies need is a justice and a theology favoring—or opting—for an imitated union that does not destroy differences. Rather, this justice and its theology harness differences. This is what we mean by analogical imagination, i.e., understanding, through patristic witnesses, what the hypostatic union is, and going to do likewise, not exactly (cf. Luke 10:37).[30] To go and do likewise concerns renewing our being and our common actions together. Biblical/doctrinal interpretations are pivotal to realizing this going to do likewise. Yet, we must first, agreeing with James Breztke, imagine "what the going and the doing of the 'likewise' means for us."[31]

Hypostatic Union and Reconciliation as Renewal

What the God-man renewed was not the structure of being human (i.e., body and soul). Patristic witnesses like Maximus the Confessor and John of Damascus insisted that if Christ's humanity changed the structure, then human nature would have been destroyed since the given structure would have been altered. Hence, what happened through Christ's humanity was the renewal of human nature. This position will critique, therefore, some justice processes that look at offenders (persons/groups) from the perspective of natural disposition (pathology); hence the necessity to alter it. A former Prime Minister of Britain, Tony Blair, once proposed that perhaps there should be pre-natal testing to look for the criminal gene and alter it before birth. Restorative justice's position is contrary to Tony Blair's. Original restorative justice discourse seems agreeable to the patristic understanding of hypostatic union that the structure of human nature is a given. It cannot be altered without destroying its integrity. Thus, what is important after violation of non-recognition is the renewal of human mode. Hence, restorative justice emphasizes restoring relationships. We see this position also in Margaret Walker's thesis that moral repair is the just and ethical obligation after humans' default zones of trust has been gravely violated. In the final chapter of her *Moral Repair*, she appears to locate the ability for moral

---

30. Bretzke, *Morally Complex*, 95.
31. Bretzke, *Morally Complex*, 95.

repair in restorative justice ethos and practice, even with historical wrongs like slavery and racism in the United States.[32]

Consequently, restorative justice's emphasis on restoration of relationships resonates with this Christian doctrine of renewing relationships and common actions. Perhaps, renew instead of restore evokes greater promise and realism because restore appears to signify passivity—just pour back what was previously lost. This gives the impression that human beings are containers of dignity, and violence pours this dignity away. So, justice re-stores, i.e., pours back the depleted dignity into the containers. However, for conceptual precision, no one ever takes dignity away. For various reasons, it might be eclipsed (i.e., the failure of non-recognition). It is never poured away such that we need to restock (restore) the warehouse of dignity. Alternatively, renew implies that there has been a distortion regarding relationships and necessary common actions across the various levels of common actors.

Hence, renewal through justice is about unplugging the rot, finding creative ways to regenerate the relationships and the affected common actions in their respective degrees. Although all human persons are human, we have degrees of relating as humans (e.g., friends, neighbors, citizens, residents, enemies, foreigners, refugees, etc.). Accordingly, we are always in relationships, though the intensity differs. Even if there is no prior affective relationship, we are already related by the virtue of sharing the same nature. Consequently, justice is about the recognition of that humanity, the responsibility to those relationships, and the imperative common actions implied from that given.

It is this justice, in my estimation, that can bring about the renewal, which gives the possibility for common actions through mutual co-operation, and through the determination of the not yet reconciled parties. While the guilty party responds through "costly repentance"[33] (with all the concrete material and symbolic implications), victims hopefully will respond with mercy, because at times even justice and costly repentance might not still unburden the perpetrator. At that point, it might be acts and gestures of mercy, not excluding forgiveness, that can liberate. It is in this co-operation and co-participation that the new creation is born—a radical difference, though not radical discontinuity: "the experience of becoming 'godlike' through Christ in a 'wonderful exchange' (*admirabile commercium*) underpinned the conviction about his identity: 'it was God who became human

---

32. Cf. Walker, *Moral Repair*, esp. 207–29.
33. Moule, *Forgiveness and Reconciliation*, 23.

that we humans might become divine."[34] We experienced new creation because a radical other chose to be united with an-other in "'a condescension of compassion, not a failure of power.'"[35]

Hypostatic Union and Rights Discourse in Justice and Reconciliation Projects Today

In the contestations against the Nestorians, who understood the hypostatic union as a conjunction, like a husband and wife having a union of wills, and not organic/integrated, one can realize an important message for today's politics and projects. The argument for the union as conjunction, with the analogy of a married couple, signifies equality of honor. However, fathers like Cyril of Alexandria contested. According to Cyril, "equality of honor does not unite the natures. Peter and John, for instance, are of equal honor with each other, as both apostles and holy disciples, but the two are not made into one."[36] Now, if equality of honor (or what today will translate as equality of dignity and respect for rights) does not unite separate spheres of realities, it does provoke, from a Christian perspective, a critique about the near-exclusive focus on rights discourse as we see in post-apartheid South Africa, and most transitional societies. According to Steven Robins, a South African scholar, one of the remarkable things people noticed about the post-apartheid ANC government is the seismic shift from liberationist vocabularies to "tamer words such as rights, citizenships, liberal democracy, nation-building, transformation, black economic empowerment."[37] For Robins, this is a welcome development because people's invocation of rights talks is strategically valuable in post-apartheid South Africa. His book is a case study of the role of the civil society and NGOs that have galvanized the masses to embrace rights talks in their struggle for basic amenities.[38]

Respect for rights and dignity does not necessarily unite people. Indeed, though Robins argues that there has been a remarkable display of the embrace of rights discourse in post-apartheid South Africa,[39] it is not thick enough to reconcile South African peoples and bring about an authentically human rainbow nation, judging from current goings-on and statistics.[40] The

34. Gregory of Nazianzen, "Third Theological," 308.
35. O'Collins, *Christology*, 158.
36. Cited in Daley, "Nature," 179.
37. Robins, *From Revolution*, 3.
38. Robins, *From Revolution*, esp. ch. 1.
39. See Robins, *From Revolution*, ch. 1.
40. See, for instance, Potgieter, *SA Reconciliation Barometer*.

discourse insufficiently challenges humans to go and do likewise as inspired by the hypostatic union, because it does not confront stakeholders strongly enough to move towards an organic union between existing persons/peoples united in substance, but different only in their origination. Robins offers in his concluding chapter that despite his opening thesis on the role of rights discourse in post-apartheid South Africa, the rights discourse has ambiguous and contradictory characters in mass mobilization because the discourse takes the fundamental criticism about rights discourse for granted: "the individualising, fragmenting and depoliticising nature of rights discourses."[41] This criticism, which neglected "the national and community dimensions,"[42] leveled against the TRC and the dominant religious understanding of reconciliation as spearheaded by Tutu, shows a striking similarity between the TRC's restorative justice and this thin rights discourse.

Many societies rank high in the observance of legal honor, but are not effectively reconciled. They might be pragmatically working along, but one cannot confidently affirm that there is reconciliation between the peoples. Belgium is a prime example, though probably not the only one in the West.[43] The union of separate spheres of realities in various contexts today (without violence, without the annihilation of differences, without anarchy) needs a more than normal/contractarian approach. Perhaps, what we need to inspire such contexts is rediscovering the meaning and practical sense of covenant.[44]

Although Rabbi Jonathan Sacks arrives at this conclusion from his Jewish Rabbinic tradition, a Christian can arrive at a similar conclusion within his/her Christian tradition on the hypostatic union discourse. Sacks and the Christian are both emphasizing one issue: for the kind of the notion of reconciliation being pursued in this work, *we need persons/peoples concerned to enter into a deep relationship with those whom they are sharing the same geopolitical space.* Consequently, one can dare to say that the hypostatic union challenges us to move beyond the liberal and politically correct concept of common ground to that of higher ground, as some conflict resolution experts proposed some time ago.[45] Common ground is the overlapping of contending self-interests. However, where there are intangible elements, like identity, recognition, and status, then

---

41. Robins, *From Revolution*, ch. 8, quotation on 172.

42. Chapman, "Introduction," 12.

43. Massart-Piérard and Bursens, "Belgian Federalism," 18–20; Deschouwer, *Politics of Belgium*.

44. Sacks, *Dignity of Difference*, 202–9, quotations on 206, 209.

45. Dukes et al., *Reaching for Higher Ground*.

there is the need to explore the higher ground. Higher ground inspired, for instance, by the hypostatic union, demands contextual sensitivities, viable strategies for goal implementation, follow-up evaluations, and financial support. This implies that justice and reconciliation projects should not just be prescriptive (a critique raised earlier against Tutu's theology of reconciliation). Rather, it should be an expression of a higher vision for a humanly possible and meaningful future.

Hypostatic Union, Reconciliation Project and Historical Consciousness

The inner disposition of divine activity as revealed in Christ is the norm and source of priorities in an ethic of compassionate responsibility in Christian Ethics: "Jesus articulated our fundamental attitude in the double commandment of love (*agape*) . . . the commandment to love God is in fact the basic and comprehensive circle which includes the commandment of love of neighbour."[46] This is the meaning of participating through *imitatio Christi* in the incarnated person of God the Son. Through this participation, he continues his victory over sources of evil that wreak havoc and tear apart people hitherto living in peace.[47] However, when violators damage this peace, this norm flowing from God's message through the hypostatic union shows how we can go about renewing it. First, we realize that true peace can come if we adopt a model that is not implicated or trapped in the vicious cycle of destructive mimetic rivalry.[48] This is one of the advantages of a Christological framework for a just peace because Christ's redemptive act through his incarnated personhood is ongoing. Hence, the Christic and redemptive personhood is like a beacon beckoning us to reach deeper into the various hitherto neglected areas of human liberation and reconciliation.

Second, we recognize again from the hypostatic union that peace is elusive if one does not adopt a historical consciousness model i.e., one that takes the historicity, particularity, and context of the other moral agent into consideration. Any non-contextual approach is hardly an ethical model of grace and realism. On the contrary, a moral option (by a moral agent) that respects the intrinsic nature of humans as social beings will pay attention to the need for what Janssens refers to as "co-existence, co-operation, and co-participation" being integral to "*ordo caritatis*" that is necessary for realizing ethics of love

---

46. Janssens, "Norms and Priorities," 207 (emphasis original).
47. Collins, "Girard and Atonement," 148.
48. Schwager, "Christology," 354.

and responsibility.⁴⁹ Thus, the aptness, in my opinion, of Gregory of Nazianzus's classic formulation: "the unassumed is the unhealed."⁵⁰

Hypostatic Union and the Limits of Analogical Imagination

Despite the promises of bringing the hypostatic union into a theology of reconciliation, we should reiterate that we have a limit to analogical imagination. For instance, while the paradox of hypostatic union is already a given (with "assumption of coherence"),⁵¹ whose explanation we eke out endlessly, the paradox of post-conflict unity and reconciliation of two or more radical nations is a *telos* sought with hopeful realization, even contrary to an expectation and history of similar radicalness. Consequently, the mode of union and outcome will not be as radical and unique as the hypostatic union (contra Tutu's grandnarrative theology of exceptionality, uniqueness). Though all are equal substantially, they are not relationally.

Furthermore, with the caveat about analogical imagination, our invocation of the hypostatic union in the context of this study is not hankering to unqualified *imitatio Christi*. Rather, we present afresh an age-long tension: how to make sense of a given (hypostatic union) with disparate spheres of realities—yet working perfectly for its (soteriological) *telos*. Consequently, we need to understand our contexts today, how contrasting spheres of realities are together in a way that we can achieve and not derail the overarching *telos* (redemption/reconciliation). The togetherness again (reconciliation) has no tinge of totalitarian sublimation. Many brutal post-colonial African nation-states might broaden their horizons on how to transcend an existence that swings between radical separation and totalitarian sublimation (even in democratic contexts).

Accordingly, the hypostatic union expresses a union more promising than radical division which makes reconciliation after a brutal past impossible. Additionally, this Christian classic is far more valuable than what the Yorùbá call '*àmúlùmálà*'—a potpourri of confusion. Furthermore, it transcends the temptation of totalitarian annihilation of the weak and vulnerable. It is also not a union of radical separation where, within the same space, the constitutive elements move in different and parallel orbits (e.g., loose confederation). This is why Daley suggests that the union of Christ's personhood should be understood relationally, rather than as a spatial mixture that would have yielded "amalgamation or hybridization in a

---

49. Janssens, "Norms and Priorities," 221.
50. Gregory of Nazianzen, "To Cledonius the Priest," 440.
51. Coakley, "What Does Chalcedon," 155.

single hypostasis."⁵² This point is significant for post-colonial nation-states like Nigeria and South Africa that colonialists fused through the process of political amalgamation. Without due consideration for the histories and multi-faceted dynamics of the original nations, the amalgamation sowed the seeds of the fissures characterizing most post-colonial African states. This is why the hypostatic union can trigger a horizon thought in divided geo-political space about the mode of the union that will bring about the most valuable and most humanly meaningful outcome for the constituent elements. They can then go and do likewise.

Towards a Theology of Restorative Justice

Some theologies of reconciliation do not show the awareness that, even to restorative justice advocates, the term means different things to different ideological camps. I agree with George Pavlich, who at times brings a freshness of post-modern reasoning into the restorative justice dialog. He notes that the conservatives prefer restorative justice because it focuses on the plight of victims, the role of the family, offender responsibility, cost savings, and communitarian utopias—like the good old days. However, for the liberals, their attraction is premised on the promise of dealing with offenders and the community without necessarily banking on retributive/coercive justice, while still attempting to deal with the scars of crimes left on the victims and the other stakeholders. Reformers, on their own, are attracted because of the vision of social and community transformation such that it can be referred to as well as "Transformative Justice."⁵³

Tutu falls within the conservative camp of Pavlich's classification. Hence, warm and lofty ideas similar to the communitarians mark his theology. One of those lofty ideas is that of brotherhood/sisterhood on the assumption that people shared some deeply entrenched emotional relationships before violent and traumatic rupturing of the relationships.⁵⁴ This puts undue pressure on victim-survivors to return to that lofty state. However, a more realistic theology that will not pressure stakeholders to resume that warm relationship should be guest-centered. What this presupposes is that a theology

---

52. Daley, "Nature," 177.
53. Pavlich, "Deconstructing Restoration," 90.
54. Scheid offers a similar position, when she contends Philpott's take on the relationship between forgiveness and reconciliation. For Scheid, it is possible to forgive without the desire for the restoration of relationship with one's violators. Hence, it makes sense to distinguish between minimal and maximal reconciliation. Cf. Scheid, "Christian Peace Ethics," 280–81.

of restorative justice does not, as a matter of principle, prioritize embrace (*ubuntufication*) with all the presuppositions of friendship. Another component of *K* (reconciliation) i.e., *a* (love-as-mercy) will pursue that.[55]

Restorative Justice and Christian Ethics of Hospitality

Contrary to Tutu's amplified ethics of embrace (*ubuntufication*), a theology of restorative justice, with its penultimate status, prioritizes ethics of hospitality. It is a renewed disposition of persons encountering themselves in a non-adversarial atmosphere. This ethics presupposes the opening up of the host to welcome the guest. Fanie du Toit, a South African theologian, invoked this ethics of hospitality in his reflection on the TRC and its relevance to the country's then-emerging political discourse.[56] The TRC was an event where some stakeholders opened up to the 'stranger' i.e., the qualified victims of some of apartheid's crimes. Yet, the interaction had to be in an atmosphere that did not seek to subdue the other i.e., the perpetrators. du Toit took inspiration from Miroslav Volf's concept of embrace.[57]

Volf construes embrace as a metaphor denoting openness, yet in anticipation. It does not impose or grab. Rather, it allows freedom of the other to take her time. This embrace is active and passive: holding and being held at the same time. It is free, liberated, and un-condescending so that in the embrace both are enriched by the other's particularity. In other words, individual or collective differences are not threats to peace, such that one has to subsume or obliterate them. They need to be preserved, Volf argues,[58] just as the *perichoretic* dance of the Trinitarian persons does not endanger or blur the relational particularities of the Triune persons. This embrace, however, is unconditional. It is the only way to guarantee non-exclusion. Hence, embrace is grace; and for the Christian, this might not be without *via Dolorosa*.[59] For Volf, therefore, embrace is the metaphor for reconciliation. This implies that final reconciliation is a work of grace, whereas non-final reconciliation implies self-sacrifice and the choice to readjust one's identity because of the other's radical difference.[60] Of course, the hermeneutical trajectory of this

55. For the distinctions and interrelationships implied here, see *infra* Appendix 2.
56. Cf. du Toit, "Public Discourse," 340–57.
57. See Volf, *Exclusion and Embrace*, 140–65.
58. Volf, *Exclusion and Embrace*, 145–46.
59. Volf, *Exclusion and Embrace*, 146–47.
60. Volf, *Exclusion and Embrace*, 109–10. Volf takes on this apparent unconditionality in the reconciliation process in a later work, *The End of Memory* (2006). Cf. Volf, *End of Memory*, esp. 39–65. For a summary of this book's thesis, see Volf, "Difference," 3–12.

book contests this position, along the same line as Tutu's theology of reconciliation. It appears that Volf, like Tutu, collapses the distinction between unconditional forgiveness and reconciliation which, as I am arguing in this book, cannot be premised solely on the supererogatory.

Though du Toit invokes Volf's embrace, he does not presuppose the warm lofty communitarian utopia of Tutu (and Volf). du Toit's theological construal of the goings-on during the TRC hearings differed significantly from Tutu's.[61] I identify more with du Toit's theological ethical construal of TRC's restorative justice. For now, in similar contexts to Nigeria's postcolonial volatility, a theology of restorative justice based on hospitality towards the guest holds more promise than the lofty communitarian utopia of conservative restorative justice ideologues. The preferred ethics of hospitality starts at the anthropological level. Pavlich expresses this appropriately: "moral responsibility—being for the Other before one can be with the Other—is the first reality of the self, a starting point rather than a product of the society."[62] This is akin to Emmanuel Levinas's ethical responsibility, which is anchored on the call of the Face (weak and powerless) to the self; and the response of welcome concretizes the heteronomous relationship in the face-to-face encounter.[63] Hence, in hospitality to the other as guest, which is central to this theology of restorative justice, one receives the other (guest/stranger) into one's space in empathy and respectful listening. Hospitality demands a concrete response for justice, in empathy and respectful listening, to words spoken, blinding tears, and incomprehensible groans of persons and peoples affected by extraordinary evils and the more banal ones.[64] At this level, the responsibility to the guest/stranger is beyond accountability for direct culpability and guilt. This is the core of heteronomous responsibility, which can be defined as an activity of moral agents towards a goal that is beyond the pure Kantian deontology, i.e., duty "determined by universal rationality free of subjective considerations."[65] Accordingly, when we turn attention to the imperativeness of justice, it is not only the identifiable authors of extraordinary evils that are liable to make reparation for peace on the way towards reconciliation.

The theology of restorative justice I am articulating presupposes that the theological ethical disposition of hospitality is flexible in responding to the guest as victim, victimizer or victimized community because rigidity in

---

61. Cf. du Toit, "Public Discourse," 344–46.
62. Pavlich, "Towards an Ethics," 6.
63. Aina, "Levinas' Post-Holocaust," 22–26.
64. Aina, "Levinas' Post-Holocaust," 32–38.
65. Poe, "Peace Is Not," 38.

dispensing justice had often led to unjust justice. According to renowned Levinasian scholar, Roger Burggraeve, "The good is literally overturned into 'the evil of the good' and thus ends up in 'the terror of the good' whereby ethics is destroyed in the name of ethics."[66] This caveat implies that in the movement towards justice, the subjects are never sacrificed if the project will not end up as a perverted good. Consequently, the real justice issues emerge and are dealt with in the concrete encounter of the subjects (persons/peoples). This theology presupposes that there is no predetermined program for quick fixes, unlike the medico-therapeutic short-term catharsis of the TRC. If there is no predetermined agenda, then there should be equality in the restorative justice process.[67]

This equality in the Levinasian perspective has to be explained, for another concept—asymmetry (located in the heteronomous responsibility)—is better known than equality. Levinas's appeal to equality gives an ethical grounding for hospitality between humans without necessarily being related biologically. He refers to it as "the kinship of humanity" beyond the commonness of race, which cannot bring everyone together.[68] Equality implies mutual welcoming with responsibility between the other and the self; it is not a one-way traffic.[69] Despite this mutual welcoming and equality, fraternity and discourse that resist totalization must be asymmetrical.[70] This might sound paradoxical, but I think this emphasizes that the asymmetrical space between humans must not give rise to paternalism and passivity. The one that is an "Other" to another subject is at the same time a self confronted by an Other. This is a different way of saying respect, recognition, and consideration must always characterize the space between human subjects.

Consequently, those facilitating the restorative justice process must not lose sight of the paradoxical asymmetric dimension between the subjects. Since the concept of hospitality is flexible such that stakeholders fit into it, then, theologically, there is space for redemption in restorative justice. This redemption implies that no person or group remains infinitely stigmatized. It presupposes that no person is beyond rehabilitation, i.e., the possibility to be brought back into the mainstream of post-conflict life. However, this redemption depends on justice. In original restorative justice, this consists of three pillars: Needs-Accountability-Engagement.[71]

66. Burggraeve, "Other and Me," 349–50.
67. Pavlich, "Towards an Ethics," 11–17.
68. See Levinas's discussion on this: *Totality and Infinity*, 212–16, quotation on 214.
69. Levinas, *Totality and Infinity*, 214.
70. Levinas, *Totality and Infinity*, 216.
71. Cf. Zehr, *Little Book*, 22–25.

Taking a critical look at these pillars, only the Engagement pillar appears to be entirely symbolic. The other two, "Needs" and "Accountability," include the material and the symbolic.

Conclusion

This chapter argued that the hypostatic union as a theological analogue in peacebuilding and reconciliation projects is more realistic because it relates aptly to human experience and living conditions. Christ, in bringing about his reconciliation, through a "sacrifice" that is "dreadfully expensive,"[72] did not dispense of human reality for the sake of an idea that needed to be realized. Therefore, Christian theology, specifically theological ethics of restorative justice, peacebuilding, and reconciliation ought to be concretely incarnational and non-divisive. We premise this ethical praxis on the belief that God concretely acts in and through human history and agents. Traumatized persons and peoples in transitional societies need justice, peace, and reconciliation projects as envisioned in this chapter to regain control over their destiny. The next chapter analyzes the discussions in restorative justice and critical criminology on how to view the complex needs structure of victims of crime and their desire for justice that might contribute to overcoming their toxic emotions. In particular, I shall tease out the more hopeful three pillars of restorative justice and more than hopeful expectations of post-conflict restorative justice. These expectations are justice that heals, justice in dialog, and justice beyond frozenness and death.

---

72. Moule, *Forgiveness and Reconciliation*, 22–26.

5
A Christian Ethical Exposition on the Three Pillars of Restorative Justice

NEEDS-ACCOUNTABILITY-ENGAGEMENT.[1] THESE PILLARS ANCHOR original restorative justice. They are both the expectations and guides for a reconciliation process that will rebuild trust in a *postbellum* society. The hope which restorative justice promises must be expressed in a fitting conceptual framework that guides actions. That's why a Christian ethical reflection on its meaning and plausibility follows each component of the framework that I shall present. This is to make a case for the compelling story and promises of restorative justice particularly in peacebuilding in transitional societies.

Restorative Justice and Pandora's Box

Restorative justice's story and theory can remind one of the Greek myth about Pandora's Box. In *postbellum* contexts, some actors usually invoke the myth on the need to "kill" some stories so that a plethora of embarrassing effects will not follow. Sometimes, powerful stakeholders deny victims justice because some want to avoid opening their Pandora's Box, as was the case, for instance, with Nigeria till 1999. The fear of unleashing the negative forces from Pandora's Box has overshadowed the complete message from this Greek myth. The last force in Pandora's Box is positive, not negative. It is the force of Hope. So, the myth teaches that despite, or because of, the negative forces unleashed from Pandora's Box, we need to help the last positive force in the box—the force of Hope—to tame the negative forces.

Restorative justice comes with a compelling reminder that the dominant criminal justice system today appears to focus so much on the negative forces human beings unleash when acts of criminality and cruelty take place.

---

1. Zehr, *Little Book*, 22–25.

However, restorative justice insists that we should give a space for the last force in Pandora's Box in the post-victimization justice process. Accordingly, restorative justice tries to express the belief that we have hope for a more peaceful tomorrow, beyond the angst of yesterday's imposed toxic emotions.[2] So, criminologists, peacebuilders, and policymakers in contexts similar to Nigeria should not shy away from a criminological approach that takes "situatedness, variations, differences, of all kinds, and positionality/relationality very seriously in all their complexities, multiplicities, instabilities, and contradictions."[3] I ground this exhortation in a Christian ethical perspective that is sensitive to the human person adequately considered.

Hope generally informs the exposition in this chapter and subsequent chapters. Hope in the human person and the society makes one realize that reparation and forgiveness, crucial for sustainable peacebuilding projects, are expressions of mercy. Mercy, as invoked here, takes inspiration from Saint Caesarius of Arles. It is the concern, expressed in acts, about the hardships of those suffering. It does not exclude anyone. The crucial criteria are hardships concrete persons/peoples face and the proactive things to do about the hardship—sometimes through institutional acts of justice. This view of mercy is only possible when it is informed by love, which is the positive disposition and concern for the wellbeing of the other. This necessarily leads to collective peace.[4]

Reparation is an act that expresses concern for the hardships one caused the suffering other. Hence, the perpetrator becomes the merciful person when s/he acts to alleviate the suffering. On the other hand, forgiveness is an act of a victim that acknowledges and shows one's concern for the hardship—out of violence and past violation—the perpetrator suffers because of a burden of the past that even reparation cannot lift. At other times, forgiveness is equally an act of mercy that third parties can encourage victims to offer as a way of alleviating their hardships and sufferings, which even justice may not yet offer.

Restorative Justice as Justice that Heals

Given the tension between satisfaction, procedural fairness and reconciliation, we should consider the following as essential to justice that restores hope:

2. Cf. Braithwaite, "Emancipation and Hope," 79–98.
3. Clarke, *Situational Analysis*, xviii.
4. On Saint Caesarius's tract, which does not cover all that is stated here, see Saint Caesarius, "Reading from the Sermons," 354–55.

a. commensurate reparative acts;

b. space for disclosure and closure;

c. a commitment against mutual re-victimization, even if anger and shaming persist.

We acknowledge that restorative justice does not intrinsically reduce recidivism. This justice does not imply that people will not re-offend. In ethical terms, one can say that the existence of a justice practice does not automatically translate to healing justice. The process as well as other components of every human act as a moral event determines the success of the justice. The components of the moral event include the goods sought after, the intentions, the circumstances and motivations of the respective stakeholders. As a moral event, healing justice goes beyond a system of justice that focuses on physicality e.g., "did you or did you not do this certain action?" An envisioned healing justice pays equal attention to other things before the moral agent acted. For instance, without intentionality accounted for in the moral evaluation of an act, one may not pass moral judgment on the act.[5] This ethical reasoning requires a fine distinction of the human act—through the principle of "*debita proportio*."[6] This principle, though marginal in some aspects of Roman Catholic moral tradition, is the bedrock of Aquinas's elucidation of human acts, especially when it concerns an act in which there are two different effects.[7] For an action to be morally good, things chosen in service of the end are "properly proportioned according to reason to the required end (*debita proportio*)."[8]

If we bring this ethical reasoning to the context of justice that serves victims, it can assist us in judging if a justice process is satisfactory. If the process is fair, the encounter creates an avenue and hope for change and human development—for victims, offenders, and the larger human community. When there are parties with conflicting ends in view and narratives that sustain these, satisfaction should be weighed proportionately to guarantee fairness. Proportionate reasons, for instance, that balance satisfaction and desire, on the one hand, and fairness, on the other hand, in some concrete circumstances, must pay attention to some six conditions.

---

5. We should understand this against the insight that human actions consist of two orders: the "order of intention" and "order of execution." Of these two, the "order of intention" is the primary one, and it consists of desiring, willing, deliberating and choosing particular things in service of the end (order of execution). Cf. Aquinas, *Summa Theologiae*, IaIIae, quæ. 1, art. 1, *responsio*, art. 4, *responsio*, quotation at art. 4, *responsio*.

6. Janssens, "Ontic Evil," 128.

7. Aquinas, *Summa Theologiae*, IIa-IIae, quæ. 64, art. 7, *responsio*.

8. Janssens, "Ontic Evil," 128 (emphasis original).

The first is that actors must consider the foreseen social implications of the choice in the name of justice. Second, they must choose a course of action that is universally tenable. They must consider if people in similar circumstances will choose this action. Will it bring harmony and human wellbeing if practiced everywhere? Third, they must discern if contextual conditions are in favor of the action or not. For instance, the outcome stakeholders envisage should not provoke public outcry or anarchy. Fourth, they must factor in the wisdom of past occurrences. Fifth, there should be widespread consultation for input on discernment and experiences of appropriate justice outcomes. Sixth, they must have room for religion-informed contribution, because religion has a role to play even in non-transitional, secularized, societies. Jürgen Habermas, one of the staunch "defenders of modernity," even recognizes the revalorization of religion in the post-secular age. Religion helps in the formation and consolidation of value commitments even in public.[9] Hence, religiosity is now seen more as a resource for human development rather than as a threat.

The bottom line from these six conditions is a dialectical relationship between personal discernment of the stakeholders and communal discernment on what is good and the common good,[10] which should be based on an adequate understanding of human aspirations and needs of concrete persons and peoples. Accordingly, the good(s) achieved or sought after will remain endangered if justice actors do not have an eye, through these criteria, on other components and factors that bring satisfaction in the justice process to all persons involved (and not just the victims). Yet, we cannot afford to endanger the ends sought (i.e., peace, prosperity, and freedom). So, justice processes, especially the ones dominant in international criminal justice today and statist diplomacy, are not ends in themselves. They are simply at the service of these ends. This is why one can insist that they should have a reasonably proportional and "friendly but cautious"[11] approach to Common International Law. This law should be seen as principled guidelines that shed light on legal systems (but not necessarily controlling the systems through rigid interpretations/applications).

Contextual realizations of the ends sought demand contextual appreciation and approach in the justice system in post-conflict societies. So,

---

9. Habermas, "Religion in the Public," 1–25; Junker-Kenny, "Capabilities," 153.

10. This is the "sum total of social conditions which allow people, either as groups or as individuals, to reach their fulfilment more fully and more easily." See Pontifical Council for Justice and Peace, *Compendium*, no. 164.

11. De Wet, "'Friendly but Cautious,'" 1529–65, esp. 1564–65.

responses "*must* be tailor-made for each circumstance through careful diplomatic consultation with all affected parties."[12] This requires:

a. paying greater attention to the higher status of each nation's constitution, at times over the Common International Law—provided the Constitution itself is a product of "peace agreement" (like South Africa's post-apartheid interim constitution);

b. there is the equality of arms. This underscores the necessity for procedural equity for all parties involved in the judicial process (victims, perpetrators, the communities) as part of a non-discriminatory rule of law.

Hence, multilateral justice institutions should express, and constantly be examined, if they still carry the goal entrusted to them—"our shared commitments and hopes"[13] of moral human rights heritage. Unfortunately, the kind of justice envisioned here that heals all persons affected by a destructive past has not often materialized due to the protection of ideology and idealism: "we have sometimes settled for vague and noble-sounding words rather than engaging in the difficult social and political work necessary to build justice on the ground where rights often conflict and hard choices must inevitably be made."[14] Surakiart Sathirathai's point finds resonance with Charles Villa-Vicencio, who defends the route taken by South Africa's TRC against the unsparing criticisms of those he refers to as the "human rights purists."[15]

We can infer that respect and responsibility are crucial to the process of recovering human agency after trauma (i.e., healing as defined above). For instance, in Howard Zehr's opinion, South Africa's TRC's narrative option is one of its enduring values.[16] His experiences with victims and offenders made him appreciate the power of narrative discourse. In storytelling, we express our identities and attempt to recreate them after conflict and trauma. Non-expression of these stories is tragic because repressed memories are dangerous, as I demonstrated regarding Nigeria's history of mass violence. Painful experiences cannot be denied no matter how hard some may try.

12. Sathirathai, "Renewing Our Global Values," 2 (emphasis original).

13. Sathirathai, "Renewing Our Global Values," 3, 10.

14. Sathirathai, "Renewing Our Global Values," 6. Sathirathai was the preferred candidate of the ASEAN Community for the post of the Secretary General of the United Nations that was eventually filled by Ban Ki Moon. Sathirathai's ideas for global peace-building come close to that of Boutrous Boutrous-Ghali's "Agenda for Peace" (1992), which had been toned down under the leadership of the former UN Secretary General the late Koffi Annan. See Gray, *International Law*, 284–85.

15. Villa-Vicencio, "Transitional Justice," 390.

16. Zehr, "Journey to Belonging," 26–28.

Rather, the wise thing to do is to incorporate them into who we are. Stories of shame and humiliation, if told in an atmosphere of respect and acceptance, can turn the stories into ones of courage and dignity. Stories told in public transform both the storyteller and the listening public, which now recognizes the stories of those who were on the fringes of the political discourse. This leads to a richer and more inclusive and common national narrative. Communities living side by side need to recover this manner of groaning for victims to recover, to move on (and this concretely is healing).

Reasonably, healing is effectively part of justice if one works within a frame of an "ethic of responsibility and solidarity" implied in the triadic ethical model of the three sense levels in ethical reasoning. The first sense level is the level of signification—the visceral level that seeks to understand the subjective significance of a moral event, i.e., the contextualized intention. This level cautions that one should restrain from giving judgment before one has entered into the narrative of the actors, to understand why they acted as such. The second sense level confronts the actor with the objective fact, beyond the mere intentions. This level contests a tendency towards uncritical mercy. A merciful attitude can degenerate into easy tolerance, due to false pity. Hence, the ethicist can be implicated in evil if s/he opts for the ethical paradigm of deculpabilization. The third sense level is the level when the actors can truly seek the authentic human good for them under the prevailing conditions and circumstances. This is where the truly human meaningful act will combine the beautiful and the good. This is the level that helps to build on the possible areas for growth in the actors. Though there is contingency and evil, there is also space for growth. Love is the basic ethical disposition operative in the three sense levels. If we focus only on the consequences of the evil done without, at the same time, trying to make a space between the actors and their acts, we risk operating a stark ethical Manichaeism—the tendency of an unmitigated deductive ethical approach, and a law-centered ethics.[17] This three-sense level ethic should underpin contemporary criminal justice. This ethical responsibility, which challenges us to see healing as part of justice to the human person adequately considered, is real, experiential, consequential, historical, and proportional.[18]

a. Real: Doing the good is based on the concrete human experience. So, one must accept the provisional feature of one's conclusions, even as we are not exculpated from keeping up our vision, i.e., attaining human wholeness;

17. See Janssens, "Norms and Priorities," 207–38.
18. Cf. Gula, *Reason*, 242–49.

b. Experiential: Moral arguments/conclusions are based on experiences—past and present;

c. Consequential: Actions and conclusions have costs—in the short and long run. So, one must pay attention to the complexities of consequences due to ambivalence of values in conflicts;

d. Historical: This considers the contingency of human agents and the "senses" in their actions;

e. Proportional: Given the complexities of values, costs, and human limitations in actions, we are challenged to achieve the greatest good over evil (or the lesser good). Thus, prudence and moral guardians towards prudential judgments are indispensable.

"Justice that heals" underscores the importance of attentiveness to stakeholders in their contexts because of a non-negotiable trio (love, justice, and peace). *Love* (e.g., mercy, remorse, empathy), *justice* (e.g., truth, equity, reparation), and *peace* (e.g., fidelity, assured safety) are inextricably bound. Love in action is no shallow emotion. For instance, love without justice is dishonest; justice without love is excruciating and repulsive. Love is authentic when it is an expression of justice. Marc Lalonde describes this kind of "just love" that contributes to healing as "a self-emptying kenotic love capable of granting primacy to the needs of the other human being over those of the Self."[19] Yet, what Carol Gilligan says about caring that empties oneself is noteworthy. Caring that sustains the web of relationships includes the one who cares. Prudential judgment demands that we should balance the tension between care for others and care for oneself.[20]

So, just love aims at bringing order where there is chaos. Equally, loving justice relies on the moral agency of human persons as responsible, co-participative, and cooperative subjects to begin the process of the (re)creation of the chaotic space for the sake of ongoing redemption of the world.[21] Accordingly, the justice promised by restorative justice holds a greater hope for the incarnation of the trio above. These presuppose an openness of dynamic movements towards sustainable peace, characterized by "an ongoing process of listening, adjusting, and understanding" that "the peace we seek will not be the peace of the status quo."[22] For some, this position raises the ethical question on the (in)compatibility of love and justice. However, love-as-mercy is, biblically speaking, saving help,

---

19. Lalonde, "Critical Theory," 362–63, esp. 363.
20. Cf. Gilligan, *In a Different Voice*, 61–62.
21. Janssens, "Norms and Priorities," 221.
22. Sathirathai, "Renewing Our Global Values," 7.

or redemptive assistance. Consequently, all concrete persons and peoples need this redemption from a destructive past. Love-as-mercy should fill any human assistance towards human wellbeing after violence and conflict. Justice, thus, is (and must bear) a structural expression of this redemptive assistance—not only to victims and their communities, but also to perpetrators and their communities. Justice for concrete persons and peoples cannot foreclose its essential features of redemption and assistance. In other words, justice is foundationally non-utilitarian, i.e., it (justice) is expressed for the sake of all stakeholders, even perpetrators. Justice is not simply a message of deterrence for others. A critical question, therefore, faces us: Is a perpetrator, for instance, entitled to empathy and altruistic acts, which are acts performed for the sake of the other, notwithstanding the other, and without the thought of benefit to the doer?

As one considers this intriguing question, perhaps a passage in the New Testament can inspire insight on what redemptive assistance aims at, and who is entitled to it. The writer of 1 Peter concludes the letter by trying to encourage the suffering recipient community. He writes: "And after you have suffered a little while, the *God of all grace*, who has called you to his eternal glory in Christ, will himself *restore, establish, and strengthen you*" (1 Pet 5:10, RSV; emphasis mine). Some other English translations based on some other ancient manuscripts read: "The *God of all grace* who called you to his eternal glory through Christ (Jesus) will himself *restore, confirm, strengthen, and establish* you after you have suffered a little" (1 Pet 5:10, NAB; emphasis mine).

With due respect to biblical scholarship on the contributions of first Peter to the New Testament's covenant of peace,[23] we can see this passage as an expression of a belief in God's redemptive assistance to persons and human communities in need of just peace. God aims at *restoration*, i.e., a life freed from victimization and trauma. In other words, victimhood and

---

23. Willard Swartley's seminal work on peace and justice in the New Testament is a useful contribution. He devotes some pages to 1 Peter, where he remarks that this letter has been largely neglected in Christian peace studies. However, in recent decades, Swartley asserts, the letter has made the transition from being a "victim of benign neglect" to being a valuable canonical contributor on Christian doctrine of "non-retaliation" and "non-violent resistance" (cf. 1 Pet 2:21–25; 3:9–18; 4:12–18). God, for the writer of 1 Peter, is "the final arbiter and creator of justice." See Swartley, *Covenant of Peace*, 263–73, quotations on 263, 264, 268.

However, Swartley does not consider 1 Pet 5:10, which gives the reader an idea of what the grace of God intends for the victim(s), and its implication for us—to be steadfast in that grace (cf. 1 Pet 5:12), through an ethics of "redemptive assistance" for those suffering. This will connect the doctrine of non-retaliation and non-violent resistance with the demand of justice that heals. See Van Rensburg, "Code of Conduct," 496, 504–6.

trauma are not permanent because they do not have an ontological status. It is being-at-peace with self and others that is ontologically congruent with human persons. Without this, human life and the world cannot have a taste of happiness. Accordingly, the grace of God aims at assisting suffering persons/peoples to recover that condition of being-at-peace. It is not a return to pristine Eden, because the scars of suffering remain. Nevertheless, recovery is a gracious commitment towards that necessary good and happy life despite the destructive past.

Furthermore, the grace of God *strengthens*. Strength means empowerment. The restoration of God is not magic that leaves the victim(s) as passive agent(s). Even if the grace of God will restore, human agents are equally crucial in bringing this about. They need to keep the hope alive that there will be light at the end of the tunnel. Indeed, agreeing with Jürgen Moltmann, and Elie Wiesel, those who do not have hope die—not just physically, but existentially and spiritually.[24] So, a humane and divinely-inspired redemptive assistance aims at preventing and/or overcoming apathy, which, as stated in an earlier chapter, can paralyze victims to the point of becoming frozen in time. The process of narratival reconfiguration and reframing is essential to redemptive assistance. It is about making traumatized persons powerful enough to see the past and the actors involved in a different light to the extent that the imagination they have will not hold them prisoners of that same past. We cannot experience restoration without empowerment towards creative re-imagination. This point reminds us of Saint Augustine's words, paraphrased thus: The God who created us without our cooperation will not save us without our cooperation.

Finally, the grace of God *establishes*. Establishing can mean to make secure. As chapter 1 highlighted, those victimized are generally living on the fringes of society. They are further marginalized by the fact of their victimization, and its imposed toxic emotions. Redemptive assistance, therefore, aims at bringing the victims out of their closets into the realm of human security. This contributes to human wellbeing, which has both spiritual and material features/significance. Accordingly, divine *grace* that *establishes* human wellbeing, for victims, in a way that *strengthens* and *restores* them, is the just way God wishes to *confirm*, i.e., validate the (innocent) victimhood of those who are suffering in 1 Pet 5:10. Summarily, therefore, *justice that serves victims/human community heals via the trajectory of redemptive assistance (love-as-mercy)*. Now, from a multi-victim perspective, although there may be primary victims, the effects of victimization and atrocities are so expansive that justice must factor, as much as possible, the widened

---

24. See Muller-Fahrenholz, *Kingdom*, 17, 21; Wiesel, "Urgency of Hope," 48–49.

net of victimhood/suvivorhood. In a truly humane society, thus, we cannot exclude perpetrators from redemptive assistance offered above. It may seem to some critical readers that one may be surrendering to the rhetoric that we are all victims now by insisting that perpetrators should be factored into the net of redemptive assistance. By no means.

We have times when the lines of victimhood and perpetration are clear and when they must be made clear. However, as amply demonstrated in the first chapter, these clear-cut lines are few and far between in the various conflicts and violence that have been part of Nigerians' narrative. Nigerians inflict sufferings on one another, and they all suffer together. Our vision of sustainable peace and healing justice (for Nigeria) must pay attention to this fact. The concrete expressions of this vision through the structures and cultures that will contribute to nation re-building will have to be creative in widening structural expressions of *merciful love* that *restores, strengthens, confirms, and establishes* as much as possible. Nevertheless, one cannot rule out the possibility and even desirability of punishment and coercive measures at times, as argued earlier concerning the preferred Christian ethical realism. Yet, all actions and options made for loving justice and just peace must aim at restoring, strengthening and establishing the human person(s)/peoples that are suffering, except we want to claim that those being punished are not suffering and that degradation is inevitable. It is utilitarian to see punishment that degrades as inevitable. It turns the human agent into a means for social cohesion. Hence, this view of punishment gives a wrong diagnosis. Consequently, it cannot lead to the healing of the parties in the long run.

Restorative Justice on "Justice and Dialog"

Freedom from fear and despair and freedom to hope and trust are crucial to dialog for justice. "Freedom from" to "freedom to" implies an ethical process of growth towards what is authentically human and meaningful. This ethical process of growth points to an ethic that can assist in experiencing the freedom to hope and trust, instead of fear and despair of the past. Consequently, we need to pay serious attention to an ethic of being. Compassionate liberality as envisioned in the "Sermon on the Mount" characterizes this ethic.[25] If people have not been empowered to transcend their fears and anger, all the economic efforts come to naught, regardless of the amount of money the World Bank, IMF, or NGOs pour into conflict-ridden zones. Time and again, we are reminded that for justice, peace, and reconciliation to build

25. Cf. Miller, "Girardian Perspectives," 34–35.

up in conflict zones, the heart is indispensable, because the heart is the seat of emotions that is crucial to the founding of principles and ethics.[26] So, the heart is necessary for a way of life (ethic of *be-ing*) that restorative justice presupposes.[27] We need this ethic if our ethics of public actions (e.g., the criminal justice process) shall be meaningful and fruitful. Ethics of being (e.g., virtue ethics) is concerned with whom to become and how to be within a community of persons. Human character is central to this ethic. Character flourishes when it is habitually cultivated, and acted out. In other words, this is about a consistent way of living and acting that corresponds with and expresses the kind of person one is/one envisions to become, and the kind of "people we want to be and the community we aim to have."[28]

Admittedly, the vision of justice, intricately connected with dialog as argued above, is easier said than done. In the context of mass violence and trauma, public hearing (like South Africa's TRC; Nigeria's HRVIC) is one of the ways of bringing in as many stakeholders as possible. However, the public hearings of Nigeria's HRVIC were more of talking, even shouting, cursing, and theatrics, than hearing and listening to the other. It was more like a conversation between deaf mutes. Status differential caused muteness on the side of lowly citizens and deafness on the side of the powerful citizens, who at times did not even desire dialog. They preferred the *status quo*. So, how much hope, then, does justice founded on dialog have in this kind of context? It will depend largely on the hearts of those involved. They cannot achieve much if they are filled with rage, denial, suspicion, and fear, because nobody can force reconciliation—even if self-preservation can induce conciliation between parties. Furthermore, we can achieve little without the political will to make dialog happen publicly and seek out all stakeholders that agree on the rules of engagement without blacklisting or diabolizing them.

One can see a problem with dialogical justice. It challenges stakeholders to be open to answers to this question: why did this happen—to us/you/me? We may not get a universal answer. John Bowker affirms quite rightly that "virtually all human judgments [sic] of any interests are open to contest."[29] Hence, he suggests in his *Sacred Neuron* that stakeholders with conflicting narratives should adopt "intelligent rationality" within concrete history as a court of appeal when there is narrative discordance. Though this

26. Cf. Vacek, "Passions and Principles," 83–86.

27. Vacek explores the role of emotions (affectivity) in the pursuit of justice: "'The heart of justice is care and compassion, and without that there can be no justice, no matter how equitable matters may seem.'" Vacek, "Passions and Principles," 86.

28. Villa-Vicencio, "Transitional Justice," 388.

29. Bowker, *Sacred Neuron*, 10.

sounds modernist with a strong emphasis on reason, it is necessary (though not exclusively) because appeal to value can be part of the human court of appeal.[30] However, adopting this positive option means we cease to have enemies whose existence gives us so much attention and emotional kicks (sense of purpose, making us feel alive). We are faced with a drawback. We need enemies to serve as substitutionary objects that immune us from our collective communal guilt and even intra-communal divisions and injustice. So, an ethical option of mutual demonization serves that scapegoatist purpose of social cohesion of an awkward communal unity. This is why many Nigerians will acknowledge their awkward intra-ethnic unity in the face of various political and ideological divisions other ethnic or religious groups. For instance, the Yorùbá have age-long divisions among the various sub-ethnic groups, e.g., Ijebu vs. Egba (in Ogun State); Ekiti vs. Ibadan. This is replicated all over Nigeria, e.g., Anambra Igbo vs. Owerri Igbo; Hausa vs. Fulani; Fulani vs. Nupe; etc. To persist in the state of denial, we accentuate the enemy without to romanticize about a communal unity that is not there or very weak. So, we must be open to the truths of other stakeholders about themselves, us, and values that unite or separate us when we engage in dialog to solve conflicts and search for sustainable justice.

Again, we see the indispensability of a political will to follow through the process. This is important considering the ill-fated Nigeria's HRVIC. The end of the Commission showed that the civilian government of former president Olusegun Obasanjo and his political cronies were ready to follow through as long as the Commission favored them. Accordingly, the president established the Panel without constitutional legitimacy needed in a constitutional democracy to forestall the likelihood of the Commission going in the way they did not desire. Former military president Ibrahim Babangida finally used this lacuna at the Supreme Court to declare that the "illegal" Panel violated his human rights by including his name as one of the gross violators of human rights in Nigeria. The Supreme Court granted his prayer.[31]

We see here a telling danger about any justice founded on dialog without sufficient safeguard for satisfaction. We see the continued reign of impunity through a tragic expression of the coarseness of the heart not touched by the blinding tears of the suffering other, which many Nigerians saw during the public hearings for justice. Justice as beyond frozenness and death is closely connected to the blinding tears of the eyes.

30. Bowker, *Sacred Neuron*, 71.
31. See Yusuf, "Country Studies," 333–39; Kukah, *Witness to Justice*.

Restorative Justice Beyond Frozenness and Death

Justice beyond frozenness and death affirms implicitly that hope necessarily has a preeminent place in the post-conflict justice process. From a Judaeo-Christian perspective, hope is the virtue that instills humans with the self-assurance that they can reach difficult goals.[32] This virtue is decisive for humans who live in a liminal state, i.e., a life of in-between and tension. Two things characterize this state. On the one hand, the state is oriented towards fulfillment. On the other hand, it is aware that due to human finitude the future will not be fully achieved in the here and now. This state emphasizes that humans are pilgrims, who are constantly on the way, yet persistently challenged to be confident that "ultimate blessedness will not be betrayed."[33] The *Compendium of Social Doctrine* is on target here in one of its concluding paragraphs: "*Christian hope lends great energy to commitment in the social field, because it generates confidence in the possibility of building a better world, even if there will never exist 'a paradise of earth.'*"[34]

One can notice an affinity between Judeo-Christian belief and restorative justice ethos. According to Judeo-Christian belief, impediments and disillusionments, due to tragedies and even sins, cannot frustrate the loving designs of God for a life of blessedness ultimately. Similarly, restorative justice ethos insists that victimhood is a transient state. The human subject is before and endures beyond victimhood. No matter the depths of trauma and frozenness, the subject can rise beyond this and very likely drop the toga of victimhood through a transformation of past narrative. Hope that stubbornly springs up within the human subject and the human community is inherent in the Judeo-Christian belief and restorative justice ethos. According to Thomas Aquinas, hope, as an emotion, has four characteristics: good; future-oriented; arduous; and possible. This is why in spite of its arduousness, hope "involves a psychological tendency towards a good."[35] Hope is not wholly subjective, because the good sought or the evil being avoided can come about not just through one's efforts. It can be mediated through the assistance of others, who are linked with one or who identify with one's hoped for destiny.[36] While Aquinas, in the referred above, identifies God as the other that mediates hope, we may not necessarily restrict it to God.

32. Wadell, "Hope," 438.

33. Wadell, "Hope," 438.

34. Pontifical Council for Justice and Peace, *Compendium*, no. 579 (emphasis original).

35. Cf. Aquinas, *Summa Theologiae*, Ia-IIae, quæ. 40, art. 1, *responsio*; quotation at art. 2, *responsio*.

36. Cf. Aquinas, *Summa Theologiae*, IIa-IIae, quæ. 17, art. 1, *responsio*.

The human community and its institutions can equally offer assistance to achieve the good (justice) and avoid the evil (injustice) when people find themselves in tension in their liminal state.

While Judeo-Christian belief in hope counters despair, restorative justice's beyond frozenness and death emphasizes that no one is beyond restoration. No situation is beyond repair. No one can be bracketed out of mercy and the ability to overcome toxic emotions. Invariably, we see an ethical realism that connects Judeo-Christian belief of hope and restorative justice's ethos of beyond frozenness and death. Evil is never absent in the human community and the world. Yet, beyond the depths of evil and its consequences on persons and the human community, humans are redeemable (i.e., restored; renewed). Paradoxically, some can experience this realism as a stumbling block if care is not taken. On the one hand, the particular restorative justice ethos under discussion seeks to protest and protect against the deficit of hope (e.g., despair, paralyzing sadness, frozenness). On the other hand, it can be liable to the excess of hope.[37] This can happen when there is the overconfidence that victims, whose contrast experiences were occurrences of disempowerment, can be empowered simply by giving them space to narrate their stories (i.e., symbolic reparation). If care is not taken, we can display disproportionate confidence that victims will always or are expected to show mercy (especially forgiveness) once offenders show remorse. This excess of hope can pay undue attention to the symbolic at the expense of some other elements of justice for collective survivors battling in their liminal state.

The expectations of justice "beyond frozenness and death" emphasize that restorative justice should contribute towards undoing oppressive structures and conditions. These expectations pay attention to the connections between structural location and people's wellbeing and its absence. These are part of the promises of restorative justice. If these promises shall be realized, then hope is crucial to restorative justice in peacebuilding. Yet, hope is not a strategy. Hope must be expressed in a fitting conceptual framework that guides actions.

---

37. Deficit of hope gives the message that one can be of no good or cannot reform. It further implies giving up on the possibility of grace and mercy which bring about redemption of one who had fallen into sin. Excess of hope, conversely, expects pardon without repentance, mercy without merits. Cf. Aquinas, *Summa Theologiae*, IIa-IIae, quæ. 20, art. 4, *responsio*; quæ. 21, art. 1, *responsio* (in that order).

Conclusion

The renewal of the mode of being together between different spheres of reality is the principal insight from the discussion in chapter 4 on the hypostatic union. This insight inspired this chapter on Christian ethical reflection on the discussions in restorative justice and critical criminology on how to view the complex need structure of victims of crime and their desire for justice. The chapter concurred that the three-pillar approach of restorative justice might contribute to victim-survivors' healing, i.e., reaching the state of reorganization of their distended self-narrative and their assumptive world. This gives restorative justice the clearest image as a redemptive approach since it offers imagination and conceptual thinking that proposes hope after frozenness in time. This conclusion might give the impression that the realistic theology of restorative justice as inspired by the hypostatic union offered in this chapter takes care of the limitations in Tutu (cf. chapter 3) and even restorative justice in general. By no means. Although thus far there is a strong argument for restorative justice and its compatibility with Christian ethics, in two instances (Nigeria's HRVIC and South Africa's TRC), restorative justice has shown its propensity towards excess of hope, which theologically speaking is a sin against hope. This tension in restorative justice regarding the vices of justice and hope shall be explored in the next chapter.

6
A Theology of Reconciliation for My Neighbor-Turned-Enemy

WHEN THE DRUMS OF war and conflict fall silent, the communities start to take stock. When they look across the borders or the fence, who do they see? Enemies with whom they have unfinished business in future? Or human beings with whom they share *ubuntu*? Their perspectives after the war determine their efforts. We seem to have great resources, brains, and brawns when it comes to prosecuting wars. It looks as if it is easy to mobilize to wage war and destroy, but difficult to muster the same people to build and maintain the foundations of fragile peace. Perhaps, this contrast made Sir Henry Maine say, "'War appears to be as old as mankind, but peace is a modern invention.'"[1] Although Maine's statement is academic, difficulties in resolving conflicts give this impression. We have tried military might with its retributive judicial system. We have tried peace enforcement and blanket amnesty. We have tried incarceration and execution as deterrence. Yet, peacebuilding is not as successful as war-mongering. Then restorative justice comes into the murky waters of peace-building. How can one talk of "restoration" in the face of irreversible effects of war "evil men" committed, some passionately question, like the victim in the Prologue to this book? Can we continue to pass on this cycle of violence to our generations? Are we so powerless that we cannot restore justice without bloodshed and hatred?

As part of the inspirations and challenges of restorative justice, this chapter presents how Christian theological ethics can courageously and realistically respond to the issues of Go(o]d, evil, victimization and justice based on the criminological imagination and practices laid out in the previous chapters. This chapter suggests how Christian theological ethics can approach issues critical criminologists are bringing forth today based on

1. Howard, *Invention*, 1.

their work with victims of conflicts and various violations. When theological ethicists bring their imagination in contact with criminological and victimological imaginations and trends, then they (theological ethicists) can be seen as serious dialog project partners and justice activists for collective victims/survivors who continue to inhabit the same geographical and geopolitical spaces.

A Theology of Reconciliation for My Neighbor-turned-Enemy

By now, we realize that restorative justice is concerned about creating an environment of justice for peace to dwell. Unlike Tutu's position, restorative justice, at singular moments like the HRVIC/TRC, is not *the* moment of justice because of time perspectives tied to peacebuilding. When we factor in these time perspectives in the complex need structure of guests, we further appreciate that material and symbolic dimensions of justice must be maintained in creative balance. The HRVIC/TRC did not satisfactorily achieve this balance because of the predetermined horse-trading. I am arguing that the original restorative justice does not prioritize one need over the other in the complex human need structure. This is reasonable from a personalist ethical approach because the complex human need structure reflects the multidimensionality of the human person. Hence, personalist care ethic fits the theological framework of hospitality to the neighbor-turned-enemy. Below is an illustration of the shape of things to come via restorative justice.

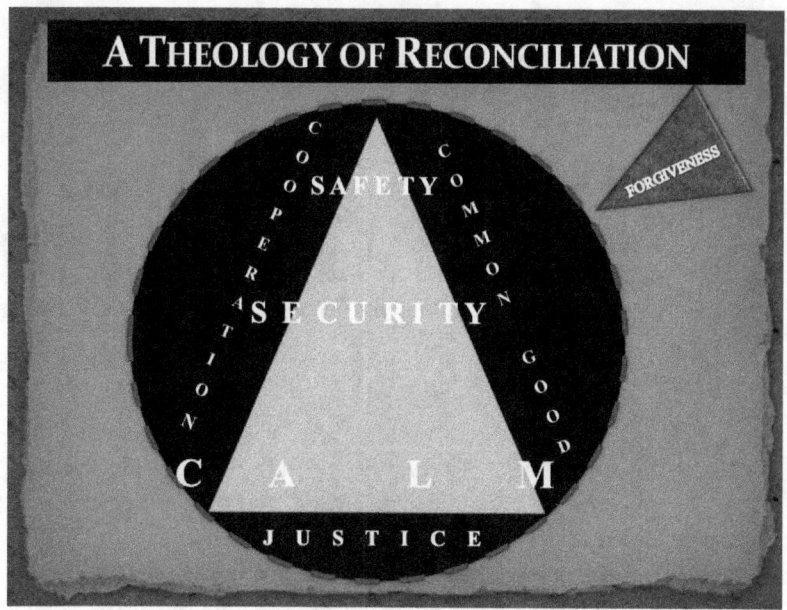

Courtesy of the Author

Legend

Triangle: Representing the three sides for *Reconciliation*:

- *Cooperation*: This underscores that pivotal place of diversity; it emphasizes relationality, characterized by paradoxical ethical asymmetry (equality and heteronomy) that guards against both defect and excess of justice.

- *Common Good*: This refers to the common purpose of life together. It is pursued in trust to the extent that it moves towards a higher ground where the calculus of the pan scale yields to covenanting disposition.

- *Justice*: Normative practice (materially and symbolically) that pursues the reconfiguration of distended narratives and renewal of peoples' modes of relations joined in common good and coexistence.

Dotted Circle: It represents the *Environment* where the Triangle of Reconciliation can happen. Equally, it is what the triangle should bring about. In other words, the triangle's sides and the circle's composition reinforce one another:

- *Safety*: The cessation of overt hostilities through a combination of unilateral and bilateral ceasefires, and imposed peacekeeping.
- *Security*: The reduction of toxic fear; also it means the predictability of a safe life after the cessation of hostilities.
- *Calm*: Unhindered space and opportunity to pursue personal and collective development, and human wellbeing.

Triangle within Dotted Circle: This refers to the *incarnation of reconciliation* with the vision of My Enemy–My Guest who might become a Neighbor.
Triangle outside the Dotted Circle: Forgiveness

- *Forgiveness*: Its pointed edge shows its capacity to break through the reconciliation process. However, strategically, it is outside the carefully crafted policies toward reconciliation. Forgiveness is an esteemed value added. It can close the dotted circle, ensuring a more perfect union between persons living side by side irrespective of group differences. Realistically, stakeholders can do without it in the pursuit of reconciliation as illustrated and explained above. Although parties may be better off with it, they cannot rush it or force it, or even predict it. I premise the placement of forgiveness and the caveat above on what we regard as the feature of a gift: one can do without it, one cannot demand it, but a gift can enrich the recipient because it symbolizes a relationship of love between the giver and the recipient. Gifts are exchanged only among friends and partners. One never exchanges gifts with enemies. A gift does not demand anything in return to the giver, but one can show appreciation. This disposition about the feature of gift presupposes habitual cultivation. Hence, forgiveness, as a gift, presupposes that it is a virtue. It is not normative in the sense of a principle we demand as a matter of justice.

Consequently, one can realize how this book's theology of restorative justice, in agreement with its original context, sees violations done to and by human persons and peoples. They are harms done to the dignity of human persons. Yet, these persons have rights to respectful coexistence, common good, safety, and a serene environment. Hence, such persons and peoples demand justice as a non-negotiable right. This justice must seek to redress, to the extent possible, the violations to their complex need structure. I anchor this theology of restorative justice on a realistic and humble anthropology. Humans are part of an imperfect, though good, creation. Imperfection implies the subduing of chaos through separation at creation. In this sense, separation is good. Hence, I included the right to respectful coexistence with and in differences in the illustration above. Yet, chaos rears its head time and again toward the elimination of separation, through projects of totalization and sublimation. Consequently, after chaos, we have an ethical responsibility to reaffirm the fundamental goodness of separation/difference. This responsibility after chaos in the human community is a normative expression of the right to exist, not as sublimated differences into a dominant identity, but as diversity in unity. This ethical responsibility after chaos, which goes by another name, i.e., justice, is a work of healing, not necessarily in the medical-therapeutic sense. On the contrary, it is deeply anthropological.

Postbellum justice is a fundamental expression of care for the disenfranchised other, who is equally a "stranger" such that it renews and reaffirms the sublimated subject's right to be a stranger. Or as Roger Burggraeve states in his *Wisdom of Love*, "Levinas' concept of justice is indeed intended in the broad sense of the word, as doing justice to the Other, respecting him or her as Other and in this light promoting his or her concerns before one's own."[2] This is an ethics of excess, as in every relationship that has space for love. Towards the end of his article on the Golden Rule, Paul Ricœur acknowledges that the interpretation of the Rule anchored on superabundance, and not equivalence, "elevates the principle of morality above itself, close to its breaking point, to the point where it would turn once more to the non-ethical."[3] A disinterested responsibility ethic characterizes this principle of superabundance. Disinterestedness does not mean a lack of concern for the other. On the contrary, it means, *pacé* Kant, being so concerned for the other that one does not show interest in one's comfort.[4] That's an ethics of excess.

One can, therefore, suggest that Aquinas's discourse on the normativity of vengeance as an ethical response to unjustified violence and excessive responsibility seem capable of reinforcing each other in Christian theological ethics of restorative justice. Summarily, according to Aquinas, vengeance (*vindicatio*: the root of vindicate, vindication) is a moral obligation. Vengeance (*vindicatio*) is "accomplished by some punishment being inflicted upon one who had given offence."[5] Disinterestedness characterizes this form of punishment as *vindicatio*, as opposed to revenge. The punisher metes out the punishment without hatred, and without the intention of taking delight in the punishment. The punishment is simply to correct, redress,

---

2. Burggraeve, *Wisdom of Love*, 103.
3. Ricœur, "Golden Rule," 397.
4. Cf. Cottingham, *Western Philosophy*, 506–12.
5. Aquinas, *Summa Theologiae*, IIa-IIæ, quæ. 108, art. 1, *responsio*.

and protect God's honor or keep the offender in custody to protect order and the common good. Vengeance, therefore, is for the sake of the other, not the self, i.e., it is a presumption against the violation of one's neighbor (i.e., a presumption against injustice). Vengeance, as a responsibility to redress, is a peculiar expression of care for the neighbor.

The following are the characteristics of vengeance as a moral obligation: reasonable; calculated; emotion-less (disinterested); non-malicious; humane (?); and sensible. These characteristics do not favor what Aquinas refers to as the two vices against vengeance—"excess" (e.g., inhumanity; disproportionality) and "defect" (e.g., impunity; amnesia).[6] While Levinas's notion of justice as expressed earlier, in response to totalizing projects in human societies, makes case for the otherness of the Other, Aquinas's morality of vengeance offers an ethical framework within which the ethical responsibility must operate so that we do not replace one evil with another. In this way, Levinas's ethics of the excess will not lead to an excess of justice.

On the one hand, ethical responsibility after chaos must guard against degrading vengeance. It must not displace the toxic emotions felt by the hitherto disenfranchised other on an Other (Aquinas's excess). On the other hand, the response must not do too little. It must not avoid doing what is necessary to redress the violations against victims of totalizing projects (Aquinas's defect). While the HRVIC (and the TRC) avoided Aquinas's excess, these commissions' restorative justice embraced the defect, through the acceptance of the exclusionary mandate, which paid insufficient attention to the ethical demand of presumption against injustice: *doing justice to the Other, respecting him or her as Other and in this light promoting his or her concerns before one's own.* That's why the commissions, due to their unrealistic construal of restorative justice, will be remembered as partly being ethical failures, because they accommodated unacceptable impunity, despite their touted success.[7] Without simultaneous ethical obligations to make direct material reparation to victims, these restorative justice-like initiatives lacked two concepts that are closely related to humane justice after chaos. Empathy and liberation are indeed needed for the return from exile (i.e., alienation or sublimation through the disenfranchising project of totalization).

Theological ethics of restorative justice in contexts of chaos has an eye on integral reconciliation—i.e., $K = (a + d = e)$.[8] The justice needed for reconciliation must respond to residual issues from the micro (personal),

6. See Aquinas, *Summa Theologiae*, IIa-IIæ, quæ. 108, art. 1, *responsio*, ad 1, ad 2; art. 2, *responsio*, ad 1, ad 2, ad 3.

7. Aina, "Nigeria's HRVIC," 55–86.

8. *Katallage* (reconciliation) means an environment of *agape* (love) and *diakaiosune* (justice) experiencing *eirene* (peace) with a higher likelihood towards rebuilt trust.

meso (cultural; group dynamics), and macro (systemic) levels. This construal of justice is processive, gradated, and ongoing, though with a projected timeline and costs. Perhaps an analogy from the hospital might explicate this point. Indeed, a hospital analogy can be criticized as an indication of inconsistency since earlier I appeared to have sympathy for the criticism against the Tutu and the TRC for using a medico-political imagination in dealing with South Africa's project of totalization.[9] There is a qualitative and time perspective difference between this analogy and TRC's medical inspiration (psychotherapy). The analogy looks at the gradation of response in the hospital to victims of an accident. However, TRC's medical analogy is indeed located in one phase—the final phase, i.e., the OPD phase. This shall become clearer below.

Victims of totalizing projects (e.g., apartheid; genocide; religious/ethnic/gender discriminations) are like accident victims rushed to the hospital (i.e., justice system). Offering first aid is the first thing to do for such persons. When they get to the emergency department, the medical personnel offer them a treatment that helps them stabilize. Thereafter, the medical staff is likely to transfer the victims to the medical ward for further observations and treatment for various wounds sustained. While on admission, beyond the purely medical attention, there is space for spiritual/pastoral care for those disposed. When they have been certified well enough to go back home, they are discharged but probably are referred to the Out-Patient Department (OPD) for physiotherapy, psychotherapy, or other assistance to get back to their optimum level as much as possible. Hence, while accident victims receive relief and stability at the emergency and medical/surgical wards, the OPD is for optimal post-nightmare performance. Indeed, as stated in chapter 4, all analogies limp. For instance, while the hospital personnel do not look for or pursue the cause of the accident, justice, even restorative justice, does not focus exclusively on the victim. The offender must be held accountable, for the costs that will be incurred in bringing relief and stability to their victims.

The Place of Justice towards Reconciliation

The victims of totalizing projects (not on case by case alone, but as groups) are entitled to the demands of justice. This coincides with Priscilla Hayner's first index of reconciliation. Violence must end and security is guaranteed.

---

9. *Supra*, chapter 3 of this book, under the header "Tutu's Theological Discourse and the *Aporia* of Healing."

There is no reconciliation as long as threats of violence continue to exist.[10] After the community has achieved some relief, then members can turn their attention to guaranteeing stability and sustainability. There are various considerations for what can bring stability and sustainability, depending on the respective states of the victims. So, it is crucial to create conditions in and around the victim-survivors that will guard against any form of relapse. At this level, what is crucial for relief is profoundly rooted in corporeality, without necessarily bracketing out the symbolic dimension. This assertion is not different from the promise of God's salvation in the Hebrew Bible. The promise of blessing for God's people (Gen 12:1–3a; Num 6:22–27) implies wellbeing that is "*deeply materialistic*,"[11] i.e., "a changed circumstance in the world, a safe, secure place given to what are perhaps a landless seminomadic or a peasant people. The gift of God is a deep socio-economic novum in their life."[12] Hence, ethical responsibility ought to be "propelled by promises that make this option of land concretely possible."[13]

Accordingly, accessibility to justice as corporeal reparation must be of utmost priority, not just to a select few, but to the mass victim-survivors. Without this corporeal dimension of justice needed for relief and stability, there is no possibility of reconciliation. This resonates with the second to the fifth indices of Hayner's reconciliation. These are: second, acknowledgement and reparation; third, cooperative projects that bring hitherto conflicting parties together; fourth, tackling structural inequalities and material needs; and fifth, institutional reforms that reflect the other four elements.[14] Truly, one is not implying that only the corporeal dimension of justice will bring reconciliation. As noted severally already, the symbolic dimension is crucial in overcoming a toxic past, just as the symbolic and non-medical interventions of pastoral agents are crucial for some patients' healing. What I am reiterating here is the firm stance that disproportional emphasis on the symbolic dimension of justice[15] is inimical to the stability and sustainability of reconciliation in the long run.

Consequently, one will realize that Tutu's theology of restorative justice, exhibited during the TRC, appeared to jump from the first aid/emergency treatment to OPD assistance—with his active and unrelenting nudge

---

10. Hayner, *Unspeakable Truths*, 163.
11. Brueggemann, "Law as Response," 90 (emphasis original).
12. Brueggemann, "Law as Response," 90.
13. Brueggemann, "Law as Response," 91.
14. Hayner, *Unspeakable Truths*, 164–66.
15. E.g., storytelling before the public and before the violators as therapeutic and cathartic; truth disclosure; acknowledgement, etc.

towards forgiveness. This critical observation makes sense that Tutu's notion of reconciliation and restorative justice built on short-term cathartic purgation, truth, and forgiveness, at least during the TRC, without an expansive notion of justice making a strong appearance. This movement does not resonate with severely wounded victims' needs generally. Realistically, when people are traumatized and still in the early phase of moving beyond the trauma, the first and most appropriate response is not forgiveness, but justice. This justice consists of both the symbolic and the concrete. When this has been done, then one can realistically raise the issue of forgiveness, as an appropriate response to the limitation of non-negotiable justice. We know that no matter how expansive, justice cannot make up for the irreversibility of the moral evil that had occurred. As such, whatever punishment meted out to the perpetrator remains disproportionate to the pains inflicted on and carried by the victims.

So, I premise the criticism about the jump in Tutu's theology on earlier observations that his interventions during the TRC did not guarantee or engender public safety, security, and mass relief. The long-term justice that brings relief and stability was largely absent or at best weak. Even in the medical treatment of severely traumatized patients, if treatment moves rapidly through first aid treatment to OPD referral, patients risk re-traumatizing. This was equally the case in post-apartheid South Africa. With the collaboration of Tutu's theology and advocacy, several victims of South Africa's project of totalization were left re-victimized. This time they became victims of naïve and/or outfoxing politicians, pragmatic technocrats, and some *baruti* (e.g., Tutu). Their good intentions lacked sharp postcolonial social analysis and hermeneutics of suspicion of the crafted mandate of restorative justice-like initiatives.

Consequently, one can notice another qualitative difference between original restorative justice and Tutu's construal. Original restorative justice's principal focus, unlike Tutu's restorative justice, is on public safety, sanctioning, rehabilitation and victim services. Even the cathartic purgation in restorative justice that Tutu (and Nigeria's Kukah)[16] made so much argument for is processive in original restorative justice. The short-term medico-political model is foreign to original restorative justice. The reason for the limitation of healing and the long-term achievement of the TRC/HRVIC

---

16. Kukah criticizes HRVIC's critics on the Commission's disproportionate emphasis on the symbolic and supererogatory issues like forgiveness, leaving material reparation under recommendations. Kukah claims the critics are "armchair critics," who have paid scanty attention to what victims, the public, and learned colleagues appreciated about the Commission's creativity for justice. For Kukah, these views are what matter. See Nwogu, *Shaping Truth*, x–xi; Kukah, *Witness to Justice*, 460–68.

comes down to the non-appreciation for this processive cathartic dimension in original restorative justice.

What the analogy above inspires and reiterates repeatedly is that for original restorative justice, if parties in post-conflict contexts want the reconciliation, then authorities must boldly create a safe atmosphere before, during and after the initial and short-term dialogical interfaces. Without this expansive and bold justice project that gives assurance against re-victimization and disenfranchisement, there will be no future. Again, contra Tutu's "No Future without Forgiveness," this theology of restorative justice, inspired by original restorative justice, proposes that *there is no future without a corporeally conducive atmosphere for all victims of past projects of totalization.*

Restorative Justice in Peacebuilding and the Recognition of 'Ẹiyẹ Kíńkíń'

There is no future without a corporeally conducive atmosphere for victim-survivors of the past.

I offer the statement above because of a danger noticed both existentially and mythically. We have seen how, for whatever reason, powers that be and their *baruti*-collaborators reduce the intensity and depth of the peoples' lack of justice, peace and reconciliation to extraordinary evils, and personalized therapeutic storytelling of trauma. This glorifies victims of extraordinary abuse. Consequently, justice actors exclude the victims of banalities of evil and everyday violations (the insignificant). Existentially, the dangerous twists and turns in post-war Nigeria and post-TRC South Africa are largely located in the feeling of exclusion by a majority of those countries' citizens when political stakeholders were designing justice for the crimes of their locust years. The reasoning shall not be rehashed here, since we have dealt with these in chapters 1 and 4.

However, I wish to reintroduce an inspiration for my theological ethical position above. I did so initially in the first chapter when outlining the ethical trajectory for unearthing unpeaceful relationships and for moving beyond toxic emotions. It is the mythopoetic rendition from Yorùbá oral tradition, "*Ìtàn Ọba Aláràn-án àti Ẹiyẹ Kíńkíń*," or "The Story of King Aláràn-án and the Tiny Bird." The story of Ọba Aláràn-án and Ẹiyẹ Kíńkíń and the lessons from it point to a role of justice that gives due recognition, especially to the *Kíńkíń* of post-conflict contexts. Nothing crushes human hope and belief like dashed expectations. In *Consolations of Theology*,[17] there is an entry on disappointment that brings this home. Brian Rosner's article on Bonhoeffer and disappointment suggests how one can calculate the degree of disappointment:[18]

> "Prodigious Prospects" + Devastating Failure = Major Disappointment;
>
> High Hopes + Dismal Failure = Major Disappointment;
>
> Inconsequential Hopes + Negligible Failures = Minor Disappointment.

Despite the high hopes preached about TRC, Blacks still live in their world (of poverty and disillusion), while the Whites live in their world (of affluence, indifference, and illusive safety).[19] Similarly, confronted with what has changed after the TRC, or its achievements, Christo Thesnaar remarks, "only a few of the survivors from South Africa's past received economical, physical and social redress."[20] Hence, communities in the rainbow nation are still burdened by past injustices.[21] One can restate what Villa-Vicencio stated years ago. He said one of the missed opportunities of the TRC was the failure to be more proactive towards reducing the Gini coefficient, with South Africa having the highest in the world at the end of the TRC.[22] More than twenty years later, much has not changed. Millions of Ẹiyẹ Kínkín are still neglected. Their suffering and poverty, unemployment and avoidable illnesses are on the increase. Hence, reconciliation is still low in post-TRC South Africa.[23] Nigeria is no different. As stated in chapter 2, Nigeria is low on positive peace, while it has become the poverty capital of the world. Hence, "The fate of the 'poorest of the poor' has a causal link with stability and security. . . . there is a relationship between the various types of violence in the modern state and the neglect of the insignificant in the land."[24] The forgetfulness of the Ẹiyẹ Kínkín is not peculiar to Nigeria's HRVIC (and South Africa's TRC). They appear ingrained in restorative justice-like practices in *postbellum* contexts.

---

17. Rosner, *Consolations of Theology*.

18. These have been adapted slightly from Rosner, "Bonhoeffer," 108 (emphasis mine).

19. Cf. Kukah, *Witness to Justice*, 437.

20. Thesnaar, "Restorative Justice," 55.

21. Thesnaar, "Restorative Justice," 55.

22. Villa-Vicencio, "Neither Too Much," 28.

23. Meiring, "Bonhoeffer," 22.

24. Aina, "Good Governance," 221.

Although some programmes have attempted to generate new national narratives to identify the in-groups and out-groups, many of them were utilised as the opportunity to push forward the new political authorities' propaganda, as was seen in Rwanda. While each of these examples presents a unique set of lessons, they demonstrate one common underlying issue: Such state-driven mechanisms have failed to acknowledge the various needs of victims and wider community members in dealing with social narratives and psychological challenges.[25]

This is why restorative justice advocates acknowledge as much as I do that in transitional justice stakeholders must bridge the gap between three spheres of justice in *postbellum* restorative justice—retributive, distributive, and social.[26] This is how restorative justice in peacebuilding clearly can demonstrate that it is "a mechanism for responsive law, hence making a strong case for it moving beyond micro issues to 'Restorative Peacebuilding.'"[27] *Postbellum* justice should offer assurance against re-victimization. It ought to allow victims to feel being in control of their life again. Also, victims must experience meaningful life *postbellum* to the extent possible.[28]

Let us, therefore, return to our foundational heuristic: $K = (a + d = e)$.[29] In this sense, when justice (d) that is attentive to wounded sensitivity and committed towards general relief and stability is added to love-as-mercy (a), we should experience peace (e). The presence of the trio of love, justice, and peace should bring about the reconciliation of peoples caught in mass violence and destroyed truth. While not focusing *in extenso* on the a and e components in this book, I suggest the components for a and e in my scheme of things.[30] The heuristic presented at the beginning of this book does not guarantee the reconciliation envisioned absolutely. Probability is associated with mathematical equations and symbolic logic, though probability assists to predict logical sequences and possible outcomes. Hence, we come back full circle to the original symbolic formulation.

---

25. Lee and Clements, "Conclusion," 245.
26. Aina, "Nigeria's HRVIC," 61–64; Kukah, *Witness to Justice*, 433–34.
27. Aina, "Nigeria's HRVIC," 57.
28. Reychler, *Democratic Peace-building*, 31.
29. *Katallage* (reconciliation) means an environment of *agape* (love) and *diakaiosune* (justice) experiencing *eirene* (peace) with a higher likelihood towards rebuilt trust.
30. See Appendix 2.

A THEOLOGY OF RECONCILIATION FOR MY NEIGHBOR-TURNED-ENEMY

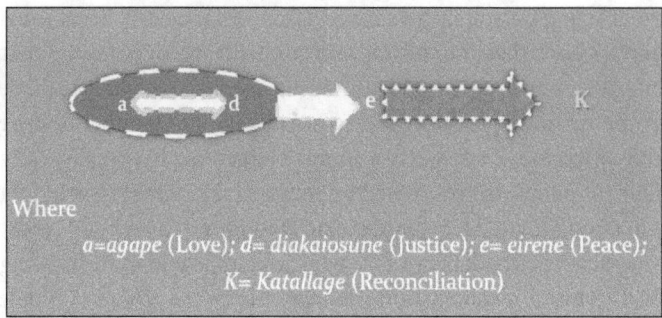

Where

a=agape (Love); *d= diakaiosune* (Justice); *e= eirene* (Peace);
K= Katallage (Reconciliation)

This symbolic formulation has been highlighting the following so far:

1. There is an intricate, often muddled, relationship between justice and peace; love and justice; peace and love. When conflicts arise, peace is the buzzword out of the three: "we want peace"; "let peace reign." Yet, what peace on the way to reconciliation means and how to reach this peace is diverse. When people say "we want peace" or "let peace reign," what are they saying? What do they desire? How do they realize their desire? When people say "we want peace" or "let peace reign," they are affirming an existential reality about their lives at that point. They are in a state of discontentment and troubled agitation. Discontentment and troubled agitation imply being ill at ease within oneself, being ill at ease with others, and the community (e.g., the polity), and being ill at ease within itself. This is the state of lack of peace. So, peace, on the way to reconciliation, is affirmed when discontentment and grave agitation are eliminated or ameliorated. However, what can bring this peace?

2. We cannot reach peace without justice. Yet, justice that cares less about the elimination of discontentment and grave agitation cannot midwife peace. Justice that leaves discontentment and troubled agitation intact creates a situation of the rooster and the rope. There is a Yorùbá expression: "*Adìẹ bà l'ókùn; Ara ò rọ okùn; ara ò rọ adìẹ*"—"The rooster perches on the rope; the rope is ill at ease; the rooster is not at ease." The Yorùbá use this to express a situation where parties in a conflict are experiencing instability in their relationships despite what has been done; hence danger persists. In this state, various expressions of suspicion (an indication of lack of fundamental trust) exist.

3. Trust is a rational disposition of confident expectation that regardless of prior trauma or relational toxicness, a person or persons will act "in a competent and acceptably motivated way so that despite vulnerability,

the trusting person or persons will not be harmed."[31] Trust inherently implies hope that one will act with goodwill and decency on matters of interest among parties. Hence, we say political reconciliation, defined as the rebuilding of bridging trust between conflicting, traumatized, and suspicious peoples, is a moral obligation. It is realistically possible for people to trust based on recognizable indices, even if they are still struggling to let go of the toxic emotions of anger and resentment towards the offenders or those who are implicated in the hurting past. Furthermore, reconciliation can happen between groups of people (e.g., between Yorùbá and Igbo, between Hausa and Tiv, between Christians and Muslims, etc.). The groups, through their representatives, and at various levels, can work together in trust for their common goods and those within the geographical space they share. Govier and Verwoerd define the kind of reconciliation still missing in several transitional societies: "We interpret reconciliation as requiring the establishment of trust, and sustainable trust within healthy relationships cannot be developed when widespread abuse is ignored or discounted."[32] However, trust, a crucial index of reconciliation that peace seeks, cannot be legislated. Trust regarding "attitudes, relationships, and activities"[33] must be actively cultivated and nurtured.

Therefore, this book's heuristic affirms the following:

a. There is something supererogatory about peace. Peace is prefaced by love (the domain of supererogation; superabundance) and justice (the domain of normativity; equivalence). This means that justice is between love and peace. Justice is neither the first nor the last word. Being *in-between* is intrinsic to justice. Love (the logic of superabundance) is the first word in human experience. We experience love long before we know what justice (the logic of equivalence) is. Hence, love precedes expressions of justice. Love is also not the final word. This is based on the ethical principle of "*ordo bonorum*" (order of the good),[34] which states that "in a case of conflict, it is a human and Christian good to seek to secure this good of my neighbour."[35] This love morally qualifies our decisions and actions, i.e., the presence or lack of this love makes human decisions morally good or morally

---

31. Govier and Verwoerd, "Trust," 185.
32. Govier and Verwoerd, "Trust," 183.
33. Govier and Verwoerd, "Trust," 182.
34. See McCormick, "Ambiguity," 46–47.
35. McCormick, "Ambiguity," 47.

evil.³⁶ So, if those who experienced disempowerment, exclusion, and vulnerability due to legalized crime of the past are considered neighbors by negotiators and other decision-makers, then a process that does not consider these neighbors is ethically fraudulent. This is based on my understanding of "virtually exceptionless material norms," i.e., norms that affirm that there may not be a proportionate reason to justify some human actions because these acts destroy whatever values "human reason" might have thought to be protecting in the long run.³⁷ Any reconciliation project without the kind of *just love* as pursued in this book is "a mere salve for the consciences of the privileged"³⁸ and any process associated with this kind of project, in my opinion, cannot be trusted. Thus, love must never lose sight of justice if the demands of the right relationships among neighbors shall be sustained or repaired after violence. We must always avoid the aforementioned condition of the rooster and the rope.

b. Transgressions against right relationships cannot be repaired sustainably without love. When love and justice are combined, irrespective of tensions, peace has hope. When there is peace among people/persons who have experienced transgressed relationships, then they may be able to rebuild their trust in one another and their relationships. When this happens, they can affirm to be living in a state of reconciliation, i.e., $K = (a + d = e)$. Yet, reconciliation should not be hurried. It must be incarnated, praxis-driven, and contextual to recreate the right relationships between the stakeholders (i.e., neighbors-turned-enemies). Neighbors-turned-enemies remind us that these parties will continue to share the same geographical space. Hence, their future life together postbellum must always dominate the choices and narratives, unlike international wars and stakeholders who will go their separate ways once they arrive at acceptable solutions. They are not closely related neighbors whose lives are intertwined at every turn.

c. Reconciliation must also involve a reasonable balancing of fundamental values and human needs dear to the parties; these values and needs should not be played against one another. As we pay attention to victims' traumas, we should pay attention to perpetrators' fears, which led them to inexcusable atrocities. Freedom from fear (by

---

36. Aquinas, *Summa Theologiae*, Ia-IIæ, quæ. 24, art. 1, ad 1, art. 2, *responsio*, ad 3; Harak, *Virtuous Passions*, 77.

37. Cf. Knauer, "Good," 75n7; Gula, "Meaning," 483–84; McCormick, "Ambiguity," 42–43.

38. Cf. Research Institute on Christianity in Africa, "Faith Communities," 59.

neighbors-turned-enemies) measured by safety and relief is crucial, especially after intergenerational projects of totalization. One of the intercessions of Lauds in the Liturgy of the Hours inspired this point: "Let us bless our Saviour, who by his rising to new life has freed the world from fear."[39] From the introductory words of the intercessions for Tuesday, Psalter week 2, we get a picture of what the church-at-prayer sees as the implication of Jesus' resurrection. The implication, in my opinion, should inspire human action at the service of conflict transformation. As argued in chapter 4, with Jesus' resurrection, God broke the chain of estrangement between the Godhead and humans, without leaving the victim (God-man) in death (or frozen time). Humans (past, present, and future) are no longer scared of revenge from the victim. Hence, freedom from fear, for humans, means there is no fear of revenge (on the part of the perpetrator) and no fear of reoffending (on the part of the victim). This freedom from fear signals the beginning of the expectation of reconciliation. So, parties' history of suvivorhood is as important as contending histories of victimhood. Survivors have to write their history despite the past and not replicate the past today. This implies giving all parties a voice that is equally heard on the kind of justice processes that would be beneficial in confronting proactively their collective past. If the post-conflict establishment of trust is the basic index of national reconciliation, then relevant agents must work towards reconciliation among peoples with disparate narratives of primordial identities and loyalties.

d. Justice evokes fairness and balance. It is not simply a judgment, which is a sentence, i.e., a decision taken at the end of a trial. Hence, justice as argued in this chapter and this book as a whole emphasizes the ethical balancing involved in this aspect of the post-conflict reconciliation process. The Reconciliation Chart (Appendix 2), which $K = (a + d = e)$ inspires, does not in any way suggest hierarchization between reconciliation and love, justice, and peace. The chart simply attempts to show that reconciliation is a complex compound, consisting of several elements, which can even be further broken down into specific elements. Hence, post-conflict reconciliation is like a chemical compound (e.g., water) that comes about through a delicate balancing of several elements (H_2O). Accordingly, a post-conflict justice practice (especially restorative justice) must fit into this delicate balance. It must neither destabilize nor impoverish reconciliation. The success or ambiguity of restorative justice shall be judged against this caveat—because

---

39. Sacred Congregation for Divine Worship, *Divine Office*, week 2, Tuesday (185).

"beyond rhetoric and aspiratory goals"[40] of restorative justice, we must evaluate these to see if they have tangible impacts on survivors' post-conflict life (*ethical realism*).

Ultimately, the larger-than-life rhetoric and aspiratory goals of restorative justice in Tutu's theology and advocacy, on the one hand, and the TRC (two realities that cast spell on many imaginations across the world), on the other, have made many to mistake the hope promised by their version of restorative justice for achievement. Consequently, I come back to the questions at the end of my symbolic thesis: *To what extent is RJ synonymous with d? Is RJ sufficient as d in transitional societies?*

The Relationship between Book's Diakaiosune (d) and HRVIC/TRC's Restorative Justice

Though Nigeria and South Africa are examples of transitional societies that appealed to restorative justice, Nigeria's case is special. Due to the fate of the HRVIC's *Report*, the commission remains an incomplete job, in addition to the incompleteness inherent in all truth commissions with regards to justice needed in transitional societies.[41] Hence, there will be disproportionate references to the Nigerian and the South African experiments since there are more extant materials to prove and evaluate the critical reception of TRC's restorative justice project.

First, *d* (*diakaiosune*) and *RJ* (restorative justice) as deduced from Tutu's theology and TRC are not contiguous. If one recalls the analogy from the hospital response to accident victims and the story of Ọba Aláràn-án and Ẹiyẹ Kínkín as well as the lessons drawn from this mythical story, it is understandable why one can insist that there are qualitative differences between *d* (*diakaiosune*) and HRVIC/TRC's restorative justice. Both *d* and *RJ* have a common point of departure. However, while *d* continues through the intensely corporeal long-term treatment, HRVIC/TRC's restorative justice appears more concentrated on what might fit OPD procedures. Hence, *d*, due to its components, guarantees stability and relief. HRVIC/TRC's

---

40. This phrase, though used in a different context, aptly expresses a crucial observation about restorative justice. See Jamison, "Might of Metaphysics," 9.

41. Bishop Kukah titled the final chapter of his memoir on Nigeria's HRVIC "Reconciliation Delayed?" He struggles with HRVIC's fate and the possible truncation of national reconciliation. In the end, he affirms that the Truth Commission was successful because it afforded many people to tell their stories, which they never imagined would happen in their lifetimes (p. 477). However, justice is more than the symbolic catharsis. Kukah, *Witness to Justice*, ch. 13.

restorative justice did not guarantee stability and relief, even if democracy in these two countries is close to three decades (South Africa) and two decades (Nigeria). Perhaps, this was out of the mistaken confidence that once the transition was steadied, every other outstanding issue of concrete justice would be dealt with in a progressive liberal democracy. It was naïve confidence because it underestimated the role of power and idolatrous self-interest with the socially irresponsible elites pursuing "self-interest in a society where mutual trust did not exist beyond the narrowest of circles."[42] Robin Lovin, a Christian ethicist, offers what should characterize Christian ethical realism in the twenty-first century. Widespread liberal democracy has achieved a status of normativity and triumphalism to the point of subtly resembling the political idolatries of the past—the will to power and self-interest. Christian ethical realism in the twenty-first century, therefore, must never lose its critical vigilance and hermeneutics of suspicion in its public intervention. We crucially need this to guarantee happiness within the polis. This happiness in the polis will be guaranteed in the "institutions by which we provide for our families, educate our children, share and preserve the experiences of our culture, and organize the production and distribution of goods and services."[43]

Furthermore, while *d* has an eye on what concretely will contribute towards reconciliation between groups, through attentiveness to micro, meso, and macro residual issues, HRVIC/TRC's restorative justice overtly focused on *reconciliation* minus the meso and macro residual issues, due to what I pointed out earlier as the fallacy of composition inherent in Tutu's theology/TRC/HRVIC. For instance, this fallacy equated apology and forgiveness between a handful of the twenty-seven thousand official victims of TRC and their perpetrators with forgiveness and reconciliation between the groups from which they came. This was possible because the confessional trajectory actively found a kindred spirit in its secular counterpart—the particular medico-political psychotherapy that the liberal human rights approach adopted. In addition, *d* is not dualistic unlike Tutu's theology of restorative justice. The components of *d* cover both the body and the spirit, with the body and its needs taking priority over the spirit at the critical phases. The transethical (forgiveness; remorse) is beyond the scope of *d*.

Second, contrary to what TRC presented as the kernel of restorative justice, especially the over-prioritized forgiveness and the symbolic reparation, *RJ* is not synonymous with *d*, even if admittedly it is a contributory inspiration for my schematic representation. Some give the impression that

42. Lovin, "Christian Realism," 676.
43. Lovin, "Christian Realism," 678.

the restorative justice the TRC adopted is synonymous with the kind of justice necessary for *postbellum* life together among South African peoples. They hinge the impression on the amnesty-for-truth clause and the symbolic reparation provided to most of the twenty-seven thousand official victims. On the contrary, the restorative justice presented by Tutu/TRC lacks the feature and character to be synonymous with *d* presented above. Tutu's/TRC's *RJ* critically failed at the crucial moment to include the residual issues from the meso and macro levels. It failed also to assign culpability and responsibility for decisive partners at two crucial levels (i.e., the bystanders and beneficiaries). In other words, given that the forces of seductive, outfoxing, and punitive capital markets held Tutu's/TRC's *RJ* hostage, their *RJ* lacked a fundamental feature, i.e., the intersection of the three spheres of justice, which the reformers within the restorative justice movement envision.[44]

Third, Tutu's/TRC's *RJ* did not incarnate *d*. There are two reasons for this conclusion. On the one hand, as compelling as Tutu's theology of restorative justice is, it does not present itself compellingly enough as capable of incarnating secular-derived original restorative justice. Perhaps, it is even not appropriate to look for a theology that can incarnate original restorative justice. Conceivably, this was Tutu's mistake, thinking that this theology of *ubuntu*—rainbow nation of God—was sufficient to just co-opt and use the language of restorative justice. Tutu's theological method about its relationship with original restorative justice can be another example of a method in contextual theology that Steven Bevans refers to as the Translation method. According to this method, "[T]here is always something from the outside that must be made to fit inside; there is always something 'given' that must be 'received.'"[45] Tutu's theology is like the norm, we have to make original restorative justice fit into this norm. Accordingly, original restorative justice, just like other things considered extraneous to this theology, will have to be adapted to fit this theological norm, without causing chaos or heresy. If one considers this observation critically, then the restorative justice that comes out from Tutu's theology cannot be synonymous with *d* that remains faithful to its non-theological and realistic background. On the other hand, TRC's restorative justice was equally incapable of incarnating *d* due to its severely compromised status. Hence, with a compromise that excluded the meso and macro residuals as normative, and for slipping into the fallacy of composition in the way it conceived reconciliation, the *RJ* of TRC was too restricted and constrained to be affirmed as *d* that contributes to reconciliation between groups, through attentiveness to all the residual issues.

44. Aina, "Nigeria's HRVIC," 61–64.
45. Bevans, *Models*, 30–46, quotation on 33.

Fourth, HRVIC/TRC's *RJ* is insufficient to be *d* in transitional societies. One sees that TRC's *RJ* was insufficient given that as late as 2019 some South Africans still asked about the kind of justice that would bring reconciliation to South Africans.[46] In addition to the millions of the excluded majority, many of the official victims, since the 2000s, have been pursuing civil suits in Europe and the United States of America, against the South African government for reparations. This is another instance that the *RJ* in practice was grossly insufficient. One of the TR commissioners, Yasmin Sooka, observed with some regret that

> the TRC dealt with "outward manifestations of apartheid" while it excluded "the economic system served by those abuses" which is an echo of the "blindness" of "human rights." If I have to do it again I would look at the systems of apartheid . . . I would look at the systematic effects of the policies of apartheid.[47]

More than a decade later, not much has changed in this regard. According to the 2019 SA Reconciliation Barometer, 77.1 percent of respondents say South Africa still needs reconciliation. Given that inequality has worsened since the end of the Apartheid/TRC,[48] the survey asked respondents what had contributed to this reduced bridging trust. Responses varied. Corruption (84.4 percent), political exploitation of primordial faultlines (74 percent), and lack of justice from historical wrongs (74.4 percent) are the major barriers to reconciliation.[49] Gugu Nonjinge, project leader, Afrobarometer, captures the mood of South Africans and their dashed hopes about reconciliation: "'If you can't get to a point where everyone gets equal access to resources—in economic terms or in social terms—we can't begin to speak about reconciliation.'"[50]

Indeed, the lack of *d* as envisioned above in post-TRC South Africa makes the country to be ill at ease within itself and between its multiracial and multiethnic groups, despite the external impressions of forgiveness and truth disclosure. I arrived at this conclusion judging by various multilayered perspectives and by personal experiences during some visits to provinces considered the poorest and unattractive to tourists (Free State, and North-West Provinces), despite being homes to some of the largest farms and mines in South Africa. More than a decade later, the latest data

---

46. Potgieter, *SA Reconciliation Barometer*.
47. Klein, *Shock Doctrine*, 211.
48. Potgieter, *SA Reconciliation Barometer*, 51.
49. Potgieter, *SA Reconciliation Barometer*, 24–25.
50. Potgieter, *SA Reconciliation Barometer*, 80.

show things have worsened.[51] South Africa's bridging trust has reduced. On the contrary, bonding trust is on the increase. Bonding trust refers to being more at home with and trusting one's relatives/neighbors, i.e., people who are like one, than trusting out-groups. Hence, racism and xenophobia have not been addressed decisively.[52] Truly, the future is another land; and it might not yet be in sight in South Africa, more than two decades after the TRC and its restorative justice.

Nigeria does not fare better. In addition to Nigeria's current state as presented in chapter 1, the 2021 Social Cohesion Index shows that Nigeria is not a socially cohesive society. Its social cohesion has taken a dip since 2015. Social cohesion means "the willingness of citizens of a country to cooperate and work together towards ensuring the survival and prosperity of the country."[53] According to the survey, there is "growing citizens [sic] distrust towards the state and fellow citizens; as well as a proclivity towards ethnicity over nationalism."[54] With a computed score of 44.2 percent in the social cohesion index, Nigeria falls "below the average threshold of a socially cohesive country."[55] Nigerians say they have more trust in religious leaders (55 percent) and traditional leaders (44 percent) than President Muhammadu Buhari's government (26 percent), the judiciary (26 percent), the National Assembly (22 percent), and law enforcement agents (22 percent).[56]

The low scores of political, judicial, and parliamentary institutions are based on the perceptions about social justice. Significantly, about 74 percent of respondents say that "all Nigerians are not equal before the law."[57] Furthermore, 58 percent of respondents say "the Federal Government isn't making enough effort to promote a sense of inclusion for all ethnic groups in the country."[58] All of these reveal that Nigeria is stronger in bonding trust than in bridging trust. As seen with South Africa's state above, bonding trust is a barrier to reconciliation, whereas bridging trust is crucial for reconciliation. Consequently, Nigeria ranks low in reconciliation. So, both South Africa and Nigeria might just get to the promised land (reconciliation) someday.

A Scripture passage sharpened this conclusion (Num 14:1–25, NRSV). This pericope presents what we can see as the divine dialectic between

---

51. Benyera, "South Africa's Truth," 198–99.
52. Potgieter, *SA Reconciliation Barometer*, 65.
53. Ihua, "Nigeria Social Cohesion."
54. Ihua, "Nigeria Social Cohesion."
55. Ihua, "Nigeria Social Cohesion."
56. Ihua, "Nigeria Social Cohesion."
57. Ihua, "Nigeria Social Cohesion."
58. Ihua, "Nigeria Social Cohesion."

forgiveness and non-reconciliation after Israelites' rebellion and ingratitude. God forgave rebellion and ingratitude for the non-recognition of God's role in bringing the Israelites to the point they were—from Egypt (the land of slavery through the Red Sea) to freedom (on the way to the promised land). Hence, like *Ẹiyẹ Kínkín*, the Yorùbá mythical story related earlier, God decided to punish the Israelites. However, like the *Babaláwo*, Moses pleaded with God, the victim, unlike the *Babaláwo* that pleaded with the offender. God took Moses's plea to heart and forgave Israelites, but God did not let go of justice, though forgiveness (a manifestation of love-as-mercy) mitigated the severity of the punishment. In Num 14:12, God promised total extermination of the offenders. Nonetheless, after Moses's plea, this severe punishment gave way to a less severe one: though their lives would be spared, the offenders would not enter the promised land (cf. Num 14:22).

From the dialectics between forgiveness and punishment in this passage, we can have forgiveness without reconciliation, especially because of the persistence/non-repentance in burdening, testing and consistently showing lack of trust from the offending party (cf. Num 14:11). Therefore, the guilty were forgiven even without expressing remorse; thanks to Moses's intercession (cf. Num 14:13–19). Yet, due to intransigence as a people, they would not enter the promised land. Even so, we have an exception to the rule. Caleb, the one who trusted, i.e., who had a "different spirit" (Num 14:24), would enter the promised land. Caleb had a different spirit from his intransigent people. One can deduce that reconciliation implies being of a different spirit—of bridging trust and faithfulness—in the Other, such that they can enter the promised land, i.e., the future hoped for and promised. Reconciliation can take generations sometimes because of a lack of a "different spirit" of trust and faithfulness in the Other.

South Africa and Nigeria have left their "Egypt" (the past characterized by projects of totalization and sublimation). However, they are still wandering in the wildernesses with a lot of testing and intransigence, especially from the beneficiaries of the past projects. Consequently, entering the promised land will depend on South African and Nigerian peoples being of a different spirit—like Caleb, trusting and keeping faith with one another. Probably something else is needed to make *d* flourish in South Africa and Nigeria decades after TRC's/HRVIC's *RJ*. It is something that cannot be included in the symbolic hypothesis but will have to make its way into the reconciliation process.

Restorative Justice, Reconciliation, and Spirituality

If d will flourish in transitional societies, to the degree stability and relief permit, then forming a new generation with a different spirit is crucial so that even if their forebears cannot or will not enter the promised land, the new generation will get there someday. The hope for reconciliation lies not in those severely affected by the toxic emotions of yesterday. The hope lies with the generation with a critical distance—in time and emotions—from the toxic past. It will take time, sweat, and tears.

Hope is grounded on the reality of the openness to cooperation. According to the 2021 Social Cohesion Index, "63% of citizens are 'Extremely or Somewhat Willing' to cooperate with fellow citizens to make Nigeria more united."[59] This is where one can see a crucial role for religions (especially Christianity) and the humanities (especially arts, media, and educational institutions) in building up a new generation with a different spirit concerning love, justice, peace, and reconciliation. Since religious leaders rank highest in the trust indicator, they have a lot to contribute to helping Nigerians change their narratives of toxicness to bridging trust. Hence, religions will have to redefine their roles to form the new generation in virtue that assists our reconciliation thesis. This assertion follows up on an earlier observation concerning the limit of predictable calculus for reconciliation.

The probability clause acknowledged earlier reinforces the claim that restorative justice is not simply principilist. It does not just stick to the various elements of d to bring about K; or what in ethics is called an ethics of action. Restorative justice is equally an ethics of being, ethics of disposition, encompassing empathy, and liberation. Ethics of being inform concrete actions. This is why virtue ethics is crucial for restorative justice. This theology of restorative justice will succeed only if there are agents of social transformation who will pass on this imagination in the ongoing process of reconciliation that is characterized by the eschatological language of *already and not yet*. Now, some remind us that virtue ethics does not focus on structural change. Some might even go as far as suggesting that person-centered virtue ethics cannot be transferred to the collective.

Reinhold Niebuhr's *Moral Man and Immoral Society*, originally published in 1932, is a classic text on this point. According to Niebuhr, there is a significant distance among human persons in modern society. His ethical realism led him to acknowledge that while individual persons could practice virtues and even practice self-sacrifice, structurally, their societies ran

---

59. Ihua, "Nigeria Social Cohesion."

on the will to power and self-interest.[60] Hence, a change could not come by appealing to reason, not to talk of conscience and virtue. The change would come through revolution. Yet, this does not guarantee the reign of morality because the revolutionaries sometimes turn out worse than those they ousted. So, Niebuhr was not very supportive of revolutionary change, out of fear of the chaos that might result. While Niebuhr was optimistic about the human person ("Moral Man"), he was pessimistic about modern society ("Immoral Society"). He was a man of his time—a time of *realpolitik*. So, his ethical interventions and analyses were within this political practice. At any rate, the non-violent and swift transformation the Civil Rights Movement brought severely challenged Niebuhr's ethical realism.

Those Niebuhr's ethical realism influenced are not very optimistic about the capacity of person-centered virtue ethics to transform structures. Understandably, perhaps virtue ethicists equally begin and end their discussions on the person, taking it for granted that once the person changes, the society will change without giving a clear indication on how this will happen. However, as Lovin points out in his discussion on the swift transformation that swept through Eastern Europe (and South Africa) in the eighties and nineties, Niebuhr's ethical realism underestimated the role of imagination in structural change: "In other words, a realistic calculation of what is likely to happen must include the fact that people on both sides of the barricades are capable of envisioning something different."[61] If there is a dialectical relationship between creators of structures and structures themselves, then a change in imagination, even at the institutional levels, through various levels of ethical discernment, can transform structures. To deny this will imply that once humans create institutions and structures, these, in turn, activate their auto-drivers, functioning henceforth independently, and irrespective of human intervention.

Due to the eschatological component (already and not yet) in reconciliation, hopefully, the imagination to be passed on in the ongoing process will presuppose openness to something new—the inbreaking of the eschatological moment in reconciliation at the micro, meso, and macro levels. This eschatological sensitivity equally infuses humility in us that we cannot predict with absolute certainty when reconciliation will flourish, despite the working proposition. Yet, we do not need to grieve when reconciliation is delayed here and now despite what we have done. Even if reconciliation is yet to flourish, the imagination of agents of social transformation will increase the hope to build peace with the least of violence and bloodshed;

---

60. Niebuhr, *Moral Man*, chs. 4 and 10.
61. Lovin, "Christian Realism," 674.

with the least exclusion of the *Kińkiń* of the *postbellum* societies. Necessarily, a change of mindset makes room for solidarity towards and participation of those cruelly affected by policies of a fascinated century.[62] The change signals a resolution to will the good of the other, characterized by reciprocity, conversation, participation and communion, as against desire/utility.[63] This goodwill, according to Aquinas, ensures a life of happiness, "the destiny of human life."[64] Happiness, as an ultimate end for humans, so fulfills an individual human's "whole desire that nothing is left beside for him to desire."[65] This will happen at the reunion with God in heaven i.e., the beatific vision. The beatific vision, nonetheless, is an inspiration and a source of renewal for humans. This happiness can be tasted in this life, but only through commitment to a life of virtue. This is because happiness as ultimate fulfillment is not automatic. It must be striven for by living in the likeness of God, according to human nature and capacity.[66] Once again, we are reminded that religious perspectives on virtues and spiritualities of virtuous living are important for reconciliation.

If one can say that, theologically, reconciliation is like rising from the ashes of a violent and fearful past, it is possible not only by our actions and delicate balancing. It is possible also because of the transethical—grace. The book of Psalms reminds us, "Except the Lord builds the house, those who build it labor in vain. Unless the Lord watches over the city, the watchman stays awake in vain" (Ps 127:1). This resonates in Ricœur's insight, according to Maureen Junker-Kenny in a contribution on the role of religion and public theology in a post-secular age: "The 'predisposition for the good' is constitutive, and the 'propensity for evil' is factual. Yet the struggle between the two cannot be resolved by powers on their own. It calls for the initiative of a God who must be more than a judge."[67] Religious contributions through engaging spirituality cannot be bracketed out in the pursuit of *postbellum* sustainable peace and reconciliation.

---

62. This paraphrases a statement credited to Enrique Iglesias, former president of the International Development Bank at the end of the last century. Cf. Gutiérrez, "Liberation Theology," 104.

63. See Aquinas, *Summa Theologiae*, IIa-IIæ, quæ. 23, art. 1, *responsio*; ad 3, also p. 5 [note a, b].

64. Aquinas, *Summa Theologiae*, Ia-IIæ, prologus.

65. Aquinas, *Summa Theologiae*, Ia-IIæ, quæ. 1, art. 5, *responsio*; quæ. 3, art. 5, *responsio*; quotation from quæ. 1, art. 5, *responsio*.

66. See Aquinas, *Summa Theologiae*, Ia-IIæ, quæ. 1, art. 8, *responsio*; quæ. 3, art. 2, *sed contra*; quæ. 3, art. 5, *responsio*.

67. Junker-Kenny, "Capabilities," 161.

Spirituality is not just a pietistic option. Christian spirituality, for instance, for love, justice, peace, and reconciliation might reveal two crucial things for those devoted to these issues. First, motivations, commitment, and actions should rest on God. It should be attentive to and inspired by God's saving acts in the world. Second, they should be Christocentric because they flow from being-in-Christ, guided by and flowing from the community of God's family. Michael Allsopp explains that these dimensions of Christian spirituality incorporate "the totality of our *relational* and *emotional* (affective) skills, training, education, and experience."[68] This is a spirituality of active contemplativeness. This spirituality recognizes that spiritual concerns inevitably become political concerns when the milieu of our faith and that of our peoples has changed. Even though the spirituality of reconciliation is attractive, it has a spin. It is an article of faith—in God, in humans, and in our capacities to create a "hope-full" world here and now. This is a spirit inspired way of being-with-one-another.[69]

Consequently, I applaud Tutu's contribution to the theology and praxis of restorative justice by emphasizing the role of spirituality. We recall a quotation from a biographer of Tutu concerning his theological contributions: "His thinking is expressed more in sermons, devotional talks and addresses than serious theological writing."[70] Hence, his contributions to justice and reconciliation are heavily infused with his preferred Christian spirituality; and they are always situated within the context of his pastoral ministry. This emphasizes that the work of reconciliation and the outcome are not entirely out of human ingenuity. There must be space for religious imaginations and insights. It is commendable that Tutu gives further backing for religious imaginations and spiritualities in peacebuilding and reconciliation processes.

Nevertheless, we know by now that there are serious reservations about the kind of spirituality and religious imagination that Tutu brings. A spirituality that flows from the translation model of contextual theology is deficient for the pursuit of justice and reconciliation elucidated upon so far. It appears that his brand of spirituality is too triumphalistic, naïve, and weak on postcolonial critique. This is not peculiar to him alone. It seems the ambivalent relationship the church had with the state during a painful past makes official theology and spirituality to be idealistic, muddling the water of justice and reconciliation. Perhaps, the political correctness of official

---

68. Allsopp, *Renewing Christian Ethics*, 155–63, quotation on 221 (emphasis original).

69. This is an inspiration from earlier discussion in chapter 4 on the hypostatic union and the subsequent ethical interpretation.

70. Du Boulay, *Tutu*, 87.

theology, and now the spirituality, of justice and reconciliation, as gleaned from Tutu, has been the reason why critical criminologists and some critical advocates of restorative justice do not see—and do not miss—ecclesial actors and their theology as helpful dialog partners. Paradoxically, perhaps it is this same politically correct theology and spirituality that makes ecclesial actors like Tutu be so easily courted by the state, and the international community. Robin Lovin states that a pliant ecclesial intervention along the line observed above runs the risk of making the church look more like a "'Constantinian' church that takes responsibility for the more or less that political compromise requires in return for a place at the table in the public discussion."[71] This pliant outlook implicitly accepts the idolatry of "'the primacy of the nation state'"[72] that is still surviving to date. To be regarded as helpful partners, the church (through all its faithful, especially its leaders and theologians) has to rehabilitate its theology from political correctness. Perhaps, it is high time the church courted some irresponsibility. It must distance itself from hegemonic circles that hold levers of control on what is given space in public discourse concerning the kind of justice that responds to the crucial three levels (micro, meso, and macro) necessary for sustainable peace and reconciliation.

Consequently, in my opinion, the church can begin from the kind of spirituality that shall form a new generation with a different spirit. A non-politically correct spirituality for a different spirit should flow from what might be called a liberative praxis model of contextual theology. We can define this as *any kind of intentional and purposeful activity based on reflection and human engagement in a particular context aimed at creating a social transformation that is favorable to human flourishing in that particular context in the short and long run.*[73] This praxis has concrete relevance to Africa (with its wars, low-density violence, and poor social cohesion) because of the ineluctable connection between sustainable justice and peace process, on the one hand, and issues of social justice, on the other.

Conclusion

The theology offered in this chapter thrives on a specific theological imagination (hypostatic union; renewal of mode of being together). Yet, it does not lose sight of social analysis and postcolonial sensitivity for most

71. Lovin, "Christian Realism," 679.
72. Lovin, "Christian Realism," 679.
73. Inspired by Aristotle, *Nichomachean Ethics*, bk 5; Habermas, *Knowledge and Human Interests*, 301–14.

transitional societies. Hence, the chapter argued that spirituality, which religious actors will predictably promote, must inspire liberative praxis in such societies. Politically correct theologies and praxis of restorative justice discredit such actors and the religious traditions they represent. Finally, the conclusions of this chapter, especially on restorative justice and spirituality, give added inspiration for religious contributions in peacebuilding. At least within contexts like Nigeria, the church is a crucial member of the civil society, given the reality that religious leaders appear to be the most trusted on the trust index of the national social cohesion survey. Hence, restorative justice as envisioned in the previous chapters and the current one should inspire the church to embrace liberative praxis concretely. In traumatized and perplexed contexts, this praxis makes the church an effective agent of social transformation. The next chapter teases out some suggestions that can flesh this praxis.

7

Nigeria and Beyond

An Agenda for Christian Ethics in Restorative Peacebuilding

A COMPREHENSIVE DEMAND OF *postbellum* justice in transitional societies necessarily includes victim reparation programs, a truth commission, criminal prosecution, counter-impunity agencies, and institutional capacity building. These comprehensive components of restorative peacebuilding prevent gross human rights violations from repeating. They drive social cohesion and transformation. The body of Christ in transitional societies must adequately respond to these comprehensive demands for transitional justice in the throes of mass violence. As such, how shall Christian peace ethics factor these demands in its contributions? From the beginning, we have argued that overcoming toxic emotions is a key entry point into these discussions. The importance of overcoming toxic emotions remains an enduring inspiration for restorative justice. This emphasis holds that apart from the interest-based approach, which hardcore realists favor, the psychological aspects (emotional components) must not be overlooked in negotiated peace agreements, especially in transitional societies. The emphasis on the emotional components, especially in intrastate conflicts (like Nigeria; South Africa), cautions against naïvety, which some restorative justice advocates had been liable (e.g., Arch. Tutu). They appear to think that once parties have been able to stem the tide of violence or reign of terror, people will embrace themselves in bridging trust, thus leading to rapid social cohesion. Indeed, as Robert Rothstein observes, despite negotiated peace agreement, psychological and subjective factors have yet to be overcome, and "the past is neither forgotten nor forgiven, whatever the nature of the peace agreement."[1]

---

1. Rothstein, "Fragile Peace," 238.

This chapter teases out some proposals regarding the role of the church and its members. I premise this role on the revalorization of religion in the public sphere, the importance of religion's deprivatization, and the decisiveness of religion in the global south. Hence, it is unsurprising that Christianity has been involved in a lot of transitional processes in recent years. But then, what type of ecclesial praxis is at work in transitional societies like Nigeria? This is critical because of the paradox of religious intensity in the country, on the one hand, and a culture of impunity, on the other. How has the Christian religion contributed to this paradox? How can Christianity be challenged to take multi-victim justice perspective and impunity serious? A recommendation of Nigeria's HRVIC *Report* drives these questions. The *Report* recommends that Nigeria needs a "robust and active civil society" for a more peaceful and reconciled country.[2] The Catholic Church (like other religious communities), for instance, is part of civil society. Hence, it is most suitable, as other religions, to be the locus of micro and macro loving justice that gives a toxic emotion-free future to a traumatized nation, suffering from "recurrent incendiary political violence and anomic political behavior."[3] The findings from the country's national social cohesion survey make the argument more compelling.

We remember, as the previous chapter pointed out, religious leaders are the most trusted in Nigeria. Of course, religious leaders and traditional leaders, instead of national leaders, being the most trusted in the country underlie a troubling reality. These trusted leaders are the custodians of two primordial categories in Nigeria—religion and ethnicity. Hence, they are more prone to promoting bonding trust than bridging trust and linking trust. Bonding trust refers to the disposition of being at ease among people in the same group (ethnic, religion, gender, class). Bridging trust refers to the rational disposition of confident expectation and cooperation between different groups. Linking trust refers to the confident disposition that makes various groups in society connect positively with the various institutions in the society, especially the state and its organs.[4] Many see religion as a centrifugal force. Hence, they see religions as only capable of promoting bonding trust. Nevertheless, this chapter and the next reiterate that religions are as much a centripetal force as they are centrifugal. The submissions in this chapter should be viewed as a proactive response to the HRVIC recommendation for programmatic action for transitional societies like Nigeria so that diversity and unity may no longer be undermined.

2. HRVIC, *HRVIC Report: Volume One*, ch. 3, no. 3.242.
3. HRVIC, *HRVIC Report: Volume One*, ch. 3, no. 3.227.
4. Cf. Potgieter, *SA Reconciliation Barometer*, 29.

This chapter's task begins from a somewhat unusual angle. However, this angle should make lots of sense given what I presented in chapter 3 concerning what happens to victims of violence: the collapse of their assumptive world. This collapse contributes to the flourishing of toxic emotions. Hence, social agents of transformation need to help these victims to make sense of these emotions and get over them. Truly, religious contributors focus on overcoming toxic emotions among persons/groups. However, hardly do they pay attention to the toxic emotions that victims of violence and calamities have towards God. Yet, religious contributors, who are attentive to and inspired by developments in critical criminology, are best primed to function in this area. How can there be loving justice, peace, and reconciliation between divided persons and groups if those persons' and groups' toxic emotions towards God remain untouched?

Human Responsibility Regarding God's Acclaimed Omnipotence

How can a loving God allow unspeakable evil to happen to non-precipitating victims of mass violence? If God is indeed omnipotent why could that same God not stop the endless pogroms and sectarian violence in Nigeria from 1966 till as recent as November 2021, or any of the wars ravaging Africa? If God is almighty and all-loving how could he allow scores of worshipers be bombed out of existence on Christmas Day in 2011 right inside St Philip Catholic Church Madalla? If God is so active in the world, where is that same God in a world where female rape continues unabated as an ordinary weapon of wars? It seems we know more of God's silence in the world than God's activity. The idea of a compassionate and omnipotent God cannot be sustained in a world that catastrophes ravage.[5] It seems we cannot sustain this idea of a compassionate and omnipotent God. The following paragraphs reflect on these troubling theological questions. However, all too often people begin their queries with an inappropriate question. After articulating the reason for this claim, I offer a proposal concerning how Christians especially can have a more realistic belief in God's activity in the face of endless violence and catastrophes. Hopefully, the themes in these reflections can further strengthen the agenda for Christian peace ethics in transitional societies, especially for victims, who are wrestling with their toxic emotions towards God, and how they can still believe in and worship the same God who appeared to

---

5. Laato and de Moor, "Introduction," ix.

have let them down. These reflections dovetail into a particular theological challenge for the church as the body of Christ.

Not "Where Was God?"

Quite often when bad things happen to people we ask, "Where was God?" Rarely do we ask: "Where was humanity when this was allowed to happen and when it was happening?" Humanity dies gradually when evil happens, and we do nothing. As Wole Soyinka's prison memoir aptly states: "The man dies in all who keep silent in the face of tyranny."[6] If we are gifted with the ability to forgive, even God, and make sense of life again after a ruinous past, then we can ensure that the same past does not repeat itself. As Kristiaan Depoortere argues, "love is challenged by suffering and suffering challenges love."[7] Evil shifts us from our over-confidence in God's omnipotence to attitudes of humility and realism that are consistent with this book's ethical position. Hence, the second part of Depoortere's words confronts us with our task of co-creatorship and the call to justice in love-as-friendship. This task asks humans to enter a "'pathic' moment"—the moment we have "the courage to be afraid,"[8] when we are no longer blind or indifferent to suffering. Rather, we allow the suffering to enter into real life—with all its unpredictable ripple effects. If only we spend as much ink and time in asking not just "What is God doing about this horrible situation of evil?" but "What are we doing about this evil that is eating the humanity in us away?" We should be more worried about what we are doing or not doing than what God is doing or not.

Humans are not privy to what God is doing at any material point in time. Anything we say about what God is doing is conjecture or calculated guesswork, even if often laden with faith. On the contrary, what stakeholders are doing or should do is important, especially in sub-Saharan African contexts like Nigeria, where God is most often seen as one that has the magic wand that stirs the pool. So, everybody huddles around the pool waiting for the "miracle" (cf. John 5:1–9).[9] Instead of being active participants or active co-creators for a more just and fully reconciled context, most stakeholders see themselves as passive recipients of God's miraculous

---

6. Soyinka, *Man Died*, 13.

7. Depoortere, *Different God*, 71.

8. Depoortere, *Different God*, 99.

9. See Leonard Cohen's "Waiting for the Miracle," https://www.youtube.com/watch?v=LXvGoSMP7tw

interventions. So, they keep "waiting for the miracle to come" for a renewed creation from the ashes of their ruinous past.

This is quite inappropriate about the religious response to evil in Nigeria, like lots of countries in sub-Saharan Africa. Almost everything is left at God's doorsteps and people just go around looking up unto the heavens from where help shall come (cf. Ps 121). Religious charlatans among the people are very adept at relieving people of their human vocation to be up and about doing something about the evil in the world. For instance, Daniel Smith, in his seminal anthropological exposé on corruption in Nigeria, attests that the domestication of morality in Nigeria especially, though not exclusively, by the new generation churches detracts people from paying attention to the social origins and structures of sins in Nigeria. Hence, this moralistic predilection does little in members to engender actions for social engagement and transformation.[10] Instead, the people, believing strongly in God's omnipotence, spend a lot of their waking moments and moments of fantasy to dream up the spectacular miracle that will counter the evils of sectarian violence and impunity, vindicate the victims, and soothe their physical and emotional pains. It does not work that way, as Harold Ellens offers—we have a caring obligation towards victims just as God has his obligations. If we do not work towards reconciliation, God will not force his way down: "if we do not reach beyond the alienations and transcend the terror of terrorists, God cannot save us."[11]

Accordingly, solidarity with those suffering because of evil and fundamental resistance (like Jesus) is the right attitude that we ought to express. This is a service (or ministry) to sufferers that fuses theory, praxis, and experience, or even has priority of praxis over theory, or sermonizing. This is similar to what some refer to as mercy as economics. This is the ethical responsibility that sees its pure and good intentions expressed not just in good words, but in visible economic assistance, by using our socio-scientific, technological, and fiduciary resources for the other in need.[12] If the other is tangible and the suffering is tangible, the humanitarian assistance that is meaningful and helpful must be tangible and effective in its tangibility. This response to evil is something that we can learn about what the Bible attempts to say on God's response to evil.

Heb 12:2–4 is an example: "looking to Jesus the pioneer and perfecter of our faith. . . . Consider him who endured from sinners such hostility against himself, so that you may not grow weary or fainthearted. *In your struggle*

---

10. Smith, *Culture of Corruption*, 207–20.
11. Ellens, "Revenge, Justice, and Hope," 234–35.
12. See Burggraeve, *Wisdom of Love*, ch. 4; Burggraeve, "Good," 88–89.

against sin, you have not yet resisted evil to the point of shedding your blood" (NRSV, emphasis mine). God, then, in and through Jesus's death on the cross, shows us what he is doing; and it is not palatable: God resists evil even if the evil (apparently) subdues him. God prefers to resist evil even if at a very costly price. It is preferable to do this than to be contaminated by evil and let evil become God's communion partner. On this point, I will concede to N. T. Wright. From Genesis (after the fall), the Scripture is an account of the "messy way in which God has had to work to bring the world out of the mess."[13] God faced the question "Where was/is God?" Jesus answered that question, not by explaining it but by living it.[14] Given the affirmations above about the decisive role humans have to play for God to realize God's ethically just intentions for creation, the following subsection offers a rereading of divine omnipotence in the light of the dipolar theism above that takes evil seriously, yet does not give it the final word. The bottom line is that evil, no matter how brutal, cannot change God's decisive intention for the world.

God Is Not Fetishly Omnipotent, but Compelling

Earlier, we referred to Heb 12:2–4 as a text from which we can glean what God is doing about evil in the world. Beyond that, or in addition to it, I wish to suggest also that the same passage (amongst many others) puts forward the following thesis: *The God of the Bible is not a "fetish,"*[15] *omnipotent and almighty God who does anything without us.* On the contrary, based on the dialectics between God, creation, and humans as created co-creators, *God is a compelling God.* This God, who is the *Holy One*, created humans as distinct like the rest of creation. Through and with their distinction and separation from him, humans can become committed to God as partners in an established covenantal relationship. A paradox, therefore, confronts us: the "heteronomous autonomy" of human beings.[16]

Heteronomy evokes the status of creaturehood as given, while autonomy evokes the reality of creaturehood as a gift human beings own. Yet, this gift precedes the exercise of freedom. Hence, love as a gift precedes the response of love. Nonetheless, the response of love is possible because God the creator gives us the space to be human to respond to this particular gift of love. So, the response of love (by humans) to the gift of love (from God) by

---

13. Wright, *Evil*, 58–59.
14. Depoortere, *Different God*, 48.
15. This means a particular patriarchal image of God: "a male God who controls everything." Dombrowski, *Not Even a Sparrow*, 78.
16. Cf. Burggraeve, "Conversational God," 345–46.

being at the service of love in and through creation reveals something about God. God is in retreat—an act of *anachoresis*, i.e., "the withdrawal, or also the kenosis or self-emptying of the Holy One. 'The marvelous contraction of the Infinite One... the Infinite in the finite.'"[17] Thus, a God whose powerful love gives such latitude is still worth praying to, worth thanking, and above all worth responding to his compelling wooing love, even if one questions, and might even dare forgive, such God for dashed expectations.

The concepts of compelling God and co-creatorship are pertinent to tackle what up till now has been implicitly referred to but not named: the heresy of a kind of docetism. It is the heresy that does not see God getting messy and getting messed up in the dirty affairs of the world. God is really above that mess, very majestic. So, that is also the response of the church. The church, paraphrasing Max Weber, should not get its hands muddled in dirty politics. Ecclesial actions in transitional societies must always avoid this Docetism.

A Compelling God and Ecclesial Mission Today

If the compelling God and human co-creatorship contest a Docetist outlook among Christians, especially in public projects responding to the tears and groans of victims, there was bound to be tension, especially in Roman Catholic magisterial discourse, on what constitutes ecclesial mission: justice or charity? While the Synod of Bishops in 1971 affirmed that justice is constitutive of the church's mission of proclamation of humanity's redemption from oppressive situations,[18] Pope Paul VI, in his *Evangelii Nuntiandi*, seems to repudiate this by declaring that evangelization (though with variegated elements) is constitutive of the church's mission.[19] Hence, justice (or development as Pope Paul VI prefers) becomes just one of the elements.[20] This seems to be the tendency in the church's magisterial position today. The implication, therefore, is that justice is not seen to be at the heart of Christian proclamation (i.e., an activity that the church must engage in beyond supplying moral imagination for justice). So, justice is like a value added. It seems, to gloss over the tension in magisterial documents, the *Compendium of the Social Doctrine of the Church* does not include synods of bishops among the sources of the church's social doctrine, even if it includes Roman

---

17. Burggraeve, "To Love 'Other-Wise,'" 10–11.
18. Cf. Synod of Bishops, "Justice in the World," nos 6, 35, 36.
19. Paul VI, "*Evangelii Nuntiandi*," no. 14.
20. Cf. Paul VI, "*Evangelii nuntiandi*," no. 24.

congregations (see "Index of References").²¹ Accordingly, we get the impression that justice is not at the heart of the church's mission. The church sees justice as an instrument of evangelization.²²

This phrase—"justice as an instrument of evangelization"—is problematic because it appears theologically misleading. An object considered as an instrument is extrinsic, not intrinsic, to revelation. In other words, the end sought (evangelization of peoples) will still be achieved even in the absence of this particular instrument, which can be regarded as merely circumstantial. On the contrary, instead of being an instrument, justice is the matrix where the subject of revelation unfolds in the world outside the church's liturgy. It is in the church's praxis of justice and love that the Christ of its evangelization is revealed to people outside the church. Concretely, the church cannot make justice extrinsic to its evangelization projects. It is intrinsic to it since it is constitutive of an equilibrated Christian identity that Gregory of Nyssa writes about in one of his treatises on "Christian Perfection":²³ "There are three things which characterize the life of a Christian, action, speech, thought. . . . After thinking comes speech, which reveals in words the idea which has been conceived in the mind. After thought and speech in the third place comes action which realizes the thought in deed."²⁴ Through this equilibrated Christian identity, Gregory continues, the church can share "in all the titles used to describe Christ, in soul, in word, and in the habits of our daily life, so as to reveal the name of Christ."²⁵ Louis-Marie Chauvet similarly affirms in his *Symbol and Sacrament* that this balanced Christian identity can be represented as the body endowed with the power of cognition (the Head). This body corporately recognizes the gratuitous gift of God and celebrates it (the Heart); then it moves to act out its gratitude in the world (the Hands).²⁶

Despite some patristic accents and contemporary development in the theological understanding of Christian identity, Pope Benedict XVI's *Deus Caritas Est* confirms the disproportionality between justice and charity. It affirms that charity, not justice, is constitutive of the church's mission. Justice is for the state and lay members of the church involved in the political

---

21. Cf. Aina, "Catholic Theology," 92.

22. Cf. Pontifical Council for Justice and Peace, *Compendium*, esp. nos 60–86; cf. nos. 67–68.

23. Saint Gregory of Nyssa, "On Christian Perfection," 224–25.

24. Saint Gregory of Nyssa, "On Christian Perfection," 224–25.

25. Saint Gregory of Nyssa, "On Christian Perfection," 224–25.

26. Chauvet, *Symbol and Sacrament*, 170–82, esp. 178–80.

plane.[27] The job of the church, therefore, will seem to be supplying motivation on how the world can build justice. Consequently, the church is not ethically obliged to take ecclesial/institutional action (e.g., to seek redress, or take initiative to seek redress) on behalf of justice for oppressed peoples and persons. The task of the church, according to the *Compendium*, is to teach and "announce moral principles" and "to make judgments" needed for human development.[28] In *Caritas in Veritate*,[29] Benedict XVI continues this trend by offering the theological position that informs his contribution in his encyclical: "Charity is at the heart of the Church's social doctrine.... It gives real substance to the personal relationship with God and with neighbour; it is the principle not only of micro-relationships ... but also of macro-relationships.... Love is God's greatest gift of humanity, it is his promise and our hope."[30] This charity, nevertheless, is not an expression of mere sentimentality. Accordingly, truth defines the charity *Caritas in Veritate* expounds: "Truth is the light that gives meaning and value to charity."[31] This is informed by the personal dimension of biblical faith in God. It is bipolar: "Charity and Truth, Love and Word."[32] 'Gratuitousness' and 'grace' characterize this charity.[33] This understanding of the nature of biblical charity gives character to the mission of the Catholic Church in the polis: it is the "proclamation of the truth of Christ's love in society."[34] This ecclesial mission is a service to charity.[35] By emphasizing truth giving meaning to charity, Benedict XVI follows the position of the *Compendium* that ecclesial mission is to proclaim enduring truths in charity in the world so that authentic human development will blossom.

The pontificate of Pope Francis seems to echo strongly the position of the 1971 Synod of Bishops regarding the place of justice, especially advocacy, in ecclesial mission. According to Pope Francis, the Christian mission cannot remain silent in the face of politics and economics of exclusion, "inequality and lack of integral human development."[36] So, for the pontiff, peace, the friendship of the *anawim* of the land, and the preferential option

27. Cf. Benedict XVI, "*Deus Caritas Est*," nos. 28–29.
28. Cf. Benedict XVI, *Deus Caritas Est*, nos. 69–71.
29. Benedict XVI, *Caritas in Veritate*.
30. Benedict XVI, *Caritas in Veritate*, no. 2.
31. Benedict XVI, *Caritas in Veritate*, no. 3.
32. Benedict XVI, *Caritas in Veritate*, no. 3.
33. Benedict XVI, *Caritas in Veritate*, no. 5.
34. Benedict XVI, *Caritas in Veritate*, no. 5.
35. Benedict XVI, *Caritas in Veritate*, no. 5.
36. Francis, *Fratelli Tutti*, no. 235.

for the poor are the starting blocks for sustainable peace. Seeking and promoting consensus in the land is not always the best strategy for peace in the land. Advocacy for the sake of "the least of our brothers and sisters"[37] is part of the Christian response for sustainable peacebuilding.

The current magisterial position takes seriously the fact that the church cannot remain indifferent to the sufferings of the people. This is an ethical responsibility for which it must act in response to the command: love thy neighbor (cf. Luke 10:30–37). The church has this ethical responsibility even if it is not at fault. If the church indeed is the body of Christ, it presupposes, therefore, that the church can be touched, i.e., it is corporeal in the sense that it has a heart of flesh, which is sensitive (capable of being emotionally touched) and vulnerable (having the capacity to be converted from its self-absorption). This can be unpleasant because it can push the church out of its comfort zone, beyond its knee-jerk reactions—ranging from sending relief materials to making promises of/contributing money to the aid agencies that are committed to alleviating suffering and miseries. Nonetheless, when the spirit of the body (of Christ) is poked and touched spiritually, thus giving rise to concrete ecclesial responses to victims who are suffering physically, psychologically, socially, and spiritually, then the church can be considered ethical. When the church becomes involved in the suffering of the Other then we become ethically responsible beings, who heed the command: "Thou shall not kill." It is a command and a vocational call to "non-self-evident altruism."[38]

Therefore, and agreeing with Max Weber, one can affirm that the courageous Christian is one "who is not afraid to get his or her hands dirty."[39] God resists evil in the messy world of human beings to the point of being messed up. Why should the church and Christians be any different? The cross of Jesus faces us every time with the judgment that evil is serious. We must take evil seriously and do serious things about it, not in churches and revival grounds alone; not just through documents churned out in large volumes and conferences far removed from actual sufferers; but in the messy world of aching victims, of self-deceived perpetrators, of justice-seeking to create peace. This is why the cross and the many other biblical stories create for us what Reimund Bieringer (and Mary Elsbernd) refer to as the "normativity of the future": a dialogical and future-oriented hermeneutic, which steers human history towards its final goal. This normativity compels

---

37. Francis, *Fratelli Tutti*, no. 235.
38. Burggraeve, "Conversational God," 344–46.
39. See Verstraeten, "Tension Between," 182, 183.

human beings with their co-creatorship responsibility to participate in visions and acts that liberate, heal, (re)create, and transform.[40]

This point is crucial if we shall overcome a principal curse (*impunity*) that negates justice and works against peace in Africa, more so in Nigeria; and we can bring soothing relief to people stuck with toxic emotions for decades on end. The impunity that causes social harm is not related to war or mass violence alone. It also includes corrupt practices influenced by patrimonial predilections and the state's complicity in corporate crimes. The church in such societies must face up to these, in proactive engagement. It must not just be contented with giving proclamations of enduring truths for authentic human development, or else the church faces a harsh judgment of history in future. In the opinion of John Waliggo, a few years before the shame of the Rwandan genocide: "The future of the Christian Church will be slippery if Christianity fails the African people in the hour of their dire need. The future generation will want to know where the Church was when people were suffering; what message was given to bring hope, challenge, reprimand."[41]

If one uses Nigeria and South Africa, the two regional powers in Africa that have featured prominently in this book, as case studies for an appropriate ecclesial mission, at least in sub-Saharan Africa today, one might appreciate that reconciliation is a preferred mission in the face of untold horrors and tears in Africa. This mission of reconciliation seeks justice, makes and builds peace, heals people's memories, and rebuilds the societies fractured by violence and distrust.[42]

The Church in Nigeria: Learning from Europe's Deprivatization

Religious actors do not need to be apologetic and defensive on the valorization of religion in the modern state. One takes inspiration from the purposes of the three occurrences of deprivatization mentioned in chapter 3. There are many contexts, especially transitional societies, in need of the active involvement of religion in building authentically democratic states. Accordingly, the church in transitional societies will have to revisit its mission and role because the sins of the past are not past: they are still manifesting themselves today. Hence, seeking transformation in liberation is a

40. For a comprehensive reader on "normativity of the future," see Bieringer and Elsbernd, *Normativity of the Future*.
41. Waliggo, "Making a Church," 24.
42. I have extensively argued this elsewhere. See Aina, "Mission," 218–65.

fundamental *telos* in ecclesial mission, and Christian ethics by implication, in transitional societies. In the following pages, I shall be outlining some proposals on how the Catholic Church in Nigeria, for instance, can face up to the issues bordering on justice, restorative peacebuilding, reconciliation and human flourishing for God's people. The suggestions are pointers on how the Catholic Church in Nigeria can concretize what it is wrestling with. In this regard, one should commend the Catholic Laity Council of Nigeria for devoting its annual conference at the beginning of the millennium to the role of the church in national reconciliation.[43]

Mission and task in the modern state, where there is "the universalism of suffering,"[44] are decisive to the church's self-understanding today. Suffered evil and attendant toxic emotions, like the ones recurring in this book, are realities confronting the Catholic Church in Nigeria and its theology. Hence, its responses must go beyond logic and hope to proactive engagements as a crucial member of the civil society. If the church sees itself, in a political space like Nigeria, more aligned with its peoples wrestling with issues related to delayed nationhood, and less aligned with the state, then the church must respond to the biblical call to be "co-creators." Being a co-creator implies molding to bring about a creation that continues to radiate the goodness that was present at the primordial creation. Hence, the church must clear the landscape first as part of its co-creation. Accordingly, the church will have to excavate the ties and economic conditions in contexts like Nigeria to discover the underlying social and human psychologies that make people so susceptible to manipulation of their primordial ties or their economic conditions (e.g., prebendalism, patrimonialism, class struggle, methodological individualism, and identity markers for bonding trust).[45] Furthermore, unearthing especially these human psychologies should probably unravel why people persist to give in to manipulations when they already know that opportunists are simply manipulating them. Understanding the values and rationality behind atrocious acts of otherwise normal people is part of the task of a redeeming co-creation that shows ethical resistance to such acts. Accordingly, in confronting the past, we must attend to the role of emotions. What follows might help to deal imaginatively and proactively with these emotions, their sources and their effects.

---

43. See Awan et al., *Jubilee Celebration*.
44. Metz, "Toward a Christianity," 252, 253.
45. Cf. Aina, "Religion," 336–46.

Overcoming Toxic Emotions and Restorative Peacebuilding: The Church as a Locus

In chapter 1, I referred to prophetic witnesses in transitional societies needed to foster a climate of loving justice and rebuilt trust. Such prophetic witnesses, especially religious communities as vital members of the civil society, can create situations or a *habitus*, which can make people empower themselves and come to terms with their past and its pains. This will enable them to decide to move forward such that the painful and hateful past will no longer be the epicenter of their lives and identities. For the Catholic Church in Nigeria, this is constitutive of the ministry of reconciliation, and the message of reconciliation entrusted to it (1 Cor 5:16–20).

Hugh McCullum reminds us,

> The concern for justice must permeate every action by churches; and justice involves looking at the murky political issues which cause massacres and refugee exoduses and denouncing injustice without taking partisan positions. It seems in the case of Rwanda the de-politicized emergency aid is easier than long-range initiatives for justice, peace and reconciliation.[46]

Yet, as Elias Opongo agreeably argues, the ambulance approach is no longer suitable for responsible institutions committed to peacebuilding.[47] So, part of the proactive engagements in a nation like Nigeria marred by evil is to make the ecumenical community the locus of justice and reconciliation (and forgiveness). The ecumenical community in Nigeria ought to create havens for survivors who want to venture out of their closets of imposed toxic emotions to share their stories as the beginning of the healing of bad memories. This led to an earlier proposal for an ecumenical summit for national reconciliation in Nigeria.[48] In a divided country yet in grave need of reconciliation, this proposal "might be a graced event that can bring together all the Christian denominations and their experts in the various fields and sectors concerned about helping Nigeria move beyond the ever-present 'toxic emotions' of its citizens."[49]

This is one way the ecumenical community in Nigeria, united in the crucified yet risen Christ, can fan alive once again the flickering flame of hope "'even in the gravest moral crises.'"[50] This is necessary because empirical/

---

46. Cf. McCullum, *Angels Have Left*, 44.
47. Cf. Opongo, *Making Choices*, 54–60.
48. Aina, "Ecumenical Cooperation," 65–69.
49. Aina, "Ecumenical Cooperation," 65.
50. Cahill, "Goods for Whom?," 211.

mechanist institutions and structures working for peace do not easily pay attention to irrational factors for peace or violence. This is clear with regards to Nigeria as presented in chapter 1. From previous chapters, one realizes also that some of these factors (e.g., getting people to overcome hatred and fear, taking responsibility for an irresponsible past, and forgiveness) are matters of the heart, imagination, and spirituality. What Mark Amstutz states on post-genocide Rwanda is apt for Nigeria, South Africa, and several transitional societies.[51] As long as "distrust and fear dominate ethnic relations, the consolidation of constitutional government and the development of the national economy will not be possible."[52] Christianity in Nigeria is eminently qualified to act in the best way in overcoming these irrational factors. Like all authentic religions, Christianity is there to help us unlearn the mimesis of violence, and learn that of nonviolence. It takes inspiration from Jesus, whose commitment to universal restoration, and reconciliation, led to the creation of a new worldview and new ethic—an ethic of being.

The rebuilding of a broken world is as much a material effort as it is an intensely interpersonal, communitarian, and spiritual effort. For many people, this is what peace entails after any form of disaster. Peace is a journey, starting from the interior of the persons involved, but destined towards a recreation of the chaotic space aided by justice contributing to processive reconciliation. Yet again, we are reminded that for $K = (a + d = e)$ to become possible in Nigeria, the heart is indispensable. It is about time Christians in Nigeria worked in the messy world of God and humans to help all cultivate empathetic hearts for peace, justice, and reconciliation. Justice towards reconciliation does not necessarily depend on retributive punishment, and not even truth commissions. There is the assertion that the movement towards higher ground includes the transethical, like forgiveness. The higher ground does not even depend unconditionally on reparative justice.

Time and again we are reminded that retributive punishment—even in very strict and stark manifestations—does not serve as deterrence. The adoption of the "Convention on the Prevention and Punishment of the Crime of Genocide (Paris; 09.12.1948)"[53] has not stemmed mass murders, genocide and crimes against humanity: "stricter international and domestic laws cannot change the morality of people."[54] Instead, the underlying social causes have to be proactively addressed. Lee Earl gives a succinct description of what he sees to be the mission of the church—a mission of

---

51. Amstutz, "Is Reconciliation Possible?," 541–65.
52. Amstutz, "Is Reconciliation Possible?," 564.
53. See Suy, *Corpus Iuris Gentium*, 426–28.
54. Vorster, "Preventing Genocide," 394.

restoration, not only about development: "The Church must be about the business of community restoration prior to community development.... Communities can have significant impact on crime, and the church has the power to be a key player and motivator behind the community."[55] Accordingly, the church, which has strong mediating roles in fractured societies like Nigeria and South Africa, with other social institutions must complement themselves to see to the positive change in people's morality, to "create a moral-cultural foundation that honors human rights."[56] They will have to play a major role in reforming values and attitudes. This ultimately helps the traumatized and disconnected societies to transcend irrational factors that fueled past acrimonious life.

So, a National Ecumenical Summit on Justice and Peace might afford the ecumenical community in Nigeria to walk, work, and breathe together on issues of justice and peace, and the rebuilding of trust. It might contribute equally towards proactively punctuating the spiral of toxic emotions in the country.

Overcoming Toxic Memories and HRVIC'S Report

Specifically, the Catholic Church in Nigeria has to decisively face the culture of impunity in the country. This subsection offers another suggestion that the Catholic Church in Nigeria, in particular, might find useful in doing this. Continued lack of interest in the HRVIC's *Report*,[57] especially by the church, is giving supremacy to the Nigerian state. It seems the state is more interested in its status and defending the interests of its patrons and godfathers/mothers over a project (the HRVIC) that carried such great legitimacy in the eyes of Nigerians. The HRVIC is even more legitimate than South Africa's Truth and Reconciliation Commission, which did not have such widespread legitimacy among South African peoples then or now.

Civil societies as voluntary bodies in the public working beyond the control of the state for the common good will have to take this lack of interest serious. Since the church is a valued member of the civil society, its proclamation, theology, and mission will have to take this to heart also. Against the backdrop of the theological ethical positions laid out thus far, "being response-able" is a principle of action incumbent upon the Catholic Church in Nigeria in creating alternative imaginations. These imaginations envision "new and better ways of conceiving those everyday struggles and

55. Earl, "Spiritual Problem," 245.
56. Amstutz, "Is Reconciliation Possible?," 560, 564.
57. Kukah, *Witness to Justice*, xviii–xix.

aspirations which lie at the basis of a people's social existence."[58] We can achieve the alternative imagination through a methodological approach called "the network of representation of life stories," which explores the "boundaries of narratives."[59]

Accordingly, creating, developing and teaching this methodological approach is an area that the church can be helpful. The church, because of its nature as an anamnetic community, can significantly contribute towards exploring those boundaries of narratives in the country, precisely because those boundaries have held many persons, peoples and even the nation hostage for close to six decades. This proposal echoes Miroslav Volf's call for the purification of memory in a way that the memory of the past does not keep today and the future hostage.[60] The significant difference is that Nigeria is already held hostage by its peoples' varied toxic memories. Due to the hostage situation, I agree with the WCC's resource book on churches' ministry of reconciliation in situations of violent conflicts. WCC states that the church has a pivotal role in overcoming toxic emotions seeping out through prejudicial stereotypes that fuel the politicization of victimhood.[61]

Giving space for traumatized survivors and survivor communities to reconfigure their narratives of selfhood might be one of the ways the church can help to subvert these myths. It is through the narrative of pain that humans begin the movement from disorganization to reorganization. The successful movement from disorganization to reorganization brings renewal of persons, equally contributing to the social capital. This movement reveals an interpersonal, and ritual-like, private/public process in the human community where victims are present. We can appreciate hence that the church at the service of reconciliation in transitional societies needs to explore the interface between love (the logic of superabundance) and justice (the logic of equivalence). Accordingly, the Catholic Church in Nigeria has some things to learn from Paul Ricœur. For instance, Ricœur's pardon-return metaphor offers the symbolism of redemption at the micro-level, while his metaphor of mourning offers a symbolism of redemption or transformation both at the micro and macro levels. Ricœur regards "work of memory and work of mourning" as human labors seeking to work through the past as it struggles for reconciliation after the "loss of objects of love"—at various

---

58. Katongole, "Violence and Social Imagination," 163.
59. Smith, "Narrative Boundaries," 22–23.
60. Cf. Volf, "Difference, Violence, and Memory," 10–11.
61. World Council of Churches, *Participating in God's Mission*, no. 85.

levels and fora.⁶² Ricœur's metaphors can inspire peacebuilding projects by the church or supported by the church at various levels.

The genius of Ricœur's metaphor is that it recognizes the power of memory, and the intricate link between memory and toxic emotions: *toxic emotions keep memories alive; memories reinforce/validate toxic emotions as long as the memories remain untransformed.*⁶³ Nevertheless, Ricœur's metaphor recognizes that there are contending memories at different levels. Hence, we have to engage these collectively and at various levels. This implies that the work of memory and mourning is not a punctual event; it is processive. The church will have to envision a viable framework that can help in overcoming toxic emotions at the micro-level and at the structural/systemic level. This will be a massive contribution towards redressing what Michael Ignatieff suggests as the massive moral weakness of contemporary life: it is "not, as some people think, a general lack of moral principles, but on the contrary, indignant moral posturing by people too lazy to think through the consequences of strong emotions."⁶⁴

The following offers what a work of reconciliation aims at doing, from the perspective of Ricœur's mimetic arc.⁶⁵

---

62. Ricœur, "Memory and Forgetting," 6–7.

63. Ricœur, "Difficulty to Forgive," 14–16.

64. Ignatief, "Imprisonment and the Need," 98.

65. For a typical Ricœur's mimetic arc see for instance Duffy, *Paul Ricoeur's Pedagogy*, 121.

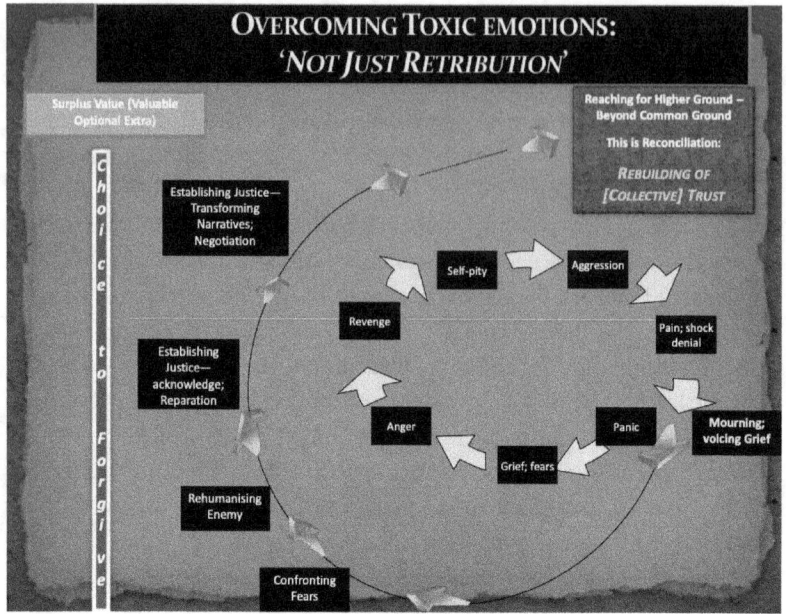

Adapted from Botcharova[66]

The church, due to its anamnetic nature (with various rituals of *remembering* and healing), in principle offers possibilities for this work of memory and mourning at various levels. At a base level, people can have rituals of memory encounter and transformation. These rituals will have significant movements: from mourning and confronting fears, with empathy, to an acknowledgement of truth from divided sides, and even possibly symbolic or real reparation. While this is going on, some magisterial/interventionist religious actors can equally be cooperating at the higher level for a similar trajectory between representatives of divided communities to the point of having strategic policy changes along the following lines:[67]

i. Agreement to abandon rhetoric for various audiences that keep up inherited mentalities fueling distrust;

ii. dominant groups agreeing to make short-term sacrifices (either out of altruism or self-interest), while all the groups, especially the minority and marginal ones, make concerted efforts to rein in their extremists and closed in revolutionaries;

---

66. Botcharova, "Implementation of Track Two," 298.
67. Cf. Rothstein, "Fragile Peace," 244.

iii. creating space for apologies for past transgressions against inter-group relationships;

iv. engaging creatively with the issue of punishment and redress in a way that helps to reduce animosity and intransigence;

v. Creating an economic blueprint that balances efficiency and equity, even with the possibility of sacrificing efficiency in the short term, so that expectations are well-managed without dangerous disillusionment in the long run as it appears to be in post-TRC South Africa.

However, due to the simultaneity of the process at the base and the Track I levels, parties at Track I level may lose sight of what those that will normally be marginalized are saying. Since the system does not see the tears of persons, but religion does, the church's contributions at the base levels through its rituals and processes can help bring these blinding tears for justice to the public. What I am suggesting here is not simply an act of charity. The movements are helping the cause of loving justice so that enduring peace might come and people might someday enter into reconciliation. According to our previous interpretation of Ricœur's pedagogy of reconciliation in the secular society, love is distinct from justice though interrelated and contributing critically to justice: "Love does not turn into justice, but does appear to be capable of transforming the *sense of justice* that lays at the basis of systems of justice."[68] Love thus educates the principles of justice for the sake of "social reconciliation" which is "the re-construction of the 'moral order.'"[69]

This complex proposal coming from the metaphor of *labor of memory and mourning* is sensitive to reconciliation. In transitional societies where cruel pasts have divided communities and groups, reconciliation is impossible without loving justice both at the micro and structural levels. I premise this caveat on what reconciliation means as chapter 5 offered. Reconciliation is not necessarily a warm feeling towards the other. So, rebuilding of bridging trust is a definition of reconciliation that can stand the test of interpersonal demands of relationships as well as inter-communal/inter-group (racial; ethnic; gender; religious) demands of relationships within the same geographical space. The web of relationships below shows the implication. The web shows the various levels of relationships violent conflicts affect, and how they all need to be worked on in double movements; thus the double-edged arrows.

---

68. Duffy, *Paul Ricoeur's Pedagogy*, 115 (emphasis original).
69. Duffy, *Paul Ricoeur's Pedagogy*, 114.

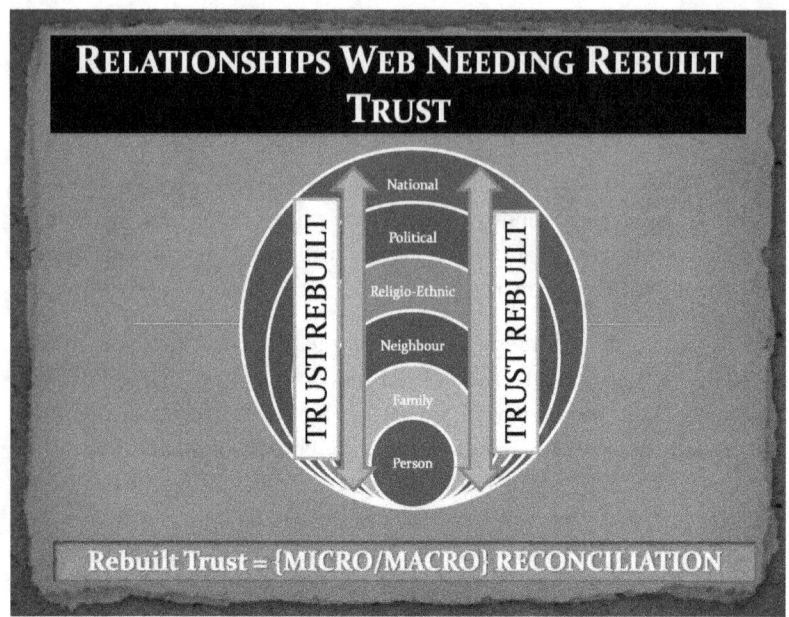

Courtesy of the Author

If we take the caveat and relationship web offered above to heart, then the Catholic Church in Nigeria will recognize that it has a strategic role to play in overcoming toxic emotions in that country. To play this role effectively, the Catholic Church in Nigeria has to confront itself with the same question that Chris Cunneen asks advocates of restorative justice: *"how do we respond to both recent (and not so recent) systematic, fundamental and large-scale abuses of human rights perpetrated and often legitimated by modern states?"*[70] When victims/citizens suffer due to the criminality of the faceless, how does the church respond to the need for culpability, responsibility, and reparation? We must face these questions because of some paradoxical responses from the modern state. Responses after mass violence, especially concerning accountability under the rule of law, vary depending on the particular contexts. There are places where the political institution is willing and able to confront impunity (e.g., South Africa; Namibia), while some other places are willing but not able (Rwanda). The third response is able but not willing (El Salvador; Nigeria); and the fourth is not able and not willing (Haiti).[71]

---

70. See Cunneen, "Exploring the Relationship," 356 (emphasis mine).

71. I have adapted this from Mani's *Beyond Retribution*. Mani presents the grid to reiterate that just as there are different contextual situations after conflicts, stakeholders should have different contextual responses. Yet, she offers, the international community

Given that most countries in Africa fall within the second and third categories, it is pertinent for the church to seriously consider how it can respond to the culture of impunity that is implied in these categories. Some nations face some difficulties that make some of their political leaders adopt the responses noted above. Hence, the church can concretize the hope it preaches in some contexts where political leaders have adopted some responses that border on impunity. The church has done this in some places. For instance, the Roman Catholic Church established Guatemala's "Project for the Recovery of Historical Memory" because the Guatemalan political leaders were able but not willing to embark upon the journey towards recovery through truth-building.[72] By inference, therefore, the Catholic Church in Nigeria has a critical role to play towards justice, peace, and reconciliation, not just by platitudes and palliative care, but by actions, especially as Nigerians are faced with the culture of impunity fueling conflicts and sectarian violence in Nigeria (the widespread violence in the Niger-Delta region, the southeast zone, and ethnic violence in Northern Nigeria are relevant pointers).

Nigerian citizens look up to the church (within the civil society) to provide inspiration and imagination on ways to confront the culture of impunity through similar projects like Guatemala's "Project for the Recovery of Historical Memory"; the Horn of Africa's "IGAD" initiative that includes middle-level actors of the civil society like churches and NGOs.[73] Some required steps towards reconciliation do not necessarily need a state mandate. These include relinquishing old inherited mentalities that keep peoples apart in distrust, or creating multilateral initiatives across divided groups to generate cooperation and familial spirit, or stemming the tide of historical revisionism through critical engagement with respective collective memories living on in peoples' minds. Admirably, without waiting for the state's mandate, the Catholic Secretariat of Nigeria in collaboration with The Kukah Center kick-started a national conversation some years ago of the kind of network of representation of life stories that I referred to earlier. They even documented this conversation.[74] Unfortunately, the CSN did not step this process down to the base levels for more impact. So, we cannot evaluate the medium and long-term impact of this admirable initiative.

---

still opts for "one cap fits all" response to all situations. However, "a one-size-fits-all approach is unlikely either to regain public confidence, or restore the rule of law." See Mani, *Beyond Retribution*, 70–76, quotation on 76.

72. Shriver, "Repairing the Past," 216.

73. On these, see Appleby, *Ambivalence*; Lederach, *Building Peace*, 153–61; Schreiter, "Peace-Building," 51–56.

74. Omonokhua et al., *Peace and Reconciliation*.

Yet, the church is specially placed to make these conversations happen. Given this, in addition to offering traumatized persons, peoples, and communities the space to begin their journeys from disorganization to reorganization, the kind of havens I referred to earlier can offer the opportunity to reflect and pray together about the narratives of Nigeria's past as contained in *The Report*. This opportunity can be a salutary way to begin to make sense out of and come to terms with the forthright reflections and conclusions *The Report* provides. This can be a modest contribution of the church towards Nigeria becoming a nation, beyond being a nation space. The various base Christian communities, which, hopefully, will embrace Nigerians of various denominations, are most suitable for these grassroots engagements. Whatever the outcome and conclusions of these base-informed engagements are can be published as a report on what significant sections of Nigerians say about *The Report* and persons and institutions mentioned therein. The report of the church-inspired civil society's Justice Project should be made public as one of the first steps towards a reconfigured national/regional shared narratives. I have been inspired by a similar trajectory the South African Catholic Bishops' Conference adopted when it decided to assess race relations in the church a decade after apartheid. After various levels of discussions, reflections, and para-liturgical ceremonies, the findings were published as a report on the state of the Roman Catholic Church in post-Apartheid South Africa as of 2005.[75]

Due to the circumstances surrounding *The Report*, some figured perpetrators may not be prosecuted in the nearest future. This should not dampen spirits because there are more pressing things to do as one can appreciate so far in this book. So, the hunt for such perpetrators should not override the complex justice process this book favors. As expressly stated at the beginning of this chapter, "processing for penality"[76] is just one aspect of the demands of justice in transitional societies. Processing for penality is not the most decisive. The most decisive issues include the reconfiguration of narratives at the personal, interpersonal, and (inter) national levels. Do Nigerians necessarily need perpetrators in the dock before they can begin their reconfiguration? Probably not, because as demonstrated in chapter 1, when affected Nigerians cannot get their perpetrators, they get trapped in their victimhood.

So, the care of traumatized survivors is a more pressing issue. To prove that victims are dignified and cared for even without the presence of the perpetrators, the church, or the civil society, strives to fulfill this more pressing

---

75. See SACBC Justice and Peace Department, *Race Relations*.
76. Findlay and Henham, *Transforming International*, 313.

obligation due to political leaders' unwillingness or inability. In the meantime, the church and non-state actors for justice and peace will make it clear to perpetrators that the prosecution truce is limited, and the unwillingness and inability of the state are not going to last eternally. The perpetrators can use the time of grace to embark upon their process of self-redemption and reintegration because, at the end of the truce, they shall face retributive justice. Yes, one should pay attention again to Ricœur: justice must not exclude love expressed through "consideration." Hence, justice processes must be just also. Justice should be consistent, guaranteeing "equality before the law and more attentive to the narrative identity of those who appear before it."[77]

However, the space for the prosecution of unrepentant perpetrators is proof of their inconsideration to be part of the post-conflict reconfigured political space. Therefore, if they are found guilty, they cannot be part of that space. As noted earlier, prosecution alone cannot bring the kind of reconciliation we construe for Nigeria. Elicitive peace education is equally crucial for Nigeria. Again, the Catholic Church in Nigeria has a pivotal role to play.

GST 222: Peace and Conflict Resolution Studies

Many peacebuilders focus on the role of education in reconciliation talk and culture due to the veracity of the cliché, "children live what they learn." There is a need for educating for peace. In the words of Saint James, "Those conflicts and disputes among you, where do they come from? Do they not come from your cravings that are at war within you? You want something and do not have it; so you commit murder. And you covet something and cannot obtain it; so you engage in disputes and conflicts. You do not have, because you do not ask" (Jas 4:1–2, NRSV). Wars begin in the human mind and heart. It is human consciousness that first needs reforms. Education, to a large extent, defines human consciousness. Consequently, it has a strategic role in creating peace (and reconciliation) in the world by educating children for coexistence through multicultural learning. This is a rewarding tool of social reconstruction in a radically pluralist society. Maaike Miedema recalls what some youths said at Geneva in November 1998 in preparation for the Hague Appeal for Peace: "Many felt that before taking a wider global perspective, we needed to first find peace in our homes, schools, and communities. It was agreed that themes of justice, tolerance and peace had to be woven into the education of children of the world, as they are the future leaders of the 21st century."[78] In a world where the dominant

---

77. Ricœur, *Memory, History, Forgetting*, 474.
78. Miedema, "Introduction," 268.

political theory of realism underpins public structures and policies including education, peace-education needs to inculcate in children that national armies, regional defense systems, and nuclear deterrence/proliferation are not reliant on building peace and reconciliation. Rather, "all citizens have to be taught to use modern conflict-resolution technologies (like mediating, empathetic listening, negotiation and bargaining) at interpersonal and inter-group levels."[79] This boils down to education for "ethics of disposition and ethics of principle" to protect them against cognitive moral confusion, which is part of the "failure of value-free education,"[80] where the young generation is just clueless about what is right and wrong in their dealings with people. Some basic moral values are important, which educators need to pass across in developing a culture of justice and peace anchored on reconciliation. We live in a moral world, and we must respect and protect it because it is fragile. The crimes against humanity in our contemporary history should, without doubt, convince one that the human conscience is feeble to confront "its inner demons."[81] Jonathan Sacks quotes Edward Shils to affirm this point in his *Politics of Hope*: "Human beings do not fare well in a disordered world. They need to live within the framework of a world in which they possess a chart.... The destruction of these cognitive, moral, metaphysical and technical charts is a step into chaos."[82]

Nigeria's National Universities Commission (NUC) has tapped into this global best practice on education for peace.[83] To proactively deal with Nigeria's poor history of violence, in 2005, the NUC mandated all tertiary institutions to include "Peace and Conflict Resolution Studies" as a General Studies course. Leveraging on this mandate, Catholic education must focus on the youth so that they can be living witnesses (salt and light) of Christ in the continent that overflows with toxic ideologies which further jeopardize the desire for justice, peace, and reconciliation (JPR). Witness ethic and spirituality are crucial to Catholic education. Human beings create and sustain cultures and systems. These human beings need role models who are artisans of JPR. These models give concrete hope that another world—of JPR—is possible in Africa. There are pedagogical challenges. First, internalizing the principles and *telos* of Catholic Education at the service of JPR demands teaching modules, tools and kits, which, for now, the Catholic Church in Africa does

---

79. Miedema, "Introduction," 270.
80. Sacks, *Politics of Hope*, 183.
81. Geffre, "God of Jesus," 75.
82. Sacks, *Politics of Hope*, 181.
83. The following paragraphs summarize a previous contribution on this subject. See Aina, "GST 222," 249–67.

not have, unlike other places. Second, Catholic Social Teaching (CST) is largely virgin territories in Catholic institutions in Africa except for major seminaries. Hence, building a curriculum at the service of JPR will take a lot of time and resources of experts who might not be professional teachers and pedagogues. Nevertheless, these challenges are surmountable.

Even though the Roman Catholic Church proclaims that Catholic education is at the service of JPR, does the Pontifical Council for Christian Education—or even SECAM—have a curricular framework, for instance, for JPR in our Catholic schools? Is there any even for the seminaries, and other houses of formation? Yet, graduates of Catholic educational institutions generally become civic leaders, pastors and pastoral agents in many local communities in Africa. As it is, these graduates, when faced with crises threatening their communities' fragile justice, peace, and reconciliation, are normally left to improvise through trials and errors. This has to change, and Nigerian theologians who are involved in the educational sector should take the lead. As stated severally, reconciliation means a process of rebuilding relationships of trust. Therefore, our educational interventions on justice, peace, and reconciliation must develop modules and action plans on the *relationships web needing rebuilt trust at the micro and macro levels.*

For this to happen, the Catholic education curriculum for JPR should adopt a psycho-cultural educational model. This model can help Catholic education at the service of JPR because it echoes the *telos* of Catholic education: to build up women and men who pass through Catholic educational institutions to live lives of virtue and justice in the light of CST's overarching principles. Both Catholic education and the psycho-cultural, praxis-oriented educational model focus on the totality of the human person. Hence, students have to acquire critical thinking skills to question facts, understand concepts, evaluate facts, motives and policies, and formulate opinions. The peace education curriculum must be interdisciplinary in content and scope. Hence, experts from related disciplines (e.g., biblical theology, philosophy, and history) should be invited to team-teach. Theologians and other academics should explore the possibility of tapping into their professional and disciplinary diversity to come up with a comprehensive trans-disciplinary curriculum for JPR for use in Catholic schools.

Education for peace will have a positive long-term impact. However, this is insufficient in the face of incessant attacks and insecurity. What about armed violence as justified self-defense? During the 2021 Annual (Virtual) CATHAN Conference (April 6–10, 2021), members were evenly divided on the appropriate Christian response to religious terrorists, bandits, and armed Fulani herdsmen. After all, do we not all want terrorists and kidnappers neutralized permanently? If we say no to violence, and no also to absolute pacifism, what concretely must we do to promote security in the interim? Is absolute pacifism not counter-intuitive? Can an unabashed renunciation of violence safeguard peace and stability? Most importantly, can absolute rejection of armed violence triumph over the evil of war, ethnic cleansing, suicide bombing, and kidnapping for ransom? This conference of Roman Catholic theologians could not generate unanimous answers to these questions. I simply use this to illustrate how all Nigerians, even professional theologians, are still struggling with issues of unjust aggression, counter-response, and ethics of means of redressing mass violence. Hence, I am revisiting these questions and tensions as part of my contribution to a *postbellum* ethical realism that may stretch the restorative justice ethos in peacebuilding.

Actions to Counter Incessant Insecurity and Ideological Violence: Beyond Just War Tradition?

Some scholars have argued that the early Christians had a reason for their pacifism. They were pacifists out of realism. At that time, the early Christians, as a minority in the Roman Empire, had no "territory to defend nor law and order to maintain."[84] When Christianity became the official religion after Constantine's conversion, that pacifism was tested. Christianity later turned to violence when it became Roman Empire's official religion. Violence and use of coercive force supplanted early pacifism, non-retribution, and nonviolence. Christianity no longer had that luxury of absolute pacifism because Christians in charge of the empire had to defend their territory and maintain law and order. Hence, Christian apologists began to articulate the just war reasoning. The theological warrant for violence and persecution of the religious other (e.g., Jews, heretics) was less from the Scriptures. Rather, the warrant came from a historical interpretation of Christianity's experience. According to Lloyd Stefen,

> Christians came to understand that their rise to power was an expression of God's will, the successful advance of Christianity evidence that God was authorizing Christians to seize the power of the sword in order to use it to God's greater glory. On this understanding, Christians were authorized to use coercive power to maintain the supremacy of Christian faith against all adversaries, be they from within the faith or external to it.[85]

---

84. "Introduction to Part I," 9.
85. Steffen, "Religion and Violence," 118–19.

Indeed, the just war reasoning's history is complex and problematic.[86] It has a pre-Christian tradition, although it became identified with some realist schools of thought within Catholic moral tradition to date, especially Saint Augustine and Saint Thomas Aquinas. However, there are three core issues behind the just war tradition. These are presumptions against unjust aggression, right to self-defense, and reasonable proportionality in the use of force. Just war thinking was dominant in Christianity's realist ethic of countering violence. It was so until the latter part of the twentieth century. The evil regimes of Hitler and Stalin reinforced the importance of the impracticability of absolute pacifism. We should bear in mind that just war thinking presupposes the obligation of justice and protection of the weak.[87] According to Reinhold Niebuhr, though Jesus's ethic of forgiveness and universal love is absolute and definitive, it is "not immediately applicable to the task of securing justice in a sinful world."[88]

Conditions for Just War

Our guide here is Saint Thomas Aquinas:

> *I answer that*, In order for a war to be just, three things are necessary. *First*, the authority of the sovereign by whose command the war is to be waged. For it is not the business of a private individual to declare war, because he can seek for redress of his rights from the tribunal of his superior. . . . And just as it is lawful for them (civil authorities) to have recourse to the sword in defending that common weal against internal disturbances, when they punish evil-doers, . . . so too, it is their business to have recourse to the sword of war in defending the common weal against external enemies. Hence it is said to those who are in authority (Psalm 82:4): "Rescue the poor: and deliver the needy out of the hand of the sinner" . . . *Secondly*, a just cause is required, namely that those who are attacked, should be attacked because they deserve it on account of some fault. Wherefore Augustine says (QQ. in Heptateuchum, Q10, super Jos.): "A just war is wont to be described as one that avenges wrongs, when a nation or state has to be punished, for refusing to make amends for the wrongs inflicted by its subjects, or to restore what it has seized unjustly." *Thirdly*, it is necessary that

---

86. For recent discourses on the history and developments, see Scheid, "Christian Peace Ethics," 254–56; Cahill, "Just War," 170–80.
87. Niebuhr, "Why the Christian Church," 45–54, esp. 50–54.
88. Niebuhr, "Why the Christian Church," 49.

the belligerents should have a rightful intention, so that they intend the advancement of good, or the avoidance of evil.... For it may happen that the war is declared by the legitimate authority, and for a just cause, and yet be rendered unlawful through a wicked intention.[89]

From the foregoing, the Roman Catholic tradition developed the following principles (conditions) for waging a just war:

i. Right to resort to war—legitimate authority, fully informed of the relevant facts.

ii. Right intention—advancement of the good, avoidance of evil; there must be no cruelty, desire for power and booty, no passion for inflicting harm. War must be fought with sobriety.

iii. *Ius ad Bellum*—the resort to war is just, and the last resort.

iv. *Ius in Bellum*—the right conduct is followed in war; proportionality.[90]

Christians who argue for just war against *Boko Haram* and violent Fulani herdsmen, for instance, probably presume that Christians have the right—even the obligation—to declare just war in the face of *Boko Haram*'s ideological violence and religious terrorism. Even if we concede that Christians can possibly declare just war, the question is: who is the legitimate authority to declare this? Just war was originally articulated within the context of sovereign empires. So, does it make sense that Christians should declare just war? Is the church a sovereign state? Who is the legitimate authority in Christianity that can declare just war?

Let's look at the other conditions. There might be a right intention to wage war, i.e., to redress suffered evils and avoid greater evils. Nevertheless, the just war theory originally mentions the ethics of means. The war must be waged justly. Part of what this entails is that the enemies must be clearly defined and identified so that non-combatants will not be hurt. That means there must be an identified group of combatants. Who is the enemy Christians have to confront in Nigeria? Is it the Muslim *Ummah*? Is it *Boko Haramists*? Who are they? Where are they? Have we exhausted all possibilities such that war is truly the last resort? But there are other possibilities, ranging from dialog and police action to security intelligence and undercover operations.

---

89. Aquinas, *Summa Theologiae*, IIa-IIae, quæ. 40, art. 1, *responsio*.

90. There is a contemporary addition: *Ius post bellum*—The Right to conclude a post-conflict settlement. Pabst, "Can There Be," 724; Scheid, "Just War Theory," 100–101.

Perhaps it is an exercise in futility to include just war as a possible response to security challenges in Nigeria. However, what of armed resistance or violent self-defense? This question raises the important issue of the ethics of vengeance (ethics of fire for fire). We explored Aquinas's proposal on the possibility of *vindicatio* (vengeance) as lawful and a virtue. *Vindicatio* is concerned with a repayment (redress) owed in terms of evil perpetrated. According to Aquinas, vengeance (*vindicatio*) is "accomplished by some punishment being inflicted upon one who had given offence" upon some conditions.[91] Vengeance, therefore, is for the sake of the Other, not the self. It is a presumption against the violation of one's neighbor (presumption against injustice). "Vengeance," as a responsibility to redress, is a peculiar expression of care for the neighbor. Yet, clear boundaries govern *vindicatio*. We should learn some things from Aquinas. Seeking redress against injustice is bound by ethics. In other words, we must not displace our toxic emotions by placing them on others, even if they are our enemies. Empathy and other emotional skills are necessary for moral living, which the sociopath/psychopath lacks. Empathy is linked to mercy (*misericordia*, which Aquinas translates as compassionate heart) towards the misfortune of others: "As Augustine says (*De Civitate Dei* ix, 5), mercy is heartfelt sympathy for another's distress, impelling us to succor him if we can. For mercy takes its name *misericordia* from denoting a man's compassionate heart [*miserumcor*] for another's unhappiness."[92] Enemies are not excluded from the obligations of mercy and charity.[93] We must love them, not because they are our enemies. We must love them "only in so far as they, like us, are human beings who desire happiness."[94]

From Aquinas's position on the ethics of *vindicatio* (vengeance), just love for peace and reconciliation in any transitional society has a presumption against injustice, abandonment and death. We are touchable; hence, we are open for the other. The first law of a just love is: "Thou shalt not kill." Rather than seeing this as a prohibition against murder, we must see this as a command beginning with an act of restraint, or refraining from intimidation and deception, of non-indifference, or non-tyranny, since tyranny reduces the other to an object.[95] This calls for conscience with scruples, not necessarily a scrupulous conscience. A sensitive conscience is concerned not to do violence to the other. We must be proactive, even if our actions

---

91. Aquinas, *Summa Theologiae*, IIa-IIae, quæ. 108, art 1, *responsio*.
92. Aquinas, *Summa Theologica*, IIa-IIae, que. 30, art. 1, *responsio*.
93. Aquinas, *Summa Theologica*, IIa-IIae, que. 25, art. 8, ad. 2.
94. Aquinas, *Summa Theologica*, IIa-IIae, que. 25, art. 6, *responsio*.
95. Burggraeve, "Other and Me," 344–45.

are not entirely free of ethical ambiguities. We might argue for the practical reasonability of armed resistance, for instance, by appealing to the ethical principle of *minus malum* (lesser evil). The concern and questions about conditions for justified violent self-defense or just war echo the concept of lesser evil: about human behaviors/actions that are not ideal but are chosen for a minimum of humanity. The concept of lesser evil is a form of realistic mercy and justice in the face of reality and a good dose of common sense. This is acceptable because we want to prevent to the extent possible something that might cause some moral revulsion.

Yet, the impermissible cannot be completely avoided. Hence, we need ethics that mediates between the ideal and humanly desirable action in specific contexts. Having said this much about sensitive ethics and the reasonability of *minus malum*, lesser evil ethics has some notable limits. This ethics—as in just war and violent self-defense—does not stimulate or summon us towards growth in human quality. This is why we must move beyond the logic of the lesser evil to the small good, which summons sinful yet fundamentally good moral agents to move beyond avoiding the weightiest consequences. It summons them towards the greater good, based on the principle of gradualness.[96]

Just War Reasoning Today and Tomorrow

The church is largely moving away from the justification of the use of coercive force. In a contemporary contribution, Kristopher Norris locates the notable shift in Pope Paul VI's *Humanae Vitae* (1968), and Pope John Paul II (1985, 1995, 2000, and 2003). Pope Francis's *Fratelli Tutti* joins the list of magisterial documents that express strong presumption against war. He builds on Pope John XXIII's earlier reservation that it is meaningless to claim that war can be a legitimate instrument of justice and peace.[97] Hence, *Fratelli Tutti* declares: "We can no longer think of war as a solution because its risk will probably be greater than its supposed benefits. Given this, it is very difficult nowadays to invoke the rational criteria elaborated in earlier centuries to speak of the possibility of a just war. Never again war!"[98] Norris also includes the United States Conference of Catholic Bishop's *The Challenge of Peace* (1983), which states the magisterial stance of the "strong

---

96. See Francis, *Amoris Lætitia*, no. 295.
97. John XXIII, *Pacem in Terris*, no. 127.
98. Francis, *Fratelli Tutti*, no. 258.

presumption against war."[99] Scholars like Norris and Lisa Cahill[100] date the shift to the post-conciliar period.

Yet, this shift predated the magisterial documents above. Pope Benedict XV, nicknamed "Pope of Peace," started this movement from the magisterial angle. In a series of interventions at the outset of WWI, he upbraided the practices of war and violence.[101] He went ahead to condemn even the distinction of just war. The very concept of war is unjustifiable. Hence, all forms of war must be abrogated.[102] He called for the abrogation of all forms of the arms race.[103] Even though Pope Benedict XV's interventions did not meet with immediate success, his advocacy on hindsight led to "an 'increasing rejection of the use of violence to resolve conflict.'"[104] The movement from the just war reasoning signals a movement towards the original evangelical injunction of a nonviolent ethic. This movement is striking since, for most of the twentieth century, Christians were at the receiving end of violent actions and persecutions. In response, they opted for martyrdom, by accepting suffering and violence for the sake of the kingdom of God.[105] We cannot talk of a Christian ethic of peace and conflict resolution without returning to the original vision. Yet, the ideal still has to be tempered with ethical realism. Christian ethics has a presumption against injustice, especially against one's neighbor. Hence, to use a contemporary expression in international politics, we have the responsibility to protect our neighbors that are unjustly treated. Christian ethical realism endorses lobbying for military action from the international community as a last resort in the face of unrelenting impunity and loss of lives and territories. Of course, one should exhaust other forms of hard diplomacy. Yet, if they fail, then the restrained use of military force is justified.[106]

Consequently, I agree with the ethical realists Cahill highlights in her contribution to just war.[107] We must reaffirm our primary evangelical vision of nonviolence. Due to our responsibility to protect those unjustly treated, there are grounds for "the moral legitimacy of specific uses of armed

---

99. Norris, "'Never Again,'" 119.
100. Cahill, "Just War," 169–85.
101. Benedict XV, "Apostolic Exhortation."
102. Cf. Fröhling, "God, the Lord of Peace," 210–11.
103. Benedict XV, "Note."
104. Fröhling, "'God, the Lord of Peace,'" 213.
105. Fröhling, "'God, the Lord of Peace,'" 213.
106. *Catechism of the Catholic Church*, no. 2309.
107. Cahill, "Just War," 177–80.

force."[108] This is part of loving justice. My understanding of restorative justice in peacebuilding does not preclude the demands of responsibility to protect, which may include the restrained use of military force. When Christians consider the transformative possibility after violence, they are not just viewing the violence and the rite of passage solely from the transcendental standpoint. This standpoint considers the *postbellum* possibilities from the prism of eschatology and soteriology, with less attention "to the rational moral meaning" of crucial after-words in the throes of violence: justice, truth, mercy, peace, and reconciliation.[109] Grace and reason must always go together in dealing with violence and its after-words. My stance is based on Catholic social thought's anthropology, which is capacious. Human nature has a divine origin. Yet, the human person is sinful and fallible. Hence, it must always be guided by practical reasoning. All that we will or must do are in eschatological tension between now and not yet. There are unceasing imperatives. Yet, our actions and responses are flawed, based on the doctrine of original sin. Consequently, Catholic social thought is neither exclusively utopic (transcendental) nor promising heaven on earth (immanence). We must always maintain a creative balance between two or more goods we are pursuing, or the instruments for realizing these goods.

The Church: *"Communio Sanctorum"* et *"Communio Peccatorum"*

Restorative Justice recognizes and encourages the role of community institutions, including the religious/faith communities, in teaching and establishing the moral and ethical standards, which build up the community. A Yorùbà saying goes thus: "*Ẹni tí yí ò bá dá aṣọ fún èniyàn ti ọrùn rẹ ni a ò kọ́kọ́ wò*"—"We will first look at attire of the one who wishes to renew another's wardrobe." This is usually offered against the pretentious magnanimity of one who lacks the means (or credibility). I premise this on two critical virtues the church and its members need. These are realism and humility. Given realism and humility, the Catholic Church remembers that it is not just part of the solution. Some times, it is part of the problem due to the religionization of politics and politicization of religion—especially in Nigeria, as noted in chapter 1. I remember the words of Josephine, a Rwandan genocide survivor, "we will never go back to that church. . . . The angels have left us."[110] The church in Rwanda was heavily implicated

---

108. Cahill, "Just War," 177.
109. Steffen, "Religion and Violence," 132.
110. McCullum, *Angels Have Left*, xix.

either through atrocious acts, complicity, or inaction when thousands were mowed down.[111] Hence, Josephine's words epitomize the tragic consequence of this abuse of religion.

The church might have to leave its moral high ground and acknowledge clearly and explicitly even before the "crazy empires"[112] of the world that the church had sinned against justice, and needs the mercy of God.[113] This makes sense if the church truly takes to heart the exhortation of the 1971 Synod of Bishops: "While the Church is bound to give witness to justice, she recognizes that anyone who ventures to speak to people about justice must first be just in their eyes. Hence, we must undertake an examination of the modes of acting and the possessions and lifestyle found within the Church herself."[114] Collective responsibility implies the church is both *communio sanctorum* and *communio peccatorum*. Bradford Hinze argues that so long as the church gives space for the developing doctrine of social sin, which invariably implies collective responsibility and accountability, then we must add "*communio peccatorum*" to the ancient doctrine of "*communio sanctorum.*" We situate this within a larger discussion on the tension between the objective dimension of ecclesial repentance and the subjective dimension.[115] Writing from an African context, a South African theologian, Neville Richardson echoes Hinze: "History is replete with examples of the fact that there is sin in the empirical, institutional church—it is *peccatorum communio*, a community of sinners. Only through faith can the empirical church be perceived as *sanctorum communio*."[116] The church as an institution, the church as a community, bears *some degree of guilt* for some of the present-day evils, even in Nigeria. We participate in this guilt as representatives of the past.[117] This is akin to John Paul II's "social sin" in *Sollicitudo Rei Socialis*.[118] This sin makes sense because many structures of sin remain entrenched not only because some persons introduced them but because some beneficiaries of the sinful structures maintain them.[119]

---

111. See Hollenbach, "Report from Rwanda," 13–17; McCullum, *Angels Have Left*, 65–94.

112. Cf. Wright, *Evil*, 99.

113. Cf. Hurley, "Ecumenical Methodology," 364–65; Sobrino, "Christianity and Reconciliation," 87.

114. Synod of Bishops, "Justice in the World," no. 40.

115. Cf. Hinze, "Ecclesial Repentance," esp. 220–35.

116. Richardson, "Sanctorum Communio," 106.

117. Jimmy Bellita offers that collective responsibility can be seen linked to a "social situation". Belita, "When Sin Defines," 198.

118. John Paul II, "*Sollicitudo Rei Socialis*," no. 16.

119. John Paul II, "*Sollicitudo Rei Socialis*," no. 36.

This is indeed a difficult proposition because it raises questions and fears about the infallibility of the Catholic Church and the fear of scandalizing the youths of today if the church has to publicly ask forgiveness. There are theological grounds to go this route.[120]

Many of the statuses and privileges that Christianity is still enjoying today in Nigeria, just like in many parts of Africa, are rooted in the religion's ambiguous relationship with the colonialists and imperialists. So, the Catholic Church, as an empirical reality, cannot deny being without sin in Nigeria and not without the responsibility to publicly acknowledge its sins, for instance, the historical sin of cooperation with the colonial enterprise. Today, we can add the Catholic Church in many ways being sucked into ethnic politics, ambiguity regarding just remuneration of wages, and clericalism; and seek satisfaction. Christians cannot disconnect themselves from this history, although we can make it clear that the Catholic Church and its faith are more than that its sobering past. If one encourages variously disappointed and traumatized survivors in Nigeria, to forgive and reconcile with the church, the question is: *what are they reconciling with: a church that bears some degree of responsibility for what happened to them and their people, or with sinful sons and daughters of a perfect mother church?* This kind of distinction serves as a barrier for a church that has a vocation to be a locus of justice, peace and reconciliation.

Part of the ethical responsibility the Catholic Church in Nigeria also has is to acknowledge that the guilt of some past evils concerns the church as an institution and not cases of isolated Christians. The fear that acknowledging the church's failures (especially for the Roman Catholic Church) will compromise the infallibility of the magisterium should not paralyze it to the extent of not seeing that there is corporate responsibility. Nevertheless, this kind of conclusion should not be used to extrapolate guilt on individuals of a new generation. There should not be a collective responsibility that will foster the cycle of transferred "trauma, endangerment and revenge."[121] Being guilty in the primary sense is not the same as being implicated in the guilt (secondary guilt, or being guilty to some degree). This is similar to the distinction Hannah Arendt made between the notions of guilt and responsibility: "While there can be only individual guilt, responsibility, on the other hand, is vicarious, always provided that we belong to a group or collectivity. Feeling oneself to be responsible is the price we pay for not living on our own but among other people."[122] This distinction, without lessening the

---

120. See International Theological Commission, "Memory and Reconciliation."
121. Mitchell, *Can Love Last*, 128.
122. Cited in Dupuy, "Approach," 188.

seriousness of evil that occurred, is crucial for breaking the cycle of violence and unforgiveness, and reconciliation.

Primary guilt is for those who are directly responsible and those who participated in the atrocities, as well as those who were in a position to do something and refused to do it. These are people who in international law would be guilty of failing to act according to the due diligence principle.[123] Secondary guilt is for those who share in the narrative of violence, prejudice of the past, and privileges of past complicity. The task of this class is not to seek forgiveness or be forgiven for the horrors of the past (that is absurd and impossible). However, this class is implicated in continuing the suffering of those who share in the narrative of suffered evil and pains. This class's task is to seek ways of accepting reparative sanctions (and possibly asking forgiveness) for the continued suffering due to their history. This is part of the act of releasing the present-day generation of the full weight of the past to lay a firm foundation for future transformation.

This reflection on the church as *communio sanctorum* and *communio peccatorum* aims at making humans, especially Christians in Nigeria, appreciate the seriousness of colluding with or surrendering to evil instead of resisting it. It makes one more dreadfully aware that individual actions of Christians have universal consequences. The church must deal seriously with its failings as much as it deals with the failings of the crazy empires. Evil runs through us all—even those in the church. So, we all need to be humble and realistic. However, we should not be paralyzed by primary/secondary guilt. The church needs to forgive itself for failing victims and even perpetrators. This kind of forgiveness is "the most hopeful sign of community restoration and healing known to the human race."[124]

Conclusion

This chapter offered that Christians in transitional societies or situations of violent conflicts need to spend more time on concrete praxis and less on waiting for the miracle that dulls their sensitivity to what needs to be done to overcome toxic emotions in their lands. To arrive at this conclusion, the chapter suggested that Christians and the church should rethink their notion of God—not as one that is omnipotent like the traditional patriarchal

---

123. This principle states that there is corporate responsibility and culpability by parties to international law for acts of agents under their control, and for the acts of omission to prevent or adequately respond to gross human rights abuses. Barnidge Jr., "Due Diligence Principle," 81–121, esp. 86–87.

124. Wright, *Evil*, 103.

God. Rather, in the history of salvation as mediated through the Scriptures and human experiences, God is powerfully compelling. God's compelling love, which should inspire human praxis, is a guarantee that evil will never have the last word. Nevertheless, the evil that will not have the last word to a great extent depends on human openness to liberative praxis. God needs humans to overcome humans' toxic emotions. Paradoxically, we need courageous ministers to overcome their toxic emotions towards God. Hence, ecclesial mission is not simply philanthropic charity and proclamation of enduring truths. Overcoming toxic emotions is an ethical imperative; it is an option for justice.

This loving justice in multifaceted modes is the matrix of revelation outside the church's liturgical assembly. The chapter developed this assertion on the role of the Catholic Church in Nigeria with regards to overcoming toxic emotions through actions expressing loving justice for the sake of peace that might bring divided peoples into reconciliation. The chapter offered that the Catholic Church in Nigeria must find bold and creative ways to institutionally embody the compassion it so much preaches and writes about, because "when we lose our compassion, we lose our souls. When the heart stops beating, the body dies."[125] If the church does not want to court mortality any longer, then it will do well to institutionally find ways to show solidarity to those sufferings various kinds of evil, especially due to the curse of impunity. This institutional expression of solidarity is justice, which is constitutive of the church's mission of reconciliation in the world today.

Ultimately, this chapter intended and hopefully demonstrated a possible thematic framework of Christian theological ethics that is attentive, intelligent, reasonable, responsible, and loving towards the fact and narratives of victims of mass violence. Hopefully, when Christian theological ethics and Christian ethicists work through this kind of thematic framework, they will be regarded as helpful dialog partners with critical criminologists and traumatologists, especially in restorative justice discourse and advocacy. With this sensitivity, they can collaboratively come up with concrete and viable ways to respond to the needs of victims and their demands for/of justice, especially when they are trapped in a culture of impunity. Finally, then, the church united in suffering, responding ecumenically to heal the past, helps the present to midwife a future full of hope based on just peace and reconciliation.

---

125. Jones, *Jesus*, 248.

General Conclusion

Adìẹ bà l'ókùn; Ara ò rọ okùn; ara ò rọ adìẹ

The rooster perches on the rope; the rope is ill at ease; the rooster is not at ease

IT HAS BEEN A long way from the beginning, yet never far from it: *the challenges of toxic emotions of peoples in transitional societies and the realistic role of restorative justice in peacebuilding.* This book contributes to restorative justice finding its balance in transitional justice and peacebuilding. In doing this, and trying to avoid the fate of the rooster and rope above, we did several complex and intricate balancing, and critical engagements. This concluding chapter offers the fundamental positions of this book, with some reflections on the relationship between Afro-Christian reconciliation ethics and the conditions for post-conflict justice on the way to reconciliation. This will clarify certain accents especially regarding forgiveness in transitional justice.

An Afro-Christian Ethics for African Peoples in Transition

This book has grappled with an underlying question confronting post-colonial and post-conciliar Africa's hermeneutic of identity: What is the value-setting of African peoples, which need to bear on their Christian identity, vocation and mission? We have grappled with this question in the spirit of the theological necessity of an African Christian Ethics. Agreeing with Bujo and Odozor, we recognize that Afro-Christian Ethics must be "anamnetic— in a more inclusive way than that identified by Bujo as the case in African traditional ethics."[1] One must remember and begin with Jesus Christ, and all

1. Odozor, *Morality Truly Christian*, 165.

the saints; one can insert ancestors worth remembering here. Yet, one must remember those ancestors whose ruinous neglect contributed to Africans' anthropological poverty and perennial internecine wars.[2] Memory must move beyond the ruinous past and the culpable to constructive ethics of reconciliation (within post-colonial African contexts of my enemy-my neighbor). So, Afro-Christian ethics must be based on the current realities of the bleeding yet Christian continent. The African moral theologian that is truly attentive to his/her context must find a way of healing memories in Africa via conflict resolution. So, a fully inculturated moral theology should have a close connection between ecclesiology and moral theology: "the encounter between gospel and culture must necessarily pass by way of the church—that is the church as 'real, incarnate body of Christ, the Church as it is with all its blemish, and not abstract, idealized in our minds.'"[3] African moral theology that is truly Christian and truly African must be at the service of the church as "a community of moral discourse" that "deliberates on and teaches about what should be done or left undone in Africa and by African Christians in the light of the teaching, deeds, and life of Jesus."[4]

An authentic African moral theology must be "dialogical and an ethics with big ears," in dialog with African tradition and Christian tradition simultaneously.[5] In the final analysis, African Christian ethics must be ethics of discipleship and ethics that pays serious attention to what Jesus did. The central concerns of African Christian ethics as an imperative must include practicing forgiveness as a central Christian exhortatory imperative. For this ethics, love is the epicenter of the Christian life. It is concerned about the preferential option for the poor and vulnerable. It promotes equality and human dignity irrespective of ethnicity, gender, and religion.[6] While it is important to take cultures serious in the construction of theologies responsive to Africans' hermeneutics of identity and global relevance, one must adopt an attitude of eternal vigilance vis-à-vis culture (whether African or ecclesial). One must not harbor or condone vices (practices, thought) that are harmful to the welfare of the human person integrally and adequately considered.

2. Odozor, "African Moral Theology," 609.
3. Odozor, *Morality Truly Christian*, 271.
4. Odozor, *Morality Truly Christian*, 271.
5. Odozor, *Morality Truly Christian*, 294.
6. Odozor, *Morality Truly Christian*, 297–98.

Responsibility to Relative Identities and Loyalties: Agenda for Christian Ethics

Violent conflicts fueled by toxic emotions in Nigeria, like most post-colonial states, in their contemporaneous natures, stem from the false articulation of the nation-state in Africa at the dawn of colonialism. Chapter 7 identified overcoming this burden of the past as an ecclesial mission for the survival of places like Nigeria. Consequently, Christian ethics in Nigeria has to re-vision its role, in fidelity to the gospel, and even Aquinas's definition of the natural law, which informs his anatomy of the moral event. The role of Christian ethics in transitional societies is to provide a map and a compass with which persons within the Christian tradition might travel. This should serve as a corrective of predominant emphasis in Christian ethics in Nigeria (like many countries): an emphasis on avoiding specific sinful actions instead of ethics anchored on the human person adequately and integrally considered. In the Roman Catholic tradition, this is seen in the penitential-oriented approach in moral theology to the extent that persons rarely situate their daily acts within the larger picture of the ultimate end of a Christian way of life.

This book pushes for a transition to a more praxis-oriented and historically conscious Christian ethics and ecclesial mission seeking to give concrete answers to questions posed by concrete persons and peoples living in transitional societies like Nigeria today. Hence, the answers that Christian ethics need to come up with revolve around responsibility towards multiple identities and loyalties of Nigerian peoples for instance. Chapter 7 contains an illustration of the web of relationships needing rebuilt trust after mass conflicts. Between the innermost layers (person; family) and the outermost layer (national), other layers are competing for loyalties. They equally shape the identities of persons (of the same family). In other words, beyond the dogmatic and particularistic notions of identities fueling inter-group conflicts in Nigeria, as elsewhere, persons and peoples have multiple and relative identities.

In particular, religion is not the sole decider of the post-colonial African's identity. There are about ten categories of social identities. These are "locational, clan, ethnic, subnational, ethnolinguistic or larger religious, national, regional, and racial factors."[7] Accordingly, these relative identities and concomitant responsibilities towards them and not just to an ideologically overblown one should be a major preoccupation for Christian ethics. Then it shall be recognized as a partner towards the development of national

---

7. Paden, *Muslim Civic Cultures*, 34.

consciousness and reconciliation in any transitional society like Nigeria. We understand that grandchildren resolve the issues of their grandparents. Due to historical and emotional distance, grandchildren, if properly formed, can transcend the irredentism and exclusivism of their grandparents, which their parents were unable to do, probably because they were too traumatized about the past. Hence, chapter 7 suggested that seminaries, houses of formation, and other higher institutions of learning should have modules on justice and peace education. If done, with Christian ethicists taking the lead role, then Nigeria, like other transitional societies, might be raising a new generation of pastors and pastoral agents schooled and skilled in sustainable peacebuilding and culture of nonviolence devoted nonetheless to real justice. These, in turn, will be equipped to teach, preach, and promote national consciousness and civic responsibilities beyond the formation the immediate post-War generation, for instance, received.

Religion as Centripetal Force for Reconciliation

Religion has a higher possibility of mobilizing for violent behaviors in a pluralist religious community if there are low levels of human development. So, religion *per se* is not the problem. The triple deficit of politics, law, and economics is a common Achilles heel in Africa. The triple deficit has stunted the human development of Africa's epicenters of religious violence, for instance, Nigeria. How can protagonists and survivors of mass violence move from a propensity towards violence to a nonviolent disposition? The protagonists in these countries need to view violence from another prism. Instead of the zero-sum cycle of toxic emotions (*aggression-pain-counter-aggression*), we need to see violence as a rite of passage. We do not need to be stuck in the past as we repeat the aggressions and pains on one another. We can adjust our collective "lens" to see our common experience of violence as *kairos*. As a rite of passage, we can emerge from violence to transform our identities (*from competing victims to collective survivors*) and narratives (*from mythical stories to harmonized narratives of neighbors*). Due to its transformative capacity, religion is a resource for the transformation of violence.

We now turn to the transformative power of Christianity, and its possibility today. What Christianity has done with the cross is our point of departure. Christ's crucifixion was an unjust and heinous crime as an innocent victim. Hence, ordinarily, the cross ought to have been an object of derision to Christ's followers, and a basis for violent mimetic rivalry with other religious and cultural traditions. However, the cross has transformed "from a symbol of violence into one of salvation and eternal life, and on such a reading the cross is actually a good thing indeed."[8] The transformation of the cross from a violent symbol to a life-giving one makes sense from Jesus's ethic as the Gospels recorded them. Justice as equitable distribution of resources, reconciliation, and forgiveness are the hallmarks of Christ's ethic. In particular, the ethic of forgiveness and reconciliation impresses it on Christians that they must love their enemies; they must return good for evil instead of applying *lex talionis* towards one's persecutors. The message of non-retaliation and the logic of superabundance of love towards those undeserving is very strong in the Gospel.

The Sermon on the Mount emphasizes that God's kingdom "would exclude those not willing or ready to accept" the ethic of non-retaliation.[9] The faithful Christian lives her/his life "in and toward love of God and neighbor and opposed to violence, vengeance, retaliation, and hatred—all that is opposed to love of God and neighbor."[10] Christ's ethic of post-violence, which Christianity tried to live by, is quite remarkable. It is incredible considering that "the early Christian community became a victim of state-sponsored violence due to repression by the Roman authorities, and suffering persecution at the hands of governmental authority."[11] Despite the violence and persecution, ancient Christians did not alter the religion's ethic. They very likely took inspiration from the words of Jesus, when he was facing the prospect of violent death as an innocent victim. Jesus could have resorted to coercive force, which was within his power. Instead, he was faithful to the rejection of *lex talionis*. Jesus said at his trial before Pontus Pilate, "My kingdom is not from this world. If my kingdom were from this world, my followers would be fighting to keep me from being handed over to the Jews. But as it is, my kingdom is not from here" (John 18:36, NSRV). This evangelical ethic has informed Christians' notion and praxis of reconciliation.

Reconciliation is the process of unlearning the evils of sin which had separated people, and learning to live together under the same roof of the House of Love. It is both diachronic and synchronic. On the one hand, parties learn from traditions of persons who have embodied the art of forgiveness. On the other hand, the parties learn today about those who among us are excelling in the craft and how they are living it out or practicing it. Perpetrators cannot be blind to this; victims should not turn their backs on this, while all parties should be aware of this. We can achieve reconciliation only through the cultivation of virtues, which are by no means

---

8. Steffen, "Religion and Violence," 130.
9. Steffen, "Religion and Violence," 115.
10. Steffen, "Religion and Violence," 115.
11. Steffen, "Religion and Violence," 112.

easy to develop. It is grace that can enable us; it is not just about therapy. This is why all transitional societies need moral agents that will help to create the culture and help develop the craft of reconciliation. Miroslav Volf points this out in his admonition to theologians (and I will include all those devoted to peace-building): "Theologians should concentrate less on social arrangements and more *on fostering the kind of social agents capable of envisioning and creating just, truthful, and peaceful societies, and on sharing a cultural climate in which such agents will thrive.*"[12] Creating an identity that will bring reconciliation has to be cultivated and nurtured. It is about developing an ethics of character/virtue.

A Christian Ethic of Reconciliation, Forgiveness and Vengeance: Echoes from *Fratelli Tutti*

In chapter 7 of *Fratelli Tutti*, Pope Francis attends to the lack of peace in many parts of the world due to unhealed and festering open wounds. In this context, the world needs peacemakers and peacebuilders.[13] The seventh chapter offers us some interesting positions from the Holy Father. First, he accepts an insight from relational psychologists that reconciliation does not mean returning to the *status quo antebellum*. Humans change all the time. Conflicts and violence change us. Hence, a realistic conflict resolution must begin from the fact that conflict and violence had changed the interlocutors. So, if there will be renewed encounters without demanding a return to life before the violent conflict, then peace action must pursue the truth about the violent past. It is the first step towards peace. Truth is a component of justice. It is a human right.[14] Second, there is a part of the demands of *postbellum* conflict transformation in *Fratelli Tutti* that echoes the lesson from our study of the hypostatic union, even if the pope does not appeal to a Christological foundation: "The path to peace does not mean making society blandly uniform, but getting people to work together, side-by-side, in pursuing goals that benefit everyone."[15] This echoes an insight from the hypostatic union. Based on the *communicatio idiomatum*, distinct properties (divine, human) are not sacrificed because of reconciliation. Reconciliation does not demand that we dissolve differences: "hypostatic union is not a destruction of what

12. Volf, *Exclusion and Embrace*, 21 (emphasis original).

13. Francis, *Fratelli Tutti*, nos. 225; 228–32. The pope likens peace to a building (architectural piece) that needs to be built *ad infinitum*. We must keep working for peace. We never finish the peace architecture, but we must keep at it.

14. Francis, *Fratelli Tutti*, no. 226.

15. Francis, *Fratelli Tutti*, no. 228.

exists."[16] Rather, it is about renewal. It is about repairing "the 'mode' of our being, i.e., renewing who we are and how we are in relation with our relationships and those we share common actions."[17]

Renewal refers to the mode of how we live with one another in the world after violent conflict and estrangement. Renewal and change go together. There is no renewal without change. We must change how we live with one another in the world. This change becomes more relevant concerning the exercise of our freedom in the choices we make. We must change to live according to virtue as against vice, which led to the estrangement and violence in the first place.[18] The significant change estranged partners must experience is growth that despite our qualitative differences, "co-existence, co-operation, and co-participation"[19] are possible. This is part of the Christian affirmation of graced *ordo caritatis* (order of love) that is necessary for realizing ethics of love and responsibility in the world. The Holy Father teaches similarly, "we can work to overcome our differences without losing our identity as individuals."[20] Third, peace has a higher probability of success when we rehumanize our enemies. God in Christ Jesus never lost sight of our intrinsic dignity and identity as one created in his image and likeness. He never demonized us. We must do likewise: "'If only we could view our political opponents or neighbors in the same way that we view our children or our spouse, mother or father! How good would this be!'"[21] Consequently, reason must take precedence over vengeance; people take precedence over *realpolitik* of law and politics. Peace processes must include the stakeholders. The principles of subsidiarity and participation must always be respected.[22] These two principles are at the heart of *Fratelli Tutti*'s unrelenting calls for "'a culture of encounter'" that is indispensable for building "the unity of the nation."[23]

Fourth, Christian pacifism does not imply inaction and acquiescence to injustice. We cannot remain silent and passive whenever and wherever the human person's dignity suffers either singly or collectively. Yet, actions cannot be violent because violence does not end in a solution. That is why violent public demonstrations must be eschewed. Such demonstrations do

16. Aina, "Catholic Theology," 84.
17. Aina, "Catholic Theology," 84.
18. Aina, "Catholic Theology," 85.
19. Janssens, "Norms and Priorities," 221.
20. Francis, *Fratelli Tutti*, no. 230.
21. Francis, *Fratelli Tutti*, no. 230.
22. Francis, *Fratelli Tutti*, no. 231.
23. Francis, *Fratelli Tutti*, no. 232.

not always have clear objectives; hence, they are easy to be manipulated for partisan interests.[24] Christian peaceful actions for peace imply conscientization, mobilization, and participation for justice in the land, especially for the most impoverished in the land. Christian mission cannot remain silent in the face of politics and economics of exclusion, "inequality and lack of integral human development."[25] So, for Pope Francis, peace, the friendship of the *anawim* of the land, and the preferential option for the poor are the starting blocks for sustainable peace. Seeking and promoting consensus in the land is not the only best strategy for peace in the land. Advocacy for the sake of "the least of our brothers and sisters" is part of the Christian response for sustainable peacebuilding.[26]

After making these points, the pope turns to the relationship between forgiveness and reconciliation in the Christian faith. The lack of conceptual clarity leads to "fatalism, apathy and injustice, or even intolerance and violence."[27] In nos. 238 and 240, *Fratelli Tutti* articulates the tensions in Christian faith about forgiveness and pacifism, on the one hand, and giving a nod to legitimate conflict, on the other.[28] Importantly, Christian understanding of forgiveness and pacifism does not mean preaching 'cheap grace' that expects one to renounce one's rights or confronting corruption, criminals, and those debasing human dignity. Forgiveness does not condone evil. Even though we are called to be merciful towards even our enemies, the Christian faith teaches us that this does not mean we must allow the oppressor to keep oppressing us. We must not let the oppressor think or believe that what is happening is acceptable. True love for the enemy includes finding means of making the oppressors stop their oppression; "it means stripping him of a power that he does not know how to use, and that diminishes his own humanity and that of others."[29] Forgiveness does not preclude just redress for criminal harm one or loved ones suffered.[30]

In the same breath, Pope Francis reminds us that our Christian faith teaches that the pursuit of justice must not fuel anger or obsession for revenge. There is no future for any family or nation if what forcefully binds the members is revenge and hatred.[31] We overcome a past of injustice,

---

24. Francis, *Fratelli Tutti*, no. 232.
25. Francis, *Fratelli Tutti*, no. 235.
26. Francis, *Fratelli Tutti*, no. 235.
27. Francis, *Fratelli Tutti*, no. 237.
28. Francis, *Fratelli Tutti*, nos. 238–39, 240.
29. Francis, *Fratelli Tutti*, no. 241.
30. Francis, *Fratelli Tutti*, no. 241.
31. Francis, *Fratelli Tutti*, no. 242.

hostility, and lack of trust through virtues associated with reconciliation, solidarity and peace.[32] Authentic reconciliation means confronting the past bravely, not silencing the past. Authentic reconciliation involves a paradox, according to Pope Francis's teaching. This is because true reconciliation is "achieved *in* conflict, resolving it through dialogue and open, honest and patient negotiation."[33] Without honest discussion of differences anchored on justice, we cannot rebuild trust (which is reconciliation). Reconciliation leads to unity that does not absorb differences or create a "syncretism."[34]

Forgiveness, within the scheme of reconciliation, insists on remembering, and not forgetting. Paradoxically, therefore, we remember and forgive; we forgive and remember. Forgiveness does not mean we must hurriedly turn a new page, and move on. We move forward by looking backwards (remembering). If we will progress *postbellum*, we must remember truthfully and clearly.[35] There is no room for parsimony and the sin of omission[36] for those desiring rebuilt trust. Pope Francis shows here that he is aware of a contentious issue, which many transitional societies like Nigeria are battling. It is the nature of forgiveness. Does reconciliation mean amnesty? Amnesty without expiation leads to amnesia—forgetting is the second murder.[37] So what are we talking about? How can the two go together? This is what Jean Elshtain calls "knowing forgetting" in her article "Politics and Forgiveness."[38]

Amnesia is dangerous and unhealthy. To exorcise the memory that is too overwhelming and gloss over reparation, we become beings without memories. Our future is doomed to be empty because we remember so little of our past. We become beings without identity. On the other hand, knowing too well brings the rupture full circle: "'those who don't know their history are doomed to repeat them' (Santayana)."[39] Yet, those who know their history too well are condemned to repeat them.[40] So what can we do? This is where the proposed thesis of Elshtain's "knowing forgetting" becomes relevant. It is a conscious act of releasing the present-day generation of the

32. Francis, *Fratelli Tutti*, no. 243.
33. Francis, *Fratelli Tutti*, no. 244 (emphasis original).
34. Francis, *Fratelli Tutti*, no. 245.
35. Francis, *Fratelli Tutti*, no. 249.
36. In this context, the sin of omission refers to the deliberate dissemination of half-truths as the whole truth to authenticate one's stance for or against an issue or problem. Francis, *Fratelli Tutti*, no. 249.
37. Francis, *Fratelli Tutti*, nos. 250–53.
38. Elshtain, "Politics," 32–47.
39. Elshtain, "Politics," 35.
40. Elshtain, "Politics," 35.

full weight of the past to lay a firm foundation for future transformation because they are not pressed down by the weight of the former generation's guilt. When we remember too well we grow with the mindset that there is only one option of reaction. We have the option of either that of the victim or that of the perpetrator. But "knowing forgetting" brings us to the consciousness that there are no completely innocent or guilty parties. It makes us face the reality: though we are victims, we also know our sins. We remember the past and the extent of the influence they exert on the present, and how it should shape the present events.[41]

There is no common purpose of forgiveness, even among Christians.[42] Some say forgiveness is intended for reconciliation.[43] Some define forgiveness as the mean between mercy and justice, or as the blending of mercy and justice. As defined elsewhere, forgiveness is "an expression of Love-as-Mercy that lets go of toxic emotions towards one who had unjustly caused the collapse of one's assumptive world. It is a choice because it is one of the relationship processes followed after transgressions against relationships."[44] The choice of letting go of one's toxic emotions towards a perpetrator of evil shows the gratuitousness of forgiveness. It is a gift. It is non-programmatic. It is unpredictable. That is the interruptive power of the Spirit of grace. Michael Henderson agreeably says: "I stand in awe of the courage and generosity of many people who have been ready to forgive in circumstances that are outside the experience of many of us. . . . It is about conscience—and, for those who think in such terms, the prompting of the spirit."[45] It cannot be forced. It is entirely at the prerogative of the victim-survivor.

This is why we should couple forgiveness with mercy or love, not reconciliation. Accordingly, we need to create havens and structures that help people to be more open to forgiveness, where they can confront or be confronted with the challenges of unforgiveness without being condemned for lack of forgiveness. No one relishes being in a state of unforgiveness. The costs are too enormous to bear. Yet, the handicap can be so great that some people prefer to opt for unforgiveness and its costs. Conceptually, reconciliation can happen at the personal, group, ethnic, religious and national levels. Reconciliation can happen at every level of the web of human relationships. It is not an exclusively personal act like forgiveness. Reconciliation is not a gift one gifts to the other. Reconciliation, conceptually and in reality, is

---

41. Elshtain, "Politics and Forgiveness," 34.
42. See Taylor, "Role and Meaning," 39–55; Cervantez, "What If," 135–46.
43. Cf. Cervantez, "What If," 137.
44. Aina, "Overcoming 'Toxic' Emotions," cii.
45. Henderson, *Forgiveness*, x–xi.

what happens to one's web of relationships after serious conflict. Paradoxically, there is one thing that connects the probability of reconciliation and the state of unforgiveness (refusal/inability to forgive). Unforgiveness is a stress reaction. If the injustice gap increases, reconciliation will be delayed. There can be no reconciliation without justice. If justice increases also, the refusal to forgive reduces due to the process of detoxification, which we call the cooperative process of "removing relational poison."[46]

Overcoming Toxic Emotions and Restorative Justice in Peacebuilding

This book, motivated by Nigeria's (and to some extent South Africa's) recurring self-implosion and a restorative justice-like practice (HRVIC), offers an analytical generalization on the plausibility of a common pattern beyond the particular reference points (Nigeria; and South Africa). With the concept of toxic emotions, the book offers that beyond focusing on objective interests needed for stability, transitional societies must pay attention to subjective factors, especially toxic emotions (e.g., mistrust, anger, denial, pity, shame, humiliation, guilt) in processes towards peacebuilding. This analytical generalization can be rationally understood in contexts beyond Nigeria, and South Africa. This book has articulated how overcoming toxic emotions is a core of restorative justice's promises. With this articulation (cf. chapters 1 and 2), this book contributes to the ethical reasoning of restorative justice's promises that stakeholders can utilize in other transitional (and even non-transitional) contexts experimenting with restorative justice. With the concept of "overcoming toxic emotions," this book lends its voice to some advocates of restorative justice who are increasingly attentive to the importance of trauma and its demands on "after-word" justice. Unresolved trauma puts any nation or society at risk regardless of monies spent on rebuilding infrastructures after trauma. More importantly, the book equally underscored the importance of the toxic emotions of Ẹiyẹ Kínkín—mass victims of atrocities, often of everyday normalized evil. Whether in a transitional society like Nigeria or non-transitional societies, like those in the global north, unless we pay qualitative and quantitative attention to various forms of victimization, the human family is at risk of sliding into barbarity, even risking annihilation, because inaction puts wounded victims at criminal risks due to anger arising from neglect and injustice.

Due to particular emphasis on the "toxic emotions" of Ẹiyẹ Kínkín, this book raised issues with restorative justice in peacebuilding, at least from the

---

46. Worthington, *Forgiveness and Reconciliation*, 49, 197, 212–17, quotation on 216.

two practices described and analyzed (Nigeria's HRVIC and South Africa's TRC). On the one hand, restorative justice in peacebuilding comes with its promising message of wanting to maintain a creative balance between objective interests and subjective factors. Such transitional projects will move beyond the mechanist peacemaking approach that looks at particular conflicts as a cause and not a case. Restorative justice claims that it views conflicts as case, a problem-event that offers an opportunity to revisit old wounds, engage in daring hermeneutics, and possibly restructure the political landscape. Hence, restorative justice claims to bridge the spheres of justice. On the other hand, restorative justice in peacebuilding, at least from Nigeria and South Africa, has largely operated as an approach that is closer to the cause outlook than the case one. Perhaps, this is because the restorative justice that has been practiced appears to buy into the dominant notion of human rights, which focuses strongly on responding to egregious human rights violations.[47] If one adjudges this approach from the perspectives of peacebuilding and reconciliation as defined, then this book offers another insight. We seem to see a conceptual muddiness in the phrase "restorative justice in peacebuilding" that has to be stridently and consistently avoided. Conventionally, restorative justice seems to be more of an approach closely related to peacemaking than peacebuilding. Restorative justice, contrary to some conventional construal, is not synonymous with peacebuilding because restorative justice is "an interpersonal response to particular (violent) incident on the microlevel."[48] Restorative justice prefers that offenders who pose significant safety risks and are not yet cooperative be placed in settings where the emphasis is on safety, values, ethics, responsibility, accountability, and civility till they learn empathy and values of reintegration.

Nevertheless, restorative justice can and contributes to peacebuilding. Indeed, since peacebuilding is processive and based on "time perspectives" as stated in the general introduction, restorative justice advocates will have to continue to insist that restorative justice in peacebuilding is not synonymous with Truth (and Reconciliation) Commissions, which have functioned largely within an intermediate space between peacemaking and peacebuilding. I hope that this book will prod criminologists, transitional justice experts and restorative justice advocates, who still see the potential of restorative justice in overcoming toxic emotions. One hopes they will develop process-oriented and nested paradigm practices, which can respond to the various demands of the time perspectives of the peacebuilding

47. Some contributions on criminology, human rights, and criminality raise this issue, with some throwing the kind of challenge that this book has raised severally. See Parmentier and Weitekamp, *Crime and Human Rights*.

48. Cf. Rohner et al., "Challenging Restorative Justice," 17–19.

defined and favored in this book. In this regard, the book offers a proposal that shows the promises and inspirations of restorative justice in peacebuilding with the aid of Paul Ricœur's hermeneutical mimetic arc. It shows that restorative justice in peacebuilding can help towards overcoming toxic emotions at various levels of society, with the crucial contribution of the religious institutions, for instance. Overcoming toxic emotions and the accompanying conceptual formulation can serve as another inspiration for transitional justice experts and criminologists interested in restorative justice's potential in peacebuilding. The role of restorative justice in peacebuilding cannot be located only in truth commissions. Hence, experts will continue to articulate their expectations for meaningful faith-based interventions and collaborations in peacebuilding and reconciliation projects. This is promising because the experts' expectations will be seen to be sensitive to and inspired by a Christian notion of reconciliation, and not perceived as another secularization agenda.

Hence, I will like to clarify the function of the heuristic offered at the end of the general introduction and the scheme in the appendix referred to severally in this book. The heuristic has hermeneutical and evaluative functions. Hermeneutically, I originally formulated it to conceptualize the promise of restorative justice, at least in the original context. According to original restorative justice, the renewal of the human mode of relationship is important after a violation. Hence, restorative justice's emphasis is on renewing relationships. This renewal through justice is about unplugging the rot, finding creative ways to regenerate the relationships and the affected common actions in their respective degrees. Even if there is no prior affective relationship, subjects before the justice system are already related by the virtue of sharing the same human nature. Consequently, justice is about the recognition of that humanity and responsibility to those relationships and the necessary common actions implied from that given. However, this view of justice is more than the stark retributive option we are used to. Even if restorative justice advocates do not mention it, for this justice to reach its *telos*, love-as-mercy is imperative. Some terms deployed about restorative justice (embrace, mourning, re-humanization, etc.) conceptually and ethically speaking echo love-as-mercy. Yet, these are important if the justice on the way towards the renewal of relationships after violence and conflicts will achieve its *telos*. Hence, love-as-mercy reinforcing justice will create an environment of calm, which might even encourage the promise not to repeat the past. This is peace. This book's heuristic, therefore, offers a schematic representation that makes sense of what restorative justice promises to be doing. So, from a Christian ethical perspective, one can use this heuristic to understand and possibly question what restorative justice is doing in practice, and the dimensions of its focal points, at least in transitional justice.[49]

This brings me to the second function of the heuristic, i.e., its evaluative function. As demonstrated throughout this book about the Nigerian and South African experiences of restorative justice in peacebuilding, the heuristic can, at least from a Christian ethical perspective, help to evaluate the consistency of restorative justice in transitional justice and peacebuilding projects because of reconciliation, the ultimate *telos*. The heuristic presupposes the following question that we can pose to adaptations of restorative justice in transitional contexts: how much or less of loving justice for the sake of peace on the way to reconciliation can actors point? So, the heuristic and especially the scheme in the appendix (cf. Appendix 2) can be a useful tool for transitional justice experts and restorative justice advocates at least to ethically evaluate the degrees of love-as-mercy, justice, and peace with reconciliation in the target societies. Furthermore, the scheme can help experts to make ethical sense of the degrees of the precious quartet in transitional societies.

The twofold function exemplifies how religious ethics of a particular orientation can offer a valuable contribution to restorative justice advocates in peacebuilding. Religious ethics have a more realistic and challenging contribution than a rather more traditional approach. Hence this book questioned why there appears to be a preference for *baruti* discourse (e.g., Tutu's) than religious ethicists with a phenomenological orientation (e.g., Ricœur). Restorative justice and Ricœur, for instance, have a lot in common, e.g., phenomenological research and conceptual approach especially hermeneutics, and these can deal with those knotty and grey areas criminologists and transitional justice experts are constantly wrestling. This book asked and answered this implicit question: between *Baruti* and experts in religious ethics whose approach is much more realistic for the kind of works criminologists dealing with restorative justice in peacebuilding are involved with? Assuredly, I am not suggesting that there has to be an either/or approach regarding these different religious contributors. What I am suggesting is that there is the need to explore greater collaboration with those who have some conceptual approach that can complement, inspire, or even challenge experts in criminology and transitional justice beyond that of some highly inspirational religious contributors.

Furthermore, when Christian ethicists work through the kind of thematic framework offered above, they might be more resourceful dialog

---

49. Some criminologists with interest in transitional justice and restorative justice have offered something close to this, even if their present representation can be clearer. See Parmentier and Weitekamp, "Political Crimes," 138, fig. 4.

partners from the Christian tradition with criminologists and transitional justice experts. This stance did not come out of a vacuum. It is based on an incarnational theology of reconciliation.

An Incarnational Christian Theology of Reconciliation and Restorative Justice

Incarnational as used here means two things. First, it means Christian theology of reconciliation takes inspiration from the mystery of the incarnation and the doctrine of the hypostatic union. In other words, a Christian theological ethical reflection on this mystery and doctrine is confronted with a perduring lesson intended for the believers: reconciliation between God and humans came about because the victim of sin (God) chose to give the perpetrator (humans) another chance by renewing their modes of relationship. God did this by bridging the spheres of realities (divinity and humanity) in the God-man, to heal the estranged relationship from the roots (*sanatio in radice*). Second, incarnational means Christian theology of reconciliation is decisively corporeal, i.e., pursued and effected in the body—anthropological, cultural, political, and ritualized. In other words, incarnational Christian theology of reconciliation seeks to boldly bridge the symbolic and the corporeal dimensions of reconciliation needed by estranged parties (My Neighbor–My Enemy). This articulation contends that even if some grave errors and moral evils in human institutions had implicated some interpretation of Christian doctrines (e.g., patriarchal interpretation of God; unnuanced divine omnipotence), the same religious tradition, with the inspiration of some doctrines, can contribute to healing within the tradition and even within the larger society. Hence, the specific contributions of this book to restorative justice in peacebuilding unreservedly took inspiration from the hypostatic union.

So, dipolar theism implied in this theological ethical approach contends that God, the creator of the world, is not the omnipotent patriarchal God that believers have been traditionally taught to believe in; a belief which in some cases leads to passivity and privatization of morality, and the glorification of prayer warriors that relentlessly encourage individual victims and even the masses to wait for the miracle of the intervention of the omnipotent God. Due to various dimensions of trauma and suffered evil, admittedly there is a complex needs structure of survivors, more so in postcolonial contexts like Nigeria and South Africa. An incarnational Christian theology of reconciliation, this study severally suggests, must not lose sight of social analysis and postcolonial sensitivity for such contexts.

Hence, beyond the micro-focus that features prominently in some articulation of Christian theology, associated with magisterial religious contributors, we need an equal and simultaneous emphasis on the meso- and macro- dimensions of justice, peacebuilding, and reconciliation. Accordingly, I suggested that responsibility to the other should take priority over guilt, yet without denying demands arising from guilt.

Ethical responsibility in transitional societies has been framed within a Judeo-Christian biblical tradition that recognizes that there was unfinished chaos at creation. So, there remains the pull in creation towards obliteration of separation and difference brought about by creation. Chaos (as different forms of evils, both natural and moral) threatens and works against the goodness of creation (separation and difference). Therefore, justice in the throes of different forms of chaos must proceed from an ethical responsibility to affirm the goodness of separation. I articulated this in the normativity of the right to exist, not in sublimation, but as diversity in unity. This accent of justice is a work of healing, i.e., care for the disenfranchised other who is a stranger, yet without ceasing to be a stranger (irreducible alterity).

I developed this accent of justice as a work of healing in the discussion on the promise of Aquinas's ethic of *vindicatio* and Levinas's ethic of responsibility being held in creative tension in/for transitional societies. While Levinas's notion of justice, in response to totalizing projects in human societies, makes a case for the otherness of the other, Aquinas's ethic of *vindicatio* offers an ethical framework within which ethical responsibility must operate in order not to replace one evil with another evil. In this way, Levinas's ethics of the excess (i.e., ethics beyond ethics/equivalence; love) will not lead to an excess of justice, i.e., the supererogatory must be ethical. Consequently, reconciliation across the web of relationships in transitional societies is not unconditional. The book has argued that there are three broad preconditions for reconciliation—love-as-mercy, justice, peace. Of the trio, it appears that the role and place of justice are the most knotty, even in this book. Justice as an *in-between* project on the way to reconciliation must serve life comprehensively. The whole can be healthy only if constituting units are healthy and strong individually and collectively. Thus, justice, inspired by heteronomous responsibility, should not focus only on the identifiable authors of extraordinary evils as those liable to make reparation. This study's Christian theology of reconciliation insists that concrete responses to justice in empathy and respectful listening to the spoken words, blinding tears, and incomprehensible groans of persons and peoples must factor in the effects of both the extraordinary evils and the banaler (every day, faceless) ones. Subjects of justice (especially the *Ẹiyẹ Kíńkíń*) should never be sacrificed if the justice project will not end up as a perverted good.

Due to paradoxical asymmetry (equality and heteronomy) between human subjects, one can say that theologically there is space for redemption (*re-conciliation*) in a restorative justice-inspired transitional project. However, this redemption depends to a large extent on justice, which has several spheres (cf. Appendix 2). The spheres consist of both the symbolic and the material, which must be held in a delicate balance. These represent the expectations emphasizing that restorative justice should contribute towards undoing oppressive structures, conditions, and political ecology, especially as impinging particularly upon the Ẹiyẹ Kínkín. These expectations pay attention to the connections between structural location and people's wellbeing. Of course, hope is crucial to restorative justice in peacebuilding. Nevertheless, hope is not a strategy. We must express it in a fitting conceptual framework guiding actions for justice for peace to dwell as people journey towards reconciliation. From the foregoing, this book's Christian theology of reconciliation challenges restorative justice to give priority to the sphere of social justice. For instance, acute sensitivity to social justice needs of dispossessed Ẹiyẹ Kínkín in some transitional societies recognizes the necessity for a reparation package that looks beyond those who have primary guilt.

If according to biblical tradition justice humanizes as much as it vindicates and punishes, then a Christian theology of reconciliation as offered in this book equally insists that justice must contribute decisively (i.e., material, sociopolitical, symbolic, and economic) to the humanization of victims of everyday evils and faceless crimes. Accordingly, those who share in the narrative of violence, prejudice of the past, and privileges of past complicity must make reparation also, and not just magnanimous gesture; or else the fate of victims remain unchanged. The task of this class is not to seek forgiveness or be forgiven for the horrors of the past (that is absurd and impossible). However, this class is implicated in continuing suffering of those who share in the narrative of suffered evil and pains. This class's task is to seek a way of accepting obligation for reparation for the continued suffering due to their history to which they have some degree of responsibility. This is part of the act of releasing the present-day generation of the full weight of the past to lay a firm foundation for future transformation.

Going Forward: Lessons from the Hypostatic Union and *Fratelli Tutti* for Christian Mission in Nigeria

1. Based on the *communicatio idiomatum*, distinct properties (divine, human) are not sacrificed because of reconciliation. Reconciliation

does not demand that we dissolve differences. Reconciliation does not mean returning to the *status quo antebellum*. Humans change all the time. We must change to live according to virtue as against vice, which led to the estrangement and violence in the first place. Just as God in Christ Jesus never lost sight of our intrinsic dignity and identity as one created in his image and likeness, and never demonized us, so also we must do the same.

2. In our advocacy for the traumatized Ẹiyẹ Kińkín of transitional societies, we must balance soft and hard diplomacies in our Christian mission and proclamation for the kingdom of God. Following Boutros-Boutrous Ghali's *Agenda for Peace*, the ecclesial mission includes preventive diplomacy (fact-finding missions; developing early warning mechanisms;[50] remembering that we are sentinels—exercising our prophetic role of standing in eternal vigilance to warn our people of danger before it comes; we must be awake and never complacent [Ezek 33.7]). We must invest more in peacekeeping. These include soft diplomacy like mediation, negotiation, arbitration; campaigning for demilitarized zones, possibly creating sanctuary cities, where individuals from warring sides might want to move to and stay together even if the larger societies are still at war. IDP camps today are like sanctuary cities. Christian ethical realism that I referred to earlier has room for hard diplomacy, which includes campaigning for sanctions against intransigent violators of rule of law[51] and lobbying for military action from the international community as a last resort in the face of unrelenting impunity and loss of lives and territories. If peaceful means fail, the use of military force is allowed "to maintain or restore international peace and security in the face of a 'threat to the peace, breach of the peace, or act of aggression'";[52] to "respond to outright aggression, imminent or actual."[53] Hard diplomacy also includes peaceful adjudication via the International Court of Justice (World Court). The World Court is an essential (under-utilized) component of peacemaking.[54] For instance, in Nigeria, the Catholic Church can challenge its Catholic lawyers to take up this advocacy. The pastors' task is to animate and harness the various charisms in the church for the building up of God's kingdom. They need to partner more with

---

50. Ghali, *Agenda for Peace*, nos. 20–25.
51. Ghali, *Agenda for Peace*, nos. 42.
52. Ghali, *Agenda for Peace*, nos. 42.
53. Ghali, *Agenda for Peace*, nos. 44.
54. Ghali, *Agenda for Peace*, nos. 39.

civil rights activists, just as the leadership of the Catholic Secretariat of Nigeria did during the military dictatorship. The church and the civil societies have to work closely and not at cross purposes.[55] *Postbellum* advocacy includes peacebuilding, which promotes and facilitates cooperative projects that "link two or more countries in a mutually beneficial undertaking that can not only contribute to economic and social development but also enhance the confidence that is so fundamental to peace."[56] These cooperative projects contribute to rebuilding trust. Peacebuilding includes education for peace that seeks to reduce "hostile perceptions through educational exchanges and curriculum reform may be essential to forestall a re-emergence of cultural and national tensions which could spark renewed hostilities."[57] Then, there is capacity building that is concerned with building strong democratic institutions. It also includes various interventions of institutions like Caritas Nigeria, Catholic Relief Services, Kukah Center, various diocesan JDPC aimed at promoting social justice in the land. Social justice is "as important as strategic or political peace."[58]

Methodological Promise of Interdisciplinary Research in Faith-based Interventions

The research leading to this book confronted me time and again with the role of religious institutions, especially the church, in transitional societies. Indeed, if the church has a redemptive role in the world today, it is faced with a question: how does it go about incarnating it? To answer this question, the Roman Catholic Church (RCC), for instance, acknowledges that to incarnate this redemptive role, it must pay attention to the issues at hand. Hence, the church affirms that it engages in interdisciplinary collaboration on those issues relating to human persons and the goods of the human society. Nevertheless, one can notice that there is a research approach that is characterized by methodological disjointedness in preference to methodological consistency. The RCC, for instance, describes a *status quæstionis*, sometimes with the help of the descriptive component of interdisciplinary research. However, at its analytical, hermeneutical, or practical part, responses are almost always based on the deposit of faith as contained in the social doctrine of the church,

---

55. Aina, "Catholic Identity," 462–64.
56. Ghali, *Agenda for Peace*, nos. 56.
57. Ghali, *Agenda for Peace*, nos. 56.
58. Ghali, *Agenda for Peace*, nos. 59.

without necessarily showing how the hermeneutics methodologically flows from the data previously described. It is like giving forthright answers to questions not asked. It is as if data is forced into the doctrinal corpus. This deductive approach has been referred to as a "translation method," which has been argued as being insufficient in interdisciplinary engagement, especially with non-theological disciplines.

Perhaps this is one of the reasons why serious-minded transitional justice experts and criminologists tend to overlook faith-based contributors when it comes to serious conceptual discussions and evaluation of their projects. Admittedly, this may be changing given the fruit of an extensive collaboration between scholars in the social sciences, especially criminology and sociology, humanities, especially theology, and law.[59] The collaboration aimed at "a conceptual framework for peacebuilding grounded in a relational approach that is contextual, comprehensive, integrative, and holistic."[60] Curiously, the book, *Restorative Justice, Reconciliation, and Peacebuilding* has just one theological entry, which explores restorative justice and forgiveness.[61] Though this volume explores various conceptual foundations and relationships involving restorative justice in peacebuilding, the theological contribution is on forgiveness and restorative justice. It is as if theology's relevance in an interdisciplinary discourse on restorative justice is limited only to forgiveness. A later publication by theologians confirms this.[62] The volume explores just the relationship between restorative justice and forgiveness. All discourse about justice, peace, love, and truth are discussed under forgiveness and restorative justice. This gives an impression of overemphasis on forgiveness in restorative justice discourse. This is a challenge for theologians to ask themselves why this is the case.

So, informed by its inductive approach, this book has shown how faith-based interventions can take data from non-theological disciplines serious and follow up on these logically till the end without presupposing answers, yet without losing its faith-inspired critical edge. This book has offered, through its theological analogue (hypostatic union), a possibility to redress the rather disproportionate emphasis on some patristic teachings and monastic practices as sources. Confronted with the data thrown up by victims as in restorative justice discourse and practices, this interdisciplinary research provides a broadened horizon on justice that renews after a harrowing past, contrary to some Catholic authors that see a

---

59. Llewellyn and Philpott, *Restorative Justice*.
60. Llewellyn and Philpott, *Restorative Justice*, ix, 8–9.
61. Pope, "Role of Forgiveness," 174–96.
62. Blyth et al., *Forgiveness and Restorative Justice*.

Catholic-inspired restorative justice focusing on mediation, rehabilitation of prisoners, parole, education, and substance abuse treatment. This book shows that there are actors in faith-based organizations that can collaborate meaningfully, while equally enriching interventions and evaluations regarding peacebuilding processes and reconciliation projects for instance. Accordingly, this book can contribute towards greater collaboration between non-theological experts and faith-based actors, especially ethicists, in peacebuilding and reconciliation processes in transitional (and non-transitional) societies where religions play crucial roles.

Final Clarification and Reflections

Forgiveness and Decisive Precondition(s) for Reconciliation

I stated above that love-as-mercy, justice, and peace are three decisive preconditions for reconciliation. Some may pose a question on this book's stance: What about forgiveness? I offer two answers, which summarize the positions I have taken in this book. First, the hermeneutical framework offered in this book challenges the disproportionate accent on forgiveness in transitional justice processes and reconciliation projects. There is no causal relationship between forgiveness *per se* and reconciliation. In other words, there is no evidence that forgiveness causes reconciliation. Given this observation, experts in transitional justice, and even Christian ethicists and *baruti*, have to acknowledge and insist that there is a rather nuanced and delicate relationship between forgiveness and reconciliation. These two are not sides of a coin, as conventionally thought and taught. For this reason, it appears that Stephen Pope's contribution in *Restorative Justice, Reconciliation and Peacebuilding* referred to above lumps restorative justice, reconciliation and forgiveness under justice. This is at odds with my fundamental distinctions in this book. Yet, a careful reading of Pope's contribution will reveal that forgiveness as understood by Aquinas conceptually falls under love-as-mercy (the logic of abundance), and not justice (the logic of equivalence). When love and justice meet, the offender is gifted with some degree of just love.

Second, though forgiveness belongs to the sphere of love-as-mercy, it has a unique place within this sphere. Unlike other dimensions of love-as-mercy, forgiveness, from the Christian ethical perspective articulated in this book, is not an entirely human action. Grace plays a decisive role in forgiveness. Hence, to what extent can we make this forgiveness a precondition for reconciliation? Like other dimensions of love-as-mercy, forgiveness is important in overcoming toxic emotions. Nevertheless, we must exercise patience in waiting for it to make its epiphany. What we can do in the interim is to create conditions that can be conducive for forgiveness to appear and blossom when it chooses. When it makes its epiphany in places where stakeholders are still struggling to renew their mode of relationships after a chaotic past, forgiveness will add value to the web of relationships, directly and indirectly as the case may be, on the way towards reconciliation, which we might not reach in this world. So the unique place of forgiveness in this book serves as a critical eschatological proviso. There may be reconciliation to some degree (due to other dimensions of love-as-mercy reinforcing justice considering peace). Nevertheless, reconciliation may not happen to some degree, because some relationships are still waiting for the promise and hope of forgiveness; and this may not come till death. On the contrary, we can have forgiveness and yet reconciliation still does not happen. This makes sense and we can accept it if we take heteronomy—the radical otherness of the other—serious. This position pays attention to the tension about forgiveness, especially in political projects. So, forgiveness without reconciliation is like a salute; an expression of good wishes or goodwill to the one the forgiver is forgiving. It is akin to saying to the person: "May your future be well; may the Spirit guide you," even if they go their separate ways like Esau and Jacob after an estrangement of thirty years (cf. Gen 33).

Accordingly, I have some sympathy for Michael Cervantez's stance that there may be morally justified reasons for persons "who find forgiveness beyond what they are capable."[63] This avowal of unforgiveness is not an instance of moral deficiency as some opine.[64] Forgiveness, for Cervantez, cannot be disconnected from a traditional moral principle, "*Deus impossibilia non iubet*" ("God does not command the impossible"). "God does not require individuals to do what is morally impossible for them—including forgiving one's offender, when doing so is beyond what is possible for them."[65] For Cervantez, there is no moral justification for forgiveness where is there is no "relational connection between victim and offender."[66] Forgiveness, for Cervantez, appears to mean ceasing to harbor resentment towards one's perpetrator.[67] It is morally justified in the context of My Neighbor–My Enemy. Considering the reality of the inevitability of interpersonal

63. Cervantez, "What If," 135.
64. Cervantez, "What If," 135–36.
65. Cervantez, "What If," 142.
66. Cervantez, "What If," 137.

67. Bishop Joseph Butler's definition of forgiveness probably inspired Cervantez's stance. Bishop Butler claims that "forgiveness requires the 'forswearing [of] resentment.'" Cervantez, "What If," 139.

encounters, there is the constant moral need for relational repair. He opines that those holding resentments need "to strive for the continued abatement and eventual elimination of resentment."[68]

However, I have some reservations about an aspect of Cervantez's position. His position is suitable for micro relationships. It is not entirely helpful for groups of victim-survivors and perpetrators in transitional societies, where they and their offspring will continue to share the same space. How does he handle group resentment? This brings us back to reconciliation. If reconciliation is or implies the restoration of mutual trust after a traumatic period, then this takes time even after individuals might have forgiven. Restoration or better still renewal of relationship demands care: "mended friendships demand more care than those which have never been broken."[69] Let us recall my position that justice is decisive for overcoming resentment and toxic emotions. So, justice in an atmosphere of peace increases the likelihood of reconciliation that fosters the cooperative process of "removing relational poison."[70]

Restorative Justice and Christian Forgiveness: A Tensed Relationship

Forgiveness is imperative considering the importance of its formation. Yet, it is not a deontological or legal imperative. It is exhortative. Forgiveness can contribute towards reconciliation between persons, but forgiveness, as defined in this book, does not cause reconciliation between groups. Taken to a logical conclusion, it is possible for mixed groups to live together nearby and in limited justice, even if there is a toxic atmosphere between parties; and their country functions very well. There are countries in the West whose ethnic groups are working together for decades in an atmosphere of calm (conciliation), with high standards of living, though still in search of reconciliation characterized by commitment towards the higher ground of trust. So, there can be a future without forgiveness. I agree with Michael Taylor that there seems to be an excessive assumption about the benefits of forgiveness. Forgiveness may be good, but it should not be programmatic and made to dwarf other goods in restorative justice processes.[71]

Forgiveness must always be related to a range of after-words like "change, repentance, reparation, release, humility, understanding, growing

68. Cervantez, "What If," 137.
69. Monbourquette, *How to Forgive*, 179.
70. Worthington, *Forgiveness and Reconciliation*, 216.
71. Taylor, "Role and Meaning," 54.

empathy, the ending of hostilities, foregoing ill-will, forgetting or 'not remembering', moving on, restoration and reconciliation."[72] Given these *postbellum* after-words, one can associate forgiveness and future with a nuance. This view of forgiveness helps the case of just love. This is what should motivate Christians that forgiveness is not absent in the language of the *postbellum* reconciliation process. However, forgiveness is meaningful and life-giving in a *postbellum* context when it is inseparable from the search for social justice and reconciliation.[73] This is how we can understand the exhortative imperativeness of forgiveness. Forgiveness does not function as a *quid pro quo* nor should it be viewed from a consequentialist approach that speaks of forgiveness in terms of benefits.[74]

Forgiveness remains a gift that we can bestow or not, incumbent on a mixture of variables, especially the injustice gap. Due to the *gift-ness* of forgiveness, we can have justice as a sanction (to reduce the injustice gap) without forgiveness. However, there is no perfect reconciliation without forgiveness because forgiveness as a concrete expression of love-as-mercy falls under the sphere of *agape*, which should contribute to reconciliation. Loving justice leads to peace; the presence of the trio in a community of persons after violation can be summarized as a state of reconciliation identified with the rebuilding of trust. Even if there can be some level of trust without forgiveness,[75] to insist that there can be perfect reconciliation without forgiveness implies a doctrinaire exclusion of forgiveness as a component of love.

If forgiveness, in my opinion, is the hard choice of letting go of the venom towards someone who deserves the stake due to her/his atrocious deeds, forgiveness places a moral burden on the perpetrators and the state to adequately respond to the gratuitousness of forgiveness. The forgiving victim-survivor symbolically pleads: *I forgive because I love since there can be no forgiveness without belief, and no belief without love, and no love without hope and assurance in the other. I am surely taking a risk believing in you. Do not take my vulnerability for granted. Do not kill me further with your self-deception and fragmentation.* Accordingly, forgiveness demands responses that nurture the culture of solidarity, which in turn bring the soothing balm

---

72. Taylor, "Role and Meaning," 55.

73. Taylor, "Role and Meaning," 55; Thomas, "'I Forgive,'"133.

74. Taylor, "Role and Meaning," 53.

75. It is a fact that I may bear resentment towards somebody. However, this resentment does not automatically make me lose my objectivity of the person. Despite my current state of unforgiveness, I can still acknowledge the offender as trustworthy, especially if he or she had acknowledged his or her wrong. It is just that I am still unable to forgive.

of peace, and ultimately reconciliation. Therefore, forgiveness challenges and even inspires us to live out ethics of disposition in love with the other.

In respecting plurality, the ethics of disposition, with love as its normative value, seeks to create a new post-conflict community without falling into the snare of modernity, which tends to focus on instrumental reason. If not, we remain trapped in a Manichean dualism and contesting ethical paradigms: diabolicization (used by victims; victors); deculpabilization (preferred by perpetrators); and banalization (used by bystanders and some professionals working with perpetrators). For the sake of reconciliation, we have to unlearn the rhetoric of diabolicization and/or deculpabilization and learn to walk in the path of mercy and compassion as Jesus did. This creates a new worldview and new ethic—an ethic of being characterized by "compassionate liberality"[76] as envisioned in the "Sermon on the Mount." This is an ethic that makes people live together in covenantal unity in freedom from fear, where the most crucial moral value is restoring ruptured relationships and trust.

Finally, Christians need to acknowledge that, unlike God, we do not and should not live entirely on the aneconomic level. Humans (even as Christians) live in a world that will always need the creative, even if tensed, balance between equivalence (justice) and superabundance (love), although they do not necessarily oppose themselves. Like the engine of an automobile, they rub against themselves for the smooth running of the car. Without this friction, the automobile engine will not run. However, for the sake of the friction's end (smooth running of the engine), there is the need for a lubricant (engine oil). Grace, in my estimation, is the lubricant between justice and love; and that is why in my heuristic grace does not feature under love, justice, or peace. Humans do the trio. Grace is not part of what we do. It is a gift poured upon human effort so that we might just arrive at the end (perfect reconciliation). This reconciliation has a higher probability when the new generations, like Caleb, are formed with a different spirit—of trust and faithfulness (cf. Num 14:24). Hence, even if their parents and grandparents cannot enter the promised land, these new generations will get there someday. Therefore, we cannot factor out spirituality on our journey towards reconciliation. Accordingly, one sees an important role for religions (e.g., Christianity) and the humanities (e.g., arts, media, educational institutions) as agents of social transformation and reconciliation. This is why this book's underlying heuristic for overcoming toxic emotions proceeded at different levels and sectors with various stakeholders in

---

76. Cf. Holgate, *Prodigality*, 170–83.

view so that one day, some generations with a different spirit of trust and faithfulness will enter the promised land of reconciliation.

Ultimately, restorative justice is an overtly optimistic option for conflict resolution. It is optimistic that the victim can reach out in embrace. Hopefully, the perpetrator has the nobility to ask and receive forgiveness and accept the invitation to embrace. It is positive that warring communities can create a house of love together and dismantle their huts of hatred. It is confident that the Lion and Rabbit can live together in peace. It is sanguine that the Elder, the Perpetrator, and the Victim in the Prologue to this book can one day hold hands together and dance to the song by Onyeka Onwenu, a Nigerian female musician: "One Love Keep Us Together." Paradisiacal!

Is it feasible in this world? Possibly.

Is it possible in Nigeria during my generation's lifetime? I hope!

Appendix 1

Appendix 2

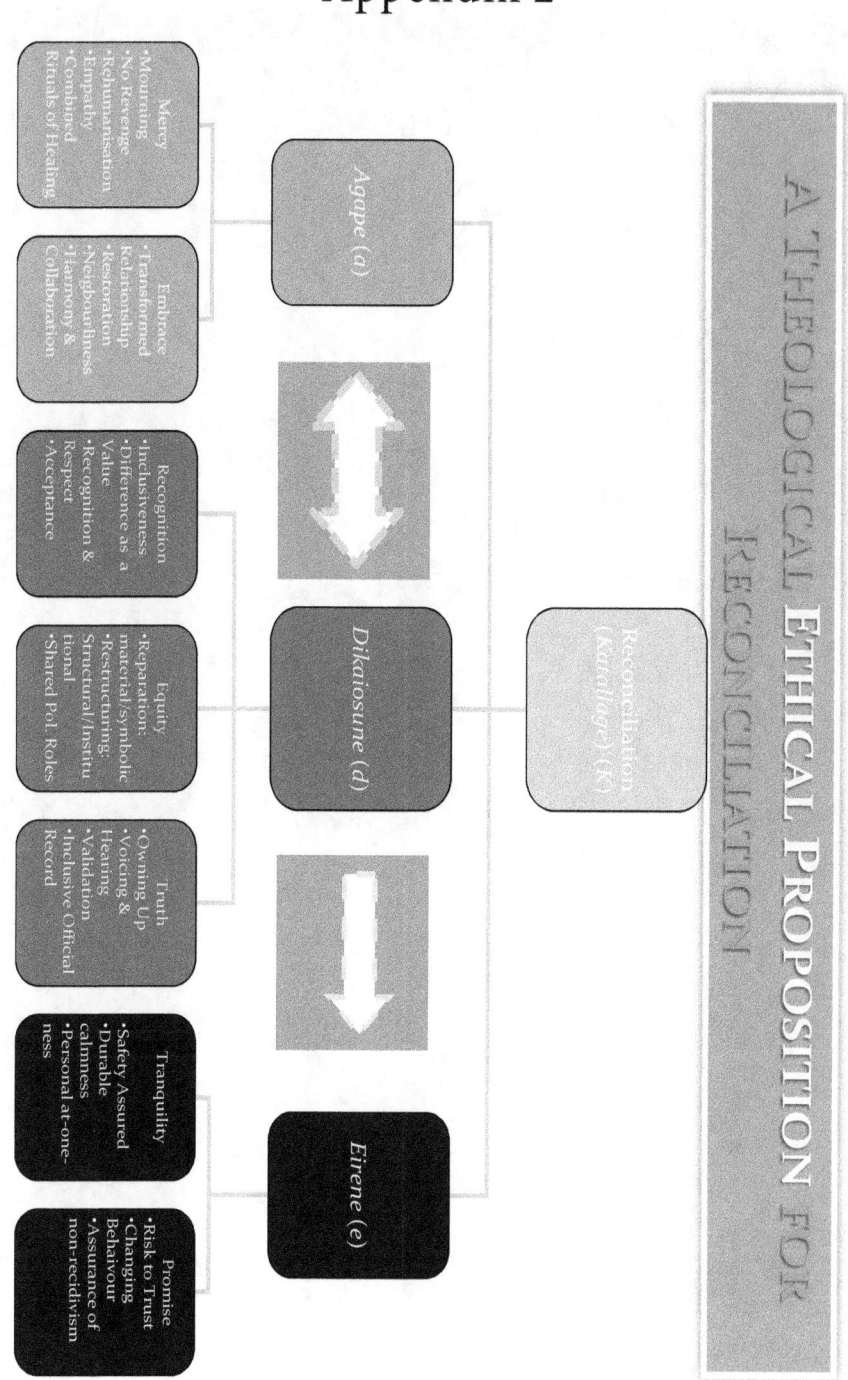

Bibliography

Abimbola, Wande. *Sixteen Great Poems of Ifa*. Geneva: Unesco, 1975.
Achebe, Chinua. *Home and Exile*. Oxford: Oxford University Press, 2000.
Achtemeir, E. R. "Righteousness in the OT." In *The Interpreter's® Dictionary of the Bible: An Illustrated Encyclopedia*, edited by Buttrick George, 80–85. New York: Nashville, 1962.
Achtemeir, P. J. "Righteousness in the NT." In *The Interpreter's® Dictionary of the Bible: An Illustrated Encyclopedia*, edited by Buttrick George, 91–99. New York: Nashville, 1962.
Adam, Heribert. "Divided Memories: How Emerging Democracies Deal with the Crimes of Previous Regimes." In *Legal Institutions and Collective Memories*, edited by Susanne Kartstedt, 79–100. Oñati Series in Law and Society. Oxford: Hart, 2009.
Adeleke, Duro. "Lessons from Yoruba Mythology." *Journal of Asian and African Studies* 39.3 (2004) 179–91.
Afigbo, Adiele. "Popular Uprising as a Reflection on Legal Justice." In *Nigerian History, Politics and Affairs: The Collected Essays of Adiele Afigbo*, edited by Toyin Falola, 571–78. Trenton: Africa World, 2005.
Agbaje, Bayo. "Proverbs: A Strategy for Resolving Conflict in Yoruba Society." *Journal of African Cultural Studies* 15.2 (2002) 237–43.
Aina, Raymond Olusesan. "Catholic Identity and Civic Demands in the Light of 'Political Homelessness': On the Revalorisation of Religion in a Post-Secular Age." In *The Christian, Elections and Faithful Citizenship in a Pluralist Society*, edited by Luke E. Ijezie et al., 460–71. Port Harcourt: CATHAN, 2019.
———. "Catholic Theology of Post-Conflict Restorative Justice: The Doctrine of Hypostatic Union as a Viable Inspiration." *Journal of Moral Theology* 5.2 (2016) 81–98.
———. "A Christian Response to Insecurity and Intractable Conflicts in Nigeria: A Challenge to the Youth." *Nigerian Journal of Religion and Society* 3 (2013) 34–52.
———. "Ecumenical Cooperation at the Service of National Reconciliation: A Proposal." *Nigerian Journal of Religion and Society* 6 (2016) 56–72.
———. "Good Governance and Overcoming Insecurity in Nigeria: An Agenda for Pastoral Leaders and Agents." *Journal of Inculturation Theology* 16.2 (2019) 218–33.

———. "GST 222: Peace and Conflict Resolution Studies in view of *Africae Munus*—Overcoming Globalisation of Intolerance and Indifference." In *Youth Formation and Globalisation in the Nigerian Context*, edited by Luke Ijezie et al., 249–67. Port Harcourt: CATHAN, 2018.

———. "The Hypostatic Union and Ethic of Reconciliation and Forgiveness: Inspirations for Christian Mission in Transitional Societies." The 35th Annual Conference (Virtual) of the Catholic Theological Association of Nigeria (CATHAN), April 6–10, 2021.

———. "Killing for God in Nigeria: Looking Forward by Looking Backward." In *Religion and Violence: The Potential for Conflict and Peace*, edited by Klaus Krämer and Klaus Vellguth, 95–103. One World Theology Series. Quezon City: Claretian, 2021.

———. "Levinas' Post-Holocaust Ethic, Responsibility Ethic, and Catholic Social Thought." *The Nigerian Journal of Theology* 32 (2018) 21–42.

———. "The Mission of the Church in Africa Today: *Reconciliation?*" *African Ecclesial Review* 50.3–4 (2008) 218–65.

———. "Nigeria's HRVIC & Its Restorative Justice: The Promises, Tensions and Inspirations for Transitional Societies." *African Journal of Criminology & Justice Studies* 4.1 (2010) 55–86.

———. "Nigeria's Post-Amalgamation Volatility: Are the Gods to Blame?" *Nigerian Journal of Religion and Society* 4 (2014) 14–31.

———. "Overcoming 'Toxic' Emotions and the Role of Restorative Justice: A Christian Ethical Reflection on Restorative Justice's Promises, Ambiguities and Inspirations towards Peacebuilding in Nigeria." PhD diss., Leuven: Katholieke Universiteit, 2010.

———. "Religion, Politics and the Angst of a Nation-To-Be: Situational Identities and the Salience of Religious Pluralism." In *Human Rights, Religion and Society (Fs Jake Omang Otonko)*, edited by Matthew Michael et al., 333–49. Jos: Eiwa, 2020.

Amosu, Akwe. "South Africa: Tutu Says Poverty, Aids Could Destabilise Nation." *AllAfrica*. November 4, 2001. Online. http//allafrica.com/stories/200111050100.html.

"All About the Oputa Panel (H.R.V.I.C)." http//www.nigerianmuse.com/nigeriawatch/oputa/.

Allan, Alfred, and Marietjie Allan. "The South African Truth and Reconciliation Commission as a Therapeutic Tool." *Behavioral Sciences & the Law* 18.4 (2000) 459–77.

Allan, Alfred, et al. "Exploration of the Association between Apology and Forgiveness amongst Victims of Human Rights violations." *Behavioral Sciences & the Law* 24.1 (2006) 87–102.

Allen, Tim. "The International Criminal Court and the Invention of Traditional Justice in Northern Uganda." *Politique africaine* 107 (2007) 147–66.

Allsopp, Michael. *Renewing Christian Ethics: The Catholic Tradition*. Scranton: Scranton University Press, 2005.

Amoda, Moyibi. "The Relationship of History, Thought, and Action with Respect to the Nigerian Situation." In *Nigeria Dilemma of Nationhood: An African Analysis of the Biafran Conflict*, edited by Joseph Okpaku, 152–228. Afro-American and African Studies. New York: Third, 1972.

Amstutz, Mark. "Is Reconciliation Possible After Genocide? The Case of Rwanda." *A Journal of Church and State* 48.3 (2006) 541–65.

Angermaier, Claudia. "Book Review: *Ending Impunity through International Judicial Institutions*." *Criminal Law Forum* 17.2 (2006) 229–33.

Anthonissen, Christine. "A Critical Analysis of Reporting on the TRC Discourses in *Die Kerkbode*." *Scriptura* 83 (2003) 258–75.

Anyadike, Obi. "Nigeria's Secret Programme to Lure Top Boko Haram Defectors." *The New Humanitarian*, August 19, 2021. https://www.thenewhumanitarian.org/news/2021/8/19/nigerias-secret-programme-to-lure-top-boko-haram-defectors.

Appleby, Scott. *The Ambivalence of the Sacred: Religion, Violence, and Reconciliation*. Lanham: Rowman, 2000.

Aquinas, St. Thomas. *Summa Theologica With Synoptical Charts*. Translated by Fathers of the English Dominican Province. 5 vols. Allen, TX: Christian Classics, 1981.

Arendt, Hannah. *The Human Condition*. 2nd ed. Chicago: University of Chicago Press, 1998.

Aristotle. *Nichomachean Ethics*. Edited by Paul Negri. Unabridged ed. Dover Thrift. Mineola, NY: Dover, 1998.

Awan, Alice, et al., eds. *Jubilee Celebration and National Reconciliation: Proceedings of the 29th Annual National Conference of the Catholic Laity Council of Nigeria, held at Lagos, December 2001*. N.p.: Catholic Laity Council of Nigeria, 2001.

Awolowo, Obafemi. *Path to Nigerian Freedom*. London: Faber & Faber, 1947.

Barnidge, Robert, Jr. "The Due Diligence Principle Under International Law." *International Community Law Review* 8.1 (2006) 81–121.

Bash, Anthony. *Forgiveness and Christian Ethics*. Studies in Christian Ethics. Edited by Robin Gill. Cambridge: Cambridge University Press, 2007.

Beigbeder, Yves. *International Justice against Impunity: Progress and New Challenges*. Leiden: Brill, 2005.

Belita, Jimmy. "When Sin Defines a Church: Towards A Kenosis Ecclesiology in Post-Colonial Age." *Hapag* 3.1–2 (2006) 185–204.

Bellitto, Christopher. "Teaching the Church's Mistakes: Historical Hermeneutics in *Memory and Reconciliation—The Church and the Faults of the Past*." *Horizons* 32.1 (2005) 123–35.

Benedict XV, Pope. "Apostolic Exhortation to the Peoples Now at War and to Their Rulers." https://www.vatican.va/content/benedict-xv/en/apost_exhortations/documents/hf_ben-xv_exh_19150728_fummo-chiamati.html.

———. "Note to the Heads of the Belligerent Peoples." http://www.academyofsciences.va/content/accademia/en/magisterium/benedictxv/1august1917.pdf.

Benedict XVI, Pope. "*Deus Caritas Est* Encyclical Letter on Christian Love." https://www.vatican.va/content/benedict-xvi/en/encyclicals/documents/hf_ben-xvi_enc_20051225_deus-caritas-est.html.

———. "Encyclical Letter *Caritas in Veritate* On Integral Human Development in Charity and Truth." https://www.vatican.va/content/benedict-xvi/en/encyclicals/documents/hf_ben-xvi_enc_20090629_caritas-in-veritate.html.

Bennett, Harold. "Justice, OT." In *The New Interpreter's® Dictionary of the Bible*, edited by Katharine Sakenfield, 476–77. Nashville: Abingdon, 2008.

Benyera, Everisto. "South Africa's Truth and Reconciliation Commission and Nigeria's Oputa Panel: Comparison, Lessons and the Future of Truth Commissions in Africa." In *Nigeria-South Africa Relations and Regional Hegemonic Competence*, edited by Oluwaseun Tella, 183–202. Advances in African Economic, Social and Political Development. Cham: Springer, 2019.

Berlant, Lauren. "On the Case." *Critical Inquiry* 33.4 (2007) 663–72.

Bevans, Stephen. *Models of Contextual Theology*. Faith and Culture Series. Edited by Robert Schreiter. Maryknoll, NY: Orbis, 2000.

Bieringer, Reimund, and Mary Elsbernd, eds. *Normativity of the Future: Reading Biblical and Other Authoritative Texts in an Eschatological Perspective*. Annua Nuntia Lovaniensia. Leuven: Peeters, 2010.

Blyth, Myra N., et al., eds. *Forgiveness and Restorative Justice: Perspectives from Christian Theology*. Cham: Springer, 2021.

Böckle, Franz, and Coenraad van Ouwerkerk, eds. *Moral Problems and Christian Personalism*. Edited by Marcel Vanhengel. Concilium 5. New York: Paulist, 1965.

———. "Preface." In *Moral Problems and Christian Personalism*, edited by Franz Böckle and Coenraad van Ouwerkerk, 1–3. Concilium 5. New York: Paulist, 1965.

Boesak, Willa. *God's Wrathful Children: Political Oppression and Christian Ethics*. Grand Rapids: Eerdmans, 1995.

Bonino, Jose. *Toward a Christian Political Ethics*. Philadelphia: Fortress, 1983.

Botcharova, Olga. "Implementation of Track Two Diplomacy." In *Forgiveness and Reconciliation: Religion, Public Policy & Conflict Transformation*, edited by Raymond Helmick and Rodney Petersen, 279–304. Philadelphia: Templeton, 2002.

Botman, Russel. "Truth and Reconciliation The South Africa Case." In *Religion and Peacebuilding*, edited by Harold Coward and Gordon Smith, 243–60. Albany: State University of New York Press, 2004.

Bowker, John. *The Sacred Neuron: Extraordinary New Discoveries Linking Science and Religion*. London: Tauris, 2005.

Braithwaite, John. "Emancipation and Hope." *The Annals of the American Academy of Political and Social Science* 592 (2004) 79–98.

Bretzke, James. *A Morally Complex World: Engaging Contemporary Moral Theology*. Collegeville: Liturgical, 2004.

Broch-Due, Vigdis. "Violence and Belonging Analytical Reflections." In *Violence and Belonging: The Quest for Identity in Post-Colonial Africa*, edited by Vigdis Broch-Due, 1–40. London: Routledge, 2005.

Broughton, Geoff. *Restorative Christ Jesus, Justice, and Discipleship*. Eugene, OR: Pickwick, 2015.

Brueggemann, Walter. "Law as Response to Thou." In *Taking Responsibility: Comparative Analysis*, edited by Winston Davis, 87–105. Studies in Religion and Culture. Charlottesville: University Press of Virginia, 2001.

Burggraeve, Roger. "A Conversational God as the Source of a Response Ethics." In *Theology and Conversation: Towards a Relational Theology*, edited by J. Haers and P. De Mey, 337–57. Bibliotheca Ephemeridum Theologicarum Lovaniensium. Leuven: University Press, 2003.

———. "The Good and Its Shadow: The View of Levinas on Human Rights as the Surpassing of Political Rationality." *Human Rights Review* 6.2 (2005) 80–101.

———. "Meaningful Living and Acting: An Ethical and Educational-Pastoral Model in Christian Perspective." *Louvain Studies* 13.1 (1988) 3–26; 13.2 (1988) 137–60.

———. "The Other and Me: Emmanuel Levinas on Interpersonal and Social Responsibility." *The Living Word* 114.5 (2008) 334–66.

———. "To Love 'Other-Wise:' Biblical Thought and Ethics [Course Note in 'Faith, Biblical Thought and Ethics']." Katholieke Universiteit, Leuven.

———. *The Wisdom of Love in the Service of Love: Emmanuel Levinas on Justice, Peace, and Human Rights*. Translated by Jeffrey Bloechl. Milwaukee: Marquette University Press, 2002.

Cahill, Lisa Sowle. "Goods for Whom? Defining Goods and Expanding Solidarity in Catholic Approaches to Violence." *Journal of Religious Ethics* 25.3 (2005) 183–219.
———. "Just War, Pacifism, Just Peace, and Peacebuilding." *Theological Studies* 80.1 (2019) 169–85. https//doi.org/10.1177/0040563918819808.
Campbell, John. "Ten Books for Approaching Religious Conflict in Nigeria." August 19, 2014. https//www.cfr.org/blog/ten-books-approaching-religious-conflict-nigeria.
Carmichael, Kay. *Sin and Forgiveness New Responses in a Changing World*. Hants: Ashgate, 2003.
Casanova, José. *Public Religions in the Modern World*. Chicago: University of Chicago Press, 1994.
———. "Religion, European Secular Identities, and European Integration." In *Religion in an Expanding Europe*, edited by Timothy Byrnes and Peter Katzenstein, 65–92. Cambridge: Cambridge University Press, 2006.
Casey, Conerly. "Mediating Justice: Youth, Media, and 'Affective Justice' in the Politics of Northern Nigeria." In *Democracy and Prebendalism in Nigeria Critical Interpretations*, edited by Wale Adebanwi and Ebenezer Obadare, 201–25. New York: Palgrave, 2013.
Cervantez, J. Michael. "What If I Can't Forgive? The Limits of Forgiveness." In *The Philosophy of Forgiveness—Volume IV: Christian Perspectives on Forgiveness*, edited by Gregory L. Bock, 135–46. Series in Philosophy of Forgiveness. Wilmington, DE: Vernon, 2019.
Chabal, Patrick, and Jean-Pascal Daloz. *Africa Works: Disorder as a Political Instrument*. African Issues. Oxford: James Currey, 1999.
Chapman, Audrey. "Introduction: Religion and Reconciliation in South Africa." In *Religion & Reconciliation in South Africa: Voices of Religious Leaders*, edited by Audrey Chapman and Bernard Spong, 1–16. Philadelphia: Templeton Foundation, 2003.
Chauvet, Louis-Marie. *Symbol and Sacrament: A Reinterpretation of Christian Experience*. Translated by Patrick Madigan and Madeleine Beaumont. Collegeville: Liturgical, 1995.
Chivers, Chris. "The Breaking of the Silence—and Then What?" *Church Times*, February 17, 2006.
Christie, Nils. "Conflicts as Property." *The British Journal of Criminology* 17.1 (1977) 1–15.
Clarke, Adele. *Situational Analysis: Grounded Theory After the Postmodern Turn*. Thousand Oaks: Sage, 2005.
"CNS Video—Cardinal Dolan on the Church in Africa." *Catholic News Service*, October 14, 2014. https://synodonfamily.wordpress.com/2014/10/14/cns-video-cardinal-dolan-on-the-church-in-africa/.
Coakley, Sarah. "What Does Chalcedon Solve and What Does it Not? Some Reflections on the Status and Meaning of the Chalcedonian 'Definition.'" In *The Incarnation: An Interdisciplinary Symposium on the Incarnation of the Son of God*, edited by Stephen Davis et al., 143–63. Oxford: Oxford University Press, 2002.
Collins, Robin. "Girard and Atonement: An Incarnational Theory of Mimetic Participation." In *Violence Renounced: Rene Girard, Biblical Studies*, edited by William Swartley, 132–53. Studies in Peace and Scripture. Telford, PA: Pandora, 2001.

Colvin, Christopher. "Shifting Geographies of Suffering and Recovery Traumatic Storytelling after Apartheid." In *Borders and Healers: Brokering Therapeutic Resources in Southeast Africa*, edited by Tracy Luedke and Harry West, 166-84. Bloomington: Indiana University Press, 2006.

Copeland, Shawn. "Black Political Theologies." In *The Blackwell Companion to Political Theology*, edited by Peter Scott and William Cavanaugh, 271-84. Blackwell Companions to Religion. Malden: Blackwell, 2004.

Corliss, Cody. "Truth Commissions and the Limits of Restorative Justice: Lessons Learned in South Africa's Cradock Four Case." *Michigan State University College Law Review* 21.2 (2013) 273-99.

Cottingham, John, ed. *Western Philosophy: An Anthology*. 2nd ed. Blackwell Philosophy Anthologies. Malden: Blackwell, 2008.

Council of Chalcedon. "Definition of Faith." In *Decrees of the Ecumenical Councils—Vol. I Nicaea I to Lateran V*, edited by Norman Tanner, 262-65. London: Sheed, 1990.

Cunneen, Chris. "Exploring the Relationship between Reparations, the Gross Violation of Human Rights, and Restorative Justice." In *Handbook of Restorative Justice: A Global Perspective*, edited by Dennis Sullivan and Larry Tifft, 355-68. London: Routledge, 2006.

Curle, Adam. "Peace Studies." *The Year Book of World Affairs* 30 (1976) 5-13.

Daley, Brian. "Nature and the 'Mode of Union:' Late Patristic Models for the Personal Unity of Christ." In *The Incarnation: An Interdisciplinary Symposium on the Incarnation of the Son of God*, edited by Stephen Davis et al., 164-96. Oxford: Oxford University Press, 2002.

Daly, Kathleen. "Restorative Justice: The Real Story." *Punishment and Society* 4.1 (2002) 55-79.

Danieli, Yael. "Essential Elements of Healing after Massive Trauma: Complex Needs Voiced by Victims/Survivors." In *Handbook of Restorative Justice: A Global Perspective*, edited by Dennis Sullivan and Larry Tifft, 343-54. London: Routledge, 2006.

Davis, Oliver. *A Theology of Compassion: Metaphysics of Difference and the Renewal of Tradition*. London: SCM, 2001.

Depoortere, Kristiaan. *A Different God: A Christian View of Suffering*. Leuven Theological and Pastoral Monographs. Edited by Terrence Merrigan. Louvain: Peeters, 1994.

Deschouwer, Kris. *The Politics of Belgium: Governing a Divided Society*. Comparative Government and Politics Series. New York: Palgrave, 2009.

De Tavernier, Johan. "Love for Enemy and Non-Retribution: A Plea for a Contextual and Prudent Understanding of Peace." In *Swords into Ploughshares: Theological Reflections on Peace*, edited by Roger Burggraeve and Marc Vervenne, 145-66. Leuven: Peeters, 1991.

De Wet, Erika. "The 'Friendly but Cautious' Reception of International Law in the Jurisprudence of the South African Constitutional Court: Some Critical Remarks." *Fordham International Law Journal* 28.6 (2005) 1529-65.

A Dictionary of the Yoruba Language. Ibadan: Oxford University Press, 1977.

Dignan, Jim. "Towards a Systemic Model of Restorative Justice: Reflections on the Concept, its Context and the Need for Clear Constraints." In *Restorative Justice and Criminal Justice: Competing or Reconcilable Paradigms?*, edited by Andrew von Hirsch et al., 135-56. Studies in Penal Theory and Penal Ethics. Oxford: Hart, 2003.

Dindia, Kathryn, and Tara Emmers-Sommer. "What Partners Do to Maintain Their Close Relationships." In *Close Relationships: Functions, Forms, and Processes*, edited by Patricia Noller and Judith Feeney, 305–24. Frontiers of Social Psychology. New York: Psychology, 2006.

Dinerman, Alice. *Revolution, Counter-Revolution and Revisionism in Postcolonial Africa: The Case of Mozambique, 1975–1994*. Routledge Studies in Modern History. London: Routledge, 2006.

Dombrowski, Daniel. *Not Even a Sparrow Falls: The Philosophy of Stephen R. L. Clark*. East Lansing: Michigan State University Press, 2000.

Dosenrode, Søren. "Instead of a Conclusion." In *Christianity and Resistance in the 20th Century: From Kaj Munk and Dietrich Bonhoeffer to Desmond Tutu*, edited by Søren Dosenrode, 277–81. Leiden: Brill, 2008.

Drumbl, Mark. "Restorative Justice and Collective Responsibility: Lessons for and From Rwandan Genocide." *Contemporary Justice Review* 5 (2002) 5–22.

Du Boulay, Shirley. *Tutu: Voice of the Voiceless*. Grand Rapids: Eerdmans, 1988.

Duffy, Maria. *Paul Ricoeur's Pedagogy of Pardon: A Narrative Theory of Memory and Forgetting*. New York: Continuum, 2009.

Dukes, Franklin, et al. *Reaching for Higher Ground in Conflict Resolution: Tools for Powerful Groups and Communities*. San Francisco: Jossey-Bass, 2000.

Dupuy, Bernard. "The Approach to the Question of Good and Evil in the Writings of Hans Jonas and Hannah Arendt." In *Good and Evil after Auschwitz: Ethical Implications for Today*, edited by Jack Bemporad, John Pawlikowski and Joseph Sievers, 179–90. Hoboken, NJ: KTAV, 2000.

du Toit, Fanie. "Public Discourse, Theology and the TRC: A Theological Appreciation of the South African Truth and Reconciliation Commission." *Literature & Theology* 13 (1999) 340–57.

Earl, Lee. "The Spiritual Problem of Crime: A Pastor's Call." In *God and the Victim: Theological Reflections on Evil, Victimization, Justice, and Forgiveness*, edited by Lisa Lampman and Michelle Shattuck, 235–49. Grand Rapids: Eerdmans, 1999.

Ellens, Harold, ed. *The Destructive Power of Religion: Violence in Judaism, Christianity, and Islam*. 3 vols. Westport: Praeger, 2004.

———. "Revenge, Justice, and Hope: Laura Blumenfeld's Journey." In *The Destructive Power of Religion: Violence in Judaism, Christianity, and Islam*, edited by Harold Ellens, 227–35. Contemporary Psychology Series. Westport: Praeger, 2004.

Elshtain, Jean B. "Politics and Forgiveness." In *Religion, Politics, and Peace*, edited by Leroy Rouner, 32–47. Boston University Studies in Philosophy and Religion 20. Notre Dame, IN: Notre Dame University Press, 1999.

Erickson, Millard. *Christian Theology*. 2nd ed. Grand Rapids, MI: Baker, 2004.

Fadipe, N. A. *The Sociology of the Yoruba*. Ibadan: University Press, 1970.

Falola, Toyin. *Nationalism and African Intellectuals*. Rochester: University of Rochester Press, 2001.

Farrelly, Collin. "Justice in Ideal Theory: A Refutation." *Political Studies* 55.4 (2007) 844–64.

Findlay, Mark, and Ralph Henham. *Beyond Punishment: Achieving International Criminal Justice*. New York: Palgrave Macmillan, 2010.

———. *Transforming International Criminal Justice: Retributive and Restorative Justice in Trial Process*. Devon: Willan, 2005.

Fisher, Ronald. "Interactive Conflict Resolution." In *Peacemaking in International Conflict Methods & Techniques*, edited by William Zartman, 227–72. Washington, DC: United States Institute of Peace, 2007.

Fitness, Julie. "Emotion and Cognition in Close Relationships." In *Close Relationships: Functions, Forms, and Processes*, edited by Patricia Noller and Judith Feeney, 285–303. Frontiers of Social Psychology Series. New York: Psychology, 2006.

Francis, Pope. *Encyclical Letter Fratelli Tutti of the Holy Father on Fraternity and Social Friendship*. https://www.vatican.va/content/francesco/en/encyclicals/documents/papa-francesco_20201003_enciclica-fratelli-tutti.html.

———. *Post-Synodal Apostolic Exhortation: Amoris Lætitia to Bishops, Priests and Deacons, Consecrated Persons, Christian Married Couples, and all the Lay Faithful on Love in the Family*. https://www.vatican.va/content/dam/francesco/pdf/apost_exhortations/documents/papa-francesco_esortazione-ap_20160319_amoris-laetitia_en.pdf.

Freeman, Mark, and Dražan Djukić. "Jus Post Bellum and Transitional Justice." In *Jus Post Bellum: Toward a Law of Transition from Conflict to Peace*, edited by Carsten Stahn and Jahn Kleffner, 213–27. The Hague: tmc Asser, 2008.

Fröhling, Edward. "'God, the Lord of Peace, Make Us a Face of Peace:' Contributions of the Catholic Church to Peace and Reconciliation." In *Religion and Violence: The Potential for Conflict and Peace*, edited by Klaus Krämer and Klaus Vellguth, 205–17. One World Theology Series. Quezon City: Claretian, 2021.

Ghali, Boutros-Boutros. *An Agenda for Peace: Preventive Diplomacy, Peacemaking and Peacekeeping*. https://www.un.org/ruleoflaw/files/A_47_277.pdf.

Geffre, Claude. "The God of Jesus and the Possibilities of History." *Concilium* 5 (2004) 69–76.

Gilligan, Carol. *In a Different Voice: Psychological Theory and Women's Development*. Cambridge, MA: Harvard University Press, 1996.

Glover, Jonathan. *Humanity: A Moral History of the Twentieth Century*. 1999. Reprint, New Haven: Yale University Press, 2000.

Govier, Trudy, and Wilhelm Verwoerd. "Trust and National Reconciliation." *Philosophy of the Social Sciences* 32.2 (2002) 178–205.

Gray, Christine. *International Law and the Use of Force*. 2nd ed. Oxford: Oxford University Press, 2004.

Green, Benedict. *Matthew, Poet of the Beatitudes*. Journal for the Study of the New Testament Supplement. Sheffield: Sheffield, 2001.

Gregory of Nazianzen. "The Third Theological Oration, on the Son." In *A Select Library of Nicene and Post-Nicene Fathers of the Christian Church—Cyril of Jerusalem and Gregory Nazianzen*, translated by Philip Schaff and Henry Wace, 301–9. Grand Rapids, MI: Eerdmans, 1978.

———. "To Cledonius the Priest against Apollinarius." In *A Select Library of Nicene and Post-Nicene Fathers of the Christian Church—Cyril of Jerusalem and Gregory Nazianzen*, 439–43. Grand Rapids, MI: Eerdmans, 1978.

Gula, Richard. "The Meaning and Limits of Moral Norms." In *Introduction to Christian Ethics: A Reader*, edited by Ronald Hamel and Kenneth Himes, 470–86. New York: Paulist, 1989.

———. *Reason Informed by Faith: Foundations for a Catholic Morality*. New York: Paulist, 1989.

Gundry, Robert. *Matthew: A Commentary on His Handbook for a Mixed Church under Persecution*. 2nd ed. Grand Rapids: Eerdmans, 1994.

Gutiérrez, Gustavo. "Liberation Theology and the Future of the Poor." Translated by Isabel Docampo and Fernando Santillana. In *Liberating the Future: God, Mammon, and Theology*, edited by Joerg Rieger, 96–123. Minneapolis: Fortress, 1998.

Haag, H. "Chāmās." In *Theological Dictionary of the Old Testament*, edited by Johannes Botterweck and Helmer Ringgren, translated by David Green, 478–87. Grand Rapids: Eerdmans, 1980.

Habermas, Jürgen. "Religion in the Public Sphere." *European Journal of Philosophy* 14.1 (2006) 1–25.

———. *Between Facts and Norms: Contributions to a Discourse Theory of Law and Democracy*. Translated by William Rehg. Paperback ed. Cambridge: Polity, 1997.

———. *Knowledge and Human Interests*. Translated by Jeremy Shapiro. Boston: Beacon, 1968.

Hamber, Brandon, and Hugo van der Merwe. "Rainbow of Reconciliation." *New People* 55 (1998) 19–22.

Harak, Simon. *Virtuous Passions: The Formation of Christian Character*. Eugene, OR: Wipf & Stock, 1993.

Harrington, Wilfried. *The Gospel according to St Luke*. London: Geoffrey Chapman, 1968.

Hayner, Priscilla. *Unspeakable Truths: Facing the Challenges of Truth Commissions*. Paperback ed. New York: Routledge, 2002.

Henderson, Michael. *Forgiveness: Breaking the Chain of Hate*. 2nd ed. Portland, OR: Arnica, 2003.

Hendrickx, Herman. *The Third Gospel for the Third World*. Vol. 2a, *Ministry in Galilee (Luke 3:1—6:49)*. 3 vols. Quezon City: Clarentian, 1997.

Hettema, Theo. *Reading for Good: Narrative Theology and Ethics in the Joseph's Story from the Perspective of Ricoeur's Hermeneutics*. Kampen: Kok, 1996.

Hiers, Richard. *Justice and Compassion in Biblical Law*. London: Continuum, 2009.

Hinze, Bradford. "Ecclesial Repentance and the Demands of Dialogue." *Theological Studies* 61.2 (2000) 220–35.

Holgate, David. *Prodigality, Liberality and Meanness in the Parable of the Prodigal Son: A Greco-Roman Perspective on Luke 15.11–32*. Journal for the Study of the New Testament. Supplement Series 187. Sheffield: Sheffield, 1999.

Hollenbach, David. "Report from Rwanda: An Interview with Augustin Karekezi." *America* 175.18 (1996) 13–17.

Howard, Michael. *The Invention of Peace and the Reinvention of War*. London: Profile, 2002.

Human Rights Violations Investigation Commission. *HRVIC Report: Brief on Memos*. Human Rights Violations Investigation Commission (Abuja, May 2002).

———. *HRVIC Report: Volume One*. Human Rights Violations Investigation Commission (Abuja, May 2002).

———. *HRVIC Report: Volume Two—International Context*. Human Rights Violations Investigation Commission (Abuja, May 2002).

———. *HRVIC Report: Volume Three—Research Reports*. Human Rights Violations Investigation Commission (Abuja, May 2002).

———. *HRVIC Report: Volume Four—Public Hearings*. Human Rights Violations Investigation Commission (Abuja, May 2002).

———. *HRVIC Report: Volume Seven—Summary, Conclusions and Recommendations*. Human Rights Violations Investigation Commission (Abuja, May 2002).

———. *Synoptic Overview of HRVIC Report: Conclusions and Recommendations (including Chairman's Foreword)*. Human Rights Violations Investigation Commission (Abuja, May 2002).

Hurley, Michael. "The Ecumenical Methodology of Forgiveness." *Irish Theological Quarterly* 68.4 (2003) 357–77.
Huyse, Luc. "Dealing with the Past and Imaging the Future." In *Peacebuilding: A Field Guide*, edited by Luc Reychler and Thania Paffenholz, 322–29. Boulder: Lynne Rienner, 2001.
———. "Dealing with the Past in South Africa." In *Peacebuilding: A Field Guide*, edited by Luc Reychler and Thania Paffenholz, 358–64. Boulder: Lynne Rienner, 2001.
Ignatief, Michael. "Imprisonment and the Need for Justice." *Theology* 45.764 (1992) 97–101.
Ihua, Bell. "The Nigeria Social Cohesion Survey #nscs2021: Nigeria Is Much More Divided Today Than 4 Years Ago." *Nigeria Social Cohesion Survey*, August 27, 2021. https://www.thenigerianvoice.com/news/301501/the-nigeria-social-cohesion-survey-nscs2021-nigeria-is-muc.html.
Ilibagiza, Immaculée. *Left to Tell Discovering God Amidst the Rwandan Holocaust*. Carlsbad: HayHouse, 2006.
Institute for Economics & Peace. *Global Peace Index 2018: Measuring Peace in a Complex World*. https://reliefweb.int/sites/reliefweb.int/files/resources/Global-Peace-Index-2018-2.pdf.
———. *Global Peace Index 2019: Measuring Peace in a Complex World*. https://www.visionofhumanity.org/wp-content/uploads/2020/10/GPI-2019web.pdf.
International Theological Commission. "Memory and Reconciliation: The Church and the Faults of the Past." https://www.vatican.va/roman_curia/congregations/cfaith/cti_documents/rc_con_cfaith_doc_20000307_memory-reconc-itc_en.html.
"Introduction to Part I." In *Princeton Readings in Religion and Violence*, edited by Mark Juergensmeyer and Margo Kitts, 7–12. Princeton, NJ: Princeton University Press, 2011.
Jamison, Christopher. "Might of Metaphysics." *The Tablet*, November 15, 2008.
Janssens, Louis. "Norms and Priorities in a Love Ethics." *Louvain Studies* 6.3 (1977) 207–38.
———. "Ontic Evil and Moral Evil." *Louvain Studies* 4.1 (1972) 115–56.
John Paul II, Pope. "*Sollicitudo Rei Socialis:* An Encyclical for the Twentieth Anniversary of *Populorum Progressio*." https://www.vatican.va/content/john-paul-ii/en/encyclicals/documents/hf_jp-ii_enc_30121987_sollicitudo-rei-socialis.html.
John XXIII, Pope. "*Pacem in Terris.*" https://www.vatican.va/content/john-xxiii/en/encyclicals/documents/hf_j-xxiii_enc_11041963_pacem.html.
Jones, Laurie. *Jesus, C.E.O Using Ancient Wisdom for Visionary Leadership*. Paperback ed. New York: Hyperion, 1995.
Juma, Laurence. "The Legitimacy of Indigenous Legal Institutions and Human Rights Practice in Kenya: An Old Debate Revisited." *Revue Africaine de Droit International et Compare* 14 (2006) 176–203.
Junker-Kenny, Maureen. "Capabilities, Convictions, and Public Theology." In *Memory, Narrativity, Self and the Challenge to Think God: The Reception within Theology of the Recent Work of Paul Ricœur*, edited by Maureen Junker-Kenny and Peter Kenny, 153–201. Münster: LIT, 2004.
Katongole, Emmanuel. "Violence and Social Imagination: Rethinking Theology and Politics in Africa." *Religion & Theology* 12.2 (2005) 145–71.
Kaufman, Jeffrey. "Restoration of the Assumptive World as an Act of Justice." In *Handbook of Restorative Justice: A Global Perspective*, edited by Dennis Sullivan and Larry Tifft, 221–29. London: Routledge, 2006.

Keenan, James. "Crises and Other Developments." *Theological Studies* 69.1 (2008) 125–43.

———. "Roger Burggraeve's Ethics of Growth in Context." In *Responsibility, God and Society: Theological Ethics in Dialogue (Fs Roger Burggraeve)*, edited by Johan De Tavernier et al., 287–304. Bibliotheca Ephemeridum Theologicarum Lovaniensium Series. Leuven: Peeters, 2008.

Keener, Craig. *A Commentary on the Gospel of Matthew*. Grand Rapids: Eerdmans, 1999.

Kharas, Homi, et al. "The Start of a New Poverty Narrative." https://www.brookings.edu/blog/future-development/2018/06/19/the-start-of-a-new-poverty-narrative/.

Kiess, John. "Restorative Justice and the International Criminal Court." *Journal of Moral Theology* 5.2 (2016) 116–42.

Kirk-Greene, A. H. M. *Crisis and Conflict in Nigeria: A Documentary Sourcebook, 1966–1969*. Vol. 1, *January 1966–July 1967*. 2 vols. London: Oxford University Press, 1971.

———. *Crisis and Conflict in Nigeria: A Documentary Sourcebook, 1966–1970*. Vol. 2, *July 1967–January 1970*. 2 vols. London: Oxford University Press, 1971.

———. *The Genesis of the Nigerian Civil War and the Theory of Fear*. Uppsala: The Scandinavian Institute of African Studies, 1975.

Klein, Naomi. *The Shock Doctrine: The Rise of Disaster Capitalism*. Paperback ed. London: Penguin, 2007.

Knauer, Peter. "A Good End Does not Justify an Evil Means—Even in a Teleological Ethics." In *Personalist Morals—Fs Louis Janssens*, edited by Joseph Selling, 71–84. Leuven: University Press, 1988.

Korieh, Chima, and Ugo Nwokeji, eds. *Religion, History, and Politics in Nigeria (Fs Ogbu Kalu)*. Lanham: University Press of America, 2005.

Krog, Antjie, et al. *There Was This Goat: Investigating the Truth Commission Testimony of Notrose Nobomvu Konile*. Scottsville: University of KwaZulu Natal Press, 2009.

Kubicki, Judith. "Sacramental Symbols in a Time of Violence and Disruption: Shaping a People of Hope and Eschatological Vision." In *Sacraments Revelation of the Humanity of God: Engaging the Fundamental Theology of Louis-Marie Chauvet*, edited by Philippe Bordeyne and Bruce Morrill, 171–85. Collegeville: Liturgical, 2008.

Kukah, Matthew Hassan. *Witness to Justice: An Insider's Account of Nigeria's Truth Commission*. Ibadan: Bookcraft, 2011.

Laato, Antti, and Johannes de Moor. "Introduction." In *Theodicy in the World of the Bible*, edited by Antti Laato and Johannes de Moor, vii–liv. Leiden: Brill, 2003.

Lalonde, Marc. "A Critical Theory of Religious Thought." *Studies in Religion* 34.3–4 (2005) 357–74.

Lederach, John. *Building Peace: Sustainable Reconciliation in Divided Societies*. Washington, DC: United States Institute of Peace Press, 1997.

———. "The Challenge of the 21st Century Justpeace." In *People Building Peace: 35 Inspiring Stories from Around the World*, edited by European Centre for Conflict Prevention, 27–36. Utrecht: European Centre for Conflict Prevention, 1999.

Lee, Sung Yong, and Kevin P. Clements. "Conclusion." In *Multi-level Reconciliation and Peacebuilding: Stakeholder Perspectives*, edited by Kevin P. Clements and Sung Yong Lee, 243–53. Routledge Studies in Peace and Conflict Resolution. London: Routledge, 2021.

LenkaBula, Puleng. "Beyond Anthropocentricity: *Botho/Ubuntu* and the Quest for Economic and Ecological Justice in Africa." *Religion & Theology* 15 (2008) 375–94.

Levinas, Emmanuel. *Otherwise than Being, or Beyond Essence*. Translated by Alphonso Lingis. The Hague: Martinus Nijhoff, 1981.

———. *Totality and Infinity: An Essay on Exteriority*. Translated by Alphonso Lingis. Pittsburgh: Duquesne University Press, 1969.

Llewellyn, Jennifer J., and Daniel Philpott, eds. *Restorative Justice, Reconciliation and Peacebuilding*. Oxford: Oxford University Press, 2014.

Lonergan, Bernard. "Moral Theology and the Human Sciences." In *Collected Works of Bernard Lonergan: Philosophical and Theological Papers 1965-1980*, edited by Robert Croken and Robert Doran, 301–12. Toronto: University of Toronto Press, 2004.

———. "The Transition from a Classicist World-View to Historical-Mindedness." In *A Second Collection: Papers by Bernard J. F. Lonergan, S. J.*, edited by William Ryan and Bernard Tyrrell, 1–9. London: Darton, 1974.

Lopez, Elias. *No Peace Without "Forgiving Justice:" Love in Politics*. Internationale Betrekkingen en Vredesonderzoek Sereis. Leuven: Centre for Peace Research and Strategic Studies, 2006.

Louw, Eric. *The Media and Political Process*. London: Sage, 2005.

Lovin, Robin. "Christian Realism for the Twenty-First Century." *Journal of Religious Ethics* 37.4 (2009) 669–82.

Luban, David. *Legal Ethics and Human Dignity*. Cambridge Studies in Philosophy and Law Series. Edited by Gerald Postema. Cambridge: Cambridge University Press, 2007.

Maclean, Iain. "Truth and Reconciliation: Irreconcilable Differences? An Ethical Evaluation of the South African Truth and Reconciliation Commission." *Religion & Theology* 6.3 (1999) 269–302.

Maier, Charles. "A Surfeit of Memory? Reflections on History, Melancholy, and Denial." *History and Memory* 5.2 (1993) 136–51.

Makofane, K., and N. Botha. "Christianity and Social Transformation in Post-apartheid South Africa: From Prophetic Quietism to Signs of Prophetic Recovery." *Acta Theologica* 39 (2019) 88–103.

Maluleke, Tinyiko. "Reconciliation in South Africa Ten Years Later." *Journal of Theology for Southern Africa* 123 (2005) 105–20.

———. "The South African Truth and Reconciliation Discourse: A Black Theological Evaluation." *Journal of Black Theology in South Africa* 12.1 (1998) 35–58.

Mani, Rama. *Beyond Retribution: Seeking Justice in the Shadows of War*. Cambridge: Polity, 2002.

Massart-Piérard, Françoise, and Peter Bursens. "Belgian Federalism and Foreign Relations: Between Cooperation and Pragmatism." In *Dialogues on Foreign Relations in Federal Countries*, edited by Raoul Blindenbacher and Chandra Pasma, 18–20. A Global Dialogue on Federalism Series. Ottawa: Forums of Federation, 2007.

Marshall, Christopher. *All Things Reconciled: Essays on Restorative Justice, Religious Violence, and the Interpretation of Scripture*. Eugene, OR: Cascade, 2018.

———. *Beyond Retribution: A New Testament Vision for Justice, Crime, and Punishment*. Studies in Peace and Scripture. Grand Rapids, MI: Eerdmans, 2001.

Mathews, Dylan. "What Lessons Can Be Learned?" In *Towards Better Peacebuilding Practice: On Lessons Learned, Evaluation Practices and Aid & Conflict*, edited by Anneke Galama and Paul Van Tongeren, 147–50. Utrecht: European Centre for Conflict Prevention, 2002.

McCormick, Richard. "Ambiguity in Moral Choice." In *Doing Evil to Achieve Good: Moral Choice in Conflict Situations*, edited by Richard McCormick and Paul Ramsey, 7–53. Chicago: Loyola University Press, 1978.

McCullum, Hugh. *The Angels Have Left Us: The Rwanda Tragedy and the Churches*. Risk Series. Geneva: WCC, 1995.

McKnight, C. "Justice, Righteousness." In *Dictionary of Jesus and the Gospels*, edited by Joel Green and Scot McKnight, 411–16. Downers Grove: InterVarsity, 1992.

Meiring, P. G. J. (Piet). "Bonhoeffer and Costly Reconciliation in South Africa— Through the Lens of the South African Truth and Reconciliation Commission." In *Ecodomy—Life in Its Fullness, Brokenness and Wholeness*, edited by Dirk J. Human, 18–34. Verbum et Ecclesia Series. Durbanville: AOSIS (Pty), 2017.

Meredith, Martin. *The State of Africa: A History of Fifty Years of Independence*. London: Free, 2006.

Metz, Johann Baptist. "A Short Apology of Narrative." In *Why Narrative? Readings in Narrative Theology*, edited by Stanley Hauerwas and Jones Gregory, 251–62. Grand Rapids: Eerdmans, 1989.

Metz, John Baptist. "Toward a Christianity of Political Compassion." Translated by Matthew Ashley. In *Love That Produces Hope: The Thought of Ignacio Ellacuría*, edited by Kevin Burke and Robert Lassalle-Klein, 250–53. Collegeville: Liturgical, 2006.

Miedema, Maaike. "Introduction: Educating Critical Citizens." In *People Building Peace: 35 Inspiring Stories from Around the World*, edited by European Centre for Conflict Prevention, 268–75. Utrecht: European Centre for Conflict Prevention, 1999.

Miller, Marlin. "Girardian Perspectives and Christian Atonement." In *Violence Renounced: Rene Girard, Biblical Studies, and Peacemaking*, edited by William Swartley, 31–48. Studies in Peace and Scripture. Telford, PA: Pandora, 2001.

Mitchell, Stephen. *Can Love Last? The Fate of Romance over Time*. New York: Norton, 2003.

Mojola, Aloo Osotsi. "The African Bantu Concept of Ubuntu in the Theology and Practice of Bishop Desmond Tutu and Its Implications for African Biblical Hermeneutics." In *Navigating African Biblical Hermeneutics: Trends and Themes from Our Pots and Our Calabashes*, edited by Madipoane Masenya and Kenneth N. Ngwa, 57–68. Newcastle upon Tyne: Cambridge Scholars, 2018.

———. "Ubuntu in the Christian Theology and Praxis of Archbishop Desmond Tutu and Its Implication for Global Justice and Human Rights." In *Ubuntu and the Reconstitution of Community*, edited by James Ogude, 21–39. Bloomington, IN: Indiana University Press, 2019.

Monbourquette, John. *How to Forgive A Step-by-Step Guide*. Translated by Kathy Poor and Bernadette Gasslem. Cincinnati: Darton, 2000.

Moule, C. F. D. *Forgiveness and Reconciliation and Other New Testament Themes*. London: SPCK, 1998.

Muhammad, Abdulrasheed A. "Religious Conflicts in Nigeria and Its Implications for Political Stability." *The Social Sciences* 3.2 (2008) 121–25.

Muller-Fahrenholz, Geiko. *The Kingdom and the Power: The Theology of Jurgen Moltmann*. London: SCM, 2000.

Naqvi, Yasmin. "Amnesty for War Crimes: Defining the Limits of International Recognition." *International Review of the Red Cross* 85.851 (2003) 583–625.

Niebuhr, Reinhold. *Moral Man and Immoral Society: A Study in Ethics and Politics*. London; New York: Continuum, 2005.

———. "Why the Christian Church Is Not Pacifist." In *Princeton Readings in Religion and Violence*, edited by Mark Juergensmeyer and Margo Kitts, 45–54. Princeton, NJ: Princeton University Press, 2011.

Norris, Kristopher. "'Never Again': Recent Shifts in the Roman Catholic Just War Theory and the Question of 'Functional Pacifism.'" *Journal of Religious Ethics* 42.1 (2014) 109–36.

Norris, Pippa. *Driving Democracy: Do Power-Sharing Institution Work?* Cambridge: Cambridge University Press, 2008.

Nwogu, Nneoma. *Shaping Truth, Reshaping Justice: Sectarian Politics and the Nigerian Truth Commission*. Lanham: Lexington, 2007.

O'Collins, Gerald. *Christology: A Biblical, Historical, and Systematic Study of Jesus*. Oxford: Oxford University Press, 1995.

O'Connell, James. "The Fragility of Stability: The Fall of the Nigerian Federal Government, 1966." In *Protest and Power in Black Africa*, edited by Robert Rotberg and Ali Mazrui, 1012–34. New York: Oxford University Press, 1970.

Odozor, Paulinus. "An African Moral Theology of Inculturation." *Theological Studies* 69.3 (2008) 583–609.

———. *Morality Truly Christian, Truly African: Foundational, Methodological, and Theological Considerations*. Notre Dame: Notre Dame University Press, 2014.

Oduyoye, Modupe. *The Vocabulary of Yoruba Religious Discourse*. Ibadan: Daystar, 1972.

Okpu, Ugbana. *Ethnic Minority Problems in Nigerian Politics: 1960–1965*. Studia Historica Upsaliensia. Edited by Sven Nilsson et al. Uppsala: Acta Universitatis Upsaliensis, 1977.

Omale, Don John. *Restorative Justice and Victimology: Euro-Africa Perspectives*. Oisterwijk: Wolf Legal, 2012.

———. *Understanding "Restorative Justice": A Handbook for Criminal Justice Stakeholders*. Enugu: Trinity-Biz, 2005.

Omonokhua, Cornelius A., et al., eds. *Peace and Reconciliation: A Nigerian Conversation*. Abuja: Catholic Secretariat of Nigeria, 2014.

Onuoha, Austin. "The Dilemma of Restorative Justice when 'All Are Guilty': A Case Study of the Conflicts in the Niger Delta Region of Nigeria." *African Journal on Conflict Resolution* 7.1 (2007) 63–88.

Opongo, Elias. *Making Choices for Peace Aid Agencies in Field Diplomacy*. Nairobi: Pauline, 2006.

———. "Spiritual-Diplomatic and Just Peace Approach to Ending Protracted Conflict in South Sudan." In *African Theology in the 21st Century: A Call to Baraza*, edited by Elias Opongo and Paul Bere, 78–100. Nairobi: Paulines, 2021.

Pabst, Adrian. "Can There Be a Just War Without a Just Peace?" *New Blackfriars* 88.1018 (2007) 722–38.

Paden, John. *Muslim Civic Cultures and Conflict Resolution: The Challenges of Democratic Federalism in Nigeria*. Washington, DC: Brookings, 2005.

Parmentier, Stephan, and Elmar Weitekamp, eds. *Crime and Human Rights.* Edited by Mathieu Deflem and Jeffrey Ulmer. Sociology of Crime, Law and Deviance Series 9. Bingley: JAI, 2007.

———. "Political Crimes and Serious Violations of Human Rights: Towards a Criminology of International Crimes." In *Crime and Human Rights*, edited by Stephan Parmentier and Elmar Weitekamp, 109–44. Sociology of Crime, Law and Deviance Series. Bingley: JAI, 2007.

Paul VI, Pope. "*Evangelii Nuntiandi*—Apostolic Exhortation." https://www.vatican.va/content/paul-vi/en/apost_exhortations/documents/hf_p-vi_exh_19751208_evangelii-nuntiandi.html.

Pavlich, George. "Deconstructing Restoration: The Promise of Restorative Justice." In *Restorative Justice: Theoretical Foundations*, edited by Elmar Weitekamp and Hans-Jürgen Kerner, 90–109. Devon: Willan, 2002.

———. "Towards an Ethics of Restorative Justice." In *Restorative Justice and the Law*, edited by Lode Walgrave, 1–18. Devon: Willan, 2002.

Perkins, Pheme. "Justice, NT." In *The New Interpreter's® Dictionary of the Bible*, edited by Katharine Sakenfield, 475–76. Nashville: Abingdon, 2008.

Poe, Danielle. "Peace Is Not Perpetual, Autonomous, or Rational." *Listening* 44.1 (2009) 37–48.

Pollefeyt, Didier. "Forgiveness and the Unforgivable after Auschwitz." In *Incredible Forgiveness: Christian Ethics between Fanaticism and Reconciliation*, edited by Didier Pollefeyt, 121–59. Leuven: Peeters, 2004.

———. "The Morality of Auschwitz? A Critical Confrontation with Peter J. Haas's Ethical Interpretation of the Holocaust." In *Good and Evil after Auschwitz: Ethical Implications for Today*, edited by Jack Bemporad et al., 119–37. Hoboken, NJ: KTAV, 2000.

Pontifical Council for Justice and Peace, ed. *Compendium of the Social Doctrine of the Church.* London: Burns & Oates, 2004.

Pope, Stephen. "The Role of Forgiveness in Reconciliation and Restorative Justice: A Christian Theological Perspective." In *Restorative Justice, Reconciliation and Peacebuilding*, edited by Jennifer J. Llewellyn and Daniel Philpott, 174–96. Oxford: Oxford University Press, 2014.

Potgieter, Elnari. *SA Reconciliation Barometer Survey 2019 Report.* https://www.ijr.org.za/portfolio-items/sa-reconciliation-barometer-2019/.

Prusak, Bernard. "Theological Considerations: Hermeneutical, Ecclesiological, Eschatological Regarding *Memory and Reconciliation: The Church and the Faults of the Past.*" *Horizons* 32.1 (2005) 136–51.

Research Institute on Christianity in Africa. "Faith Communities and Apartheid: The RICSA Report." In *Facing the Truth: South African Faith Communities and the Truth & Reconciliation Commission*, edited by James Cochrane et al., 15–77. Cape Town: David Philip, 1999.

Reychler, Luc. *Democratic Peace-building and Conflict Prevention: The Devil Is in the Transition.* Leuven: Leuven University Press, 1999.

Richardson, Neville. "*Sanctorum Communio* in a Time of Reconstruction? Theological Pointers for the Church in South Africa." *Journal of South African Theology* 127 (2007) 96–115.

Ricœur, Paul. "The Difficulty to Forgive." In *Memory, Narrativity, Self and the Challenge to Think God: The Reception within Theology of the Recent Work of Paul Ricœur*, edited by Maureen Junker-Kenny and Peter Kenny, 6–16. Münster: LIT, 2004.

———. "The Golden Rule: Exegetical and Theological Perplexities." *New Testament Studies* 36.3 (1990) 392–97.

———. "Memory and Forgetting." In *Questioning Ethics: Contemporary Debates in Philosophy*, edited by Richard Kearney and Mark Dooley, 5–11. London: Routledge, 1999.

———. *Memory, History, Forgetting*. Translated by Kathleen Blamey and David Pellauer. Chicago: The University of Chicago Press, 2004.

———. *The Symbolism of Evil*. Translated by Emerson Buchanan. Paperback Ariadne ed. Boston: Beacon, 1969.

Rigby, Andrew. *Justice and Reconciliation After the Violence*. Boulder: Lynne, 2001.

Robins, Steven. *From Revolution to Rights in South Africa*. Suffolk: James Currey, 2008.

Rohner, Holger-C., Jana Arsovska, and Ivo Aertsen. "Challenging Restorative Justice State-based Conflict, Mass Victimisation and the Changing Nature of Warfare." In *Restoring Justice after Large-Scale Violent Conflicts: Kosovo, DR Congo and the Israeli-Palestinian Case*, edited by Ivo Aertsen et al., 3–45. Devon: Willan, 2008.

Rosner, Brian. "Bonhoeffer: On Disappointment." In *The Consolations of Theology*, edited by Brian Rosner, 107–29. Grand Rapids: Eerdmans, 2008.

———, ed. *The Consolations of Theology*. Grand Rapids: Eerdmans, 2008.

Rothstein, Robert. "Fragile Peace and Its Aftermath." In *After the Peace: Resistance and Reconciliation*, edited by Robert Rothstein, 223–47. Boulder: Rienner, 1999.

Rotimi, Ola. *The Gods Are Not to Blame*. Ibadan: University of Ibadan Press, 1975.

SACBC Justice and Peace Department. *Race Relations and the Catholic Church in South Africa: A Decade After Apartheid*. Pretoria: Justice and Peace Department, 2005.

Sacks, Jonathan. *The Dignity of Difference: How to Avoid the Clash of Civilizations*. Rev. ed. London: Continuum, 2004.

———. *The Politics of Hope*. London: Vintage, 2000.

———. *To Heal a Fractured World: The Ethics of Responsibility*. London: Continuum, 2005.

Sacred Congregation for Divine Worship, ed. *The Divine Office: The Liturgy of the Hours According to the Roman Rite*. Vol. 3, *Ordinary Time, Weeks 1–17*. 3 vols. London: Collins, 1996.

Saint Caesarius of Arles. "A Reading from the Sermons of St Caesarius of Arles (Sermon 25,1)." In *The Divine Office: The Liturgy of the Hours According to the Roman Rite*, edited by Sacred Congregation for Divine Worship, 354–55. London: Collins, 1996.

Saint Gregory of Nyssa. "On Christian Perfection [PG 46, 283–286]." In *The Divine Office: The Liturgy of the Hours According to the Roman Rite*, edited by Sacred Congregation for Divine Worship, 224–25. London: Collins, 1996.

Sathirathai, Surakiart. "Renewing Our Global Values: A Multilateralism for Peace, Prosperity, and Freedom." *Harvard Human Rights Journal* 14 (2006) 1–28.

Schabas, William. *Genocide in International Law: The Crime of Crimes*. Cambridge: Cambridge University Press, 2000.

———. *The U.N. International Criminal Tribunals Former Yugoslavia, Rwanda and Sierra Leone*. Cambridge: Cambridge University Press, 2006.

Scheid, Anna Floerke. "Christian Peace Ethics Trends in the International (Anglophone) Debate." *Jahrbuch für Christliche Sozialwissenschaften* 58 (2018) 253–90. urn:nbn:de:hbz:6:3-jcsw-2018-22160.

———. "Just War Theory and Restorative Justice: Weaving a Consistent Ethic of Reconciliation." *Journal of Moral Theology* 5.2 (2016) 99–115.
Schreiter, Robert. "Peace-Building and Truth-Telling." *New Theology Review* 19.4 (2006) 48–56.
Schwager, Raymund. "Christology." In *The Blackwell Companion to Political Theology*, edited by Peter Scott and William Cavanaugh, 348–62. Malden, MA: Blackwell, 2004.
Schwartz, Murray. "The Professionalism and Accountability of Lawyers." *California Law Review* 66.4 (1978) 669–97.
Schweigert, Francis. "Undoing Violence: Restorative Justice Versus Punitive Justice." *Chicago Studies* 38.2 (1999) 207–27.
Selling, Joseph. "Authority and Moral Teaching in a Catholic Christian Context." In *Christian Ethics: An Introduction*, edited by Bernard Hoose, 57–71. London: Continuum, 1998.
———. "The Structure and Content of Ethical Discourse." In *Responsibility, God and Society: Theological Ethics in Dialogue (Fs Roger Burggraeve)*, edited by Johan De Tavernier et al., 371–87. Bibliotheca Ephemeridum Theologicarum Lovaniensium. Leuven: Peeters, 2008.
Shriver, Donald. "Repairing the Past: Polarities of Restorative Justice." *Crosscurrents* 57.2 (2007) 209–17.
Shuster, Marguerite. "The Incarnation in Selected Christmas Sermons." In *The Incarnation: An Interdisciplinary Symposium on the Incarnation of the Son of God*, edited by Stephen Davis et al., 373–96. Oxford: Oxford University Press, 2002.
Skotnicki, Andrew. "How Is Justice Restored?" *Studies in Christian Ethics* 19.2 (2006) 187–204.
Smith, Daniel. *A Culture of Corruption: Everyday Deception and Popular Discontent in Nigeria*. Princeton: Princeton University Press, 2007.
Smith, Tammy. "Narrative Boundaries and the Dynamics of Ethnic Conflict and Conciliation." *Poetics* 35.1 (2007) 22–46.
Sobrino, Jon. "Christianity and Reconciliation: The Way to a Utopia." *Concilium* 5 (2003) 80–90.
Sontag, Susan. *Regarding the Pain of Others*. Picador ed. New York: Picador, 2004.
Soyinka, Wole. *The Burden of Memory, the Muse of Forgiveness*. Oxford: Oxford University Press, 2000.
———. "Climate of Fear: I Am Right; You Are Dead (The Reith Lectures, Episode 5 of 5)." *BBC Radio 4*, May 5, 2004. https://www.bbc.co.uk/programmes/p00gm3z5.
———. *The Man Died: Prison Notes of Wole Soyinka*. Noonday ed. New York: Noonday, 1988.
———. *You Must Set Forth at Dawn: A Memoir*. Paperback ed. New York: Random, 2007.
Steffen, Lloyd. "Religion and Violence in Christian Traditions." In *Violence and the World's Religious Traditions: An Introduction*, edited by Mark Juergensmeyer et al., 109–39. New York: Oxford University Press, 2017.
Stern, Jessica. *Terror in the Name of God: Why Religious Militants Kill*. New York: HarperCollins, 2004.
Stovel, Laura. *Long Road Home: Building Reconciliation and Trust in Post-War Sierra Leone*. Transitional Justice Series. Edited by Stephan Parmentier, Jeremy Sarkin and Elmar Weitekamp. Antwerp: Intersentia, 2010.

Stover, Eric, and Harvey Weinstein, eds. *My Neighbour, My Enemy: Justice and Community in the Aftermath of Mass Atrocity*. Cambridge: Cambridge University Press, 2004.

Suberu, Rotimi. *Federalism and Ethnic Conflict in Nigeria*. Washington, DC: Institute of Peace, 2001.

Suleiman, Susan. *Crises of Memory and the Second World War*. Cambridge, MA: Harvard University Press, 2006.

Suy, Eric. *Corpus Iuris Gentium: A Collection of Basic Texts on Modern Interstate Relations*. Leuven: Acco, 1992.

Swartley, Willard. *Covenant of Peace: The Missing Peace in New Testament Theology and Ethics*. Studies in Peace and Scripture. Edited by Ben Ollenburger. Grand Rapids: Eerdmans, 2006.

Synod of Bishops. "Justice in the World: Second General Assembly (November 30, 1971)." In *The Gospel of Peace and Justice Catholic Social Teaching since Pope John*, edited by Joseph Gremillion, 513–29. Maryknoll: Orbis, 1976.

Szablowinski, Zenon. "Apology without Compensation, Compensation without Apology." *Pacifica* 18 (2005) 336–48.

Taylor, Michael H. "The Role and Meaning of Forgiveness." In *Forgiveness and Restorative Justice Perspectives from Christian Theology*, edited by Myra N. Blyth et al., 39–55. Cham: Springer, 2021.

Teleki, Mofihli, and Serges Djoyou Kamga. "Recognizing the Value of the African Knowledge System: The Case of Ubuntu and Restorative Justice." In *Ubuntu and the Reconstitution of Community*, edited by James Ogude, 303–27. Bloomington, IN: Indiana University Press, 2019.

Thesnaar, Christo. "Restorative Justice as a Key for Healing Communities." *Religion & Theology* 15 (2008) 53–73.

Thomas, Richard. "'I Forgive You:' A Pragmatic View of Afro-Christianity and Forgiveness." In *The Philosophy of Forgiveness—Volume IV Christian Perspectives on Forgiveness*, edited by Gregory L. Bock, 121–34. Series in Philosophy of Forgiveness. Wilmington, DE: Vernon, 2019.

Thoresen, Carl, et al. "Forgiveness and Health: An Unanswered Question." In *Forgiveness Theory, Research, and Practice*, edited by Michael McCullough et al., 254–80. New York: Guilford, 2000.

"TRC and the Church Conference Reconciliation: The Difficult Balancing between Justice and Forgiveness." *Ecunews* 3 (1996) 7–10.

Tutu, Desmond. *God Has a Dream: A Vision of Hope for Our Time*. New York: Doubleday, 2004.

———. *No Future Without Forgiveness*. Image Books ed. New York: Doubleday, 2000.

Umar, Muhammad S. "Hausa Traditional Political Culture, Islam, and Democracy: Historical Perspectives on Three Political Traditions." In *Democracy and Prebendalism in Nigeria: Critical Interpretations*, edited by Wale Adebanwi and Ebenezer Obadare, 177–200. New York: Palgrave, 2013.

United Nations Office on Drugs and Crime (UNODC), ed. *Handbook on Justice for Victims On the Use and Application of the Declaration of Basic Principles of Justice for Victims and Abuse of Power*. New York: Center for International Crime Prevention, 1999.

———. *Handbook on Restorative Justice Programmes*. 2nd ed. Criminal Justice Handbook Series. Vienna: United Nations, 2020.

Uwazie, Ernest, et al., eds. *Inter-Ethnic and Religious Conflict Resolution in Nigeria.* Lanham: Lexington, 1999.

Vacek, Edward. "Passions and Principles: A Sketch of an Affective Foundation for Morality." *Milltown Studies* 52 (2003) 67–94.

Van Rensburg, Fika. "A Code of Conduct for Children of God who Suffer Unjustly: Identity, Ethics and Ethos in 1 Peter." In *Identity, Ethics, and Ethos in the New Testament*, edited by Jan Van der Watt and François Malan, 473–509. Berlin: W de G, 2006.

Ventresca, Robert. "Recovering from the Past, Rediscovering History: The Problem of Memory and the Promise of History in Catholic Culture." *Logos* 8.4 (2005) 124–57.

Verstraeten, Johan. "Fundamental Changes in the Social Ethic of the Christian Churches." In *The Transformation of the Christian Churches in Western Europe 1945-2000*, edited by Leo Kenis et al., 175–93. KADOC Studies on Religion, Culture and Society. Leuven: Leuven University Press, 2010.

———. "The Tension Between '*Gesinnungsethiek*' and '*Verantwortungsethiek*': A Critical Interpretation of the Position of Max Weber in '*Politik als Beruf*.'" *Ethical Perspectives* 2.4 (1995) 180–87.

Verwoerd, Wilhelm. *Equity, Mercy, Forgiveness: Interpreting Amnesty within the South African Truth and Reconciliation Commission*. Morality and the Meaning of Life Series. Edited by Albert Musschenga. Leuven: Peeters, 2007.

Vetlesen, Arne. *Perception, Empathy, and Judgment: An Inquiry into the Preconditions of Moral Performance*. University Park: The Pennsylvania State University Press, 1994.

Villa-Vicencio, Charles. "Neither Too Much, Nor Too Little Justice: Amnesty in the South African Context." *Media Development* 2 (2002) 27–29.

———. "Transitional Justice, Restoration, and Prosecution." In *Handbook of Restorative Justice: A Global Perspective*, edited by Dennis Sullivan and Larry Tifft, 387–400. London: Routledge, 2006.

Vogel, Lawrence. "Jewish Philosophies After Heidegger: Levinas and Jonas on Responsibility." In *Taking Responsibility: Comparative Analysis*, edited by Winston Davis, 121–46. Studies in Religion and Culture. Charlottesville: University Press of Virginia, 2001.

Volf, Miroslav. "Difference, Violence, and Memory." *Irish Theological Quarterly* 74.1 (2009) 3–12.

———. *The End of Memory: Remembering Rightly in a Violent World*. Grand Rapids: Eerdmans, 2006.

———. *Exclusion and Embrace: A Theological Exploration of Identity, Otherness, and Reconciliation*. Nashville, NA: Abingdon, 1996.

Vorster, Nico. "Preventing Genocide: The Role of the Church." *Scottish Journal of Theology* 59.4 (2006) 375–94.

Vuylsteke, Tim. "Criminologist and Honorary Doctor John Braithwaite: 'Justice Is the Least Effective of All the Post-industrial Institutions.'" *Campuskrant International* (May 2008) 5.

Wadell, Paul. "Hope." In *The Collegeville Pastoral Dictionary of Biblical Theology*, edited by Carroll Stuhlmueller et al., 438–42. Collegeville: Liturgical, 1996.

Waldron, Vincent, and Douglas Kelley. *Communicating Forgiveness*. Los Angeles: Sage, 2008.

Walgrave, Lode. *Restorative Justice, Self-interest and Responsible Citizenship*. Devon: Willan, 2008.
Waliggo, John. "Making a Church That Is Truly African." In *Inculturation: Its Meaning and Urgency*, edited by John Waliggo et al., 11–30. Nairobi: St Paul, 1986.
Walker, Margaret. *Moral Repair: Reconstructing Moral Relations after Wrongdoing*. Cambridge: Cambridge University Press, 2006.
Werle, Gerhard. *The Principles of International Criminal Law*. The Hague: tmc Asser, 2005.
Wiesel, Elie. "Urgency of Hope." In *Religion, Politics and Peace*, edited by Leroy Rouner, 48–60. Notre Dame, IN: Notre Dame University Press, 1998.
World Council of Churches. *Participating in God's Mission of Reconciliation: A Resource for Churches in Situations of Conflict*. Faith and Order Series. Geneva: World Council of Churches, 2006.
Worthington, Everett, Jr. *Forgiveness and Reconciliation: Theory and Application*. New York: Routledge, 2006.
Wright, N. T. *Evil and the Loving Justice of God*. Downers Grove, IL: InterVarsity, 2006.
Wunsch, James. "*Nigeria*: Ethnic Conflict in Multinational West Africa." In *Encyclopedia of Modern Ethnic Conflicts*, edited by Joseph Rudolph Jr., 169–82. Westport: Greenwood, 2003.
Yusuf, Hakeem O. "Country Studies: Nigeria." In *Encyclopedia of Transitional Justice*, edited by Lavinia Stan and Nadia Nedelsky, 333–39. Cambridge: Cambridge University Press, 2013.
Zehr, Howard. *Changing Lenses: A New Focus for Crime and Justice*. 3rd ed. Scottdale: Herald, 2005.
———. "Journey to Belonging." In *Restorative Justice Theoretical Foundations*, edited by Elmar Weitekamp and Hans-Jurgen Kerner, 21–31. Devon: Willan, 2002.
———. *The Little Book of Restorative Justice*. Intercourse, PA: Good Books, 2002.
Ziesler, John. "Righteousness." In *The Oxford Companion to the Bible*, edited by Bruce Metzger and Michael Coogan, 655–56. Oxford: Oxford University Press, 1993.

Index

Note: Page numbers in *italics* indicate an illustration.

accountability, term usage, 43
Action Group (AG), 31
Adam, Heribert, 68–69
Afigbo, Adiele, 33n65
African peoples, moral theology of, 203–6
Afro-Christian Ethics, 11, 203–6
Agenda for Peace (Ghali), 220
aggression, cyclical pattern of, 5
Aguiyi-Ironsi (general), 31n59, 32–33
Allan, Alfred and Marietjie, 63, 94, 98n145
Allsopp, Michael, 164
Aluko, Bolaji, 44n25
amnesty, 61, 63, 78n76, 80, 83–88, 85n97, 211
Amstutz, Mark, 180
analogical imagination, limits, 118–19
Anambra Igbo *vs.* Owerri Igbo, 135
Annan, Kofi, 67, 128n14
Annual (Virtual) CATHAN Conference (2021), 191
Apartheid, South Africa, 17–18
apology, 94, 98n145
aporia
    of forgiveness, 84n96, 86, 88
    of healing, 88–95
Appleby, Scott, 69
Aquinas, Thomas of (Saint)
    debita proportio principle, 126
    on goodwill, 163

hope, characteristics of, 136
    on just war, 193–94
    reconciliation ethics, 10
    vengeance, ethics of, 143–44, 195, 218
Arendt, Hannah, 75, 90–91, 90–91n113, 200
atrocities, political elite on, 30–31
Augustine, Saint, 132, 193, 195
Awolowo, Obafemi (Chief), 3–4n5

Babaláwo ("father of mystery"), 19–20n29
Babangida, Ibrahim, 21, 56, 135
Balewa, Tafawa, 31
Ban Ki Moon, 128n14
banalization, 1, 3, 227
Bash, Anthony, 77n75, 78
"Basic Principles of Justice for Victims and Abuse of Power," (United Nations), 39
Beigbeder, Yves, 40
Belgium, legal honor recognition, 116
Bellita, Jimmy, 199n117
Bello, Ahmadu, 32, 32n62
Benedict XV, Pope, 197
Benedict XVI, Pope, 174–75
Benyera, Everisto, 41n16
"Better dead than public humiliation" (Yorùbá dictum), 26
Bevans, Steven, 157

Beyond Retribution (Mani), 186–87n71
Beyond Retribution (Marshall), 102
Bieringer, Reimund, 176
Blair, Tony, 113
Boesak, Willa, 82–83
Boko Haram, 36, 194
bombing of church (2011), 169
Bonhoeffer, Dietrich, 149
Botman, Russel, 83
Boutrous-Ghali, Boutrous, 128n14
Bowker, John, 23, 134
Braithwaite, John, 52, 54
brutality, term usage, 16
Buenos Aires, 59n2
Buhari, Muhammadu, 36, 85n97, 159
Bull, John, 22n34
Burden of Memory (Soyinka), 3n4
Burggraeve, Roger, 96–97, 122, 143
Butler, Joseph, 224n67

Caesarius of Arles, Saint, 125
Cahill, Lisa, 197–98
calm, term usage, 142
capital punishment, 84
Caritas in Veritate (Benedict XVI), 174
Caritas Nigeria, 221
Carmichael, Kay, 98n144
Casanova, José, 67, 68
case, term usage, 36
Cassin, René, 68n32
Catholic Church. *See* Roman Catholic Church
Catholic Education, 190–91
Catholic Laity Council of Nigeria, 178
Catholic Relief Services, 221
Catholic Secretariat of Nigeria, 187, 221
Catholic Social Teaching (CST), 191
cause, term usage, 36
Cervantez, Michael, 224–25
Chalcedonian Confession, 107–8, 112
The Challenge of Peace (USCCB), 196–97
Changing Lenses (Zehr), 103
chaos, 142–45, 218
Charter of Freedom (1955), 59–60
Chauvet, Louis-Marie, 174
Christ. *See* Jesus
Christian Democratic project, 68

Christian doctrine/theology, 10, 67–68
Christian ethics
    forgiveness, 87–88, 87n102, 208–13
    historical consciousness approach, 6–7
    of reconciliation, 112–13, 208–13
    responsibility, 205–6
    restorative justice, 7–8
    vengeance, 208–13
Christian identity, 10, 174, 203
"Christian Perfection" (Gregory of Nyssa), 174
Christians
    ethics of hospitality, 120–23
    pacifist theology, 192
    response to Islamic violence, 106–7
    as victims of religious violence, 4
    See also Roman Catholic Church
Christie, Nils, 1n2
citizens, response to impunity, 47, 50
Civil War (1966–1970), 14–15, 14n14
cleft country, description of, 74–75
clemency, 78n76
co-creators, 170, 172–73, 177–78
cold-blooded, term usage, 15
collective memory, 13–15
collective responsibility, 199–200, 199n117
Colvin, Christopher, 94
common good, term usage, 141
Common International Law, 127–28
communicatio idiomatum, term usage, 107–8, 219–220
community-related restorative justice, 53–54
comparative contextual analysis (CCA) methodology, 40
compassionate liberality," 227
Compendium of the Social Doctrine of the Church, 136, 173–74, 175
compensation, to victims, 84
conciliation, reconciliation and, 74–76
confession (truth-telling), 61
conflict, reasons for, 22–23
conflict resolution
    history of, 34–37
    story about, 19–20
consciousness approach, 6–7

INDEX

Consolations of Theology (Rosner), 149
constitutional conference (1966), 24
contemporary critical criminology, 10
"Convention on the Prevention and Punishment of the Crime of Genocide" (1948), 180
cooperation, term usage, 141
Corliss, Cody, 69n39
crimes against humanity, 39
criminal justice system
    International Criminal Court (ICC), 40–41
    post-colonial era, 44–48
    restorative justice as alternative, 51–56
Cross River-Ogoja-Rivers (COR), 31–33
Cunneen, Chris, 186
Curle, Adam, 16
Cyril of Alexandria, 115

Daley, Brian, 118
Daly, Kathleen, 35
dan Fodio, Usman, 63, 63n12
dance of death
    cause *versus* case, 36–37
    conflict resolution, 34–37
    ethical framework, 13–22
    ethical imperative, 25–30
    ethnic violence, 30–37
    historical statements, 30–37
    mass violence, 22–30
    memory crisis, 34–37
    overview, 12–13
    peaceful relationships, framework, 13–22
    toxic emotions, 25–30
de Gruchy, John, 61n7, 78
de Klerk, Frederik Willem, 60, 98n145
"*debita proportio*" principle of, 126
Decree 34 (Aguiyi-Ironsi), 32–33
deculpabilization, 91, 129, 227
Depoortere, Kristiaan, 170
deprivatization
    Europeans in Nigeria, 177–189
    religious, 67–68
Deus Caritas Est (Benedict XVI), 174
diabolicization, 1, 3, 18, 28, 227

diakaiosune (justice), 74n61, 76, 144n8, 150n29, 155–160
dialog, justice and, 133–35
"Difficulty to Forgive" (Ricoeur), 72
dignity, 44n31, 75
diplomacy, preventive measures, 220–21
dipolar theism, term usage, 217
disappointment, degree of, 149
discernment, virtue of, 100n153
Docetism, 173
doves, term usage, 5
Drumbl, Mark, 55n87
Du Boulay, Shirley, 95
du Toit, Fanie, 120–21
due diligence principle, 201, 201n123
due process, 46–47
Duffy, Maria, 79
Dutch Reformed Church, 111

Earl, Lee, 180–81
ecclesial mission, Roman Catholic Church, 10, 173–77
economic costs, 57
economics of reconstruction,, 41n16
education in reconciliation, 189–192
Egba people, 135
"ego-dystonic" persons, 98, 98n145
Ekiti people, 135
El Salvador, 186
election rigging (1959), 22, 22n34
Ellens, Harold, 171
Elsbernd, Mary, 176
Elshtain, Jean, 211
emotions, role, 22–30
empathy, 195
    See also mercy
endangerment, cyclical pattern of, 5–6
environment, Triangle of Reconciliation, 141–42
equality of honor, 115
Erickson, Millard, 91, 93
eschatological component (already and not yet), 161, 162–63, 198
Essack, Farid, 65
ethical imperative, of toxic emotions, 25–30
ethical movedness, 29–30
ethical realism, 99–100, 156, 161–62

ethical responsibility, 121–22, 129–130, 218
ethics
  education for, 190
  of hospitality, 120–23
ethnic violence, 30–37
Evangelii Nuntiandi (Paul VI), 173
evangelization, 10, 173–74
existential time, 14–15

face-to-face encounter, 121
Fadipe, N. A., 70
faith-based interventions, 221–23
"father of mystery" (*Babaláwo*), 19–20n29
fears, of one another, 24
female prisoners, 52
Findlay, Mark, 40
forgiveness
  aporia of, 84n96, 86, 88
  description of, 72–73
  future without, 225–28
  as gift, 226
  "No Future without Forgiveness," 73–80, 103
  as person-centered, 77
  political forgiveness, 78
  for reconciliation, 223–25
  Ricoeur on, 14, 14n8, 18, 30
  surrender and, 85–86n100
  term usage, 142, 211, 212, 224n67
  Tutu on, 61–67, 62
  in Xhosa language, 85–86n100
  See also unforgiveness
Francis, Pope
  Fratelli Tutti, 196, 208–13, 219–221
  Synod of Bishops (1971), 175–76
Frankl, Viktor, 18n24
Fratelli Tutti (Francis, Pope), 196, 208–13, 219–221
freedom, restorative justice and, 82, 133–34
Fulani people, 135, 194

Gaddafi, Muammar, 67
Germany
  Holocaust, 18n24, 26, 28, 89, 91
  Nazi program, 26, 28n52
  post-WWI, 26

Ghali, Boutros-Boutrous, 220
Gilligan, Carol, 130
Global Peace Index (GPI), 37
Glover, Jonathan, 17–18
God
  commandment to love, 117
  ecclesial mission, 202
  miracles, 87, 170–71
  omnipotence of, 169–177
  promise of blessing, 146
  "rainbow nation of God" idiom, 61
  on reconciliation, 159–160
The Gods Are Not to Blame (Rotimi), 22
Golden Rule, 29, 79n82, 111, 143
Govier, Trudy, 152
grace, 94, 198, 227
greed, term usage, 16
Gregory of Nyssa, 118, 174
GST 222: Peace and Conflict Resolution Studies, 189–192
Guatemala, 187
guilt, primary and secondary, 200–201, 219

Haas, Peter, 28n52
Habermas, Jürgen, 127
Hague Appeal for Peace, 189
Haiti, 186
Handbook of Restorative Justice (Villa-Vicencio), 71
hard diplomacy, 220–21
hardware approach, 39, 41
hate, term usage, 16
Hausa people, 135, 152
Hausa/Fulani people, 32
Hausa/Fulani *vs.* Middle Belt peoples, 31–33
hawks, term usage, 5
Hayner, Priscilla, 83, 145–46
healing, 88–95, 125–132
Henderson, Michael, 212
Henham, Ralph, 40
heteronomous autonomy, 172–73
Hinze, Bradford, 199
historical consciousness model, 6–7, 117
Hitler, Adolf, 193
Holocaust, Germany, 18n24, 26, 28, 89, 91
honor, equality of, 115

INDEX

hope
  achievements and, 67
  characteristics of, 136
  deficit of, 137n37
  need for, 132
  virtue of, 136–37
horizontal reconciliation, 107
Horn of Africa's "IGAD" initiative, 187
hospital analogy, 145
hospitality, ethics of, 120–23
HRVIC/TRC, 140, 155–160
Human Development Index (HDI), 37
human right, truth and justice, 208
Human Rights Violations Investigation Commission (HRVIC)
  criminal justice system, 44–48
  end of Commission, 135
  Kukah's views on, 147n16
  Nigeria's new government, 1, 2
  Nigeria's public hearings, 134
  recommendation of, 168
  report, 43, 188–89
  response to the past, 42–56
  United Nations and, 56n93
Humanae Vitae (Paul VI), 196
Humanity (Glover), 17–18
humanity, when evil happens, 170–72
husband/wife conflict, proverb of, 20n30
Huyse, Luc, 79
hypostatic union doctrine
  analogical imagination, limits of, 118–19
  going forward, 219–221
  just peace, 109, 109n17
  justice and reconciliation projects, 115–17
  path to peace, 208–9
  peacebuilding methods, 28
  reconciliation as renewal, 113–15
  reconciliation ethics, 110–19
  restorative justice, 107–10
  victims/perpetrators, challenges, 110–11

Ibadan people, 135

Igbo people
  Anambra Igbo *vs.* Owerri Igbo, 135
  COR group *vs.*, 31
  hostilities against, 16n18, 33
  Yorùbá and, 152
Iglesias, Enrique, 163n62
Ignatieff, Michael, 183
Ijebu people, 135
Ilibagiza, Immaculée, 78n79
"I'm Right; You're Dead" rhetoric, 26
impunity
  citizens, response to, 47, 50
  confronting, 186–87
  examples of, 46–47
  social harm and, 177
incarnation of reconciliation, 142
incarnational terminology, 217–19
insecurity, actions to counter, 192–201
institutional justice, 43
intelligent rationality, 134
interactive conflict resolution processes, 3
interdisciplinary research, 221–23
Intergovernmental Authority on Development (IGAD), 187
International Court of Justice, 220
International Covenant on Civil and Political Rights (ICCPR), 46–47, 46n42
International Criminal Court (ICC), 40–41
international criminal law, 39
international relations, 16
Islam, in post-colonial Africa, 4, 106
Islamic terrorists, 85n97

Jesus
  crucifixion of, 206–7
  forgiveness, 86, 86n101, 91–92
  kenosis of, 110–11
  nature of, 109
  on toxic emotion, 27–28, 27n49
John of Damascus, 113
John Paul II, Pope, 196, 199
John XXXII, Pope, 196
Josephine, genocide survivor, 198–99

Junker-Kenny, Maureen, 29n54, 163
just peace. *See* hypostatic union doctrine
just war
    conditions for, 193–96
    legitimate authority for, 194
    reasoning for, 192–93, 196–98
justice
    description of, 70–71
    dialog and, 133–35
    ecclesial mission and, 10, 173–77
    fairness and balance, 154–55
    healing and, 93–94
    historical statements on, 30–37
    projects today, 115–17
    reconciliation and, 145–48
    symbolic component of, 81–83
    term usage, 141
    as in-between word, 61
justice, peace, and reconciliation (JPR), 190–91
juvenile justice system, 52

Kamga, Serges, 69
Kant, Immanuel, 29, 29n54, 143
Katallage (reconciliation), 9, 74n61, 76, 79, 144n8, 150–51, 150n29, *151*
Katholieke Universiteit Leuven, 3
Kaufman, Jeffrey, 71, 72n54
Keenan, James, 96, 100n153
King and Tiny Bird story, 19–20, 148–49, 155, 160, 213–14, 218–220
Kirk-Greene, A.H.M., 24n45
"knowing forgetting," 211–12
Konile, Notrose, 85–86n100
Kukah, Bishop, 147, 147n16, 155n41
Kukah Center, 187, 221

Lagbaja (musician), 13
Lalonde, Marc, 130
"law beyond law," 42, 42n22
leadership, 168
Lederach, John Paul, 109n16
Legal Ethics and Human Dignity (Luban), 44n31
lesser evil, concept of, 196
Levinas, Emmanuel
    Aquinas and, 10
    ethical responsibility, 121–22, 218
    Other than the self, 18, 143, 144
licentiate studies in moral theology, 3
lion and the boar story, 59
Lonergan, Bernard, 6–7
love
    God's commandment to, 117
    justice and, 79
    ordo caritatis (order of love), 209
    peace and, 152–53
love-as-mercy, 72, 72n55, 74–75, 80, 131, 215
Lovin, Robin, 156, 162, 165
Luban, David, 44n31

Maclean, Iain, 82
Maine, Henry, 139
Mandela, Nelson, 98n144
Mani, Rama, 186–87n71
Manichean dualism, 81, 227
Maritain, Jacques, 68n32
Marshall, Christopher, 102
mass violence, 22–30
Maximus the Confessor, 113
Mbeki, Thabo, 67
McCullum, Hugh, 179
"*Me and You No Be Enemy (We Be Family)*" (Lagbaja), 13, 13n4
memory
    collective memory, 13–15
    crisis of, 34–37
    extreme claims, 34–35n70
    honoring the victims, 13–14
    overcoming toxic memories, 181–89
Memory, Narrativity, Self (Junker-Kenny), 29n54
mentally ill prisoners, 52
mercy, 125, 129, 195
    See also love-as-mercy
Miedema, Maaike, 189
"might is right" ethical logic, 25
miracles, 87, 170–71
Mitchell, Stephen, 5–6
Mojola, Aloo Osotsi, 62n8, 69
Moltmann, Jürgen, 132
Moosa, Cassim, 64n16
moral conscience, 18

Moral Man and Immoral Society (Niebuhr), 161–62
Moral Repair (Walker), 113–14
moral theology, 3, 203–6, 205
motivated, term usage, 16
mourning, 182–85
mythical stories, 43

Namibia, 186
National Council of Nigeria and the Cameroons, 31
National Ecumenical Summit on Justice and Peace, 181
National Reconciliation, 43
National Universities Commission (NUC), 190
Nazi program, 26, 28n52
  See also Holocaust, Germany
Needs-Accountability-Engagement, 122–24
Neighbor-Turned-Enemy, 139–140
New Nigerian (newspaper), 32
Niebuhr, Reinhold, 161–62, 193
Niger Delta, 36, 187
Niger Delta-Oil, 55n87
Nigeria
  church in, 177–189
  Civil War (1966-1970), 14–15, 14n14
  as a cleft country, 74–75
  collective violence (1966-1999), 44–48
  compassion through *kenosis*, 110–11
  contemporary critical criminology, 10
  Decree 34 (Aguiyi-Ironsi), 32–33
  democracy in, 156
  democratic culture, 21–22
  democratic rule (1999), 1
  First Republic, 31
  Global Peace Index (GPI), 37
  Human Development Index (HDI), 37
  January 1966 failed coup, 31–33, 31n59, 32n62
  July 31, 1966 successful coup, 33
  national identity, 3–4, 3–4n5

National Universities Commission (NUC), 190
positive peace culture, 57, 149
post-military rule, 42–56
post-TRC, 149–150
poverty capital of the world, 57, 57n102, 149, 231
Roman Catholic Church in, 177–189
Social Cohesion Index (2021), 159, 161
Sulhu Program (amnesty), 85n97
as transitional society, 56–57
violence, history of, 22–30
violence costs, 57
"No Future without Forgiveness," 73–80, 103
nonaccountability principle, 44
Nonjinge, Gugu, 158
Norris, Kristopher, 196, 197
Northern Peoples Congress, 31
Nupe people, 135
Nzeogwu, Kaduna, 32n62

Obasanjo, Olusegun, 42–43, 135
O'Connell, James, 21
Odozor, Paulinus, 203
Oedipus Rex (Greek myth), 22
Omale, Don John, 54–55, 55nn89–90
omnipotence, of God, 169–177
Onuoha, Austin, 53
Opongo, Elias, 109n17, 179
Oputa Panel
  Igbo people, 16n18
  legislative supremacy, 46n38
  principal expectations, 49
  younger generation, frustrations of, 22n34
  See also Truth and Reconciliation Commission (TRC)
order of execution, 126n5
order of intention, 126n5
ordo caritatis (order of love), 209
Other than the self, 18, 143, 144
Owerri Igbo, Anambra Igbo *vs.*, 135

pacifist theology, 73, 88, 192, 209–10

INDEX

Pandora's Box (restorative justice), 124–25
pardon
    conditions of, 83–85
    as excess of hope, 137n37
    as political forgiveness, 78
    punishment and, 79–80
pardon-return metaphor, 182
participation, principles of, 209
Paul VI, Pope, 173, 196
Pavlich, George, 119, 121
peace
    as a journey, 180
    love and, 152–53
    a modern invention, 139
    term usage, 72n55, 151
"Peace and Conflict Resolution Studies," 190
peace studies, 16
peacebuilding
    as architectural piece, 208n13
    based on "time perspectives," 214
    Church as locus, 179–181
    description of, 71, 71–72n53
    educational needs, 189–192
    overview, 38, 139
    programs for, 167
    restorative justice in, 148–155
    See also restorative justice
peacebuilding methods
    hypostatic union doctrine in, 28
    preventive diplomacy, 220–21
    road not taken, 56–58
    strategic methods, 2
    term usage, 38
peaceful relationships, ethical framework for, 13–22
penitential-oriented moral theology, 205
personal rights, unscrupulous infringement of, term usage, 16
physical violence, term usage, 16
police, as obstacle to restorative justice, 54–55
political forgiveness, 78
politically correct theologies, 165–66
"Politics and Forgiveness" (Elshtain), 211
Politics of Hope (Shils), 190

Pollefeyt, Didier, 28, 28n52
Pontifical Council for Christian Education, 191
Pope, Stephen, 223
"Pope of Peace" (Benedict XV), 197
positive peace culture, 57
positive sciences, 7
postbellum era
    advocacy, 221
    afterwords, 96, 226
    conflict transformation, 198
    contexts, 124, 149, 226
    ethical realism, 192
    healing, 48
    justice, 35, 143, 150, 167
    Nigeria (1970 and following), 22, 36–37, 157
    possibilities, 198, 211
    society, 124, 163
    Truth Commissions, 100
postbellum justice, term usage, 143, 167
post-military rule, 42–56, 42n22
poverty, preferential option for the poor, 204, 210
poverty capital of the world, 57, 57n102, 149, 231
preconditions, for reconciliation, 48, 218, 223–25
preferential option for the poor, 204, 210
presentism, 34n70
preventive diplomacy, 220–21
primary guilt, 200–201, 219
prison system, 45, 45n33, 52
professionalism principle, 44–45
profiling, term usage, 106
"Project for the Recovery of Historical Memory" (Guatemala), 187
prophetic witnesses, 30
psycho-cultural educational model, 191
psychology of unpeaceful relationships, 17–18
punishment, 46n42, 47, 66, 74, 80, 102, 143–44, 180
punitive sanction, 39

"rainbow nation of God" idiom, 61
recidivism, 126

INDEX

recognition, of persons/groups, 19–20
reconciliation
  authentic meaning of, 211
  barriers to, 158–59
  Christian ethics of, 112–13
  conciliation and, 74–76
  description of, 72
  education in, 189–192
  ethical reasoning concerning, 95–101
  ethics of, 10, 112–13, 208–13
  forgiveness for, 223–25
  Fratelli Tutti on, 208–13, 219–221
  God on, 159–160
  hardware approach, 39, 41
  horizontal, 107
  hypostatic union doctrine in, 107–10
  incarnation of, 142
  justice and, 145–48
  preconditions, for, 48, 218, 223–25
  projects today, 115–19
  religion, role in, 161, 168–69, 206–8
  as renewal, 113–15
  responsibility and, 61
  restorative justice and, 161–65
  software approach, 39–40
  Triangle of Reconciliation, 141–42
  values and, 153–54
  vertical, 107
  See also Katallage (reconciliation)
reconciliation, theology of
  HRVIC/TRC and, 140, 155–160
  illustration of, *141*
  justice and reconciliation, 145–48
  overview, 139–140
  theological framework, *105*
  Triangle of Reconciliation, 141–42
  Tutu's theology of, 61–67, 62, 83–88, 95–101
  vengeance, term usage, 143–44
Reconciliation Barometer, South Africa (2019), 158
redemptive assistance, 131–33
religion
  as centripetal force for reconciliation, 206–8
  as coloring relationships, 105–7

Islam, 4, 106
leaders, trust in, 168
as resource for human development, 127
retribution and, 101–4
revalorization of, 67–68, 67n26, 168
role in reconciliation, 161, 168–69
See also Christians
religious violence, 4
remedial justice, 47
renewal, term usage, 209
reparation, 80, 84
repentance, 114
resentment, 226n75
respect, term usage, 75
responsibility
  Christian ethics, 205–6
  collective, 199, 199n117
  definition of, 18
  reconciliation and, 61, 121–22
  regarding God's omnipotence, 169–177
  to seek healing, 90
responsive law, 42–43, 42n22
restitution, importance of, 21
restorative justice
  beyond frozenness and death, 136–38
  case for, 44–48
  Christian doctrine and, 10
  Christian theology and, 67–68
  claims of, 214
  comparative contextual analysis (CCA) methodology, 40
  conceptual framework, 10
  in contexts of chaos, 142–45, 218
  criminal justice system alternative, 51–56
  distinctions between concepts of, 8–9
  future without forgiveness, 225–28
  healing and, 125–132
  hypostatic union doctrine in, 107–10
  International Criminal Court (ICC), 40–41
  justice, not friendship, 74–75
  justice and dialog, 133–35

restorative justice *(continued)*
  overview of concepts, 9–11
  Pandora's Box, 124–25
  public interface, 48–51
  reconciliation and, 161–65
  restitution, importance of, 21
  summary of, 64, 74–75
  systematic theology and, 8
  theological ethics of, 105
  theology of, 119–123
  therapeutic dimension, 49
  three pillars of, 122–24
  Truth and Reconciliation Commission and, 155–160
  Tutu, Desmond and (*See* Tutu, Desmond (Archbishop))
  See also peacebuilding
Restorative Justice and Victimology (Omale), 55n90
restorative justice approach
  description of, 1–2
  primary stakeholders in, 2
  subjective factors, 2–3
Restorative Justice, Reconciliation and Peacebuilding (Llewellyn & Philpott), 222–23
restorative peacebuilding
  four principles, 38
  hypostatic union doctrine in, 28
  road not taken, 56–58
  term usage, 38
retribution, among religious actors, 101–4, *184*
retributive justice, 4–5
retributive punishment, 180
revenge, cyclical pattern of, 5
Richardson, Neville, 199
Ricoeur, Paul
  depth of fault/depth of forgiveness, 14, 30
  "Difficulty to Forgive," 72
  excessive memory, 13–14
  forgiveness, 14, 14n8, 18, 30, 72n57, 77n74
  Golden Rule and, 79n82, 111, 143
  hermeneutical mimetic arc, 215
  on Kant's Categorical Imperative, 29n54, 30
  as a mediator, 69–70
  metaphors, 182–83
  moral evil, 62n10
  public discourse on ethical reasoning issues, 100
  reconciliation, 185
  Symbolism of Evil, 80
  trace of forgiveness, 78n76
Rigby, Andrew, 90n111
Robins, Steven, 115–16
Roman Catholic Church (RCC)
  acknowledge its sins in Nigeria, 200
  Compendium of the Social Doctrine of the Church, 136, 173–74, 175
  ecclesial mission, 10, 173–77
  evangelization, 10, 173–74
  interdisciplinary collaboration, 221–23
  just war principles, 194, 194n90
  as locus for healing, 179–181
  movement away from just war, 196–97
  in Nigeria, 177–189
  penitential-oriented moral theology, 205
  preferential option for the poor, 204, 210
  role of, 202, 221–23
  saints and sinners, communion of, 198–201
  Secretariat of Nigeria, 187, 221
  social sin doctrine, 199
  St Philip Church, Madalla, 169
  toxic emotions and, 10
Roman Empire, 88
Rome Statute (1998), 40
Rosner, Brian, 149
Rothstein, Robert, 167
Rotimi, Ola, 22
Rwanda
  church in, 198–99
  de-politicized emergency aid, 179
  genocide (1994), 26, 78n79, 177, 180, 198
  impunity, confronting, 186
  mentioned, 79, 81
  postbellum practices, 150
  Tutu on forgiveness, 85n99, 91n113
  UN special tribunals, 39

Sacks, Jonathan, 116, 190
safety, term usage, 142
Santayana, 211
Sathirathai, Surakiart, 128, 128n14
scapegoat ritual (Leviticus 6:1-10), 27
Schabas, William, 39
Scheid, Anna Floerke, 119n54
secessionist groups, 36
secondary guilt, 200–201
Secretariat of Nigeria, Roman Catholic Church, 187, 221
security, term usage, 142
Sermon on the Mount, 133, 207, 227
Shils, Edward, 190
Shriver, Donald, 78
Sierra Leone, 39, 77n73
sin
    description of, 62–63, 89
    of omission, 211, 211n36
Smith, Daniel, 171
Smith, Harold, 22n34
Social Cohesion Index, Nigeria (2021), 159, 161
social identity categories, 205
social sin doctrine, 199
The Sociology of the Yoruba (Fadipe), 70
soft diplomacy, 197
software approach, 39–40
Sollicitudo Rei Socialis (John Paul II), 199
Sooka, Yasmin, 158
Søren Dosenrode, 73
South Africa
    ANC government, 115–16
    Apartheid regime, 17–18
    Catholic Bishops' Conference, 188
    compassion through *kenosis*, 110–11
    confronting impunity, 186
    democracy in, 156
    post-TRC, 149
    Reconciliation Barometer (2019), 158
    See also Tutu, Desmond (Archbishop)
South Africa's Truth and Reconciliation Commission (TRC), 2, 50, 181

Soyinka, Wole
    Burden of Memory, 3n4
    election rigging (1959), 22–23, 22n37
    "I'm Right; You're Dead" rhetoric, 26
    "To keep Nigeria one / Justice must be done," 12n1
    prison memoir, 170
    on seceding from Nigeria, 33–34
spirituality, 161–65
St Philip Catholic Church, Madalla, 169
Stalin, Joseph, 193
state agencies, 54, 56
"steal conflicts," 1, 1n2
Steffen, Lloyd, 106, 192
stereotypes, 43
Stern, Jessica, 106
stories/storytelling, 17–20, 35, 43, 59, 129, 146n15, 187
"The Story of King *Aláràn-án* and the Tiny Bird." *See* King and Tiny Bird story
Stovel, Laura, 77n73, 81n85
strategic studies, 16
strength, term usage, 132
structural/institutional approach, 39
subsidiarity, principles of, 209
Suleiman, Susan, 14
Sulhu Program (amnesty), 85n97
Swartley, Willard, 92–93, 131n23
Swiss banks, 89
Symbol and Sacrament (Chauvet), 174
symbolic component of justice, 81
Symbolism of Evil (Ricoeur), 80
Symposium of Episcopal Conferences of Africa and Madagascar (SECAM), 191
Synod of Bishops (1971), 173, 175, 199

taxidermism, 34n70
Teleki, Mofihli, 69
theologians, 191–92, 208
Thesnaar, Christo, 149
Third Way theology, 61n7
Tony Blair Foundation, 12

Towards Better Peacebuilding Practice (Dylan), 41
toxic emotions
   ethical imperative, 25–30
   Jesus and, 27–28, 27n49
   overcoming of, 167–69, 179–181, *184*, 213–17
   Roman Catholic Church and, 10
   zero-sum cycle of, 206
toxic memories, overcoming, 181–89
transgressions, 153
transitional justice, 2, 78, 79, 101–4
transitional societies, 56
transitionologists, 59, 59n2
translation method, 222
Translation method (Bevans), 157
TRC Promotion Act (1995), 63, 99
Triangle of Reconciliation, 141–42
tripartite model of justice, 45
triple deficit, 206
trust
   of leaders, 168
   rebuilding of, *186*
   term usage, 151–52
truth, definition of, 14
Truth and Reconciliation Commission (TRC)
   countries with (2001), 48
   enforcement of, 51
   four vectors of, 50
   principal expectations, 49–51
   restorative justice and, 155–160
   South Africa's, 2, 50, 181
   Tutu's role, 60
   See also Oputa Panel
truth-telling (confession), 61
Tutu, Desmond (Archbishop)
   amnesty, 83–88
   aporia of healing, 88–95
   background, 95–96
   Charter of Freedom (1955), 59–60
   confession (truth-telling), 61–67, 62
   evaluation of contribution, 67–71, 145–48
   forgiveness, 77n74, 83–88
   forgiveness-healing connection, 94
   as a pacifist, 73, 88
   "rainbow nation of God" idiom, 61
   reconciliation, 61–67, 62, 83–88, 95–101
   restorative justice praxis, 7, 10
   retribution among religious actors, 101–4
   Rwanda genocide sermon, 85n99
   spirituality role, 164
   Truth and Reconciliation Commission role, 60
   truth-telling, 61–67, 62
   Ubuntu philosophy, 60, 69

Ubuntu philosophy, 60, 69
ubuntufication, 63, 69, 120
Understanding "Restorative Justice" (Omale), 55, 55n89
unforgiveness, 73, 77, 77nn74–75, 91, 91n113, 212–13, 224–25, 226n75
   See also forgiveness
Unforgiving Servant, parable, 87n102
United Nations
   "Basic Principles of Justice for Victims and Abuse of Power," 39
   on Nigeria's HRVIC, 56n93
   remedying human rights violations, 39
   Secretary General, 67, 128n14
United States Conference of Catholic Bishops (USCCB), 196–97
Universal Declaration of Human Rights, 68n32
unpeaceful relationship, psychology of, 17–18
unscrupulous, term usage, 16
unscrupulous infringement of personal rights, term usage, 16

Vacek, Edward, 134n27
vengeance, ethics of, 143–44, 195, 208–13, 218
Versailles Treaty (1919), 26
vertical reconciliation, 107
Verwoerd, Wilhelm, 53n79, 66, 66n24, 152

INDEX

victim-offender-community mediation, 53, 53n79
victims
    compensation to, 84
    forgiveness and, 98n144
    honoring the memory of, 13–14
    hospital analogy and, 145
    Josephine, genocide survivor, 198–99
    redemptive assistance, 131–33
    of religious violence, 4
    victims/perpetrators, challenges, 110–11
Villa-Vicencio, Charles, 42, 42n22, 61n7, 71, 128, 149
violence
    actions to counter, 192–201
    conflict resolution, 34–37
    contemporary conflicts, 38–39
    definition of, 15–16, 15n17
    emotions, role of, 22–30
    ethnic violence, 30–37
    mass violence, 22–30
    mentioned, 4
    overview, 12–13
    peaceful relationships, 13–22
    religion and, 106
    as a rite of passage, 206
virtue of discernment, 100n153
Volf, Miroslav, 120–21, 182, 208

Walgrave, Lode, 102
Waliggo, John, 177
Walker, Margaret, 83n95, 102n160, 113–14
war crimes, 39
war studies, 16
Weber, Max, 173, 176
Wiesel, Elie, 132
Wisdom of Love (Burggraeve), 143
World Council of Churches (WCC), 182
World Court, 220
Worthington, Everett, 73
Wright, N. T., 172
Wunsch, James, 24n45

The Year Book of World Affairs (1976) (Curle), 16
Yorùbá people
    Àìná's heritage, 19–20
    dictum, 26, 29, 198
    forgiveness, meaning of, 30
    justice, construct of, 70–71
    philosophy, 19n29
    proverb, 20
    sub-ethnic groups, 135
    See also King and Tiny Bird story
Yugoslavia, UN special tribunals, 39

Zehr, Howard, 103, 128

www.ingramcontent.com/pod-product-compliance
Lightning Source LLC
Chambersburg PA
CBHW071243230426
43668CB00011B/1571